Love, laugh, lear[n]
Frank ✶
Within these pages there is an
exciting story of two rangers
that learned to think and act
as one. For five to six months
we were "on our own". Our first duty

OVER THE RAINBOW

assignment was to come back
alive, and The Road Taken

Frank Starr

LUMINARE PRESS
WWW.LUMINAREPRESS.COM

Printed in the United States of America

Cover and Interior Design: Claire Flint Last

Luminare Press
438 Charnelton St., Suite 101
Eugene, OR 97401
www.luminarepress.com

LCCN: 2017955458
ISBN: 978-1-944733-42-1

To:
my partner,
my best friend,
my love,
Penny Starr

TABLE OF CONTENTS

PRELUDE

Five old friends, Priscilla, Bob and Donna, Penny and I, were sitting around a table in the True Grit Cafe in the little town of Ridgway, Colorado, quaffing a few beers and swapping stories. As usual, those stories drifted into tales of bears and Penny's and my experiences in the National Park Service.

Donna said, "You've told us so many wonderful stories, but I want to know about you two, how you got together and what led you into those unusual second career/retirement positions. And another thing; you haven't often mention fears or being scared. Didn't you worry about getting sick or hurt, or being attacked by a bear or a man?"

"Frank didn't seem to, he counted on the gods or his guardian angel to take care of us," Penny said. "But I worried about all sorts of things, and was scared a lot. There was no such thing as calling 911 if you got hurt or sick, help might well be more than a week away. I didn't worry about bears; after my assault at Jewel Cave, our first season in the Park Service, I worried about people."

Priscilla, owner of Cimarron Books and Coffee House just across the street from the Grit said, "You two should put all your stories into book form. They would go great in my shop."

Bob, a retired radiologist, had a suggestion. "Great idea, your stories would make a good book. When I read a book, I look forward to learning, especially one on natural history. I think relating the things you learned are as important to this memoir as the events you experienced and the things you saw."

Penny had a thought, "You guys have really thrown us a challenge. A book would be a lot of fun, but would today's populace, who are so accustomed to instant communication, believe we spent weeks without seeing another person and could go a week or more without radio contact? It was before GPS or cell phones, much less satellite phones. Our only means of communication was by 5- or 10-watt VHF radio that was limited to line-of-site, and there were always mountains and weather between us and our base."

The stories that follow are our response to our friends' requests.

OVER THE RAINBOW

When Penny and I were 15 and 17 years old and falling in love, we decided "Over The Rainbow" was us—our song.

> Somewhere over the rainbow, way up high
> There's a land that I heard of, once in a lullaby
> Somewhere over the rainbow, skies are blue
> And the dreams that you dare to dream, really do come true

Together we could fly over the rainbow to where dreams really do come true. We could, we would, we did, we flew over that rainbow, and dreams beyond our wildest imaginations did come true!

Penny and I met and fell passionately in love while in high school, as only teenagers with surging hormones can do. It was 1948, shortly after the end of WWII. I had graduated from high school where I had been much more interested in fun and girls than in an education. I knew I wasn't ready for more book learning. I also knew I had a duty to our country to perform. Besides that, by enlisting for one year in the Navy's Enlisted Volunteer (EV) program I was assured I would be exempt from the draft. A good plan? Sure, but it put a real crimp in our love life for that year.

After my one year hiatus in the Navy, life and love returned to a more or less normal progression. I entered the Pre-Dentistry Program at Ohio State. A few months later Penny graduated from high school, and enrolled in the School of Dental Hygiene at OSU. Penny's parents had wanted her to go to college at Northern Arizona University. My parents had tried to get me to go to dental school at Northwestern in Chicago. We both knew we had had enough of being separated, and weren't at all interested in going to different schools. That one year hiatus in the Navy convinced us that we were a pair and would spend our lives together.

We were married in a quasi-Catholic ceremony. Quasi, in that Penny was Catholic, it was the Christmas season, and I had been declared a Pagan by the incensed Monsignor who would perform the ceremony. Another of those mixed marriages which Monsignor Kennedy assured us would never last. We have toasted him every winter solstice since.

Marriage in a Catholic ceremony, in those days, and perhaps still, requires the couple attend a two hour "indoctrination class" each week for eight weeks. Everything went along satisfactorily until the seventh week when the Monsignor asked me where I had been baptized. My simple reply was, "I have never been baptized." We thought the Monsignor was going to have a stroke!

He stood up, loudly declaring, "Oh No! You're worse than a Protestant, you're a Pagan!"

To which Penny stood and put her arm in-front of me saying, "Don't you speak that way to the man I love!"

Were Penny's dad not a very generous contributor to Monsignor Kennedy's St. Agatha Perish, it would have all been over right then. The good Monsignor, seeing many dollars leaving his donation box, held his tongue, excused us for the evening and confirmed that we would meet in one week for the final time before the wedding. That incident was never mentioned again by the Monsignor or us. Gone, but not forgotten!

The ceremony could not be performed in the church—Christmas time, Pagan, and all that. It took place in a small rectory with only family in attendance. The Clemens's made up for the shortcomings of the service by putting on quite a reception. Friends told us later that it was a party to end all parties, and we missed it to go on a honeymoon. Oh well!

My graduation from dental school did follow the normal progression. I received my DDS degree a year and a half after our marriage and three months before Lori was born. As things seem to go with the best laid plans of most of us, a glitch appeared. That one year EV enlistment I had taken in the Navy saved me from the regular draft, but the Doctors Draft laws required a minimum of 21 months active duty. So it was back to the military for a two-year hitch. This time in the Air Force, and with a commission no less. I feel that both military experiences were of immeasurable value. When I got out of high school I knew I wasn't ready for more formal education. Looking back, had I gone directly to college, I would most probably have joined a social fraternity, gone to too many parties, done poorly at academics, and perhaps even flunked out. In the Navy I realized I would need an education if I wanted to make a better life for myself and, in my dreams, Penny Clemens; enough impetus to turn a poor high school student into a cum laude college graduate.

My military orders said I was to report for six weeks of medical/dental officers introduction to the Air Force at Maxwell AFB, Montgomery, Alabama, on 18 September 1955. Lori was born on 14 September 1955. In order to not be AWOL, I had to leave Penny and Lori in the hospital (in those days a week in the hospital was standard after delivery) to get to the six weeks of "indoctrination class" before moving on to McConnell Air Force Base in Wichita, Kansas. Penny and Lori moved from the hospital to her parents home until I could get our furniture moved into an apartment near the base in Wichita. When we were finally together again, we realized we had no clue as to what you do with a new baby. So it was, see how fast we could learn about babies and forget about learning new country or the Air Force.

The following summer we felt the urge for a vacation. It wasn't hard to con Penny's mother into coming out to babysit Lori for us. What kind of vacation to take? Penny wanted to go to LA and visit her brother, I wanted to go camping. Time for compromise, we would do both, a few days in Los Angeles, a week camping in Sequoia National Park, and a few more days in LA. Sounded great, except Penny had never been camping and wasn't at all sure she would like it. Being a good sport and the adventuresome type, Penny thought to herself, "I'll go camping this one time, he will be happy, and that will be the end of our camping life."

I thought, "I can put up with LA for a few days if that's what it takes to get her camping." Off we went, both secure in the belief that our personal plan would prevail.

The time in LA went fine, as we knew it would. Penny's brother was gay, and a hoot. Many of his friends were actors or models, both male and female, mostly gay, but some straight. You bet we were impressed by all of those beautiful people around Pat's pool every afternoon and evening. We didn't understand the gay or lesbian thing, but we could ignore it and enjoy ourselves, while learning about a part of society we had never really been exposed to.

The critical part of this trip was, how would Penny take to camping? We pulled into Sequoia/Kings Canyon National Park with sleeping bags, a Coleman lantern and stove, a cook kit, an ice chest, and plenty of food, but no tent. First thing to do was find out where to set up camp and where to rent a tent and cots. This was the 1950s and foam pads weren't around, much less all of the high tech gear we think of as standard equipment today. The source of all information has to be your friendly park ranger and lo and behold one showed up as soon as he saw a beautiful young woman. To our amazement, in a matter of minutes, he brought us a wall tent and two cots, which he had gotten from a concessionaire, all of which would cost us one dollar per day.

Now to set up camp before dark, but where would be the ideal spot? Look around! We were in the center of a grove of giant sequoias and the ranger had said "Camp any where there's a picnic table." It turned out we were camping in what is known as "Giant Forest." The most hallowed ground in Sequoia National Park (which is now undergoing extensive restoration). We looked up at trees that had stood for more than 3,000 years. The trunks were 35 feet in diameter, the lowest branch was 150 feet up and 7 feet in diameter. The bark on these behemoths is two feet or more thick and almost as fire resistant as asbestos. That fire resistance has allowed sequoias to survive hundreds of fires that kept the forest floor clean. Then Smokey the Bear came along with "Only you can prevent forest fires." Smokey's famous comment reduced the number of fires but allowed underbrush and dead wood to accumulate, which is now the source of many large, hard to control forest fires.

And, oh yes, the ranger had also told us about bears. It seems that a black bear had staked out this camping area (it was too loose to be called a campground) as its personal mooching grounds. At any rate the ranger very carefully explained to us that all food must be stored inside a closed car when it was not actually being prepared or eaten. If not, it might well be confiscated and eaten by our furry neighbor. Also, he explained that the feeding of any wildlife was strictly prohibited. Oh, was I thrilled. We might get to see a bear up close. Penny was more than a little concerned and excited at the same time.

That evening couldn't have gone better. We went to our first ranger program where we sat around a huge bonfire listening to the ranger tell stories of bears as well as giving us valuable information about the park and what we could do the next day. It had been Penny's first real campfire and as the embers died we looked up through the sequoia branches. The stars were so big, bright, and close we were sure we could touch them. It had been a big day and finally was time for a night's sleep in the great-out-doors. I was ready for sleep but Penny thought she would read by lantern light for a while.

Next thing I knew Penny was shaking me and whispering, "Wake up! There's a bear at our tent."

Knowing there was no possible reason for a bear to be there I mumbled something like "No there isn't, go to sleep." Whereupon the bear ran its paw down the front of the tent, getting my immediate and undivided attention.

The ranger had said if a bear should come around we needed to make loud noise which would frighten the bear and it would leave. So I banged pans and Penny yelled, sure enough the bear went away. Cautiously we peaked out of the tent flap, and with a flashlight could see the bear at a picnic table a few yards away. It had found an ice chest that had not been properly put away, opened it like it knew what it was doing and proceeded to have a midnight feast. In all of our experiences with bears since, we have never met one so knowledgeable about ice chests, it actually took a 32 oz. can of juice punctured the end with a claw, tipped it up and drank the contents. Of course it had quite an audience by this time, but wasn't to be deterred from its treasure by a bunch of gawking, yelling, idiotic humans. Eventually the show ended with an empty ice chest and the bear wandering off, having renewed its faith that man was not very bright and a sure source of an easy meal.

Back in the tent I wondered why the bear would have bothered with our tent, "There couldn't be any food in here could there?"

Well it was fess-up time, and Penny, looking very sheepish, pulled a sack of Oreos out of her sleeping bag, "Only these," she said.

Fortunately for us, both of our plans had worked out, we had enjoyed LA on both ends of the camping trip, and Penny had discovered that camping could indeed, be a great experience. In fact, by the time our third daughter, Kristy, was two we were camping on a regular basis, and when she was big enough to carry her own sleeping bag we began backpacking and canoeing for a week or two at a time. A few years later the five of us were taking a month or more each summer to hike and backpack in the National Parks and Forests, mostly in the western states.

One summer, as we were returning home from an extended family camping trip, Penny casually said, "Why don't we go over to Ohio State, (which was only a few minutes from our home and from my office, and where I was an associate professor at the College of Dentistry) and take a few courses just for fun, and learn more about the world we were enjoying so much." Well, to make a long story short, seven or eight years later I had earned a MS in Wildlife Management and Penny was only a few hours short of her degree in Anthropology/Geology; all by taking one course a quarter just for the pure joy of learning. Penny chose to not take a couple required statistics courses, thus she didn't qualify for a degree.

By this time the girls were well directed on their own paths. Lori had graduated from Bowling Green State University and was married; Carin was about to finish her BS in nursing at OSU, was in love, and thinking of marriage; and Kristy was in business school at Franklin University in Columbus. Our financial obligation to the girls seemed to be almost complete.

Now I had a suggestion, "Lets see if we can get jobs as rangers in a National Park." We and our girls had always thought park rangers had great seasonal jobs. They lasted three or four months over the summer; then they returned to their real jobs as teachers, students, or whatever. We had hiked with those rangers in most of our western parks and gone to many of their evening camp-fire programs over the past years. We had always envied them their opportunity to know a park in-depth: the geology, the plant life and animal life, the workings of an individual ecosystem. Penny said, "Lets try it!"

A few years before we had met with a district ranger in Yellowstone. He had talked politely with us and let us know there was no way in hell we would ever get ranger jobs in Yellowstone or any other major park. On a trip to Mt. Rainier National Park we had talked with the Chief of Interpretation. He had sincerely told us that without experience we wouldn't qualify for any of the jobs he had. It was not long after the end of the Vietnam War, the environmental movement was strong, and a lot of young college types were applying to the Park Service. He told us he got 5,000 applications for the two dozen positions he had to fill. His recommendation was to apply to a little-known park.

Well if you are going to apply you have to apply on something to someone. When all else fails get directions! Call the National Park Service and get those directions! Penny went to the phone—phones were wired and stationary, there was no such thing as a cell phone and cordless phones were only dreamed of. She called information, got a number for the National Park Service in Washington DC and called them.A pleasant voice answered with, "Good morning National Park Service, this is Jan. How may I help you?" She sent us the applications we needed. Page after page of statements you were to score yourself one to five on your ability or knowledge. For example: rate your skill as a canoeist, a photographer, a public speaker, or a technical rock climber; or your knowledge of astronomy, geology, emergency medicine, and the Civil War. A score of one meant you were unknowledgeable; two meant you had a speaking knowledge; three you were knowledgable and well acquainted; four you were very accomplished; and five meant you were a professional or teacher of the subject. You were cautioned to not over-rate yourself, you would be summarily dismissed if you didn't possess the skills and knowledge you claimed.

The application goes on: What is your ethnic background? Penny is adopted, looks white and is probably Irish. I was conceived out of wedlock by two people who had mixed English and German ancestry, and was told, by my uncle, that I am 1/8th Native American. They wanted documentation of the last ten jobs we had held and who our supervisor was. Damn! Neither of us had held ten different jobs in our lives. Oh well! The applications were to be filled out in duplicate and "returned in the enclosed envelopes" by 15 January. We had received them on the 5th of January. Not only that, but we were permitted to make a first choice and a second choice of parks. If neither of those parks had need of us, we would never hear from them or any other park. We would receive notice that our application had been received in Washington, and would be contacted if one of our selected parks was offering us a job.

All applications are scored by computer and all jobs must be offered to the person with the highest score and down the progressive list of scores until all available positions are filled. We had taken the advice of the man at Mt. Rainier and applied to two western parks that we figured would get few applications and had the most positions to fill. We had never heard of Jewel Cave National Monument, so it couldn't be too popular a spot and they had more openings than any of the other parks that we didn't know much about. It is in great country, the Black Hills of South Dakota, so that seemed like a good place to start. Our second choice of parks, we can't even remember now.

We got our first choice, but only after a lot of effort by the Management Assistant, Al Hendricks. At the time, Jewel Cave National Monument was managed by Wind Cave National Park (and probably still is). A National Monument usually involves one significant feature and is proclaimed by the President. A National Park is usually larger, encompasses several significant features, be they geologic, scenic, historic or other and must be declared by Congress. The superintendent of Wind Cave had sworn a married couple would never work for him. He knew there would be so much friction between the couple the park would suffer, and to hell with the rule of hiring by score. We spent a lot of time laughing about what a marriage he must have had. At any rate, his two favorite rangers from the previous season at Wind Cave had gotten married over the off-season. If he wanted his two favorites back he would have to let Al hire a married couple at Jewel Cave. We were in!

Jewel Cave (JECA)

Sunday, 18 May 1980, was a most memorable day: lots of people were born, lots of people died. Fifty-seven of those who died were unfortunate enough to be in the path of the largest ash and mud slide in recorded history as it roared down the side of Mt. Saint Helens when the north side blew 1,314 feet off its top. It was an auspicious day in our personal lives too. Penny Starr was in the air flying to her first day of work in the National Park Service at the same time St. Helens was blowing.

Penny and I had agreed to start work as National Park Service rangers at Jewel Cave National Monument (JECA) in the Black Hills of South Dakota, on the 15 June. However, early in May we got a call from Al Hendricks, Monument manager, asking if one or both of us could start work in time to be on duty for the Memorial Day weekend. I had patients scheduled through the sixth of June and wouldn't cancel them. Penny didn't like the idea of going alone, but guessed she could if it really helped the park out of a difficult situation. Memorial Day weekend is one of the busiest times of the year in most parks, so Jewel Cave could expect a lot of visitation. It would be a problem if the staff was short of rangers to lead tours through the cave.

The National Park Service (NPS), like most government agencies is big on using acronyms; thus, parks are abbreviated by using the first four letters of the name, or in the case of a park with a two word name, the first two letters of each word. Also, like the military, the NPS works on a 24-hour clock, and the day precedes the month when writing the date. Thus, Penny's EOD (entry on duty) at JECA (Jewel Cave) was to be 0900 (pronounced zero nine hundred hours, or just oh nine hundred) 19 May 1980. My EOD would remain 15 June.

Jewel Cave sits just off of U.S. highway 16, between the towns of Custer, South Dakota, and Newcastle, Wyoming. It's beautiful country: stream-carved canyons and ponderosa clad hills, and happens to be on the route between Mt. Rushmore and Yellowstone. One of the most common questions in the JECA visitor center was, "How far are we from Yellowstone?"

The Black Hills get their name from the darkness of the ponderosa pine when viewed from a distance. The bark of young ponderosas is indeed, almost black. Mature ponderosas have soft russet colored bark of scaly plates with one to two-inch deep fissures between plates, giving the tree its distinctive ponderosa look. If you stick your nose into a fissure, you get the delicious aroma of butterscotch and vanilla. The spaciousness of these trees and the whisper of a breeze moving through their tops is something I haven't the ability to describe, but those of you who have sat quietly in such a setting can appreciate the feeling of peace and tranquility that is with you there. No wonder so many people want to live in a ponderosa forest, and the Monument is in the center of a stand of mature ponderosa pine.

Penny called me nearly every evening with a report on life in the mysterious Park Service. She reported that when I got there we would live in an ancient cabin on the edge of Hell Canyon, where in 1900 Frank and Albert Michaud had felt a strong breeze coming from a small hole in the wall of the canyon—directly below our cabin. A low pressure front had to be moving in, replacing a zone of high pressure and causing the cave to exhale the air that it had inhaled during the high. The temperature of the cave air is always between 46 and 48 degrees Fahrenheit, which indicates that the cave has such a large volume only a small percentage of the air is replaced by moving from a high to a low pressure atmosphere. The air temperature is the average year-round temperature of the outside air. Winds blowing in or out, through small passages in the cave, have been measured as high as 32 mph.

Until I got there, Penny would room with Cheryl in a trailer in the Park housing area. Park housing consisted of half a dozen old single wide trailers each of which had a living-room-kitchen combination and one, two, or three bedrooms where seasonal rangers would live, one per bedroom—except when two decided to share a bed for a few hours. Permanent staff occupied two nice "Mission 66" houses, with more permanent housing promised for the future.

Penny had no problem sharing an old trailer with Cheryl, but Cheryl had a boyfriend, Bill, with whom she shared her bed. Bill was a ranger too, who had been assigned housing a few doors away. Yes, we became fast learners about the ways of the generation that was maturing in the 1980s. After all, we had kids the same age as most of the rangers we would be working with, and we might as well understand the generational difference.

Penny reminded me that the year before while we were working for the National Audubon Society as instructors at their adult environmental education camp in Maine, our middle daughter Carin and her boyfriend, Mark, were traveling and stopped to visit us for a couple of days. A shock to me, but Penny took it in stride and explained that everything was OK. Lots of young people travel and even live together before they get married. The invention of "The Pill" had given women the freedom that men had enjoyed forever—sex without the concern of pregnancy.

Penny had her own room, so "go with the flow," and enjoy observing the sex life that we had missed, but that these kids could enjoy. The sounds from the bed in the next room, only inches from Penny's head, were, to say the least, interesting and enlightening but not sleep-promoting.

We were launched on what was to become the best and most

exciting times and years of our lives. As it turned out, the Park Service became our semi-retirement and second career.

Rangers are expected to be friendly at all times, look sharp, and never be late! Look sharp means proper uniforms worn correctly. Uniforms had to be ordered from a government-approved uniform supplier, either Gregory's or Fashion World; shoes, boots, socks, pants, shirts, neckties, coats, an assortment of hats: ball cap, straw flat-brim, and felt flat-brim (also known as "road kill"). All had to be ordered ahead of time so we would be ready to go to work upon our arrival at the park. Of course half of the items were back ordered or got delivered to the park instead of to your home; half of those didn't fit properly and had to be sent back. By the way, the government does give you a clothing allowance which covers most, not all, but most, of what you are required to have.

The public expects a ranger to know everything. The park expects its rangers to be prepared to answer almost any question that may come along, in a polite and friendly way. A lot of questions are going to be asked and you are expected to know the answers. "Where is the restroom? How did the cave get to be? How old is it? Who did the exploration? What is the human history of this cave?" Then there are questions like, "How much of the cave hasn't been discovered?" and "How much of the cave is underground?"

"Well mam, we know 86 miles of the cave have been explored, and there may be that much more cave that hasn't been explored," and "As soon as it isn't underground it isn't a cave. The restroom is just beyond that big sign behind you, sir." It's hard not to laugh or roll your eyes the first time you hear a really stupid question, but you don't; you save it to tell at the next party. When Penny or I didn't know the answer to a question we would find it for the person before they left the area, or we would get an answer and mail it to them.

New rangers have a lot of studying to do, books to read, and other rangers' tours to follow and plagiarize from. We were encouraged and expected to follow the leads of the experienced people on staff. They had learned from their predecessors, and learning from those who have done it before is a great way to not reinvent the wheel. A lot of that wheel of interpretation has to be your own personality and how you choose to present the park.

Surface caves like those the Anasazi used to protect their cliff dwellings are wind and/or water eroded from sandstone. The underground kind of cave is invariably in limestone deposited on the bottom of the sea many millions of years ago. Deposits of limestone are the accumulation of the shells of untold billions of tiny sea dwelling animals falling to the bottom and being joined by billions more with the same, or similar, kinds of calcium carbonate shells, as well as by bottom-dwellers like corals and clams. All of which is then cemented together by dissolved limey minerals that precipitate from the cold, dense, deep water. The limestone may be buried under deposits of other materials such as shale, sandstone, volcanic ash, or intrusive igneous material such as basalt, and spend hundreds of millions of years being compacted before being uplifted by tectonic activity.

Jewel Cave is in Mississippian Age, Pahasapa limestone deposited on the bottom of the ancient Bear Paw Sea some 350 million years ago. Eventually it was covered by sandstone, shale, more limestone and more sandstone, all deposited on the sea's floor. Finally the sea floor was uplifted during the Laramide Orogeny, the uplift which created the Rocky Mountains and the Black Hills in the late Cretaceous period, some 75 million years ago.

The uplifting created cracks in the limestone. Rainwater percolating through the duff, soil, and rock layers above the Pahasapa, picked up carbon-dioxide and became weak carbonic acid. As the weak acid works into the cracks of the rock, it very slowly dissolves the limestone, creating tunnels, passages, and rooms. This is the process by which nearly all of the world's caves are formed. It happens when the water table is high, leaving a slowly forming cave filled with slightly acidic water. At Jewel Cave, the water table fell and rose several times. When the water table was low the dissolved calcium-carbonate flowing in was deposited as the beautiful speleothems—the cave formations which visitors come to see. When the water table was high the walls were being dissolved. The last time the water table was high enough to flood the cave, a strange thing happened. Instead of dissolving the limestone walls, a supersaturated solution of calcium-carbonate precipitated out as beautiful hexagonal calcite crystals that cover the cave walls like gems, they sparkle and twinkle with every color of the rainbow when light hits them, thus giving the cave its name.

Weekends for rangers aren't often Saturday and Sunday; we work five days and have two days off, so "Friday" can be any day of the week. The Park is open seven days a week, and schedules are arranged accordingly. On one of Penny's first weekends, she was doing household chores when Al, the Monument manager and her boss, with Steve, the chief of maintenance, drove up in a fire truck and said, "Come on Penny, we're going to a forest fire." Penny said, "Sounds interesting, but no thanks, I have a lot of things I want to get done today." They laughed and, explained that they weren't inviting her to go, they were telling her she was going! When there is a fire every available person responds. That means everyone not actively on the cave tour schedule that day—whether you know anything about firefighting or not.

On-the-job training is a marvelous way to pick up knowledge fast, and you had better be a fast learner in a wild-fire situation. Penny was under the guidance and supervision of experienced forest-firefighters, who were keeping a close eye on a new ranger on her first fire. There were trees crowning, a dangerous situation. When flames in brush reach the lower branches of the young ponderosa, fire runs up the tree in seconds, essentially exploding it, and spreading the fire to nearby trees.

Penny and the park team were on a fire line next to a crew of old-time Forest Service firefighters, cutting brush and trees and digging down to mineral soil to build a defensive line that the fire wouldn't cross. After a couple hours of hard work the crew-chief called a rest-break; everyone moved back, found a comfortable seat on the ground, and started the inevitable conversation about fires. One Forest Service man bitched about the hard work, but commented that he would be glad to have the overtime hazardous-duty pay.

Penny immediately piped-in, "You mean all this fun fighting fires and we get paid too?" Of course, the whole crew broke up and resulted in the kind of camaraderie not too often seen between Park Service and Forest Service fire crews. That night over a few beers at one of the park's common potlucks, Al and Steve retold the story to the entire park staff, with lots of embellishments. That made Penny the hero of the day and instant friend of the old timers on staff.

We became quite comfortable with firefighting over the years ahead. We carried "Red Cards" for many years, indicating we had experience, training, and passed the physical requirements to be considered prepared to handle any wildfire situation. In the two seasons at Jewel, we were each on six or eight wildfires and two structural fires. That experience led us to many years as firefighters in other parks, and on our local volunteer fire department in Colorado.

Finally, I had completed my commitments to the patients I had scheduled and could head west to Penny, Jewel Cave, and the unique life she had been telling me about. We don't do well being separated, and those three weeks was a long time for us to be apart. It was high time we got back together.

Penny had told me there are three types of cave tour. Now I could understand what she had been telling me. The standard tour goes through a paved and lighted, developed portion of the cave; a historic tour enters through a man-made opening a few feet from the natural opening, which has been obliterated over the years; and a spelunking tour, led by the spelunking ranger, takes people into dark crawl-ways unavailable any other way.

The standard tour starts with an elevator ride down a couple of hundred vertical feet. Before loading onto the elevator, most of us would stop in the elevator lobby of the VC (there is that government acronym again—VC means Visitor Center) and introduce ourselves by giving our name, where we were from, and what we did in real life. Then we'd ask our visitors to introduce themselves in a similar way—name, home town, occupation, and anything else they chose to tell. We did get some very interesting comments, especially, from little kids, who can say the damndest things. The tour covers about a mile of asphalt cave floor paths, interrupted by innumerable corrugated aluminum stairs and bridges, and ends back at the elevator after about an hour.

The same carbonic acid that produced the cave is still dissolving limestone as it percolates down to the water table. As it passes through the air of the cave the water evaporates and leaves deposits of calcium carbonate, forming the speleothems. Where it flows over a surface it forms blanket-like layers called flow-stone, running down a wall it might form a fin which could grow into a "slab of bacon" an inch thick, 12 inches wide, and 20 feet long. Iron and other minerals in the water add color, producing a realistic looking slab of bacon. Water dripping from the ceiling forms stalactites, which drip to the floor and form stalagmites; when stalactites and stalagmites grow together they are called columns. A common question was: "How do you remember which is which?" The answer: "Easy! (chuckle) Stalactites hang 'tight' to the ceiling; stalagmites 'might' grow up to be columns." That usually produced some chuckles, a few laughs, and some moans, but ended with visitors remembering the difference between stalactite and stalagmite. We heard people say, "Look there's a cloud, a horse's head, my mother in-law, a cow pie." Speliothems come in endless shapes and sizes, and can be described by endless names and adjectives. Commonly used terms are: draperies, ribbons, popcorn, dripstones, and soda straws.

Minerals other than calcite can form speliothems too: gypsum (hydrated calcium sulfate), hydromagnesite (hydrated magnesium carbonate), and aragonite, (the calcium carbonate of sea shells) are a few. "Frost work" is feathery needles of aragonite that look like a dandelion bloom going to seed. Gypsum flowers curve outward from a wall, taking on odd and grotesque shapes resembling plant stems, or roots, and are found only in dryer areas of the cave. Hydromagnesite forms balloons that grow to 1.5 to 2 inches long, and are found only in remote areas of the cave. The jewels that provide the name "Jewel Cave" are the hexagonal calcite crystals, often referred to as dog-tooth spar, that literally coat the walls in many areas.

The historic tour, which only a few people chose to take, is the one both Penny and I enjoyed the most. It gives a person the feel of actually being in a place that no one else has ever been, exploring the unknown. Group size was limited to ten, as opposed to the 30 or more that we often had on the regular cave tour. Every person is given his or her own candle lantern to use. The candle lantern is a #10 can with one end cut out, and carried by a wire loop with a candle through the low side. It makes a fun, pseudo lantern, and people are free to look where they will—within reason. We would light our own candle and carry it around lighting everyone's candle. It gave us the opportunity to talk with each person individually and get a feel of what they might be like, and what they were expecting. We always had a back-up flashlight to use in case of an emergency, but requested that no one else carry a flashlight, as it would spoil the ambiance of seeing the cave just as Frank and Albert Michaud had done over 80 years before.

We had to pay careful attention that no one wandered off; it would be very easy to get lost if you became separated from the group. Being lost in a cave with only an hour's light from a candle would be a pretty scary situation for anyone. I often wonder how Mark Twain's characters, Tom Sawyer and Becky Thatcher, got along when they were lost in a cave.

Penny and I ended our tours by taking the group into a little side room well off the regular route, having everyone sit on the floor with their backs to a wall, and blow out their candle. In absolute total darkness, which few people have ever experienced, we told stories of early cave exploration. Most people loved experiencing total darkness for the first time in their life. It was so completely different from anything else they had ever experienced. Occasionally someone couldn't handle it, and total darkness would end as soon as it began. When there were little kids along, I carefully explained to them what we would be doing; amazingly most of them really wanted to do it, and usually loved the experience. On rare occasions someone was really interested in seeing the little brown bats (*Myotis lucifugus*) that spend their days in the cave. That meant showing bats to the whole group, which had to be done very carefully and with a lot of explanation on the life history of bats.

The spelunking tour required participants to crawl through an opening on the VC deck, nine inches high and 20 inches wide by about a foot long. If you couldn't get through the hole you were too big to go spelunking. That test, in itself, produced a lot of entertainment every day. People who thought they were in good shape would lie on the floor struggling, but couldn't get their chests through—fat displaces but bone doesn't give much. We discovered, in our own spelunking, that there were holes you could only get through by taking off your hard hat, pushing it in-front of you, arms fully extended, your head turned to the side, and pushing with your toes. Everyone on the spelunking tour is equipped with a battery-powered headlamp attached to a hardhat. People are warned to wear clothes they don't care about because there is a lot of manganese on the floors, and everyone comes out streaked with black mineral.

Besides cave tours, we manned the information desk, raised the flag at 0730, opened the main gate at 0800, took the flag down at 1800, and closed the gate at 1900. (Be sure you aren't more than a minute late or early in getting those assigned tasks done!) We all had rotating schedules so each of us worked eight hours a day, five days a week.

A couple of unique individuals worked at Jewel Cave in those years; Penny was one of them. When she had an early morning tour, she would breeze through the main entrance to the VC just before her tour began, in her full dress uniform, doff her felt flat-hat, bow to the crowd, and sing, "Good morning, good morning, good morning to you, and you, and you!" especially to the little kids. They loved it and that little introduction assured that she would have an attentive audience for her tour.

The visitors to Jewel Cave are an eclectic group, from families with kids and pets (who didn't get to go on a tour), to professional geologists, biker gangs on the way to or from their rendezvous in Sturgis, South Dakota, to oil field workers whose t-shirts said "If You Ain't Oil Field Trash You Ain't Shit!" All interesting people, and most of them fun. It was not too unusual to have a group of 30 from one extended Mormon family touring the cave with you.

Evenings were completely free of visitors (or Pilgrims as we often referred to them). Closing the gate and having no one in the park except us rangers, and some family members, after seven o'clock was delightful, and conducive to parties at someone's trailer or house several times a week—a totally different way of life for us. The parties were always potlucks. You brought what you had, what you could make quickly, or what you could dream up. One of the maintenance men had dairy cows and sold us raw milk. We would skim the cream off the milk, and give it back to him to make butter. Or, save the cream to make ice-cream for a potluck, throw in some fresh strawberries or peach chunks—talk about good eating—Oh my!

Since we were living with the next generation, it was time to learn to speak the language of our young friends. We were not unaccustomed to profanity. We used it in jokes and at appropriate times, but this generation seemed to include "potty talk" as a part of normal conversation. It took me back to my time in the Navy when I had learned some pretty descriptive terms. Now we were learning that profanity was a normal part of every-day conversation. Our education continued!

WE HAD BOTH BEEN RUNNERS FOR YEARS, AND WERE DETERMINED to keep running. Penny ran five days a week, from the cabin out to the highway and up the road about two miles, to the entry gate of Jewel Cave, then back. I ran three or four days a week, down the trail from the cabin, a little over a mile, to the VC and back. Penny always did her run at 0600. She had started running the middle of May, when the sun was well up. Now it was late August and she was running toward Venus, the morning star, at first light.

She crested a rise and noticed something different—an orange object in the roadside ditch. As she got closer, that orange object became a stocking cap on a man's head. The head had a nylon stocking over the face and was attached to a man with a six inch survival dagger in his hand. He was jumping from the ditch! He grabbed the startled runner before she could turn and flee. Arm around her neck, knife in her back, he was yelling, "Get in the ditch and I won't hurt you. Every thing will be all right." She refused; they struggled there on the road; he kept telling her to get in the ditch or he would kill her. She realized she had stronger legs and he had stronger arms. They fought on, but she was able to stay on the road and out of the ditch. He kept yelling that he would kill her, but she realized he wasn't doing it. The knife in her back hurt, but her struggling had moved it to a place where, she was sure, if it went in it wouldn't kill her. She managed to work her mouth free of the hand which he had clamped over her face. She yelled, "I'm a federal officer. If you harm me the FBI will get you." At that, he seemed to panic and let go. She ran down the road as he yelled, "If

I ever see you again I'll kill you." She must have run a three minute mile coming down that hill to our cabin.

Penny had run four or five miles a day for probably fifteen years. She hadn't finished her planned run, and wouldn't go to work without finishing. So she and I ran for another half hour. That extra run sounds nuts, but it may well have saved her from serious mental consequences. She reminds me, "I lost my sense of freedom that day! I remember; I went on duty, and just about lost it in the cave. On a platform, I told the visitors, 'Just look around, drink in the beauty of this place.' I stepped back, got control, and off we went. That night I cried, and you held me all night long."

We, of course, notified the Park Service and the local sheriff. The only LE (law enforcement) person in the park was our boss, Al Hendricks, and he was on leave. Penny couldn't give a positive identification from mug shots since the man was masked, so the sheriff felt he didn't have enough evidence for a conviction, even though he was sure the attacker was a known molester, and the son of a local big-wig. Consequently, the DA declined to prosecute the case and it went into the books as an unsolved crime.

When Al got back, he decided it would be better if we moved to the park housing area with the rest of the rangers. Penny refused to give up her runs, so morning runs were done inside the gated park in the company of me or one of the other rangers who had volunteered to run with her.

One of our new neighbors had a three-year-old daughter, Mandy, who soon became a favorite of us both. She was popular with everyone, but seemed to take a special liking to us—probably the "grandparent syndrome." Mandy had cute little expressions that everyone enjoyed; every time she smelled a cattle feed-lot she would say, "Smells like money." Penny had a phrase that she used regularly. When an inappropriate, funny, or strange comment was made you would hear Penny say, "Oh, save me!" Mandy, when she heard Penny's phrase, would pipe up with, "I will save you Penny."

One early morning, before the world was up, we were enjoying ourselves by making love. At a most inappropriate moment, a tiny voice a few inches from our heads said, "What doing, Fwankie?" The spell of love was broken. We could only laugh and say, "Good morning Mandy."

CAVING OR SPELUNKING (SPELUNK IS LATIN FOR CAVE AND A lunker is anyone crazy enough to do it), is another game we took up in the off hours when we had the cave to ourselves. Exploration was an ongoing enterprise led by Herb and Jan Conn. Herb and Jan had mapped Jewel Cave from the historic entrance, before much of it was open to the public. We are still amazed by the feat they performed. Lighted by carbide head lamps, using a hand-held Burton compass and a fifty-foot tape, they did a complete survey of the cave as they explored. When the park decided to put in an elevator, in order to make more of the cave accessible to the public, Herb and Jan told the engineers where the elevator shaft should be. That was several miles distant from the natural entrance, by way of the convoluted cave passages; up, down, sideways, walkways, crawlways, every imaginable direction. The exploratory drill shaft came in less than two feet from where they had expected it.

We became good friends with the Conns. We were about the same age, and they decided we should learn spelunking properly. They took us into parts of the cave that few others had ever seen, They showed us how to do serious rock climbing—in the dark, with no equipment other than our hands and feet, hard hats, and carbide head lamps. Jan described Spelunking this way:

> There's duckways and crawlways and bottomless pits:
> You're sore and you're tired, and scared out of your wits.
> If you slip from your footing, you'll likely be dead,
> But you can't straighten up without cracking your head.

An interesting, challenging, and scary experience that truly challenged all of our physical and mental abilities. If the scuba diving we had done and loved was a visual experience, spelunking was a visceral one; in that you proceed by instinct rather than by intellect.

Jewel Cave had been a marvelous introduction to the Park Service, but after two years underground, we felt like we might be qualified enough to try for one of the more well known parks. That winter Penny called Yosemite, and by dumb luck reached the chief of interpretation for the Wawona district. They talked for a long time. Dan Card thought Penny sounded like the kind of ranger he wanted, asked us to apply, and told her we could expect positions as the Glacier Point interpretive rangers the following season.

Yosemite (YOSE)

I had never been to Yosemite National Park (YOSE). Penny had been there following her freshman year in college when she and three girl friends toured the west for a month. Somehow we had missed taking our girls to see the famous Yosemite, so my first visit was the day we were to report for duty in Wawona. We didn't need to check in until later in the afternoon, so we drove the Wawona road to the valley. That led us through a mile-long tunnel; we gasped as we pulled into the first available parking place at the Tunnel View, got out of the car and stood in awe as we stared into an "Oh My God!" view of spectacular beauty. The valley opened before us: Bridal Veil Falls to the right, with Cathedral Rocks behind it, El Capitan to the left, and Half Dome in the center distance. John Muir had entered the valley near here 1869 and described what he saw:

> Entering the Valley, gazing overwhelmed with the multitude of grand objects about us, perhaps the first to fix our attention will be the Bridal Veil, a beautiful waterfall on our right. Its brow, where it first leaps free from the cliff, is about 900 ft. above us; and as it sways and sings in the wind, clad in gauzy, sun-sifted spray, half falling, half floating, it seems infinitely gentle and fine; but the hymn it sings tells the solemn fateful power hidden beneath its soft clothing.

We saw Bridal Veil Falls that morning in full spring-flow, its gauzy veil spread wide, the sunlight creating many brilliant rainbows to inspire and welcome us to our home for the season.

After a delicious lunch on the patio of the Ahwahnee Hotel that beautiful spring day in early May, we drove the winding mountain road to the village of Wawona and located the ranger station. We met Dan Card and Jon Kinney, and discovered there would be just four of us, Kris Fister, Freddie Steele, and the two of us, to interpret the district for the first month. The three other Wawona rangers, due to commitments to school or real jobs, wouldn't show up until some time in June.

We were about to be rangers in Yosemite! We couldn't believe our good fortune. I credit it all to Penny's personality when she talked with Dan and Jon on the phone. Penny is an exceptionally good communicator. Dan and Jon recognized her talent and knew she had the abilities and personality they wanted. Dan was the Wawona District interpretive ranger—he ran the office and Jon was the seasonal supervisor, our immediate boss. They wanted us to know the park we would be interpreting, not only for American visitors, but for visitors from all parts of the world. They had sent us books on Yosemite, books on wildlife, plant-life, geology, natural history, and Native history—a lot to learn.

We and five other rangers would make up the interpretive staff for the Wawona District, three of us at Glacier Point, two at the Pioneer Historic Center in Wawona, and two covering the Mariposa Grove of giant sequoia trees. The valley was an entirely separate district, with its own rangers and their own training. We, as rangers in the Wawona district, would have very little interaction with the valley rangers. It was almost as if we were two separate parks. We learned to love being in the lesser district; the heavy visitation, crowds, and stress were in the crowded valley.

Training proved to be pretty loose. One morning, Dan was showing the four of us around the Wawona historic display of antique tools, wagons, and other pioneer items, when a small greenish bird flew to a nearby branch and sang to us. I asked what bird it was, Dan's reply was, "That's a 'bofus." Of course I had to know what a "bofus" is. Dan explained that, "A 'bofus' is 'both of us' don't know what that bird is." Dan knew paperwork and office management, but we needed to get our interpretive training from Jon who was a true naturalist, and a fine instructor. The two of them did make a good team, especially since Jon's wife, Jerry Andrews, was the district secretary for both interpretation and law enforcement, as well as the one who really kept the district running smoothly.

We found the history of the people who lived here before whites came to the Sierras interesting and important. In the mid 1800s the Yosemite Indian Tribe, led by Chief Tenaya, occupied the entire region, and preferred that white men stay out of the valley that was the home of a sub-group of the tribe who called themselves the Ahwahneechees—thus the name of the Ahwahnee Hotel. We found that many of the place names came from Indian names.

A colorful character named Major James D. Savage came to California in 1845 and set up a trading post on the Merced River, about 15 miles down stream from Yosemite Valley. In 1850 Indians, perhaps from the valley, raided the area, including Savage's trading post. In response, Savage organized the Mariposa Battalion, intending to force the Indians out of their stronghold without killing them. The plan called for the Indians to give themselves up to the Indian Commission and become good law-abiding citizens. Chief Tenaya, with a few of his men, did visit the white men's camp, but most of the tribe stayed in its valley. Apparently neither side was as belligerent as most whites and Indians of the day; there was no blood shed. When the Mariposa Battalion went in after the Indians, they saw the Yosemite Valley for the first time, recognized its unique beauty, and didn't commit the usual massacre of local residents.

Members of the battalion were so impressed with the valley that they wrote letters describing its wonders. After reading of the valley, James M. Hutchings, publisher of California Magazine, brought a horseback party including artists Thomas Ayres, Albert Bierstadt, and Henry Pratt, to see the wonders of Yosemite. Their accounts and sketches of the area appeared in papers all over the world. In 1864 Congress proclaimed, and President Lincoln signed, legislation making the Yosemite area a park and granting it to California as the country's first State Park.

John Muir had become captivated by Yosemite's grandeur. His writings, along with those of others, convinced the federal government to pass enabling legislation, the "Yosemite Grant," in 1890, and brought President Teddy Roosevelt to visit in 1903. In 1905 California returned Yosemite State Park to the federal government, who had created Yellowstone National Park in 1872, and now declared Yosemite the United States' and the world's second National Park.

The Sierra Nevada Mountains are arguably the most spectacularly beautiful mountains in the world. Muir called them "The Range of Light." They were uplifted during the Cretaceous Period, 95 to 80 million years ago. A geology book that Jon had sent told us that the Sierra Nevada Mountains are the result of 30,000 to 40,000 feet of sedimentary rock collecting in a geosyncline, an enormous valley, many millions of years ago. When that much sediment accumulates, enough heat and pressure are created to melt the lower portions. As rock melts it expands, pushing toward the surface resulting in a large batholith, a solidified magma chamber. Those original sediments were consumed in the molten magma, or warped, uplifted, and eroded until they are essentially nonexistent today. The batholith now appears as the nearly white Sierra granites. Geologists describe specific spots of the granitic mountains as granodiorite, quartz diorite, quartz monzonite, or many other geologic descriptive terms, but to most visitors, and us, "granite" is what they are. "Granite is an igneous rock formed at great depth; consisting of crystalline quartz and white feldspar, with lesser amounts of black mica," the book said.

The unique rock formations are the result of different portions of the batholith cooling at different rates; producing the massive unjointed rock of El Capitan, and vertical joints that resulted in

Glacier Point, Half Dome, Sentinel Dome, and the upper half of Yosemite Falls. Most of the debris created by the fracturing of those joints was carried away by the glaciers that filled the valley during the Wisconsin phase of the ice age, from about 25,000 to 10,000 years ago.

Yosemite's famous water falls are rivers that flow over cliffs that were left when the glaciers scoured away 3,000 feet of valley walls, leaving the unglaciated streams in what is referred to as hanging valleys.

Our positions in Yosemite were as interpretive rangers at Glacier Point. When we reported in Jon let us know the Glacier Point road still had several feet of winter's snow blocking access, so we weren't going to see our summer home for a few weeks.

Until the Glacier Point road was opened we would help Kris and Freddie, interpret the collection of historic buildings and equipment at the Pioneer Yosemite Historic Center in the village of Wawona, and the spectacular Mariposa Grove of giant sequoia trees. On busy days traffic control in the Grove was added to our assignments. That meant we needed to learn another subject; how to be traffic cops.

In 1875 a road from Fresno to Wawona was opened and the beautiful, still functional, Wawona Hotel was built to satisfy the wants of visitors. The Indians had to adjust to white man's presence or leave their historic home: they chose to adjust. The Pioneer Center focused, almost exclusively, on the white man's side of local history, with displays of relocated historic buildings, pioneer crafts, tools, and horse drawn coaches, ignoring the Indians.

The village of Wawona had been built around the desires of people from San Francisco in the early 1900s, who wanted a summer getaway. Almost all of the houses were older, and having been built with summer vacation in mind, many weren't heated or insulated; the place we stayed with Freddie was one of those. Spring mornings in the Sierras, at 3,500 feet, tended to be "well-digger cold," so it never took us long to get dressed after the alarm went off. It was a well equipped old house, and had a great wood burning fireplace in the living room where we often enjoy a warm fire, and a beer or glass of wine in the evenings.

The government was in the business of acquiring those old homes whenever one went on the market. We were staying in one of the government owned homes. The Department of Interior had first right of refusal on lots of places in Wawona and owned several houses where the original owners were allowed to live until they died or moved on.

We became friends with an elderly couple in Wawona who had sold their home to the government but still lived there year-round. We spent many an evening after our daily runs chatting with Myrtle, Lou, and their dog Daisy. One of those evenings, we were sitting in their yard with a glass of lemonade, when Daisy started acting really weird. She cried, wanted in Myrtle's lap, wanted down, ran in circles, tried to hide. We had no idea what the problem was, unless there was a bear around. Suddenly we felt what seemed like waves rolling under us. The 200 foot tall firs started swaying and twirling their tops. We had been near the epicenter of a 5+ magnitued earthquake, and Daisy knew it long before it actually happened. Amazing what "lesser animals" can perceive before we "higher animals."

The Mariposa Grove of giant sequoias was set aside as park land at the same time as the valley and is only a few miles from Wawona. The Grove itself is one of the most inspiring sights Penny or I have ever experienced. Jon took us interpretive rangers to the grove early one morning; fog was rising, visibility was limited. We walked through a stand of large fir, cedar, and white pine trees with diameters of four and five feet. As we rounded a curve and entered a clearing; in front of us stood the bole of a tree more than 30 feet across; we could only see 30 or 40 feet up through the fog, so it appeared the size of a house. As the fog rose, so did the tree, until we could finally see a limb, and eventually the top more than 200 feet up—the Grizzly Giant, 2,300 years old—not the oldest, nor the tallest living tree, but the most massive thing that has ever lived—except for a few other sequoias. Not far from the Grizzly Giant is the Tunnel Tree that had been carved out to allow stage-coaches to drive through it in 1895, and the Fallen Monarch, which Jon said had fallen hundreds of years ago, and still showed no signs of decay. The Historic Center has pictures of troops of soldiers standing on the Monarch in the late 1800s.

Jon was an interpreter's interpreter; he knew his subject and presented it like an actor on stage. He had the ability to mesmerize people and teach at the same time. We would be talking about the natural history of these trees for the next few weeks, and Jon made sure we knew about them. Besides their size and age, they are remarkable for their fire resistance; the reddish stringy bark may be two feet thick, and almost impervious to fire. Scars from fires hundreds of years before mark the base of most of the mature trees. Jon asked us to walk into the burned opening in the base of the Telescope Tree with our eyes closed, then open our eyes and slowly look up; what we saw was the sky at the end of a tunnel, like looking through a charcoal-lined telescope. The completely burned-out heart of the tree was surrounded by healthy wood and bark. The top was missing but the tree lived on.

With good intentions, man had decided that the sequoia trees would be best served by suppressing fire from their environment. At that time, foresters didn't know that sequoia seeds require the mineral soil and open light, left by a fire, to germinate. Without fire, shade tolerant fir and pine took over, and nearly stopped sequoia reproduction until the Park Service introduced controlled burning to clear the under-story of small trees and brush. These burns not only provide the soil and light conditions required by sequoia seeds and seedlings, but clear the brush and down-wood that could be a fire hazard when it accumulated against a sequoia trunk. Since we had firefighting experience, we were assigned to participate in controlled burning that fall—a good opportunity for us to learn another aspect of wildfire behavior and control.

When the Glacier Point road was finally cleared of snow, we saw that the Point has one of the most spectacular views in the country. You look directly at Half Dome to the east; to the north the 2,425-foot Yosemite Falls drops to the valley floor, and is backed by a panoramic view of the High Sierra's; to the west with good field glasses or a spotting scope you can watch rock climbers, looking like aunts, slowly make their way up the face of El Capitan. From the Point you look straight down 3,200 feet to the valley floor and the Merced River. South of the Point, Illilouette Creek plunges over Illilouette Falls on its way to the valley, and is only about two miles down the Panoramic Trail.

One of the most interesting challenges for us as the Glacier Point rangers was keeping people from climbing the fence that encircles the end of the Point. The fence is there to prevent people— who haven't enough sense to stay out of extremely dangerous places—from standing on the edge of the cliff. From the very edge they would have a better view of that vertical 3,200 feet to the valley floor, and people know "they would never fall." When telling a person they were breaking the law, and to get back inside the fence didn't work, we often explained that, "Someone falling was no skin off our nose. It is an example of survival of the fittest and natural selection. The the rangers in the valley have to clean up the mess and do the paperwork." That usually got their attention. That summer an attractive waist-high wall was built to replace the ugly fence. It was definitely nicer looking, but gave fools a better place from which to prove what fools humans can be.

There were four of us rangers stationed in a little residential area a half mile from the Point. Rich Romero, a law enforcement ranger, had the responsibility of "fightin' crime" on the Glacier Point Road and in Bridalveil Creek Campground. He also collected camp- ground fees and launched hang-gliders into the Illilouette Valley on scheduled days. When Rich couldn't launch the hang-gliders for one reason or another, either Penny or I had that duty.

To hang-glide in Yosemite you must show the launching ranger proof of experience and expertise to a predetermined high level. Hang-gliders are simply a swept-back wing with a trapeze-bar held across the chest used in maneuvering. A climbing-gear-like harness secures the pilot to the wing and provides support for the legs. Steering is accomplished by moving the bar and adjusting body weight. It is an adrenaline rushing experience. The pilot in his harness holds the wing above his head, runs to the edge of the 3,000 foot cliff and dives into open space. You can feel the excitement as they ready themselves and hear it when they invariably give a long scream as they dive off the edge. Rich and his girlfriend, Ann, loved the game, but we passed on their offer to take us double, which wasn't permitted in the park anyway.

Dave Balogh was the third interpretive ranger at the Point. He had worked there for several summers and brought his family along for the season. Dave, a school teacher, his wife Martha, and two young kids, David and Elizabeth, lived with us in that little area. We got along fine, and had some fun parties together over the summer.

Housing in the Park Service is always an interesting challenge. We were the new members to the Glacier Point crew, thus at the low end of the pecking order. Consequently Rich and the Baloghs lived in the two old log cabins that the park had built long ago. Our house was a converted latrine, 10 feet wide and 20 feet long. It had electricity and cold running water, which ran into a laundry sink. There was a counter in one corner where we could put our electric, single burner hot-plate—our stove. Shelves above the counter provided storage. A small table with two chairs made a dinning room. Pseudo curtains covered four shoulder high windows, we managed to trade two single beds for a double bed. It is standard in the Park Service that rangers provide all of their own kitchen equipment: pots and pans, dishes, glasses, and silverware, all linens, and what ever else you want. After two seasons at Jewel Cave we had the kitchen figured out and had a box of stuff labeled "NPS Kitchen" which we simply picked up as we loaded for the summer.

A hundred yards down the hill sat a little building with a toilet on one side and a shower on the other. That was the bathroom for the seven Glacier Point residents. The shower side even had a sink with a mirror above it, and hot water—most of the time. Of course all cleaning and maintenance of the area was the responsibility of the seven of us, and since we were a little more picky than the others, the bathroom chore fell to us.

Work was fun and always a challenge since we dealt with visitors from all over the world. Trying to interpret what they were asking in their broken English, (far superior to what we could have done in their language) was quite interesting and challenging. One of us was at Glacier Point most of the time, from when Rich opened a gate on the Point road at 0800 to 2200 when it was closed. We did a daily sunset program at the Point, led hikes to Sentinel Dome and Taft Point, talked about and explained the regional geology, trees, flowers, wildlife, and anything that visitors might bring up to ask about.

The hikes we led to Taft Point were my favorite. From a parking area a trail leads across an open meadow of sky-blue lupin, and red and orange Indian paintbrush; the aroma was like being immersed in orange blossoms. People are interested in the names of plants and animals, but rarely want more information. I usually explained ways to tell fir trees from spruce. "See the cones," I said, "On fir trees they grow up like the fur on an angry dog's back, on spruce they hang down."

"Those stand-up fir cones are torn up and their seeds eaten where they stand, mostly by red squirrel; while the hanging spruce cones are harvested whole and stored in the squirrel's midden for winter food." That led to my showing a spruce branch next to a fir branch and explaining that, "Fir starts with an 'f', the needles are flat and friendly, while spruce needles are square, and sharp, and start with 's.'"

As we walked on I would stick my knife in the side of a tree, step back, look up, and ask, "How high up will my knife be if we come back and find it in 20 years?" Most people had no idea where the knife would be, but guessed it would be much higher, a few knew it would be at the same height. Trees grow vertically only at the end of branches, trunks grow in diameter.

Someone usually asked about the fuzzy gray-green stuff hanging from branches, the goat's beard lichen. I explained that all lichen are a symbiotic relationship between a fungi and an algae. Of course I had a story that kids loved and adults could remember; "Freddie Fungus and Alice Algae lived in the forest; Alice Algae made food by combining energy from the sun, carbon dioxide from the air, and water from the ground. That's called photosynthesis. And Freddie Fungus built a house that provided shelter. They found neither could get along without the other, so they took a 'lichen' to each other, and together they lived happily ever after." That got laughs from kids, smiles from parents, and rolled eyes from some others.

Every evening one of the three of us interpretive rangers did a campfire program at the campground a few miles back up the road. It always started with the lighting of a campfire, which everyone seemed to love. They were always impressed with how beautifully our fires took off when we put a match to the tinder. We made teepee fires from a tiny bit of paper covered by shavings and splinters. Split sticks of Ponderosa formed the teepee (we didn't mention that the sticks of Ponderosa had been dipped in kerosene), plus larger pieces of ponderosa for a longer burn. When we put a match to the paper, it ignited the shavings into a nice little fire which soon reached the oily Ponderosa, and, voila, we quickly had a beautiful fire to stand beside while telling our stories.

Balough told a hilarious story about a bear that got into a dumpster and encouraged people to throw garbage in. Penny told one of a number of tales of the Mewak Indians who had lived in and around Yosemite for hundreds of years. I told my three theories of the formation of Yosemite Valley: either God said "Shazam" and there it was, or the Great Sierra Rock Squirrel chewed its way through the Sierra Mountains, and defecated in the valley to the west, creating both Yosemite Valley and the productive Central Valley of California. Finally, I would explain how a glacier came through and scoured the valley to its present shape.

We always walked the campground before our evening campfire program, talking with people, seeing how they were doing, answering questions, and just BS-ing. One evening as Penny arrived for her evening in the campground, an excited camper rushed up and told her of a man defacing a huge boulder. When Penny got to the spot she saw a man with rock-hammer and chisel drunkenly carving "GROCIA MY LOVE" into the boulder. Protecting the resource is one of a ranger's primary duties. Penny climbed up beside the perpetrator and said, "Sir; you are defacing the property of this park which is not permitted. You will stop immediately and return to your campsite." The drunk, who was eight or ten inches taller than Penny and at least a hundred pounds heavier, stood there with his rock-hammer in his hand, stared at Penny for—it seemed like forever—climbed down, and staggered back to his campsite. The group of onlookers who had gathered broke into applause. Penny climbed down feeling weak, talked briefly with a few people, and followed the drunk back to his camp. We didn't yet have law enforcement commissions, so Penny got on her radio, called headquarters and requested law enforcement back-up. Our friend Tom Cox showed up in a few minutes, cited the man for defacing government property, drunk and disorderly conduct, and probably a few other things. He gave Penny a big hug, thanked her, then gave her hell for not calling him to do the confrontation. Tom pointed out that the man could easily have killed her. At Penny's 50th birthday party a few weeks later, Tom admitted that the situation was better handled by Penny, saying if he had confronted the man the situation might well have gotten violent.

Responding to emergencies became routine for us both. The most disheartening we ever had was a call to a "Deer/visitor interaction, with visitor injuries." We arrived just after the emergency squad, to find a woman in hysterics and a dead little girl who had been gored and eviscerated by a buck deer. On the assumption that all animals in a National Park are tame and friendly, the woman had her young daughter feed nuts to the buck while mother took pictures. All had gone well until something startled the buck. It jerked its head up, antlers caught the girl below the waist, tore her intestines out and ruptured her aorta. She had bled to death in a matter of minutes—long before EMS could get there. I did traffic control, and moved the gawking public on down the road. Penny sat with the mother, and in a motherly consoling way got the woman under control. The medics loaded the child's body into the squad. Higher authority from the valley showed up, took the mother in their car, and followed the squad to the valley medical center. It is so unfortunate that people don't educate themselves before going to any natural area.

OUR CLOSEST NEIGHBORS WERE THE CREW DOING THE CONSTRUCTION of the wall around the point—their camping trailers were parked just up-hill from our quarters. Most of them were Hispanic men, and great fun to party with. They went home to Fresno every weekend to see their wives, replenish the beer supply, and get a load of fresh homemade tortillas. You have never had tortillas until you have fresh ones made today by a Mexican lady, and these guys knew how to fill them with the best concoction of stuff you could imagine. We spent a lot of evenings around a campfire—either theirs or ours—just talking, and drinking beer, eating tacos, and sharing stories. We were amazed by their intelligence and grasp of the world, and life in general. Thinking about how they compare with a lot of upper-middle class young white men we knew, it was quite clear that the differences between the two groups was not intellect. The hispanics had equal brains and skills as the whites, but had not had the education or, most importantly, the breaks offered to the whites by parents and society.

One afternoon I had a group on a walk and Balough had the day off, so Penny had the Point by herself. When "Furman the Forman," as we and his crew referred to the boss of the construction team, came up to her and said, "Penny we have a problem back at the parking lot."

Penny of course thought the worst. Furman told her there was a group of tourists gathered around a log that the crew had rolled over that morning. There was a very pissed, very big rattle snake by the log, and Furman was afraid someone might do something stupid and get bitten. Furman wanted to kill the snake with a long hoe that he had. Penny said, "No, we don't kill wildlife in National Parks. I'll get the snake-snare, catch it and move it back in the woods." She had once seen a rattle-snake in the Columbus Zoo, on the other side of a glass wall, but this was up-close and personal, and she had never even seen a snake-snare used. Snake-snares are a four-foot long pole, with a cord forming a loop at the far end and running back to the handle. The idea is to put the loop over the head of the snake, pull on the end of the cord, and have the snake under control in the loop.

All went well. On Penny's order the crowd spread to let the ranger in. Now it was up to one scared ranger to capture the snake and carry it off to a safe place. She moved to within range for the snake-snare, but out of the snakes striking range, carefully lowered the loop over its head, pulled the cord, and had the snake! Now what to do? The crowd stayed well out of the way as she walked down a side trail, with Furman going along still wanting to kill it for her. It was big, nearly five feet long and very unhappy, also quite heavy out there at the end of the pole. All she could do was carry it down the trail a couple hundred yards, then a ways into the woods where it should be safe to release the pissed-off snake. Now she wondered, how do I release this monster? She swung it and released the cord at the same time; the snake flew out over a manzanita bush, and landed with a thump. Now it was time for the ranger and Furman to get the hell out of there before the snake decided to take revenge. The snake, of course, wanted nothing but to get away from this crazy ranger lady.

After Labor Day, visitation to most parks slows to, as we like to say, "The newly-wed and the nearly-dead." A lot of the ranger staff also return to their real jobs as teachers, students, or whatever. This leaves the park short of rangers to deal with those "nearly-dead and newly-wed." The question came up; could we stay beyond our agreed departure date and add managing the campground to our regular duties at the point? Well we guessed we could; all it would require was canceling some patients, and letting our girls know we wouldn't be home for a while longer. This put us in the law enforcement division, as well as the interpretive division, so we could handle the finances involved with the campground. That meant we would have an additional supervisor, Hal Grovert, a law enforcement ranger whom we had gotten to know over the summer. We got along well with Hal and enjoyed the additional responsibilities of campground management. Dan Card, the boss of our interpretive positions, wanted to be sure we would return for the same jobs next season. Silly question, of course we would. We loved Yosemite and Glacier Point.

That fall Hal applied for the position of District Ranger at Katmai National Park and Preserve in Alaska. He was afraid he had over stated his qualifications and gotten himself in over his head. He wanted people working for him who he knew and had confidence in. He called us that winter, told us about his new position, and his desire to hire people he knew and trusted. He asked us to apply to Katmai. Penny immediately said "No! We're looking forward to returning to the great positions we had at Glacier Point." Those positions at Glacier Point are some of the plumb jobs in the Park Service. We were fortunate to have them. I was on a separate phone and said, "Yes! We'll come to Katmai." Hal didn't want to be in the middle of that argument, so he told us to talk it over and call him. I said, "We don't need to call back. We'll be there."

When I got down stairs I had some serious explaining to do. Our decisions are always mutual. I reminded Penny that Katmai was a place we had dreamed of since we had first been to Alaska in 1973. We were getting older, so if we didn't take this opportunity to work "The Great Land" we might never get another chance. I reminded her of her years of work as a lobbyist for the National Audubon Society, working on the Alaska National Interest Lands Conservation Act. She bought my argument, and it was settled right then, Katmai and Alaska were in our future! We realized that we were taking a chance passing up Glacier Point, but we couldn't turn down the opportunity to work in Katmai.

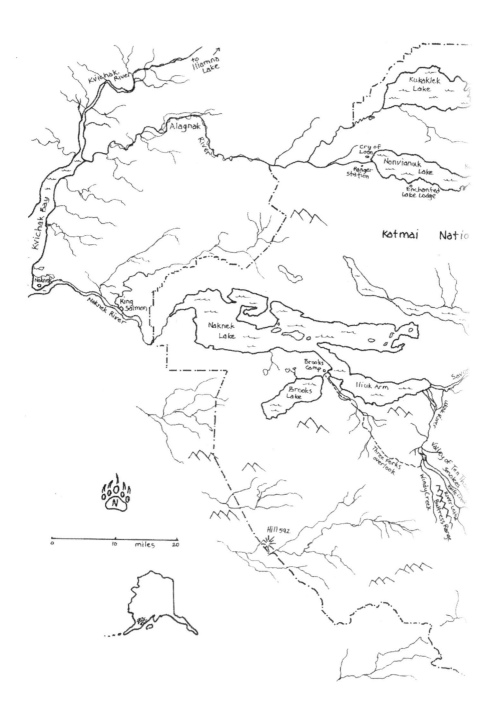

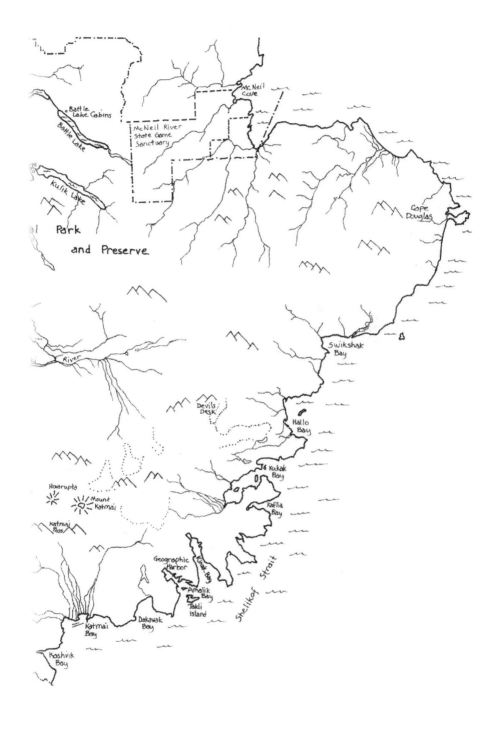

Katmai (KATM)

We wanted to know about the place we were heading. We had given up wonderful positions at Yosemite to take jobs at Katmai. What would we find? Maps showed Katmai National Park spanning the Alaska Peninsula, about 350 miles southwest of Anchorage, from the Shelikof Strait on the east, nearly to Bristol Bay on the west. The Aleutian Range of mountains forms the backbone of the peninsula and is part of the volcanic Ring of Fire that surrounds the Pacific Ocean. The Alaska Peninsula and Aleutian chain of islands are only a small part of the volcanic Pacific ring, but they play a very large role in the story of Katmai National Park. Any of Katmai's 15 volcanos could become violently active at any time. Mts. Martin, Mageik, and Trident are considered active volcanos, in that steam plumes are frequently seen venting from them. Mts. Katmai, Novarupta, Griggs, and the Kukak volcano are considered dormant. What is known as the Mt. Katmai eruption created the Valley of 10,000 Smokes and led to the formation of Katmai National Park. The park bulletin explains:

> The June 1912 eruption of Novarupta Volcano altered the Katmai area dramatically. Severe earthquakes shook the area for weeks before Novarupta exploded with cataclysmic force. Enormous quantities of hot, glowing pumice and ash were ejected from Novarupta and nearby fissures. This material flowed over the terrain, destroying all life in its path. Trees up slope were snapped off and carbonized by

the blasts of hot wind and gas. For several days ash, pumice, and gas were ejected and a haze darkened the sky over the entire Northern Hemisphere.

Still curious, we talked with former Katmai Superintendent Gil Blinn. He referred to "The Katmai" in almost reverent terms. He told us, "The Katmai is a land where man does not dominate, where time and change are measured only by the sun, the tides, and the seasons." That expresses how Penny and I now feel about Katmai. Few people will ever visit Katmai National Park & Preserve, fewer still will ever know "The Katmai." It remains a place where one must spend time observing, listening, smelling, and yes, contemplating, in order to adequately appreciate this unique natural world.

Ellen Maloy concludes her book Raven's Exile, a season on the Green River, by stating "Anyone who writes a deep map of Place fears her words will detonate the place." That certainly is our feeling of The Katmai, a place you would like everyone to know about but not to visit. Two things keep Katmai, and most of Alaska, from being destroyed by over visitation and population growth: the lousy weather and the swarms of biting insects. To be honest, the cost and difficulty of getting there also play a large roll in the park's limited use.

People visit Brooks Camp, the park's primary visitor destination, to watch the bears, and fish for rainbow trout and sockeye salmon. The salmon are there to spawn in their ancestral breeding grounds, the streams above Naknek and Brooks Lakes. The rainbow trout are there to feed on salmon eggs and fingerlings on their way to the sea. The Alaskan brown bear (Ursus arctos) is there to feed on the red, or sockeye, salmon—fresh in July, spawned out in August and September.

There are 5,000-year-old barabra pits (Native pit-houses) along the Brooks river where Aleuts lived and fished, indicating the area has been used by humans since before recorded history. The Aleuts lived a sustainable life style, all of their trash was biodegradable, tools were made from bone, antler, or stone, and their population remained well within the carrying capacity of the area. The Park Service rangers, were there to provide for the protection of the resource (plant and animal life and archeological sites) and to assist in the education and enjoyment of the visiting public.

Penny and I would be there at the request of District Ranger Hal Grovert, and because Katmai is a place we had dreamed of for years—the ultimate in natural areas of the United States. We had visited Gil Blinn when we were working at Jewel Cave and he was superintendent of Bad Lands National Park. His stories of Katmai had convinced us that we had to be a part of "The Katmai" experience.

Blinn recommended we read Dave Bohn's book *Rambles Through an Alaskan Wild* and the book *Exploring Katmai National Monument.* Both proved to be very interesting and enlightening reads on the park and its formation.

Those books gave us the sort of information we were looking for: Earthquakes shake the Aleutian Mountains frequently, so the quakes in the spring of 1912 weren't very disturbing until about the first of June. Then the quakes, centered around the Mt. Katmai area, became more frequent and stronger. The residents of the Aleut village of Katmai, where the Katmai River flows into the Shelikof Straits, saw, felt, and heard enough to expect an eruption. They abandon their village and boated south towards the village of Cold Bay. Most of the residents of Savonoski Village, to the west, where the Ukak River joins the Savonoski River near Naknek Lake, headed for the cannery town of Naknek, 35 miles away, on the shore of Bristol Bay.

On 6 June 1912 the chief of the Aleut village of Savonoski, who had adopted the name "American Pete," was heading up the Katmai Trail, along the Ukak River. He intended to retrieve gear from his hunting and fishing camp several miles up river. There had been a lot of rumbling and earthquakes emanating from Mt. Katmai and he feared his camp might be damaged and his gear lost. Not far up the trail; Pete heard, felt, and saw the eruption of Mt. Katmai and the nearby Novarupta Volcano. As he later related to National Geographic Society explorer, Robert F. Griggs:

> The Katmai Mountain blow up with lots of fire, and fire come down trail with lots of smoke. We go fast Savonoski. Everyone get in bidarka. Helluva job. We come Naknek one day, dark, no could see. Hot ash fall. Work like hell.

The Mt. Katmai eruption, which proved to be the eruption of the Novarupta volcano, was one of the largest in historic times, The Katmai/Novarupta eruption produced more than four cubic miles of pumice and ash, along with enormous amounts of volatile gasses. It was 20 times larger than the 1980 eruption of Mt. Saint Helens, (13 cu km vs 0.25 cu km) and much more powerful than the devastating 1883 eruption of Krakatau, which produced less than half the eruptive matter of the Katmai eruption. The reason Krakatau is so well known is the fact that 36,000 people were killed in that eruption, while the Katmai eruption killed no known humans. The death toll among wildlife and vegetation had to be enormous. Forty square miles of the lush Ukak River valley were obliterated by the several thousand degree hot pumice and ash which was carried along by tremendous quantities of hot gases. Wind carried ash 100 miles southeast to Kodiak Island where it accumulated three feet deep—a lantern couldn't be seen at arms length for three days. Even Seattle was dusted with ash, clothes on outside lines were damaged by acid rain. Air-born ash blocking solar radiation caused temperatures in the Northern Hemisphere to be lowered by two degrees fahrenheit for a year.

The Katmai Trail that American Pete had started up was the only route for Aleut and Russian traders as they traded between the Shelikof on the east coast and Bristol Bay on the west coast of the Alaska Peninsula. When gold was discovered near Nome, the trail became a shortcut for men heading for the 1899 gold rush. It eliminated the voyage around the Alaska Peninsula between the Gulf of Alaska and Bristol Bay. By 1900 the trail was even used by the U.S. mail service, but by 1906 the gold rush had dwindled and the trail returned to Native use.

The trail where it crosses Katmai Pass between Mt. Megeik and Trident Volcano has been known as an extremely windy and dangerous spot. In 1898 Josiah Spurr led a U.S. Geological Survey expedition across the pass. He wrote:

> Many Natives have perished here by being caught in gales, for during storms, even in summer, the wind blows with intensity and piercing coldness. At such times stones of considerable size are picked up by the wind and carried through the narrow defiles where the traveller must walk. …Owing to this danger Natives cannot be induced to cross [the pass] except in perfectly calm and clear weather.

The Katmai eruption prompted the U.S. Geological Survey, in cooperation with the National Geographic Society, to send George C. Martin, an experienced researcher of the Alaska Peninsula, to examine the site. At the obliterated Katmai village Martin found a few strands of grass and three dogs, who had somehow survived, as the only living remains. He decided all evidence pointed to the eruption of Mt. Katmai, wrote his report, and went home.

In 1915 the National Geographic Society sent an expedition headed by Robert Fiske Griggs, a botanist from The Ohio State University, to examine the biological effects of the eruption on plant life on Kodiak Island, where ash had been deposited three feet deep. Griggs found vegetation well recovered and decided to extend his biological studies to the actual eruption site. He found Katmai Bay awash in floating ash and pumice. A recent rain storm had swept down the Katmai River, erasing all sign of the Katmai

Trail and leaving knee deep ash-mud and quicksand, making the river valley inaccessible.

In 1916 Griggs, with a four-man expedition, was sent back for further research. They found conditions had changed considerably. Vegetation on the Katmai River flats was taking hold, streams had developed channels, and mountains were much greener. The team reached the rim of the Katmai caldera and were "struck speechless by the scene, for the whole crater lay below us." Looking down 1,000 feet they saw a blue-green lake with a small island in the center, and thousands of jets of steam "roaring like a great locomotive."

Descending from the crater rim Griggs and Folsom, another team member, in spite of increasing wind portending a storm, decided to hike to the pass for a view of the Ukak Valley. Griggs described what they saw:

> I can never forget my sensations at the sight which met my eyes…stretching as far as the eye could reach…were hundreds—no, thousands—of little volcanoes…sending up columns of steam which rose a thousand feet before dissolving.

In 1917 Griggs, Folsom, and D. B. Church, a student of Griggs at Ohio State, and several other scientists returned and found the "ten thousand smokes" still active. The February issue of National Geographic magazine clearly showed the geologic and scenic significance of the valley and prompted the Society to propose it be named a national park.

On 24 September 1918 President Woodrow Wilson signed a proclamation creating the 1,700-square-mile Katmai National Monument to preserve the Valley of Ten Thousand Smokes. The monument was enlarged several times, the last in 1980 when President Carter signed ANILCA, the Alaska National Interest Lands Conservation Act (in which Penny Starr had played such an important role).

Until the 1950s it was assumed that the eruption had come from Mt. Katmai. Garniss Curtis, a geologist from the University of California, Berkeley, showed the ash flows of rhyolite and andesite had come from Novarupta (Latin for newly erupted), which is now a low dome, described as a classic example of a volcanic plug. Curtis gave the most plausible theory of events of the 1912 eruption, "diversion-collapse:"

> Within a few moments, no less than 2.5 cubic miles of ash were expelled and the incandescent mass, acting like fiery-hot liquid, swept down the valley with incredible swiftness. …At or about the same time…the entire top of Mount Katmai Volcano collapsed.

Katmai Ecosystem

Everything is as it is, because it was as it was!
—Thomas Gold

Over the following decade, Penny and I had the opportunity to observe and learn a land and ecosystem that had evolved following the Pleistocene Epoch. From 1.6 million to 10,000 years ago, the northern two-thirds of North America, including most of Alaska, was covered by glacial ice, several thousand feet thick. West central Alaska from the southern side of the Yukon/Kuskoquim Delta to the Brooks Range formed an ice-free land bridge to Asia called Beringia.

Glaciers flowing from the Aleutian Range carved deep fiords on the eastern slope and emptied into the Pacific Ocean and the Shelikof Strait. The west flowing glaciers carved U-shaped valleys through the mountains, gouging out depressions that would later fill with water to become deep mountain lakes. Some of those mountain valleys have recessional moraines across them, which divide them into two or more lakes. A few of the connecting streams run over flows of basaltic lava, forming impressive water falls.

Farther west there are broad valleys where glaciers spread and carved less-deep depressions that now contain larger shallower lakes. Still further west the mountains have been left behind, but evidence of the glaciers is everywhere. Ground moraine and pothole lakes are scattered all across the lowlands. Those pothole lakes are the result of retreating glaciers leaving icebergs that melted where they sat. Lakes and lake systems soon developed connecting streams that drain them and flow to Bristol Bay.

The underlying volcanic geology and erosional activity of wind, water, and ice created a landscape which provides a habitat that plant and animal life adapted to. Katmai is known for brown bears, who earn a major part of their living by harvesting salmon migrating to spawn in their natal streams.

Sockeye, or red, salmon are the keystone species that controls life in Katmai. The cold, freshwater streams flowing from the glacier-capped mountains provide ideal breeding habitat for sockeye. In the breeding process the female digs a shallow ditch, called a redd, in clean gravel by sweeping her tail from side to side; she lays several hundred eggs in the redd, moves aside to allow a male to fertilize the eggs with his sperm. He then moves aside so the female can come back and sweep gravel over the fertilized eggs. This process may be repeated several times so that each pair leaves many hundreds of fertilized eggs. Normally the male will stay in the area to protect the eggs until he dies in a couple of weeks. The female will also die within a few weeks. Their life's work is complete. Their bodies will feed bears, wolves, eagles, raven, gulls, and innumerable other creatures. The parts of the salmon that don't get eaten by carnivores and scavengers will be consumed by bacteria and protista, who in turn will be food for insect larvae. Those insect larvae are food for young fish, or hatch into the billions of insects that feed millions of birds, and whose blood-sucking bites drive humans and other mammals to distraction.

It's the diet of salmon that has given the brown bear the growth advantage over their brethren, the grizzly bear (also Ursus arctos). Coastal brown bear males often weigh 1,000 pounds or more; that's 400 pounds more than interior grizzlies. During hibernation brown bears may lose 350 to 400 pounds. The well-fed brown bear is much more likely to be a calmer and less aggressive bear than the, primarily herbivorous, grizzly, and thus more tolerant of humans in its home.

As the old saying goes, "Does the bear shit in the woods?" You bet he does. So do the other animals of Katmai. The feces and urine, especially of the bear, fertilizes the soil, promoting the growth of plants that moose, bear, and all herbivores consume. Pollen, nectar and mammal blood feed the insects whose eggs and larvae will feed the salmon smolt and perpetuate the life that was the salmon and the life that is The Katmai.

North To Alaska

Flying into the little town of King Salmon, Alaska, in early April 1983, Penny looked out the window of the Alaska Airlines jet at rain, snow, and sleet blowing horizontally and wondered what we had gotten ourselves into. "No problem," I said, "We only signed on for six months, we can make it."

On the flight up we had the opportunity to do some reminiscing on the family that had always been such an important part of our lives and how it was evolving. We were heading to the Great Land to see and learn Katmai National Park and its brown bears. But we had another reason to be excited. Our daughter Lori had just delivered a baby girl, Claire Starr Houston.

Youngest daughter, Kristy, was still living in our home in Columbus, so we had kissed her goodbye and driven to Portland, Oregon, to see Lori, her partner John, and our granddaughter, Claire. Carin, our second daughter, had married Mark a year ago and was living in Seattle, so we would see them too.

Our first season at Jewel Cave, Carin had given us a big surprised by showing-up unannounced. Bruce, the fun-loving tease at JECA, had met her at the information desk before either of us knew she was coming. Penny and I were on cave tours, but Penny should be finishing hers shortly. Bruce took Carin down the elevator, so when Penny and her group approached to ride back to the surface, Carin stepped out and said, "Hi Mom." Penny, of course, did exactly as Bruce had expected, she screamed, "Carin! Is that you? What are you doing here?" Her group was forgotten, but enjoyed the most fun part of their cave tour, as Penny ran to her daughter for a big hug.

Lori and John had stopped at Jewel Cave, that same year, for a couple of days as they moved to Portland. We had never met John and were glad to see the future father of our grandchildren. Penny understood that generation much better than I. It was hard for me to accept our daughter living with a man before they were married, even though it was happening all around me.

Both couples had spent a few days with us in Yosemite last year. Lori had let us know then that she was pregnant, now we had added a granddaughter to our expanding family.

Carin and Mark had been married for over a year and were living in Seattle. Carin had rented a cottage on an Island in the San Juan's for us all to spend a few days before we went to Katmai. Two daughters, two sons-in-law and a brand new granddaughter, and us, spending time in a beautiful spot; what a wonderful way to get to know our growing family better.

The next several years, as we were heading to Alaska we would drive to the northwest, visit both daughters and their families, and leave our car in Portland for Lori to use, and for us to have for returning home.

The airport terminal in King Salmon sits on the SE corner of the U.S. Air Defense Command base known as King Salmon Air Force Base. The base shares its runways with a couple of commercial airlines servicing the area. The balance of the several thousand acres is the base housing and all of the facilities required for the F15s that protect Alaska and northwest America from all of those big, bad, nasty people across the Pacific Ocean. When you walk the few feet from the door of the little terminal building to the street, you look a hundred yards to the right, and a hundred yards to the left and you have seen the town. It's known as a government town because almost all of the residents work for a governmental agency such as; military, National Park Service (NPS), U.S. Fish and Wild Service (US Fish), U.S. Forest Service (FS), Alaska Department of Fish and

Game (ADF&G), or U.S. Weather Service. I am sure there are other governmental agencies that I can't think of right now, but you get the idea. There are a few civilian facilities too: two bars, one of which serves burgers and fries and even a salad, and a little grocery store.

Fortunately Hal Grovert, the District Ranger who had talked us into leaving Yosemite, met us and took us to his house. He told us we could sleep on his floor that night, and that there would be a party at Superintendent Dave Morris' house that evening. The party proved to be an opportunity to meet the other six seasonal rangers and the permanent staff of six—Dave, Chief Ranger Loren Casebeer, Hal, Resource Management Specialist Kathy Jope, Chief of Maintenance Carl Yost, and secretary Sally Orot. It turned out to be a fun party, good food and plenty of beer. We were sensible enough to not get crocked, as some of the others did. The next day we would fly to Brooks Camp, where we would spend the season.

At the party Chief Ranger Loren Casebeer seemed to take a special liking to us—or was it to Penny? At any rate it proved to be a very positive relationship for us. We flew out to Brooks Camp with Loren in the park plane, a Cessna 206 on floats, the rest of the crew flew on a Wien Air Goose. Loren gave us a very special air-tour of the area of the camp, Naknek Lake, Brooks Lake, Brooks River, low over the falls before landing on Naknek Lake, and taxiing up to the beach by the lodge. That special relationship with Loren got us a lot of opportunities to go on flying patrols that weren't offered to others nearly as often.

All of us seasonal rangers were occasionally offered the opportunity to go on back country patrols. A back country patrol involved spending your free weekend plus a few work days, patrolling various parts of the park. We jumped at the chance to experience as much of the Alaskan bush as we could. Most of the others wanted to have the weekends to relax, sleep, make-out, do laundry, or whatever fit their fancy. Consequently we ended up being the ones who were offered the chance to see places few others have ever seen. We hiked The Valley of Ten Thousand Smokes, were flown to numerous locations all over the four million acre park with a Folbot—a canvas kayak over an aluminum frame that broke down and fit into two bags, and could be reassembled wherever we went. Float plane is the only means of transportation in most of Alaska, so we were flown in, assembled the kayak, floated a river, or lake system and were picked up a few days later—weather permitting. Alaskan weather is always questionable; there were times out on the coast when we waited a week or more for weather to break enough that a plane could get in to pick us up.

Our duties at Brooks Camp were more varied than any place we had worked previously. We did an evening program about every ten days, led walks to a restored barabra (a Native pit-house), took people to Brooks Falls to watch bears fishing, sometimes catching fish in the air above the falls. We patrolled the Brooks River in hip waders, checked the campground daily to make sure food was properly stored, and took van-loads of visitors to the Valley of Ten Thousand Smokes.

Almost all visitors to Katmai are flown into Brooks Camp, where they are met by a ranger and told: "You are entering the home of the Alaskan brown bear. The bear is here earning a living; you are here to fish, watch the bears, and enjoy yourself. If the bear is interrupted at its job of earning a living, it will go into winter hibernation less nourished and fat than it would have had you not interfered with its feeding. If you are fishing and a bear approaches, get out of the river and let the bear fish through, as you would if you were a courteous golfer holding up a better golfer behind you. The bear will fish through and you may go back to your fishing spot, having had the pleasure of watching a better player in action. Should you have a 'fish on' and a bear approaches, snap your line to release the fish so that the bear doesn't associate the sound of a running reel with a human having a fish the bear could easily take. Never have more than one fish in your possession. We strongly recommend catch and release fishing, but if you catch a fish you want to keep, you must immediately take it to the fish cleaning building. Never leave a pack on the shore, a bear will investigate and, probably destroy it. If the pack should have food in it, the bear will have learned that packs are a source of food wherever that pack may be, on your back, on or her back, or on mine. NEVER take food of any kind up the river—a bear can smell it several hundred yards away and will investigate."

There is more to the introduction to being a visitor in the bear's home, but you get the idea. Some people don't take it seriously, some people ignore it, but most are very conscientious about their behavior.

Penny gave the introductory talk to a pair of men, dressed in fancy new chest waders, who had flown in from a local lodge. As she was explaining the responsibilities of being in the bear's home, one of the men said, "You don't understand, we are cardiologists from Albuquerque and don't need to hear this."

Penny replied, "If you want to fish here you will listen carefully to what I am telling you. Your life may well depend on it." Their pilot/guide had been standing behind them, and Penny could see him give her a big smile and thumbs-up. They listened! Unfortunately there are people who feel they are above being told anything, especially how to behave.

Visitors lives and the welfare of the bears depended on people knowing how to respond to suddenly being in the presence of a 1,000-pound brown bear: don't surprise them, don't challenge them, don't have food with you, and for Gods sake don't get between a sow and her cubs. If you find yourself walking a trail and a bear is approaching from the other direction, simply step off the trail to permit the bear to pass by. After all that trail was made and is maintained by the bears.

During our Park Service careers, Penny and I had the opportunity—the privilege—to work six seasons in different sections of

Katmai. We saw and learned this land as few, if any, others have. We often refer to Katmai National Park and Preserve as "The Katmai," because, to us it is much more than a park. It is a mind set, a sense of place where the world is close to a completely natural state, where life continues as it did before man's impact.

Naknek Lake and Brown Bear

Brooks Camp and the Bears of Katmai

Granite Peak, a mountain west of the Aleutian Range on the Alaska Peninsula, has streams running from it into Brooks Lake. Brooks River drains the lake and flows a couple of miles to Naknek Lake, where Brooks Camp sits. Half way between the two lakes there is an eight foot waterfall which migrating sockeye salmon must jump in their spawning migration. The falls is tall enough to slow the migration, but not too tall for a healthy fish to jump. That jump may take several attempts, many don't make it at all and quickly become bear food. There is a surge pool below the falls where salmon school and rest before attempting the jump. Once over the falls it is a clear run to Brooks Lake and the streams above where they will spawn and die. A lot of them spawn and die in the Brooks River and provide food for the bears of Brooks Camp. Many brown bears fish up and down the river and even stand at the top of the falls to catch jumping fish.

Brooks Camp itself consists of a small lodge with several cabins providing sleeping accommodations for a couple dozen guests, and cabins for the lodge staff. The Park Service has cedar-log cabins for rangers, and a building sheltering a large noisy generator supplying electricity to the whole camp. In addition there is a small ranger office and an equally small visitor center.

Our first season at Brooks Camp was a memorable one in many ways. We had arrived in King Salmon during a sleet storm in early April, been given our quarters assignments at Brooks Camp, and moved in. Those quarters were the best we ever had in our 13 years with the Park Service. A snug little one room cabin with a separate bath room, a tiny kitchen, electricity, heat from an oil stove, and to our great pleasure, hot and cold running water.

It is the responsibility of the first rangers at camp to make sure all is ready for the beginning of visitor arrivals. One of those duties is checking the small primitive campground a few hundred yards down lake. It is designed with safety being the highest priority—safety of the visitor from the bears, and safety of the bears from the visitor. There is a food cache where campers MUST store ALL edibles and cooking pots except during actual preparation and consumption of food. The cache is a mini cabin, four feet by five feet, and four feet tall. It sits on four polls elevated twelve feet to where a bear can't reach it. People reach it by setting up a hand made ladder. That ladder must always be taken down when not in use or a bear will climb it. We weren't so worried about campers' food getting taken as we were about a brown bear learning it could get food in the campground.

Not far from the cache is a three-sided log shelter for cooking and eating. There are a couple of picnic tables inside and a fire pit out front. The fire pit is for warmth and pleasure only—cooking must be done inside the shelter, on campers' own stove to assure that no food is ever in the fire pit. The closed side of the building is toward Naknek Lake with a stand of alder and poplar trees breaking the frequent lake wind. The open side faces a birch/fir forest, with the food cache to one side. The campground itself is removed from the eating area by probably 20 yards and has space for no more than 12 tents. Behind the campground is a small meadow covered by perennial grasses and wild flowers where, on rare occasions, overflow campers may be permitted to camp.

We expect the first visitors to show up in early June, when the lodge opens, for trout season. In late May as we checked on details of Brooks Camp, I was in the campground and heard a crashing sound in the forest beyond the meadow. I walked out into the meadow to see if I could tell what was going on. To my surprise a recently born moose calf came running out of the woods to my left with a brown bear in hot pursuit. The calf and bear crossed about 15 yards in front of me, ran to the far end of the meadow and made a U-turn. Dumbfounded I stood staring as the calf ran straight at me with the bear right behind. I was paralyzed, I couldn't move as they ran just a couple of yards behind me and disappeared into the woods to my left. Neither moose nor bear seemed to have noticed I was there. Soon all was quiet. I wondered what had happened, but knew what the probable outcome had been.

That afternoon Penny and I went back to see if we could find anything interesting and found the expected result of a calf being separated from its mother. Under a birch tree was the sow bear with her twin cubs-of-the-year, or COY as they are called, feeding on the moose calf, and, heart-breakingly, 20 yards away stood the cow moose watching the feasting bear. She had several long deep cuts across her back, with strips of loose skin hanging down. She had lost in her attempt to keep her calf protected. Once the cow and calf are separated there is almost no hope of the calf not becoming a meal for the bear.

We always feel sorry for the prey in such an incident, at the same time we know that is the way nature's balance works. The predators, like all of us, must eat. Without the normal predation the prey species would over populate, degrade the habitat, and end up starving which, in the long run, would bring the population back into balance with the carrying capacity of the changed habitat.

"BROWN BEAR" IS A FITTING NAME, COLORS VARY FROM BLEACHED blond, to golden honey, to light chocolate or dark chocolate, to nearly black, and any other shade of brown you would care to describe. The head and lower part of the legs is frequently dark brown. Not only is there a wide color variation, but many of them will bleach out over the summer, shed that coat and grow a new winter coat, making a bear you saw in the spring look quite different in the fall. Next spring they emerge looking like they did the previous spring. An Alaskan male brown bear often weighs more than 1,000 pounds—1,600 pounders have been recorded; females weigh more-like 600 to 800 pounds, still a very impressive animal. Most wildlife biologists agree that the brown bear and the grizzly bear are the same genus and species, (*Ursus arctos*). Not long ago there were taxonomists who described as many as 64 different species and subspecies of brown/grizzly bear. There are still a few who like to refer to the Kodiak Island bear as a different subspecies, (*Ursus arctos middendorffi*). A few people still refer to the grizzly as (*Ursus arctos horribilis*).

The most significant difference between brown and grizzly bears is their diet. Brown bears live near the coast and have a high protein diet of salmon, allowing them to grow much larger than the grizzly which lives inland with a diet of mostly vegetable matter. Both bears are omnivores, as are humans. That is, they eat almost anything. John Muir once said of the grizzly, "To him everything is food except granite." Carrion often provides the first food for bears emerging from their long winter sleep. (Carrion: the critters that died over the winter, often moose or caribou that were old, sick, or injured, and even whales that washed up on the beach.) Spring sedges and grasses are high in protein and are heavily foraged before the salmon appear. Rodents and tubers are dug at any time, and fall brings a variety of berries. Sounds to me like a pretty good well-rounded diet—fruit, vegetables, and some meat. We should eat so well!

Bears must gain 30 to 40% of their spring weight to get them through the winter hibernation. That can be as much as 400 pounds so they eat voraciously all summer.

Brown bears den up in late fall after the snows start to accumulate and their food supply has seriously depleted. Their den is dug fresh every year, an upward sloping tunnel five to ten feet long, ending in an enlarged chamber where they make a bed of leaves, twigs, dry grass, moss and most anything to provide a thermal separation from the frozen ground. They count on snow covering the opening to provide insulation—snow is permeable to air so the oxygen supply is not a problem. During their winter sleep a bear's body temperature, respiration, and pulse are lowered only slightly, whereas true hibernators have their bodily functions go to almost zero. Bears may get up and move outside the den for brief periods, but soon go back to bed. They don't eat, drink, urinate, or defecate during their four or five months winter sleep.

Fall comes early to Alaska. By mid-August leaves on the cottonwood, willows, and alder are turning to gold and copper. In early September the leaves are falling, the salmon have spawned-out, their skulls line the bank of Brooks River where the bears have dropped them or the current has taken them. The bears are fat;

eagles, raven, and the multitude of gulls and shore birds are sated; visitors have left; the lodge is closed; the rangers have headed home to their real jobs or school. No-see-ums, black flies, and mosquitoes are all gone. Penny and I were the only two rangers left in the park. We had been asked to stay late to make sure there were no problems with the closing of Brooks Camp. We were more-than happy to have the camp left to just us and the bears.

Before closing for the winter all edibles must be removed from the lodge. Anything with the smell of food would be investigated by bears. The nose of a bear is as much keener than that of a blood hound, and a hound's nose is about 100 times more sensitive than your nose. They live by their sense of smell. An old Indian saying goes, "A needle fell in the woods, a deer heard it, an eagle saw it, a bear smelled it." It is no problem at all for a bear to identify what is in a building. If something smells edible, the bear will investigate.

The lodge, at Brooks Camp, had a new manager. He apparently didn't believe that a bear could break into a secure building. All of the windows had heavy steel grating over them. The doors had "Bear Boards" in front of them—sheets of plywood with 16-penny nails driven through from the under side every two inches—not something you or I would care to step on, and bears don't either. The lodge walls were four-inch thick cedar logs. It looked like an impenetrable fortress. But not to a bear that smelled sugar inside. This one apparently hit the log wall one hell of a blow, knocked a three-foot by four-foot hole in the wall, reached in, picked up a half-full, 35-gallon can of sugar, and drug it through the hole. When we discovered the break-in early the next morning, the bear had her head and shoulders completely in the can getting a sugar fix that would keep her wound-up all day. We couldn't chase her away. We yelled, threw rocks, and shot her in the butt with a 12-gauge cracker shell—she paid us no attention. We considered bouncing a round of bird shot off the ground into her ass, but decided that wasn't necessary, and finally let the poor thing enjoy her feast. She did act weird all the rest of the day and didn't seem right the following day. She acted like a child might after eating too much candy on Halloween. She ran around acting a fool, charging into the river, and chasing other bears, but thankfully she didn't bother us. And yes, the lodge owner did get a crew out that day, to fix the hole and remove all the edibles. We inspected the lodge before it was locked up again to satisfy the case-incident report we would have to file.

We had the rather rare opportunity to sex this bear shortly after she left her sugar pot. You can guess at a bear's sex by its size, which is rather iffy, you can be fortunate enough to observe them in a sexual relation, which is a spring time "affair," and most interesting to watch. A bear with cubs is obviously a sow, which is the common way to sex bears. Or you can see a bear urinate. Males pee forward while females pee from under their tail, which is standard urination for most mammals, but not often observed in bears. We watched her pee from below her tail; no question, she was a female.

Our first season at Brooks Camp had been a beautifully successful one. We had learned more than we ever expected, we had traveled to unique places that few others had ever been or ever would be. (Those stories in coming chapters.) We had seen and done things far beyond our dreams, we were discovering what was over the rainbow.

THE EXECUTION OF SISTER

From Penny's and my log at Brooks Camp, Katmai National Park, Alaska:

Tuesday 14 June 1983

Today I killed an Alaskan Brown Bear. She was the first Brown Bear I had ever seen. Since arriving at Katmai I have seen several others, but she had been the first. A month ago Penny and I had watched her and her yearling cubs chase a beaver down the Brooks River. But since that time she had stepped beyond the behavioral pattern man has decided is acceptable for a bear. And yes, she had to be eliminated. She had become a serious transgressor and one day would have injured a human being. There are so many of us and so few of them. Now that she is gone man can tread a little more safely upon her country.

Sister had been born eight years before her execution. Her twin brother known as Brother had been killed and eaten by an adult boar when he was a yearling—not an uncommon occurrence. Mom was a poor fisher-bear, thus a poor provider and a poor teacher for her daughter. Sister grew up with the understanding that she could best provide for herself by finding scraps left by other bears, stealing from smaller or less wary bears, or simply by eating anything she might find.

The Brooks River is a world class rainbow trout fishery and is visited by serious fishermen from all over the world, as well as by ordinary people who want the experience of fishing one of the best rainbow trout streams in the world, and are willing to go the expense of getting there.

Alaskan brown bears from the central Alaska Peninsula visit the Brooks River in large numbers during the sockeye, or red, salmon run each July, and return in September when the spawned out salmon are dying and easily available in what seems like endless numbers. Add to all of this the fishermen who want the adrenaline rush of fishing in the same stream with a 1,000-pound brown bear, and people who want to watch and photograph bears. Plus the commercial photographers who are determined to get a close-up or outstanding bear photo for sale to an outdoor magazine. These people are the most difficult to convince that they must yield to a bear. They are knowledgeable enough to be sure they are safe from the bear and aren't in the least concerned with the bear earning its living. With this mix of people and bears using the river, you have the prescription for conflict and the opportunity for disaster.

The NPS rangers stationed at Brooks Camp of Katmai National Park have the responsibility of monitoring the River and camp to keep the bears and people from interacting so closely that conflict develops. We don't seem to have the ability to communicate our wishes well with the bears. Talking to them doesn't work at all; sudden loud noise frightens them; pepper spray works well at close range if the wind is from you to the bear, not at all if the wind blows the spray in your face instead of the bear's—you might suggest the bear charge you from leeward rather than from windward. Twelve-gauge cracker shells, rubber bullets, and bird shot in the rump all do OK—some times. In a life or death situation a slug from that 12-gauge shotgun works best. (How do you define a life or death situation and whether this charge is a bluff charge or if she intends to do you harm?) Rangers work hard at communicating with the bears. It's easy to give negative stimuli when a bear is caught in the act, but catching one in the act is pretty chancy. The only positive stimuli available seems to be not giving a negative. If you have trained a dog you may have a little understanding; you can't punish them if you don't catch them in the act, and a treat for being a good dog is always remembered. But how do you give a bear a treat for being a good bear? Consequently most of our communication has to be with the human visitors, and too many of them think they know too much to accept advice or instructions. In reality, people (most, not all) are much easier to train than bears.

The only way of getting to Brooks Camp, for most people, is by small float plane or amphibious aircraft. Each plane is met by a ranger and given a very serious talk on "Proper human behavior in the presence of bears." Which means anywhere in or near the river or any time a bear is, or may be, in your vicinity—that boils down to the entire time they're at Brooks Camp. Visitors are told they should behave as they would want a visitor to behave in their home, only more politely.

The incident that started Sister's demise was two fishermen, decked out in, obviously brand new Orvis fishing gear. They had had the introductory talk—I gave it. They chose to ignore it. They took a picnic lunch with them as they fished up the river several hundred yards to a beautiful spot on the bank where they could eat and watch the activity at Brooks Falls. It was an idyllic setting. They were having ham and cheese sandwiches, fruit, and cookies. The two were truly enjoying themselves when they heard a rustling in the willows behind them. Looking around they saw Sister and her two yearling cubs charging down a hill only a few yards away. They did the only thing they could, they jumped off the bank and into the river. Sister and her cubs stopped at the picnic and ate what was left, which was most of it. She and the two cubs had learned that people and their packs are a source of food. Bears learn fast and well from any experience they have. You may have heard the theory of dropping your pack if you feel threatened by a bear. That is some of the worst advice you can get. Dropping a pack leads a bear to expect the next person it meets to drop their pack. Which, if carried out a couple of times, would result in the bear searching for a person with a pack.

What should you do if a bear approaches while you are in Katmai National Park and Preserve? First step off the trail, the bear probably just wants to walk its path. Most paths in Katmai are made and maintained by the bears. Should the bear follow you, look as large as you can, stand tall, slowly wave your arms, back slowly away, and talk softly, assuring the bear that you are friendly and mean it no harm. The absolute worst thing you can do is run. A brown bear can out run a quarter horse—you can't—and running initiates a chase and catch stimulus in the bear's mind. About the only time a bear will launch a serious charge is if you startle it. You may have had a time when you were startled and were ready to fight or run—known as the fight or flight response. There is also the much more dangerous situation where you find yourself between a sow and her cubs. Sows have evolved to protect their cubs at almost any cost. I have seen sows charge a much larger bear who she thought might be a threat to her cubs. Should a bear charge to the point you are pretty sure you are about to be hit, you should yell "No," go to the ground in a fetal position with your arms covering your face, your hands behind your neck, and play dead. It worked for me one September morning when I was sure I was about to be killed. Playing dead calms the bear, it may roll you around, and bite you a few times, but if you continue to be motionless it will lose interest and leave you alone. Also, she knows she has gotten her message across that you were in her personal space and you needed to yield to the superior animal. Fighting will anger the bear even more, get you mauled and, quite possibly, killed. Playing dead takes a lot of courage and concentration, but it may well save your life.

Those two fishermen, of course were as scared as two people can be (they never related the condition of their underwear). They knew they were totally in the wrong, but as most folks will do, they had to make themselves out to be the ones who had been wronged. They rushed back to the Ranger Station to report the "life threatening attack by three vicious bears."

I was on river patrol that afternoon and had watched Sister and her two small yearlings in the lower river searching the shallows for injured fish. That must have been only minutes after the picnic, they were about 50 yards from me and paid me no heed. Almost immediately Hal, via my radio, directed me to investigate a "bear incident" just below Brooks Falls. I found some crushed brush, torn up grass, the remains of an orange, a soda can with tooth holes in it, and a shredded day-pack. Those three bears now knew that people and packs are a source of food. The incident meant that the whole camp would be on bear alert for the indefinite future, that bears were in trouble, and that I had to fill out a case incident report (rangers hate paperwork). The guilty fishermen received only a very serious talk from Chief Ranger Casebeer, and were expelled from Brooks Camp. The plane and pilot from the exclusive lodge where they were staying was at the beach waiting for them. The pilot later told us that he knew that pair would be trouble from the time they arrived at his lodge. "They were arrogant know-it-all assholes," he said.

The following night a tent in the campground was torn up. Fortunately no one and no food had been in the tent, but the smell of humans had been enough to encourage examination. Tracks in the soft earth on the outskirts of the campground showed that a small female and two yearling cubs had been the only bears in the immediate area in several days. Sister and her two cubs were the only ones who fit that description. They had to be dealt with, and soon, or a person would be injured.

Early the next morning Superintendent Dave, Chief Ranger Loren, District Ranger Hal, and Resource Management Specialist Kathy met to decide what was to be done about the three problem bears. The district wildlife officer of the Alaska Department of Fish and Game was consulted by radio. The decision was made that Sister would have to be eliminated, and her two cubs chased whenever seen.

A clearing well away from camp, but not far from the river, was selected as the execution site, and baited with garbage from the lodge. The execution squad, Hal, Loren, and I were issued high powered weapons, and instructed to fire simultaneously at Hal's command. Rangers were stationed around the area to keep other bears from approaching the garbage. There were so many fish in the river that we were pretty sure only Sister would be interested in the foul smelling easy meal. The trap was set, and, to my amazement, worked exactly as planned. At Hal's command, three weapons went off simultaneously, Sister took two steps and dropped like a rock. Careful checking showed no breathing. Much more carefully I felt for a pulse while Hal stood over her ready to shoot again if she moved. There was no pulse, she was dead. While the life signs were being checked the two yearlings were busy gobbling up the bait only ten feet away. A round of #9 bird-shot ricocheted off the ground behind the cubs was necessary to send them scurrying for the woods.

While we executioners were waiting for Sister, she had been continuing her aggressive behavior. One of our rangers, stationed on the far bank of the Brooks River, was suddenly charged by Sister and the cubs—the only time she had shown aggression toward a ranger in uniform. He wisely followed the example of the two fishermen who had precipitated the whole affair, and jumped into the river. She, of course, checked the area for food, found nothing, and followed the scent to our bait.

The cubs were not seen again that summer. One had a slight limp from the bird shot in the rump as they ran into the woods. The following year I saw a pair of two-year-old bears one of whom had a limp. I convinced myself that they were Sisters cubs and were doing

OK. They weren't seen around Brooks Camp again. We hope they had learned that they were much better off well away from humans.

Which makes one wonder, where should a bear go, what should a bear do, when it's habitat has been usurped by humans?

THE AFTERNOON OF SISTER'S EXECUTION, DICK SELLERS, THE Alaska Department of Fish and Game agent from King Salmon showed up to claim her hide and skull. That meant she had to be skinned and her head separated from her body. Hal and Loren are permanent Park Service, I was a lowly seasonal, so I got to do the dirty, hard work of helping Dick with the skinning. That turned out to be more difficult than I had expected, I had skinned a lot of small game, but a bear hide is a totally different deal. Dick slit the skin up the belly, being careful not to puncture the abdomen (that would have gotten us into a lot of blood and guts that would have to be cleaned up to make sure it didn't attract unwanted attention from people or scavengers), then the inner side of each leg had to be split to the paw. Separating the hide from the animal was a slow process. Dick insisted we not damage it with a puncture other than the three bullet holes (preservation of evidence, he said!). He had to have the hide, skull, and paws to be sure nothing of commercial value remained. The head had to be separated from the spine and the feet from the leg bones, not easy, but Dick knew what he was doing, and I did as directed.

It was shocking to see how much the naked body of a bear resembles a human body, especially with the head and feet missing. It had been more than 30 years since I had dissected a human body in my gross anatomy class, but the musculature and bones were almost identical. When the skinning was completed, we rolled her onto a tarp and dragged her to the beach. Hal showed up and helped me load her into a skiff. We took Sister's remains to the far side of Naknek Lake and deposited her on the north side of the glacial moraine that separates Naknek proper from the North Arm.

The following morning Penny and I couldn't sleep, so we got up at first light and walked the beach. Sitting quietly we heard a deep moaning sound from across the lake. We decided it was a pair of bears making love and creating a new life to replace the one that I had taken the day before.

Brooks Falls

Bear Fishing

THE BROOKS FALLS PATH

Brooks River in Katmai National Park flows east from Brooks Lake, a little over a mile to Naknek Lake, and is a prime sockeye salmon stream. About half way up stream from Naknek Lake is a basaltic cliff, which forms an eight-foot falls that the salmon must jump if they are to reach their natal streams and lay their eggs where they themselves were hatched.

The falls is a favorite fishing spot for Alaskan brown bears. As many as 18 bears will choose fishing spots around the pool at the base of the falls. Bears are normally solitary animals, not tolerating the presence of other bears. However when there is an abundant food supply, such as at Brooks Falls, they will congregate and accept the close presence of other bears.

Salmon pool-up and rest in eddies and pools near the falls before they attempt to jump to the upper river. Not many of them clear the falls in their first jump, so they offer the bears numerous chances to catch them. A good number of fish never make it over the falls at all, and end up feeding bears down stream who haven't acquired one of the coveted spots at the falls. The dominant bear, of course, takes the best spot and will defend his spot from all who might challenge for it. Other spots are decided by their desirability and the dominance of the other bears. "To the victor go the spoils," and each year the value of individual spots is settled by which bear is strong enough to claim them. The fights to claim the best fishing spots can produce some violent hide-ripping altercations, but rarely end in death, and always sort out where the individuals stand in the bear pecking order. The various spots will be occupied by different bears at different times, but when the bear who has won that spot returns for it, there is rarely another serious challenge.

A few bears develop fishing techniques that keep them out of the melee at the falls, they simply fish the river from the falls to Naknek Lake, walk back up to the falls and fish down the river again. This technique apparently began thousands of years ago, almost as soon as salmon started using the river, and has resulted in a path along the south side of the river. A visitor came into the ranger station one day and complained to Penny that, "The trails are a mess, they aren't maintained as they should be." Penny explained that nearly all of the paths in Katmai National Park were made and are maintained by bears. The woman looked shocked but had no more complaints.

People discovered and started using the Brooks Falls path not long after the bears had developed it. An archeological team, headed by Don Dumond, has found Native pit houses called "barabaras," and other evidence showing that Aleuts were fishing the Brooks Falls area at least 5,000 years ago. Not many yards below the falls, between the path and the river, there are several pits about ten feet in diameter where Aleuts built their barabaras for shelter while they fished the stream and falls for salmon. A barabara is a wonderfully designed home. A pit is dug four or five feet deep, with a diameter large enough to provide living space for a couple and their children—they managed to live a bit more frugally than most Americans. After it was dug all that remained to be done was frame a roof from alder saplings and cover the alder with thatching. Add the accouterments of a home, a fire pit for heat and cooking, and a raised platform for sleeping. They were warm in the winter, and provided shelter from rain and mosquitos in the summer.

Enough use is made of the path that things tend to happen along it. Penny was walking home along the path one evening, after a day of river patrol. River patrol meant she had walked up and down the river a half dozen times, from its mouth in Naknek Lake to the falls, a half mile up-stream. Her patrols were made in hip waders to allow her easy access to fishermen. She walked either in the river or along the path. Penny made a point of meeting every fisherman and having a conversation. She checked their license, and made sure they understood their responsibilities while fishing the same stream with brown bears, and asked if they had any questions or comments. She was limited in where she could go by being in hip waders, so some of the fishermen who were in chest waders had to move to more shallow water so she could talk with them.

Those conversations were intended to be friendly and educational, at least 95% of them were. Occasionally each of us met someone who didn't want to bother talking with a ranger and chose to be difficult. Penny was better than any of the other rangers at dealing with these nasties. She could smile in a pleasant way while she adjusted their attitude so they could understand the reasoning for the park regulations and why they had to be enforced.

She was on the path after finishing her last patrol of the day, perhaps half way between the falls and Brooks Camp, when she met Diver (we name bears so we know which animal we are referring to, just like naming a person or a river). He was coming the other way on his return upstream in order to fish down the river. Diver was the most laid-back bear on Brooks River, and, perhaps, the best fisher-bear. He had developed a technique of fishing by floating downstream with his head submerged, perhaps looking like a harmless log to an unsuspecting salmon. He, apparently, just grabbed the fish in his mouth as it swam by. Diver rarely came up without a fish, and would catch and eat several on each float of the river. To float down from the falls and walk back up, took him just under one hour—you could almost set your watch by Diver's roundtrip.

When we met a bear on the path we would step off the path a few yards to give the bear the right-of-way. Diver was standing at the top of a hill, head down swinging it from side to side, just watching the approaching ranger. As soon as Penny stepped off the path to let him pass, she stepped into four foot-tall-grass, which happened to be where a sow named Blondie with a young cub, was trying to take a peaceful siesta. Disturbing a sow with a cub is the most dangerous thing a person can do.

Diver may have saved Penny's life that day. Blondie was well aware of Diver's presence, she stood, looked at Penny, gave a threat-ening woof, but didn't charge. She and Penny were only two or three yards apart; under normal conditions the sow would have been on Penny instantly. But with Diver there she had two problems, Diver to her right, Penny to her left, so she did nothing but look at Penny and then at Diver. Blondie's indecision gave Penny the chance to slowly back down the path, away from both Blondie and Diver. That defused the situation and allowed Blondie the opportunity to make a less stressed decision.

Blondie's siesta had been disturbed, but she didn't dare leave her cub in order to attack Penny with a big boar so close (a boar will kill and eat a cub if it has the opportunity). She chose the option of moving off into the woods where neither Penny nor Diver would be a threat to her cub. Diver knew Penny, that little two-footed thing who had been walking up and down his path and river all day without causing him any problem. He seemed comfortable with Penny in his home, the sow had left, so he kept coming down the path. Penny felt comfortable with Diver, that 1,000-pound, four-footed carnivore who moved up and down the river in a predictable manner, so she kept moving back up the path—backward so she could be sure her comfort with Diver wasn't in error. When she reached a spot in the river-bank where she could step back into the stream and out of the bear's way she did, and watched Diver walk his path only a few yards away. You never can tell what kind of day you will have doing river patrol!

PENNY AND I WERE WALKING THE PATH EARLY ONE SPRING MORN-ing with Kathy, the Resource Management Specialist, when we suddenly heard a series of deep "woofs" coming from a bear about 50 yards up the trail. The bear was obviously quite agitated by our presence—we had not seen it until it woofed. It was not only warning us with its woofing, it was making short, hopping false charges at us. This is when a bear doesn't choose to charge full-out, keeping its front feet together it hops forward woofing. If you have any bear-sense you will take heed and leave—promptly. We took only long enough to decide that this bear was probably protecting a food source, before we left it to its meal.

Having a bear on food along a popular trail could cause all sorts of problems for the park, the visitors, and the bear. It was not a difficult decision for administration to say "The Falls Trail is closed due to bear activity."

Now the river patrol ranger had an extra responsibility, he/she had to make sure visitors understood that they could not use the Falls Path and why. The river ranger also needed to carefully check to see if the bear had finished its meal and moved on. This careful checking went on day after day for a couple of weeks. It was obvious that the bear had one fantastic meal, and had no intention of leaving until it was finished. Meanwhile, administration was getting all kinds of flack from visitors who had paid a lot of money to visit Katmai and watch the bears feeding at the falls. Threats were made that, "My good friend Senator Stevens will hear about this, and heads will roll." Sorry folks, we don't mess with a bear on a meal, especially not in a National Park.

The day finally came when the bear was no longer at its feast. I happened to be on river patrol that day. Seeing no bear by the path I, ever so carefully, approached the scene. An area about fifteen feet in diameter was clear, down to the duff. I found most of the skull of an adult cow moose, four hooves, and a few broken pieces of bone scattered around. A bear taking a healthy adult moose is an extremely rare event. Things didn't make sense. I needed to look further to figure out the what had happened. Under some duff and pine needles I found four tiny moose hooves. This could only mean that a calf had been taken too.

Annual predation on moose calves normally takes about a 70% toll and can go as high as 90%. As terrible as it sounds, this is a good thing. Without bear and wolf predation the moose populations would grow so large they would over browse their habitat, and exceed the carrying capacity of the land, which results in the moose suffering a much larger population crash. Human meat hunters take about 10% of the adult moose population each year, and would like to greatly reduce wolf and bear populations so that there would be more moose and caribou for them to harvest.

Reducing keystone predator populations creates an enormous disruption of natural ecosystems, with endless negative consequences. We have seen this with the elk in the Rocky Mountains. When grizzly bears and wolf populations were reduced or eliminated to protect game and domestic stock, the elk population soon exceeded the carrying capacity of their natural habitat. They moved into pastures and hay fields threatening agriculture. To mitigate this, federal and state governments started feeding programs to protect agricultural land from the elk. Hunting was increased to the extent that carefully controlled harvests are permitted in Grand Teton National Park. Of course human hunters want to take the largest animals, the prime breeding stock. Which leaves the breeding to younger or genetically inferior animals. And so it goes when man decides he knows better than Mother Nature.

SECRETARY OF THE INTERIOR JAMES "RAPE AND PILLAGE" WATT came to visit Katmai National Park and Preserve with his entourage of Secret Service body guards, and assorted VIPs. He had heard about the bears fishing at Brooks Falls and wanted to see them himself. Of course he would need a guide and the protection of his Secret Service agents to walk that "dangerous path." When someone of this importance visited, Superintendent Dave would be his personal guide, and take him wherever and whenever he wanted to go. After all the Secretary of the Interior is the ultimate boss of all Park Service personnel, and holds the purse-strings. Superintendents are never as knowledgeable about the natural history of their park as is the average ranger, but VIPs want the prestige of being escorted by the superintendent.

Off they went, up the path, to view bears at the falls, Dave leading followed by Watt, his Secret Service agent, a couple of VIPs, and a ranger, carrying a 12-gauge shotgun, to cover their rear—just in case! As they approached the falls Dave stopped to explain where they were and what they might expect to see when they reached the viewing platform beside the base of the falls. They were only a few feet from the river, and Scar Bear, the dominant bear at the falls, was returning to his normal fishing spot at the edge of the "jacuzzi"—which is what we called the turbulent area just below the falls. Scar Bear was in the river, but looked like he might come close to the VIP party. Dave knew Scar Bear, and knew there was no danger from him under these conditions. He saw the SS agent start to pull his .38-revolver from its holster to protect his boss. Dave wisely just said, "Don't, you'll just piss him off." The agent looked kind of sheepish, and returned the weapon to its holster.

To Watt's credit he wanted to know about Scar Bear, the viewing platform, and plans for the future of the park. Scar Bear had a wonderful fishing technique. He stood in the swirling foamy water, when he felt a fish brush against his leg he would simply raise his foot and pin the fish to the bottom. The fish couldn't see nor feel well enough to distinguish a bear's leg in all of the swirl and foam in the water. All Scar Bear had to do then was duck his head and pick up the fish. He always took his catch to a tiny island a couple of yards down stream, so he could enjoy it in peace. He had earned his name and his fishing spot the hard way. His face and back were terribly scared from fights for fishing rights and probably for mating rights also. The mating fights had happened a bit earlier in the year, so those wounds were still fresh when he came to claim his fishing spot. He invariably got more hide torn up securing his #1 spot at the falls. Scar Bear had held that prime spot several years and probably would hold it for a few more years before a younger, stronger bear took it from him.

Watt had had a good tour of the falls and a little scare. Dave had made points with the secretary. The agent had learned a lesson, and the "protection" ranger had a good tale to tell all of us around the fire at the evening beer session.

Penny at Battle Lake

BATTLE LAKE PATROL

Battle Lake nestles between steep mountains in a glacially carved valley in the northern part of Katmai National Park. The McNeil River State Game Sanctuary is to the east and the preserve portion of the park to the west. The lake drains, via the Battle River, into Kukaklek Lake in the preserve. (The preserve part of any National Park and Preserve is open to hunting, and thus has an entirely different set of concerns and regulations for the park administration to deal with.) There is a small group of cabins on the north shore of Battle Lake that hadn't been used for a few years. The park management needed to know if it was still not in use and, if so, that it was secure.

Penny and I would be flown to the upper end of Battle Lake with a Folbot kayak and be picked up five or six days later on the south shore of Kukaklek Lake.

Our assignment, on this four or five day patrol, was to check Battle Lake and the streams feeding into it. One comes from Pirate Lake on the boundary between Katmai and McNeil Sanctuary; the other, McNeil Creek, drains McNeil Lake in the Sanctuary. The park wanted to know if a trail could be established up either creek to McNeil Sanctuary. We also needed to check out the closed camp down lake, the Battle River, and the south shore of Kukaklek Lake. That was probably too much to accomplish on a five day patrol, but we were in our first season in the Alaskan bush and had no idea how much could be accomplished on one patrol.

Wow! What an opportunity to see and learn about a part of the park that few on staff would ever get to experience. Back country patrols were a very special deal to us. Not all of the seasonal rangers on staff were willing to participate in them since it meant working on your weekend. A five or six day patrol would normally start two days before your weekend, go through the weekend, and extend another day or two. Most of the rangers weren't interested in giving up their time-off to put in extra days of work and camp in what would probably be wet and cold conditions. We were. We jumped at any opportunity to get out and see other parts of the park. That was what we were in the Park Service for, to see and learn. The chief ranger and the district ranger were more than happy to have two rangers who wanted to work overtime with no pay, so we got a lot of back country patrols that others would turn down. In the long run, taking those back country patrols provided numerous other opportunities at Katmai and at parks where we would work in the future. We became known as a dependable team who could be sent out without there being a compatibility problem. And, if other problems arose, we would find a way to deal with them.

It was late in the day when Loren, Chief Ranger and park pilot, dropped us off from the park's "Alaskan bush-taxi," a Cessna 206 on floats. We set up camp first, then assembled the Folbot, had a freeze-dried dinner, and an evening to enjoy the wonders of bush Alaska.

Problems? We were on a sandy beach that makes easy walking so it is the path the bears use in their movements. We were above tree line so the tallest plants were seven foot tall alders that were a long way from providing a secure hanging spot for our food sack. Alder in this part of Alaska grow in thick stands of stems an inch or two in diameter with their stems only a few inches from their neighbors. We decided the only solution for our food was to separate it into two nylon stuff-sacks and stash the sacks in the safest locations we could find, then count on our luck. So the two food sacks were set at the edge of the alders, one sack a hundred yards to our left and the second that far to the right. Hopefully a bear would walk the waters edge rather than the edge of the brush, there was no food smell that we could detect, so perhaps a bear wouldn't smell anything either. There are serious rapids and a water fall on the Alagnak River which drains Kukaklek and Battle Lakes. That falls is too much for all but the strongest of salmon to negotiate. Thus there should not be a lot of salmon in Kukaklek or Battle Lake and thus few bears walking the shores—sure!

Camp was as secure as we could make it. We had our evening meal and would have a cup of hot rehydrated cider with a splash of brandy before we crashed for the night. The mosquitoes were coming out in even greater numbers than in the day, which they do every evening. Swarms of the little buggers (commonly known by rangers as "little fuckers") make the evening hours the toughest time to be sitting on shore. Our best means to defeat the mosquitoes was to be in the middle of the lake where few of the tiny vampires could reach us. We wanted to check out the Folbot anyway, so out we went. We had been on one other patrol in this kayak. Made of treated canvas with aluminum struts and plywood ribs, it is all collapsible and able to be carried in two big canvas bags. It is a great little boat and the sensible way to access the area. We loved it. How romantic; a waning silver moon was cresting the mountains to the east, there was no wind, the sky was clear, the lake was smooth, our stomachs were sated, and we were on our own for five or six days, the kind of experience we had dreamed about. As a friend likes to say, "It don't get no better."

We had flown over tundra in the park plane a few times and were anxious to hike on it. From the air, tundra looks like a lush golf course that should make ideal hiking. All we had to do to get there was to negotiate a few hundred yards of alders that lined the streams we were to examine. We knew alder thickets are a real bitch to get through, and that devils club, which was growing among the alder, was going to be an interesting part of the challenge. Devils club stands about as tall as the alder, the stem and even the leaves are covered with the damnedest sharp needles. You can't touch the plant without being very sorry, so you avoid it as much as you can. Penny has declared alder to be the mangrove of the north. You don't walk through it, you push your way through it, while calling to the bears that may be in the thicket with you. If a bear knows you are coming, you won't surprise it, and the bear will be gone before you get there. We recognize that we are interlopers in the bear's home and try to be as polite and respectful of their rights as we can.

The next morning we couldn't wait to see if our food caches had survived. To our relief they had not been disturbed, so we felt much better about leaving food in this insecure place—well maybe there weren't many bears around this lake, we hadn't seen many fish that would attract them. Better get on with our assignment!

We thought we could do McNeil Creek in one day with no problem, so off we went with our day packs which always hold rain suits, three kinds of fire starter, survival food, bug repellant, a compass, camera, binoculars, and a lunch, which normally consists of a Gerry tube of peanut-butter, several Pilot biscuits, and some dried fruit. There was, and still is, plenty of good drinking water in most Alaskan creeks. It was a steep climb, ungodly dense, over talus and glacial erratics. By 1600 we were still in the alders and gave up for the day. We knew if we went on we would never make it back to camp before dark, even if dark didn't come until 2300. We did get back to our camp a little before dark, and found our food caches still intact. It was starting to rain, so we fixed a quick freeze-dried meal and retired to the tent. We like to have a little brandy along, which is very carefully rationed to 1/2 oz. per day each, and added to a steaming cup of powdered cider. Cold, damp, tired, and thrilled. We were in a warm dry tent after a very full day, we were ready for our cup of hot spiked cider and bed.

The next day dawned to continued drizzle, which meant bush-whacking through the alder was going to be even more fun. The south side of Pilot Creek looked at least as dense as had McNeil

Creek, but it wasn't going to be nearly as steep. We had tried to navigate McNeil Creek itself and found it ran through rocks that the glaciers had deposited, some of which were larger than we were tall—no way we could make that work. The alder along Pilot Creek turned out to not be as bad as yesterday's struggle along McNeil Creek, and looked like it wouldn't be as tough a climb to the tundra. There were numerous side streams cascading in from the melting ice and snow above. We were hiking in our "Extratough" knee-high rubber boots, which Alaskans like to refer to as Alaskan tennis shoes. They had become standard foot gear for us, due to the constantly wet terrain. The side streams could be forded or even stepped across. The rain stopped before we got through the alders, and the sun was out by the time we finally reached the tundra. It wasn't yet noon, but a good time to take a break and have our peanut-butter and cracker lunch.

Tundra at last! Well of course, it wasn't what it looked like from the air. Tundra is a mixture of low lying dwarf plants that can survive winter's strong winds and constant below zero temperatures. The wind's desiccation, extreme winter temperatures, and shallow soils keep tundra plants under six or so inches in height. Some of those plants are: dwarf willow, dwarf birch, dwarf or Canadian dogwood, sedges, a variety of lichen, and mosses, with Aleutian avens growing where they can get an opening. A tough existence makes for a tough plant with stout stems that can trip you at nearly every step. All of this is growing over glacial debris, rocks from pea-gravel to the size of a bowling ball which easily turn under a persons foot. Penny describes walking on tundra as "walking on a rug thrown over soccer balls." It wasn't the golf course we thought it looked like from the air, but it was truly beautiful and exhilarating. By following Pilot Creek we made our way to a small lake where the terrain leveled out, then on up to our assigned goal, Pilot Lake. This was a doable hike if you picked the right route and weather, but not one that we would recommend for the typical park visitor.

The following morning it was pack up and head on to the Battle Lake portion of our patrol. It was the bluest of blue lakes, deep with steep banks continuing up the sides of the glaciated, basaltic and granitic mountains to their snow and ice-covered craggy peaks. Gulls were having a fit as we pushed off, we looked up and there was a bald eagle sailing by, looking for fish or maybe gull chicks.

It was late July and the wild flowers and berries were nearing their peak. By late afternoon, we were well away from the steep mountains at the east end. The lower lake had a more gradual shore where we should find some interesting flowers and berries. Berries are something we were always on the lookout for. We rarely got to have fresh fruits or vegetables in the back country so we supplemented our diet with natural berries when they were ripe. Blueberry is always a favorite. Today there were lots of them in a kind of boggy area, so we harvested them in preference to the more abundant small crowberry. The crowberry is one that we hadn't run across until we got to Alaska. It is a low, mat-forming evergreen shrub with needle-like leaves, it grows in bogs and on alpine slopes. They form small firm, juicy, rather tasteless black berries, the size of a pencil eraser. Abundant and easy to pick, but they have a seed which is quite large for such a small berry—not objectionable, but it sure makes the blueberry our preference. We noted flowers too: monks hood, great Sitka Burnet, corn lily, and Rein orchids. What a marvelous way to spend an afternoon—surveying life in the Alaskan bush! But it was getting late, and we needed to find a campsite with some shelter in case of a storm.

Another hour down lake we came to a point, around which was an ideal little cove with a sand beach. The alders were back far enough that we could set our tent near them and still leave plenty of beach for a bear to go by without us being in its way. Still nothing taller than seven feet to hang our food from, and Katmai didn't have the bear proof containers yet. So we would have to count on our luck to keep our food safe from bears. We were down to two small food sacks, which we would stash near the brush and well away from a bear's probable path along the water. One went a hundred yards to the left, the other with the cook kit, a hundred yards to the right.

We are always very careful of where we prepare our meals, never closer to the tent than 100 yards. The smell of even our freeze dried meals could attract a bear, and as much as we admire them we didn't want one visiting during the night. Penny plans the evening meal in the morning, puts a freeze-dried vegetable in a bottle of lake water to re-hydrate for the day, and decides which of our two or three main courses we will have, some of which need time to re-hydrate— some don't. I am amazed at how much the freeze-dried foods have improved since we started back-packing in the early 1960s. Some of them are actually good, and re-hydrating them for a few hours makes a great difference. Tonight's menu was shrimp-alfredo, green beans, dried fruit, and a Pilot biscuit. Of course the ambiance provided by a day in the great "Alaskan Outdoors" tends to make any food taste better, and the whole world seem better. An evening beach walk after dinner settles the food and feeds the mosquitoes. Penny's notes say "This was the loveliest day of our lives." I can't think of a better one. As frosting on the day, a gyrfalcon sailed by just before we went to the tent. We watched it as dove and flushed a ptarmigan, the falcon's favorite food. It caught the ptarmigan in its talons, flapped several times, caught a rising air current and rose to the top of a cliff where it settled. Through binoculars we could discern it was sitting at its eyrie. Did it have young in the nest? We couldn't tell from straight below.

Morning came early. We had a big day planned: check out the camp at the end of the lake, float the Battle River, and end up in Narrow Cove of Kukaklek Lake. Breakfast, as usual, would be oatmeal with raisins, tang, and instant coffee. I went out to start the Svea stove and heat water. "Oh shit!" The cook kit had tooth holes in it and the food sack was gone, the other food sack was gone too.

Not torn up with food scattered around like we would expect a bear to do, the food sacks were just gone. The tooth marks in the cook kit were too small for a bear. Could it have been a cub? No! A cub would have been with a sow and she would have left signs we could have identified. Careful examination of the crime scene revealed small foot prints, quite like those of a bear cub. It could only have been a wolverine (*Gulo gulo*), also known as "skunk bear" because of its distinctive musky aroma. The fiercest animal, for it's size, to be found in the north country. We even found its tracks leading into a tunnel of low bushes and alder stems. Where the tunnel might lead, we had no idea, except it should lead to our food. Penny was determined to follow the tunnel and retrieve our food. As she started in, I said "When you find the food, you will also find a wolverine who thinks it's his food? What do you do then?" Hmm! Better to be hungry for a few days than have a fight that you would come out on the very short end of. No way to call for help! Surrounded by steep mountains, line-of-sight radio doesn't reach far. So lets head on down lake and find Battle Lake Camp.

We found the camp only a couple of hours paddle down lake. Battle Lake Camp was very neat, well cared for. In an attractive location, at the head of a cove, with a little stream coming in close to the clustered buildings. The camp consisted of three small sleeping cabins and a lodge. Each cabin would contain two double decker bunk beds and a couple of straight-backed chairs. That would count as four "pillows" per cabin, which is the way Alaskan camps count their guest capacity, meaning this was a "12-pillow" camp. Time not spent fishing would be spent at the lodge around the fire-place having cocktails, comparing fish stories, and having meals. The lodge staff would have consisted of a fishing guide and a couple who served as manager, cook, wait-people, and extra guide. Meals would be fixed in the small kitchen and served to the guests at a long table.

We had no idea why it had not been used for a few years, unless there actually were not many fish in the lake, but we were supposed to check it out and be sure it was secure. We did. It seemed secure, except Penny found a window that she could jimmy with her knife. There could be some food inside even if it is against the law to leave food in an unoccupied building in Katmai, and we just might get hungry before we were picked up! We weren't really hungry yet, but the thought of a couple more days with nothing but berries and water didn't sound very appealing. We were well aware that weather could postpone our pick up as much as a week. No food for a week would be a grim ending for what had been a wonderful back-country experience. I don't remember the author, but someone once made the poignant comment, "The well fed person has many problems, the hungry person has but one."

Inside we found books on a shelf, magazines on a coffee table in front of the fire place, with a fire laid,. The dining table was set for eight. It looked as if the lodge was ready for guests that evening, only to have all of the people carried off by aliens. In a store room we found a canister that had just enough corn-meal for us to make one meal of mush, and a box of chocolate mints. That wouldn't make for elegant dining, but it sure would beat nothing but blue berries. We took the corn-meal and four mints.

In most of the north country taking food from a cabin isn't stealing. It is expected that anyone needing food will take what they need and replace it at the next opportunity. We weren't sure how we would go about replacing what we took, but we knew we would find a way. This ethic in the north country is vital, especially to winter-time travelers. It works, has saved many-a-person's life, and not replacing food is a sin beyond most others. We would find a way to replace the cornmeal.

The Battle River between Battle Lake and Narrow Cove was a completely unknown entity, no one from the park had ever been on it. It could be a lovely open float or it could be severe white water, where we would have to wade and line the boat along in hip

waders. We had done the unnamed stream between Murray and
Hammersly Lakes a month earlier, and were quite aware of some
of the hazards we might meet.

I NEED TO DIGRESS, AND TELL THE STORY OF FATHER BERNARD R.
Hubbard, the self named "Glacier Priest." In the 1920s and early
1930s he explored Katmai, Aniakchak, and other areas of the Alaskan Peninsula. "Explored" is a term he would have used, I think of
him as an "adventurer." He was a Jesuit Priest who traveled to some
of Alaska's most remote locations. He always took along several
big, strong, young men from his school's football team to carry all
of his gear. He also took a couple of photographers to document
the exploits. So that Father Hubbard could accentuate his many
speaking engagements with movies of the thrills and chills of his
adventures.

In the library of the Katmai Visitor Center there is one of his
movies taken in the late 1920s. Our staff loved to watch it, and laugh
at some of the outlandish predicaments they got into. The scene
that is pertinent now showed two men following Father Hubbard
into one of their most impossible situations, one man says "Tell me
Father Hubbard, why did we come this way?"

When Penny and I were lining our Folbot down the river
between Murray and Hammersly Lakes, wading over rocks and
gravel where the water could be two inches deep one step and a
couple of feet deep the next step, Penny stepped into a hole and
went in over her head. When she came up coughing and spitting
I said "Tell me Mother Hubbard, why did we come this way?" It
saved the day, changing a catastrophe into a good laugh. I built a
fire, got Penny warm and into dry clothes and finished a fun interesting adventure.

BACK TO BATTLE RIVER: IT TURNED OUT TO BE A MIXTURE OF THE
easy and difficult. Most of the way it was float, paddle, read the river

for rocks that could crush or upset the kayak, steer to stay clear of hazards, and wade when you had to. The most dangerous thing was the sweeper that we came on suddenly around a bend. A sweeper, on any stream is a tree that hangs close to the water, here it was a spruce tree that had been undercut by the river so that the trunk hung only a couple of feet from the water's surface. Sweepers have taken a lot of lives in Alaska, and would come close to taking the lives of two close friends of ours in the future. We were fortunate, in that we had time get to the far shore and work our way around the sweeper

What a day! We had lost our food, found some food, survived the Battle River, and accomplished our goal. Now we were safely on another secluded sandy beach in Narrow Cove of Kukaklek Lake. We should be picked up late tomorrow on Kukaklek's south shore.

This beach did have bear signs, tracks, and scat on the beach. Up the hill we found where a bear had dug for a ground squirrel or tubers. Around a point was a blueberry patch which attracted us, and was probably what attracted bears to the area. We would have to be careful, but after tonight's meal we wouldn't have any food for them to go after. We set the tent up on some mossy tundra far enough from the beach and berry patch for us to feel we wouldn't be examined by a bear.

As we fixed our evening meal of cornmeal mush and blueberries we watched mergansers and harlequin ducks on the river, a bald eagle sailed by. We heard our favorite sound of the north country, a loon gave its haunting call, almost a cry. It was answered by another, probably its mate. We sat as if in another world, totally fascinated as the pair met, seemed to kiss, and rub each others necks. Thrilling! They were a pair of red-throated loons. We had never had the privilege of being so close before.

Morning came, the day we hoped to be picked up, but we needed to see what the south shore of Kukaklek Lake was like. Breakfast of blueberries, pack up, say good-bye to another beautiful camp, and off in the kayak. Out in the cove the wind was picking up, by the time we got onto the lake proper it was blowing hard. Hard as we could paddle we couldn't make headway, and whitecaps were hitting us from the starboard quarter. "The wind wins" is a saying we came up with many years ago. All we could do was return to the shelter of Narrow Cove, set up camp where we were last night, and hope the plane would come. It did! Dave, our superintendent, came in low late in the afternoon, spotted us waving and set the plane down on the cove. Our Battle Lake Patrol was complete—except for the report we would write and getting corn meal to Battle Camp.

Valley of 10,000 Smokes

HIKING THE VALLEY OF 10,000 SMOKES

The Ring of Fire, which surrounds the Pacific Ocean, is the result of plate tectonics and the subduction of the oceanic Pacific Plate as it and continental plates collide. The denser oceanic plate is overridden and pushed down (subducted) by the lighter continental plate. When the subducted ocean floor meets the hot mantel, a few miles down, it melts. The hot, light, molten magma then floats to the surface and creates the volcanos surrounding the Pacific rim.

The eruption of Novarupta Volcano and the collapse of Mt. Katmai in 1912 changed a beautiful Alaskan valley into a flat, vegetation free expanse of barren volcanic ash, punctuated by thousands of high-pressure vents, known as fumeroles, blowing steam and volatile gasses hundreds of feet into the air. The ash has cooled, so steam vents no-longer exist, but the valley looks like a Mars-scape.

When we took visitors to the Valley of 10,000 Smokes on day trips, we explained the valley's history from the Three Forks Overlook Cabin, which is named for the confluence of Knife Creek, Windy Creek, and the River Lethe, which drain the valley and form the Ukak River. The cabin offers a good view up valley to Mt. Katmai and Trident Volcano. The shelter the cabin provides from the frequent strong, ash-carrying winds coming down the valley is its most appreciated function.

From the cabin, we led visitors down a path to the valley floor, a few hundred feet below, and hiked them a mile across the ash to the edge of the Ukak River. A lot of water is funneled through a narrow cut in the basalt that formed the valley floor before the eruption. That cut in the basalt is only four feet wide and who knows how deep. The roaring water, only inches below the flat basalt we stand on is a frightening maelstrom.

The only way across the stream is to jump those four feet. If you miss you are dead! It isn't too much of a jump from the near, high side, but the far side is two feet lower than the near side, making the return jump tough and very dangerous. Some of us did it during training, but we never allowed a visitor to try—it would produce endless law suits. A few people have died trying it. The day-pack of the wife of a ranger friend was found on the far side several years later; she was never found.

In order to better understand the area and prepare us to relate its story to visitors, all of us rangers were to make a four-day patrol of the valley. Penny and I would be the first of the new rangers to get this assignment. We would be dropped off at the Three Forks Cabin, hike the trail to the valley floor and across 12 miles of the flat, desolate ash to the Novarupta Volcano beside Mt. Katmai. Sounded pretty straight forward to us. Windy Creek, Knife Creek, and the River Lethe now drain the valley that was drained by the Ukak River before the eruption. In order to get up the valley we would have to ford Windy creek twice and find a place where we could cross the River Lethe farther up valley. It was mid June, just after the execution of Sister, mountain snows were melting, and the creeks were up.

It is truly an awesome place and the reason for Katmai being named a National Park. The eruption inundated a verdant unnamed valley and the streams entering from the mountains to the east in up to 700-feet of ash. The flat ash floor that was left was speckled with thousands of steam vents, called fumeroles, that were created when the hot ash vaporized the water in the streams. The steam and accompanying gasses made their way to the surface creating the "10,000 smokes" that Griggs, on his National Geographic expeditions, had made so famous.

Kathy, the Resource Specialist, took us out the 13-mile, two-track dirt road, driving across two good sized creeks, to the Three Forks Cabin in one of the vans that we use to bring visitors to the valley. She told us to be careful and watch the weather. She had heard a forecast predicting a storm. This morning looked beautiful, so we were happily on our way to experience new, different country.

The two Windy Creek crossings were interesting! Unbuckle your backpack so you can jettison it if you fall, take off your boots, and pants, put on tennis shoes, use a walking stick to create a third leg for support in the current, face upstream, step into water that was snow a few hours ago and hope you don't find a hole that's too deep. The cold fast water runs over rounded golfball to baseball size pumice rocks that are so light they often float, and tend to move when you disturb them. (Pumice is volcanic rock that consists of a highly vesicular rough texture from gasses in the cooling ash.) So that third leg is awfully important. It assures you of having two supports as you move a foot.

The bleak, windswept valley floor is something else, mostly light tan rhyolite and dark, nearly black, andesite ash that has been cemented into volcanic tuff. Every couple of hundred yards we came across the remains of a fumarolic vent where high pressure, acidic steam from the buried Ukak River and volcanic gasses made their way to the surface through the ash. We found rings of various colored glassy ash that had been formed by the superheated steam melting and fusing minerals into solid rainbows (red hematite, orange arsenic sulfide, yellow sulfur, and even blue from iron sulfide minerals).

We were having a great day, laughing and teasing about exploring with Father Hubbard and his wonder dog Blue Eyed Mageik. There was almost no wind. Noticing a string of moose prints and a short series of bear tracks, we wondered what they might have been doing out here. We located a few scattered blossoms of fireweed and avens in sheltered places. Horsetail and clumps of grass and even some dwarf willow had found a home in sheltered, moist spots. The succession of life in the valley was underway, but damned if we could find a spot to cross the River Lethe.

We had tried once; took off our boots and pants and waded into what looked like shallow water clear across. It got up to our knees and was quickly approaching our crotches. We kept on; pumice rocks floated by, one hit Penny, she said, "Damn it. Those are ice not pumice!" We were up to our asses in ice water and still were several yards short of the far shore. The chief said, "Enough," and we headed back to where we started. "OK," I said, "we'll find a better spot farther up valley."

It was getting late, 2000 hours government time, 8:00 p.m. civilian time—we were still adjusting our mental clocks. We had had too much fun and hadn't gotten as far as we intended. That was fine, we had plenty of time on this trip. We were a couple hundred yards from the Lethe and decided to set our camp by a little stream coming off the Buttress Range to our right—it would be a good source of water for cooking and drinking.

We still had to find a place to cross the Lethe, so we walked down to check it and found ourselves on the edge of an awesome canyon. We weren't crossing there! Our map showed the river dividing farther up. Tomorrow we would find a crossing.

After a dinner of ramen noodles, rehydrated minestrone soup, and a cup of rehydrated apple cider with a splash of brandy, we sat on the ash floor and contemplated the valley. The upper end gives you a slight appreciation of what this place must have been shortly after the eruption. Griggs said when he first saw it, "The whole valley as far as the eye could reach was full of hundreds, no thousands—literally tens of thousands—of smokes curling up from its floor." Father Hubbard called it, "The Abomination of Destruction." Now the steam was gone, the floor was flat, but cut by a stream rapidly eroding a canyon into the relatively soft ash. We saw a million changing moods, as many moods as there were colors with the changing angles of the setting sun. White-crowned, golden-crowned, and fox sparrows were singing; a few clouds were forming and changing the light and mood even more. We were at peace and loving our experience.

During the night a light rain started. The next morning we had our oatmeal, put on rain suits and headed out, looking for a place we could cross the Lethe. That afternoon wind started blowing ash into us, stinging our legs. We put on gaiters as the rain changed to snow and looked for a sheltered place to set our tent,—there wasn't one. The weather had gotten dangerous; Penny reminded me of Josiah Spurr's story of wind blowing rocks that had killed Natives up here. We could keep looking for shelter or use the only shelter we had, our tent. We set it up and crawled in; at least we were out of the wind, blowing ash, and snow. The rain-fly made a covered vestibule where we could cook, so we might as well relax and enjoy another of the valley's moods. We didn't see any options.

During the night the wind and rain abated a bit. By morning the sun was peeking through clouds, but the wind was back. A quarter mile to our left, we thought we could see where the River Lethe, coming off Mt. Megeik, was joined by Knife Creek which came from the Knife Creek glacier. I said, "We should be able to cross those two creeks pretty easily."

Penny, in her sensible way said, "This is our third day, the wind is still bad, we have to be back at the Overlook Cabin by seven tomorrow evening. If we spend today going on up valley there is no way we can get back in-time for our pick up."

I had to agree, but were we going to stay in the valley and be buffeted by wind and ash all day? I had a suggestion, I pointed to the west and said, "Let's cross that pass in the Buttress Range, pick up Windy Creek and follow it back."

Penny liked the idea, "That will let us see different country," she said. We crossed through the low pass and headed home by way of the vegetated valley of Windy Creek. The valley proved to have been only slightly affected by the eruption, ash had accumulated just two or three feet thick. We walked comfortably along a braided stream on the valley floor. Our pick-up was scheduled for late the next day, and we only had ten or twelve miles to go. That sounded comfortable, but it was late and time to find a campsite.

We noticed what looked like a clearing on a bench up a hill on the other side of the creek that should make a good spot with a clear view of the little valley and the mountains behind us. We crossed several shallow braids of the creek, climbed a game-trail to a lovely secluded bench overlooking the stream, took off our packs and started to make camp.

Admiring the beautiful early spring valley below us, we noticed a bear walking the far side of the creek, nose to the ground, exactly where we had walked a few minutes before. When it came to the place we had crossed the creek, it too crossed the creek. We looked at each other wondering if Mr. Bear might have us in mind for dinner. When it reached the hill where we had come up, it followed the same trail up. It disappeared from sight on the steep hillside, we stood watching and wondering. It crested the rise less than twenty feet from us, reared to its full height, got a good look at us, and fled as fast as it could. The early summer fur on that bear was the most beautiful I ever saw, gold and burgundy; it glistened in the late evening sun as he or she ran off without enjoying the dinner that we had feared. We looked at each other and laughed. We had each taken our backpacks off preparatory to making camp; after our guest left we each had our pack back on. We always help each other with our packs—not this time. We must have been thinking that we didn't want to be taken down without our gear. We will always ponder what was in our minds as that beautiful animal approached. Humans were probably the farthest thing from the bear's mind. It had been following a strange smell, probably wondering what it could be.

We had a delightful evening enjoying the view of the valley below and discussing what must have been going through the bear's mind, both before and after it saw us.

The last day of our initial patrol was an uneventful hike down a pretty Alaskan valley to the Overlook Cabin where Kathy picked us up that evening.

The Road Taken

Two roads diverged in the wood, and I—
I took the one less traveled by,
And that has made all the difference.

—Robert Frost

We, especially Penny, had always been interested in politics. Penny's Dad was a coal operator and very conservative politically. He didn't like the unions and didn't want to have to restore the land he was mining. Fulfilling those requirements cost him money. My parents had supported Roosevelt but opposed Harry Truman and had been strong supporters of Eisenhower. Having been brought up in conservative environments, we were right-leaning ourselves. We had supported Barry Goldwater by walking door to door distributing brochures for him. We had even considered joining the right wing John Birch Society. We were too old for the Vietnam War, but we flew the flag and supported our troops.

At the same time we were members of the National Audubon Society and spent summer vacations hiking, backpacking, camping, seeing, and learning the natural world across North America with our three daughters.

Penny had been a leader of Camp Fire Girls groups for years, ever since Lori, our eldest, was in first grade. She was highly regarded as a teacher and leader of young women. I had patients referred to me from all over Ohio and was a director of the

Columbus Rotary Club, so we were well known in central Ohio.

In the late 1960s, at Penny's suggestion, we both enrolled in the School of Natural Resources at Ohio State, simply for the sake of learning more about the environment and how it worked. That introduced us to a different culture than the one we knew at the dental school where I was an associate professor (on a half time basis) and Penny had been an instructor. It was a different culture than most of our friends, who today would have been considered "upwardly mobile." These university people were dedicated to teaching and learning rather than to maximizing their incomes and social status. They looked like our other friends, perhaps their suits weren't as nice and they drove smaller, less expensive cars, but we were finding we had a lot in common with them.

Associating with the faculty of the School of Natural Resources had given us a view from the progressive side of politics. The need for preservation of the natural world was being presented in class after class. A quote that I will always remember was, "Where do you throw it when there is no more away?" We were appreciating my mother's love of the outdoors, not just for its beauty but for the future of life that so depends on man respecting the needs of other life forms. We had been introduced to books such as Aldo Leopold's *A Sand County Almanac*. That book showed us that man has a responsibility beyond earning a living and respecting other peoples' rights: a respect for the land and all the lives that depend on its sustainability. Leopold told us:

> There is as yet no ethic dealing with man's relation to land and to the animals and plants which grow upon it. Land is still property. The land relation is still strictly economic, entailing privileges but not obligations. In short, a land ethic changes the role of *Homo sapiens* from conqueror of the land-community to plain member and citizen of it.

We began to understand that the Earth was not created for

humans only. This planet is shared by millions of species, from bacteria to fungi, plants, insects, rodents and elephants, most of whom have lived here much longer than man has. Those others have rights too. Each individual has rights and each right comes with responsibilities. Those responsibilities are at least as important as the rights. Until man accepts his responsibility and develops a "land ethic" he will continue the destruction of the planet we all depend on. I guess we were becoming environmentalists.

We joined a few environmental organizations and became active with the Columbus, Ohio, chapter of the National Audubon Society. Soon we were both elected officers of Columbus Audubon. A couple of years later I was asked to take the presidency of the Ohio Audubon Council. Jimmy Rhodes was governor of Ohio during my second term with OAC, and had publicly referred to me as "a damned environmentalist."

President Nixon had signed into law the National Environmental Policy Act, and later launched several environmental initiatives including the Clean Air and Clean Water Acts, the Marine Mammal Protection Act, the Endangered Species Act and created the Environmental Protection Agency. Both Governor Rhodes and President Nixon were Republicans. In spite of Nixon's environmental legislation we realized the Republican party favored harvesting natural resources as rapidly as possible. Governor Rhodes was right, Penny and I had become environmentalists and Democrats.

In the late 1970s President Carter and nearly every environmental organization in the country promoted the Alaska National Interest Lands Conservation Act (ANILCA) to protect much of unspoiled Alaska from development. The Ohio Audubon Council needed a representative to present programs state wide to any group that would listen and watch a slide show promoting the beauty of unspoiled Alaska and the need to protect it. I asked Penny if she would do that: she would love to. She presented more than a hundred programs to diverse groups from coal miners and farm bureaus to high society ladies' clubs and Rotary Clubs state wide. I joined her when I could and was impressed by the knowledge and professionalism with which she presented her programs and by the enthusiastic support that was apparent in nearly every audience she spoke to.

Penny lobbied Ohio's U.S. Senators and Representatives in Washington as well as in their Ohio offices. She debated Don Young, Alaska's U.S. Representative to Congress, live on National Public Broadcasting for an hour. She was called to testify before Congress on two occasions, and was named Ohio Environmentalist of 1980. After ANILCA passed, Penny and several other volunteers were invited to join President Carter for lunch and the signing of the bill, and were given a personal tour of the White House.

That same year, 1980, I was asked to be the Vice Presidential candidate for John Anderson in Ohio, as he ran, as an independent, for president against Ronald Regan and Jimmy Carter (Anderson was required to have a running mate from each state, who then needed to resign in September. Why, I never learned).

By 1983 we had spent four fun, very interesting and educational seasons as NPS rangers, the last being at Brooks Camp in Alaska's Katmai National Park. That fall Penny received a call from the chairman of the Ohio Democratic Central Committee. He wanted Penny to run for State Senator against an old man who had been elected time after time with no real opposition because he had an (R) following his name on the ballot in the strongly Republican district where we lived. Now he was vulnerable, old, slept through most meetings, and seldom said anything. He was known as the worst Senator in Ohio. Now the Democrats needed a known, well spoken, effective younger person to run for his seat. Would Penny do it?

The primary election was five weeks away; the Democrats had two people running, neither of whom they felt could win the general election; he felt Penny could. Would she? She attended several smoke-filled meetings in the State Office Building getting a feel of what inside-politics was like. She agreed to run in the primary that fall with the caveat that she would be given time after the primary to give serious consideration to running in the general election and pursuing a political career. They probably didn't see a viable option and agreed. Penny ran and handily won the primary.

We had come to a fork in the road. On one fork, Penny could pursue a career in politics, something she would thrive on and be good at. The challenge and exhilaration of a political contest were intriguing; the effect she could have on people's lives, the good she could do for future generations, how could she not follow that road? I had kept my dental office and opened it as soon as we had gotten home each fall. I could resume my practice of crown and bridge dentistry full time rather than half of the year. The other fork in the road would return us to Katmai next spring and to other places in future years. Yogi Berra had said, "When you come to a fork in the road, take it." But which fork?

We needed to consider our options very seriously. Hal, our boss at Katmai, had our positions saved for us. He had let us know he wanted us back. He would give us time to make up our minds but those two positions had to be filled. He wanted his staff there by mid April and couldn't wait longer than mid March for our decision.

Penny had been flooded with offers of support and any help people could give. She had a staff all lined up, a chief of staff, an organizer, a fund raiser, and a volunteer director. They were all excited and getting her campaign going. We had a great logo designed—a bright copper penny, with a silver star imposed on it, and a picture of a smiling Penny Starr's face in the center.

By this time our family was scattered. Lori, her husband, and six-month-old daughter were living in Portland, Oregon; Carin and her husband were in Seattle, Washington. Kristy was still living at home but had a good job as assistant manager of a western wear and tack store in Columbus. We talked our options over with the three of them. After all, this decision could make a big difference in their inheritance. None of them would suggest what we should do, so I marked two weeks off in my appointment book and we went to Florida to talk and think.

Side by side we walked the beautiful beaches of Captiva Island thinking and talking. This was really Penny's decision. She could choose the unknown of politics and I would continue the work of restoring mouths. She had been a great success in her work on ANILCA. She told me about talking with Senators and Representatives in their plush Washington offices, how exhilarating and challenging it was, especially when she could convince a pro-developer to support significant conservation measures. Penny had quit smoking 15 years before and hated the meetings in smoke filled rooms, so politics wasn't all fun and games.

If we chose politics and dentistry, we would be living more separate lives, Penny in an office in the State Office Building while I would return to work that I knew well and was good at, in the same office I had occupied for nearly 30 years. Or, we could return to the Park Service positions we enjoyed. We talked of the fun we had had watching the bears of Katmai, spelunking at Jewel Cave, and soaking up the beauty of Yosemite. So while we walked the beach, Penny worried and I beach-combed.

After two weeks at Captiva, Penny said, "Lets go back to Katmai. We have been so happy, having so much fun, learning and seeing new things, just the two of us together. If we take the other road we won't be together much. I like the life we have lived the past four years, us together, responsible to and for each other, each of us depending on the other." I heaved a sigh of relief, hugged her, and gave her a heart-felt kiss. That evening we celebrated the idea of being together, following the same path.

We took the road less traveled and that has made all the difference.

THE SOW WITH THREE AND ME

We saw each other at the same instant. She seemed to explode. She looked like a runaway freight train as she charged, her head down, her ears back, lips curled exposing two-inch canines. I could see the saliva streaming from her mouth. She covered the 70 feet that separated us in less than two seconds. Six hundred pounds of teeth, claws, and fury coming at me. The options were all hers, she could kill me or not.

Penny, and I had seen her for the first time the evening before as we were enjoying a peaceful canoe ride on Naknek Lake. The sow Alaskan brown bear and her three small cubs-of-the-year had not been noted by any of us rangers at Brooks Camp that season. She had been reticent and very cautious before bringing her triplets to Brooks River to feed on spawned-out salmon. Triplets are not common among Alaskan brown bears, a single cub or twins is the norm. We watched the four of them walk along the beach heading toward the river. Mom kept moving, watching for danger and always alert for food, while the kids cavorted, wrestled, pounced on sticks, and did what kids do. She had waited until late fall, when people were gone and the lodge had been closed for a week, before introducing her cubs to the Brooks River with its dead and dying salmon.

It was late September; "termination dust" had turned the mountains white. Most of the leaves had fallen from the poplar trees. The alders and willows still had golden and orange highlights. It was one of those wonderful rare Indian summer evenings and we were totally content. We were enjoying the last of our summer's wine from our drifting canoe, watching the bear family make its way along the beach to feed on the spawned-out salmon near the river's mouth, and listening to the series of ethereal, rising flute-like notes of a Swainson's thrush—perhaps the most enrapturing sound of the north.

The seasonal rangers had finished their year-end reports and gone to wherever they spent their winters. The permanent park staff had moved to the little town of King Salmon. The lodge staff had installed heavy metal grates over all doors and windows of the lodge and guest cabins before they left for the year. Penny and I were the only rangers still on duty in the four-million-acre Katmai National Park & Preserve. We were there to cover the Brooks Camp area for two or three weeks after official closing, just to make sure there were no late fall problems such as fishermen needing help or hunters looking for an easy chance to poach a bear. Water and electricity had been shut off to the entire camp. We still had heat from the oil stove in our cabin. Water we carried from the lake. We had a Coleman lantern for evening and morning light, an outhouse a couple hundred yards away, and our Svea back-pack stove for cooking.

Our normal early morning routine was, Penny checked the campground and housing area while I checked the lodge area and river just to see that everything was as it should be. We reversed that routine in the evening. During the day we walked the river together. First we headed up the riverside trail to Brooks Falls where there is a viewing platform which permits visitors and professional photographers to safely watch and photograph bears fishing for sockeye salmon. The salmon must negotiate those eight-foot falls on their migration to the spawning grounds in the feeder streams where they were hatched. Next on our agenda was on up river to Brooks Lake to check the superintendent's house as well as the housing for maintenance personnel. Our final chore for the season would be climbing Dumpling Mountain to where the radio repeater sits. That had to be put to bed for the winter, but not until our last day or we would be without radio contact with headquarters in King Salmon.

Shortly after first light the morning following our initial sighting of the bear family—it was going to be another winner of a day—I had examined the lodge area and was headed toward the river. Too happy and too relaxed, I had been talking back to a magpie who was squawking from the top of a snag by the last bend in the trail. In retrospect, that magpie may have been warning me about the bear or warning the bear about me. The bear understood the warning, I didn't. I should have been talking loudly instead of squawking to the magpie. I should have been making people noise so that I wouldn't surprise a bear. Rounding that last bend, my eyes met the bear's eyes and she charged. I did everything right, just the way we had been taught to respond in a serious bear encounter. I had experienced a few bluff charges, but this one was different. I raised my arms to look as large as possible while waving slowly, spoke softly, apologizing for being in the bear's space, slowly backed away. I backed into a tree and couldn't retreat farther. She kept coming. I knew it was over! I yelled "No," and fell to the ground in a fetal position with my fingers interlocked behind my head. Our training had taught us that if you are attacked by a black bear you should fight as hard as you can, but if you are attacked by a brown/grizzly bear you should fall to the ground, lie in a fetal position with your arm over your head and remain still, playing dead. The bear will roll you around, claw you, and bite you a few times, but if you can manage to hold still the bear will lose interest and leave you alone. I knew all of this, but could I do it? I still don't know. I think I could, knowing that to fight back is sure death.

I remember apologizing to Penny for leaving her in the terrible position of finding her husband mauled, or perhaps killed by a bear, and no one around to help. The only help she would have available to her was by radioing to Park Service headquarters in King Salmon, which was more than an hour away by air. That is, if she could reach someone by radio, if the park plane was not in for one of its routine check-ups, if the weather in King Salmon was flyable, if the park pilot was available, and more ifs—life in the Alaskan bush!

Fortunately I was not armed. We had been issued 357 revolvers for law enforcement, which we rarely carried, and 12-gauge pump shotguns for bear patrols. I had consciously decided to leave the shotgun in the cabin that morning. Experience had taught me that carrying a weapon is rarely necessary, and often a mistake. Too many bears are killed when a person panics and fires on a bluff charge, or just thinks a bear might charge. We normally load the shotgun with the chamber empty, and five rounds in the magazine starting with a cracker shell, a rubber bullet, a round of #9 bird-shot, a round of #00 buck-shot, and a slug, The order of loading is optional, some prefer the #00 buck last, this is how we chose to load. Had I been carrying the shotgun that morning, I am sure I would have used it, the cracker shell and rubber bullet would have done nothing, the #9 bird-shot would have, perhaps, blinded her—it sure wouldn't have stopped her. Had there still been time to fire the #00 buck it might have killed her, but she would surely have gotten me before she died.

Ms. bear solved our conundrum by skidding to a stop, turning, and returning to her cubs almost as fast as she had left them. Her skid marks in the duff under the tree showed that her claws were less than two feet from my shoulder, her mouth and teeth must have been inches from my head. She had gotten the message across that I was in her personal space and was too close to her cubs. She would not tolerate any invasion of that space by a person, another bear, or any animal she might perceive to be a threat.

Had that final shot been fired, the bear killed, and me mauled or killed, the NPS would have had problems to deal with—two bodies to dispose of (the bear and me), a very distraught female ranger (Penny), three cubs-of-the-year who wouldn't survive the winter without mom, and an ocean of paperwork to fill out. As it was I had a case incident report to fill out and that was it. Plus I have memories that will last forever.

Penny with Caribou Antler

HUNTING PATROLS

Katmai National Park & Preserve had fall hunting patrols occasionally in the past, but when District Ranger Hal Grovert arrived it became a really big deal. Penny's and my first hunting patrol was timed to match the first opening of fall bear season. Our patrol would be ten days of stake-out watching for possible poachers. We would have radio contact with headquarters, and were to report anything that looked suspicious. If headquarters thought it sounded like a poaching incident they would contact the Alaska State Patrol. The state controls all hunting in Alaska, including all federal lands, so they would be the ones to make actual contact with any suspected hunting party.

Our assigned location was to be hill 592, named for its designation on a USGS topo (topographic) map. When we started studying the topo map titled "Mt. Katmai Alaska, scale 1:250,000," we discovered that 592 is the elevation of a lake below the hill that we would be working from (see cover photo). The top of hill is a little over 1,000 feet in elevation, and overlooks the confluence of Angle and Takayoto Creeks near the south boundary of the park where it adjoins the huntable Becharof National Wildlife Reserve.

We were flown onto hill 592 in a helicopter piloted by Landis Lingrin, who was becoming a treasured friend. We had flown with Landis before and knew he had gotten a lot of experience flying search and rescue missions in Vietnam. We had the opportunity to fly with him numerous times in the future—to and from some "interesting" places. We learned that a lot of his so called search and rescue missions in Vietnam were "search and destroy missions."

Landis set us down on top of hill 592, which would be our primary observation location. After we had our gear unloaded our friend dove the helicopter off the steep east side and followed the creeks out of sight to the south. That left us to the peace and quiet of our hill. We reconnoitered; there is a steep glacier cut cliff on the east side that Landis had just flown down, and a more gradual slope to the north, We would be able to walk down the north side through bushes of crowberry, Labrador tea, and heather about a half mile, to access the broad valley of Lake 592 and the two braided streams. That is a walk we would be taking frequently. Every time we wanted water for cooking, washing, or drinking we would need to take that walk. We also took walks down the hill to make foot patrols of the valley. We needed to have a campsite between the hilltop, where we could expect wind and weather to be a problem, and the wet valley floor. Down the northwestern side there were more grasses, bedstraw, low blueberry bushes, plus clumps of willow and alder. That is where we decided to set our camp. We located a fairly level spot a few dozen yards from the hill's crest with low vegetation that wouldn't poke us too much when we laid on it. Mostly grasses and bedstraw over scree, it was well away from the blueberry patch where we could expect bears to be harvesting the late berries.

We would make our stake-out observations from the hilltop whenever the weather was flyable enough that someone might fly in to land in the valley. Hill 592 is fairly flat, covered in a mat of low vegetation: short tan grasses, dwarf dogwood which still had a few red berries, a carpet of mountain avens with tinny fern-like leaves and spent flower heads covering some small patches. The beautiful scarlet leaves of late fall alpine bearberry gave us a smile and a feeling of warmth. Orange, grey, black, and green crustose lichen covered the dark basaltic rocks near the edge of the cliff and gave the top of the hill a feel of an ancient fortress overlooking the valley below. Not a bad place to hang out for ten days!

The gear we put together for our 592 camp was pretty standard for us when we were going to be in one location for an extended period, and had transportation in and out. We took two North Face VE 25 tents (one for sleeping and one for cooking, gear, radio etc.), a change of clothes, full rain suits, boots, coats, toiletries (tooth brush & paste, bar of odor free soap, comb), our Svea back-packing stove, with two liters of white gas, and a bear-proof food container. A bear-proof food container is an ABS plastic tube 16 inches long and eight inches in diameter. The bottom is fused shut, the recessed lid is secured by an arm which rotates into a slot in the side of the tube by turning a recessed screw. What food is the container filled with?—instant coffee, oatmeal, raisins, and powdered tang for breakfast; Pilot-biscuits (3-inch diameter, 1/4 inch thick crackers), peanut-butter, a chunk of cheese, and dried fruit made lunches that we could carry with us on our foot patrols. An assortment of dehydrated prepared meals (usually a pasta and meat in a sauce), a dried vegetable (which we soaked in water all day), more dried fruit, and another Pilot-biscuit were standard dinner. Not gourmet meals, but enough taste and calories to keep us going and looking forward to a better meal when we were back at headquarters. Normally we took a liter bottle with about ten ounces of brandy which we carefully rationed so we had a bit to add to a cup of re-hydrated hot cider each evening.

On this patrol we even took a box of white wine. Water! There was plenty of that in the creeks at the bottom of the hill. All we had to do was walk down the brush covered slope a half mile, fill a bucket and carry it back up to camp. We would be hiking in the valley most days, so we could carry a bucket up to camp when we returned. Still we didn't waste water or use more than we had to.

Where does our waste go? There was never any food waste, the best way to dispose of extra food is to eat it. If we threw it out it would attract bears or other critters we would rather not have around. We could pee wherever we were when we felt the need. Even in the bush leaving human turds around is unacceptable. Pick a spot well away from camp, kick or dig a hole, poop in it, and scrape the dirt or duff back over the poop. Keeping a clean, odor free camp is the best way to not attract bears or other unwanted visitors.

Watching the valley for poachers, from 500 feet above, gave us the opportunity to observe moose as well as bear in their daily activities, without disturbing them. We watched several bears moving through the routine of their daily lives, well away from the chaotic kind of activities we were accustomed to at Brooks Camp. These bears were living life in the natural way—find food, eat, and rest. Finding and eating food consumes a big part of the moose day too, and resting does seem to take the balance. That doesn't hold during fall rut, which runs from early September to late November. Rut is the time bulls seem to look forward to—cows in estrus, and the chance to prove their machoism with other bulls. Estrus in cow-moose lasts about 12 days, it is the time when she is hot, or receptive. The actual estrus, when her eggs can be fertilized, is only about 24 hours. So a pair of moose usually enjoy a lot of sex over those two weeks, while the bulls act like fools for a couple of months.

We got to watch the mating game of moose the whole time we were on stake-out. We only observed actual sex once, we sure enjoyed watching the fore-play between a bull and a cow, the jousting matches between the big bulls, and the lesser bull who was trying for all he was worth and learning a lot in the process.

There was a lemming high that fall. Lemmings are the cute little mouse or vole like critters with short ears and tail, and very soft brown fur. They are known as the ones who march into the sea when their population explodes beyond the lands carrying capacity. We think they are simply looking for a place that is not too densely populated, a place where they can make a living away from the maddening crowd. Apparently the local population wasn't quite that high because a lot of them were still there when we left.

The voles appeared to think our tent made an ideal shelter from the frequent rains, especially at night when they seemed to find the warmth of our bodies, through our foam pads and tent floor, quite appealing. They crawled around under us, and were pretty disturbing until we told ourselves to "just adjust." They were a fact of life that we could fight for two weeks or accept. "Let nature have its way and things will work out." After a couple of nights with the lemmings we had another visitor, a short-tailed weasel, or ermine, discovered mecca with endless food and shelter, and moved in. Problem solved, lemmings eaten or scared off! That is, until our weasel friend decided he/she could make a nest over our heads, between the tent and the rain-fly. That was fine the first night, he/she moved around up there and was wonderful entertainment in the flashlight beam. The second night we were hoping our little friend would return, and sure enough it did. The only problem was it decided to dig and fluff up a bed. Digging with razor sharp claws doesn't bode well for the top of a nylon tent, so we had to chase it away, and it didn't want to leave. We tapped the ceiling under the weasel, it moved over, dug some more, got tapped again, moved, dug, got tapped, moved, dug, and got a hard thumping. That was enough for our friend, it left, but it had pretty well taken care of the lemming problem under the tent.

Hundreds of lemmings were still around which attracted other predators. A red fox entertained us catching voles by day. He would hold very still watching and listening. As soon as he perceived movement he jumped, and usually came up with a vole. Neither of us had ever heard of a flock of owls, but that is what we had. A group of short-eared owls found our campsite provided them with endless lemmings. Being diurnal feeders, they gave us interesting things to observe while we watched and listened for planes that might be looking for bears to poach. One evening we were going to bed as the last light was fading, and Penny counted more than 20 short-eared owls as they settled for the night. Lemmings were interesting and their predators even more interesting, but we hoped the lemmings wouldn't attract bears to camp. They didn't; there were too many fish in the streams for the bears to bother with lemmings on top of the hill.

Every evening, as the last light was beginning to fade, we would enjoy our hot cider and brandy while we watched and listened to the cacophony of thousands of long-necked, long-legged sandhill cranes as they settled into the marshes of the valley below. Wonderful ancient birds whose ancestry has been traced back to the Pleistocene epoch. Fascinating to watch, flocks of thousands would circle over us several times, calling in their low, musical rattle, before they settled for the night. At dawn they would wake us with their loud resonant bugling. We heard them before we could see them because there was usually valley fog that they rose through as they left for their days feeding preparatory to fall migration.

Our job was to watch for poachers. We only had one incident where we radioed headquarters to report a group who we thought were there to take a bear. One afternoon a Cessna 185, tail dragger on tundra tires, those wide, large-diameter tires which allow planes to land on rough terrain, came up Angle Creek low and slow, below our observation point. It circled and landed on a gravel bar not far up stream from where we sat watching. Four people got out with fishing gear, slung rifles over their shoulders, and started walking down stream. After only a few yards they spread out through the willows, so they were 40 or 50 yards apart, covering the width of the valley from the edge of the cliff, directly below us, to the creek, and continued walking down stream. Didn't look like fishing to us! We radioed headquarters, they agreed and radioed Alaska Department of Fish & Game. ADF&G agreed, and sent a flight in to check them out. The trooper flew directly up the creek, also low and slow, circled and came back directly over them, circled back and overflew them a second time. The "fishermen" got the message, they even waved to the trooper, headed back to their plane, and left. They hadn't broken a law—yet, so there was no way they could be sited. We felt we had kept them from poaching a bear. ADF&G and the park did too—we were given a "good job," over the radio, by both of them.

Right on schedule Landis picked us up on the afternoon of our tenth day of stake-out at 592. An interesting time, an educational experience, and maybe we had saved a bear's life.

THERE ARE AN ENORMOUS VARIETY OF HUNTERS IN THE WORLD today. Once, for many of the world's people, hunting was the way a family was fed and clothed. Meat, for those in the far north, was the only food available. Animal hides were the material from which clothing was made. Whale, seal, and sea lion provided food for the Native People of the arctic coasts of north America, Europe, and Asia. Seal skin and polar bear hide with fur provided them with the raw material for clothing. Caribou provided the raw materials for the food and shelter needs of the tundra Natives. Plains Indians hunted bison and pronghorn for their food and shelter. Other

Native cultures depended on hunting, as well as the gathering of nuts, fruit, and grains, but the vast majority of protein, as well as clothing, came from the products acquired by hunting.

Fruits, nuts, and the seeds of some grasses played a more important dietary role in the warmer climes, with hunting a somewhat lesser role. About 12,000 years ago people of the Middle East's Fertile Crescent started planting some of the seeds they had gathered rather than eating them all. At the same time they began domesticating dogs and sheep for a stable meat supply. Thus man changed his niche from hunter/gatherer to agriculturalist, the first and only time that a species has changed its niche without speciating. As ecologist Paul Colinvaux has said, "Perhaps the most significant event in the history of life." A species was now able to usurp the resources and thus the niches of other species, causing the continuing extinctions we are seeing today.

Wildlife spend the majority of their time hunting for food or resting. Herbivores must find the plants that fit their dentition and dietary requirements. It often looks like grazers are eating all of every plant, but careful examination will show that each species has its select plant, and portion of the plant that is selected.

Carnivores are restricted in their diet by what herbivore they can catch. Each species has a distinct hunting pattern based on their physical abilities, and the abilities of the species that are available for them to pursue. Most commonly, carnivores are able to take the old, the young, the weak, and the sick. Healthy herbivores have the ability to evade or discourage attacks by carnivores. A pack of wolves could take any moose if they were willing to pay the price. A moose is well equipped with hooves and/or antlers to defend itself. Those weapons could be quite damaging to too many members of a wolf pack. The pack is dependent on acting as a unit to subdue its prey. Should a pack of eight wolves chase and corner a healthy bull moose, then pursue their attack until the moose was taken, it is quite possible that two wolves would be killed and two more too severely injured to be functional hunting partners. The pack then, could not survive. Darwinian survival of the fittest explains that wolves who followed this type of hunting pattern did not live to reproduce. Those who were prudent and backed off survived to hunt another day and reproduce.

Hunting by humans today has been altered by technology. The advent of the high powered repeating rifle gives an inordinate advantage to human predators. Many of us still hunt for meat, and many hunt for trophies to hang on a wall. Both intend to take the largest specimen they can find, the most meat or the one which might give them bragging rights, or even be recognized by the Boon & Crocket record book. The thought that they are removing the prime breeding stock from the wild population is not considered. Removing the biggest and healthiest, of course, alters the genetic base of the following generations, and perhaps the future of the species.

On a flight home from Alaska one late fall, I sat next to a woman from Texas who's husband was "in oil" and who, according to his wife, was a big game hunter with many records to his name. Husband thought his wife should be a known hunter with her name in some record books too. She had long scarlet nails and was beautifully quaffed—not what I expected a famous hunter to look like! She was trying to set the world record for the fastest a woman could harvest a ram of five specified species of wild sheep. She already had a dessert bighorn, a Rocky Mountain bighorn, and had shot a Dall ram that morning. She would fly to Morocco tomorrow for a Barbary ram, then to Iraq the next day for her fifth, a mouflon—all in under a week! Her guides would provide all of the knowledge and do all of the work of getting her to the sheep, all she would have to do was pull the trigger. I thought, "Whoop-de-fucking-do, she will have killed five magnificent wild animals who she knows nothing about. Her only motive is to get her name in some record book, big deal!"

In Alaska the most desired trophy is a large boar brown bear. When we worked there in the 1980s and 90s the fee for a three day guaranteed bear hunt was $10,000. That meant a hunter would be taken to where he/she would be sure to shoot their bear. They had to get their bear or the guide would have to return the $10,000. It is illegal to hunt "same day airborne," it is illegal to hunt in a National Park. Hunters know the airborne rule, but they can't be sure which side of a park boundary they are on, and a lot of them couldn't care less. Normally the first two days are legal hunts, but the third day has to produce a dead bear—park or no park. Guides locate their target from the air before they establish a camp, then it is common to haze the bear to the hunter by harassing and exhausting it from a small slow aircraft. Penny and I still question whether this can be considered "hunting."

It doesn't seem like a fair hunt to us! There is no law about flying low and slow over a park, but it sure gets the attention of a ranger, if observed.

Tents Down

Cold Camp

LATE IN OUR SECOND SEASON AT BROOKS CAMP WE WERE ASKED to take on a hunting patrol for the late bear season. It would be getting cold so our Chief Ranger, Loren, talked someone at the air base into loaning him two heavy duty down sleeping bags, and two pairs those white air insulated boots. We had long underwear, turtleneck sweaters, heavy wool pants, and heavy wool sweaters. The park had their own heavy down coats we could use. Of course we had our standard two North Face VE 25 tents, cook kit, gas, extra food, radio, reading and writing material, a bit of brandy, and were ready to go "fight crime." It was mid-October but not very cold yet, so we figured it would be another fun interesting ten days in the bush.

Loren flew us into a small lake near the headwaters of American Creek in the northern part of the park. We flew up in a de Havilland Beaver on floats, a vintage aircraft, but the first choice of a lot of Alaskan pilots and lodges. The Beaver is fun to fly in, can go slower than a Cessna, can land and take off in a shorter distance, has more easily accessible storage for gear, and provides good viewing. Loren was landing us on a smaller lake than he liked, even in the Beaver. With no wind to slow the plane on landing or give him a boost on his takeoff, he was worried that he would have enough water to land on and takeoff from after he dropped us. So he flew a couple of laps to reconnoiter, which gave us a chance to take a good look at the country where we would be dropped. It was one of those pot-hole lakes left by the glaciers, in flat, open country, above tree-line. Nothing much higher than a couple of feet until you got to American Creek several miles to the south.

A beautiful day for this time of year, sunny and warm. We unloaded our pile of gear and watched Loren take off, he made it with only a few yards of water to spare. If there had been trees he couldn't have cleared them. Alone in desolate tundra country, somehow wasn't as comfortable as alone on top of a hill where you look down to a creek in habitable looking country. The fireweed had reached the top of its stem and was beginning to go to seed. The Natives had told us, "When fireweed bloom reach top, time for winter." Well, we had a beautiful day to be camping in the "Great Land." So we set up camp and enjoyed the evening while we explored the surroundings.

Hmm, not a great location; no place for shelter from wind if we had a storm. The land around the pothole lake was glacial till, the area was tundra, the only color was brown from dead leaves and dried grasses, except for the green leaves and black berries on the crowberry bushes. The berries were about gone from the high-bush cranberry and all gone from the blueberries. It looked like several miles to the nearest tree and there wasn't even a rise or a fall of more than a few feet in the landscape. We walked around the lake and saw nothing to change our minds about where we had been staked-out. We did see a couple of ptarmigan changing from their summer speckled brown to their winter white plumage. By winter the only non-white part of the ptarmigan would be its black bill and eyes.

We certainly didn't have to worry about where to get water, it was only a few yards away in the little lake. Man hasn't been in this part of Alaska enough to spread his intestinal pathogens and protozoans to the water where wildlife ingest them and spread them to other water sources, so the water would be fine to drink. No one in their right mind would camp here, except a couple of rangers assigned to hunting patrol. Most certainly no bear hunters would consider camping anywhere near this spot. Our line-of-sight radios wouldn't reach anyone unless they were in the air above the horizon. The park had told us they would be flying every day shortly after noon so we should radio-in then. A beautiful evening—relax, fix dinner, and enjoy yourselves. Loren will be back in ten days, and we will be back to headquarters, a hot shower, and a good hot meal at the base NCO Club, which the park had gotten us access to.

The next morning we woke up to another beautiful very late fall day—sunshine, little wind, and nothing froze over night. A good time to take a hike and watch for poachers. We hiked south several miles to American Creek, which confirmed where we were, but we didn't locate any poachers—amazing. We reported in shortly after noon with no problem, and were told a change in the forecast was predicting clouds and cooling in a few days. By afternoon the sky was changing, wispy cirrus clouds, looking like spider webs in the wind, were moving in. We could expect rain, or snow if it turned a little colder. By evening we had solid high clouds, and the wind was picking up. That weather change was coming sooner than expected.

Some time during the night I woke up with something pressing on my back. My first thought was, "A bear is sitting on me!" Of course, I was still not awake, it didn't move when I pushed back on it, so it wasn't a bear. I finally realized it was wind pushing on the tent. We went out, tightened the securing lines, questioned if that was enough, and placed some heavy rocks on top of the stakes to make sure the tent didn't blow away with us in it. The lines held the tent in place, but some time later in the night the tent collapsed on top of us. We were scared, but not hurt, so we just waited it out until daylight would let us see what had happened.

Daylight did finally come, after what seemed an eternity. It still wasn't cold, the wind had abated enough that we could get out and survey the damage. It was even worse than either of us had imagined. The lines that we had reinforced had held, but one of the aluminum poles was broken and sticking through the tent and rain-fly like an arrow, The other pole was bent in two places. Each of the poles of a VE 25 are several aluminum tubes strung on a bungee cord so that they snap together and make a nice flexible pole about ten feet long. The poles run from left front to right rear, and from right front to left rear, inside nylon sleeves on the exterior of the tent, forming an X over the tent dome. Well damn! we were in trouble, how could we fix this tent so that it would still be functional? We always have some duct tape in our emergency kit, so we taped the tears in the tent and fly inside and out. I held the broken pole with spare tent stakes over the fracture while Penny wrapped duct tape around them. We straightened the other pole as best we could, and the tent went back up. It didn't look good but it might hold if the wind stayed down.

By now the sky had disappeared, the ceiling was right on the deck—there would be no flying today, and no chance for radio contact. We couldn't even take much of a hike with such low visibility. All we needed was to get lost from our camp! Wait it out, it couldn't stay like this long and headquarters would be checking on us—it says here! The patrol was scheduled to last seven more days. You can't help worrying and dreaming up worst case scenarios. What if we—? What if?—What if? It does no good to worry, but it is hard not to. All would be fine!

The next morning there was snow on the ground; it had gotten cold. The Air Force had loaned us white camouflage, which we were to put over the tents if there was snow. With a white background the tan tents would stand out to anyone flying over. We had orders to stand by the the radio at all times, so we didn't feel we should both go hiking for more than a few minutes at a time. We needed to stay active for our own health, so we walked separately and were careful to keep camp in sight. We didn't dare take a chance of getting lost.

The following morning there was ice on the lake that we had to break to get water. Each morning we found the ice thicker and stretching farther from shore. It wasn't thick enough to walk on, so it was difficult to reach water and keep our feet dry. Not only was water hard to reach, but we had to break a new hole every time we wanted a drink, because the water in our bucket would freeze in just a couple of hours. Would the Beaver that brought us in be able to land if the weather ever improved enough to fly? It couldn't get to shore because of the ice, and we didn't see any way we could get to a plane at the edge of the ice.

The days passed, the ceiling stayed on the deck. Having bowel movements became a problem. The ground was too frozen to kick our little hole, we didn't want to leave human turds around. Not many choices! Penny, unfortunately solved it by not crapping—not a conscious decision, but a combination of no place to do it, concern about not getting picked up, cold, and probably other factors too. She ended up with bowl impaction, and a very uncomfortable abdomen. Just another item to make this bear hunting patrol memorable.

The ten day patrol should have ended a few days ago, our food was almost gone. Now we realized we did have cause for worry. We really had no options. The park knew we were here and would find a way to get us out as soon as they could. After 15 days of sitting in bad weather in a poor location, we heard a strange whoo-pa-ta, whoo-pa-ta sound that we recognized as a helicopter. Sure enough— Landis to the rescue! He had flown up American Creek at about 20 feet altitude and found his way to where we were sitting. Never were we nearly so glad to see another human being. And in a bird that would give us another thrilling, but very slow, extremely low ride down a winding river to safety, a warm place, an enema for Penny, and a good hot meal.

On the way out Landis told us that the official weather at the air base had shown wind gusts at 83 mph with sustained winds of 55 mph the night our tent went down. The low temperature had been -8° F a couple of days ago. As Penny likes to say "Save me!"

A few days later, our reports were completed and we were making arrangements to fly home, Landis offered to take us with him when he flew from the town of King Salmon up to the city of Kenai on the Kenai Peninsula. We jumped at the chance for a ride with Landis. He showed us what it was like to fly down a narrow river only 20 feet off the deck with clear sky, tight turn after tight turn through the meanders of the river, as fast as he could go—neither of us lost our cookies! Talk about exciting! A wild ride on a roller-coaster would be a piece of cake. The finale to that ride was to autorotate for twelve miles, clear across Cook Inlet, and into the airport at Kenai. Autorotate meant that Landis shut the engine off at about ten thousand feet, while we were over the coast of the Alaska Peninsula and let the weight of the falling helicopter keep the blades turning so that we had the most beautiful, peaceful, quiet ride we could imagine—sliding into a rising, porcelain full moon across Cook Inlet with hardly a sound. As we reached the west coast of the Kenai Peninsula, at under a thousand feet, he restarted the engine, brought us into the Kenai airport, and landed like a dove.

Law Enforcement School

Life was good for us and our girls, all three of them had graduated from college; Lori from Bowling Green State University in art and design, was married, had a daughter, Claire, and was living in Portland, Oregon. Carin had completed her BS in nursing at Ohio State, was married and living in Seattle. Kristy had graduated from Franklin University in business administration, had a good job as assistant manager of a western-wear and tack store in Columbus, Ohio, and was living in our Columbus home. We felt all of our financial responsibility to our daughters had been fulfilled. We had a beautiful home, a very successful dental practice, and a lot of good friends who thought we were nuts to go off every summer to live in a tent and work for a few bucks an hour. We told them we were having the times of our lives.

During our first two seasons at Katmai we, as a team, had been on numerous back-country patrols of three days to two weeks duration. We each had been on a few extended patrols with other rangers. We enjoyed being in the back-country, and knew other rangers who had been in remote back-country positions for all or most of a season. We asked about those season-long assignments and were told we would need federal law enforcement commissions to qualify for those jobs.

On our way home from our first season in Alaska in 1983 we had made the decision to buy some rural land somewhere in the west, retire, sell our Ohio home and build a cabin. We looked at land in Oregon, California, Arizona, and Colorado, and bought 50 acres of land on 8,000-foot-high Log Hill Mesa in SW Colorado. The land is in a pinyon/juniper forest and looks into the San Juan Mountains, with the 14,000 foot peaks of the Sneffels Range to the south and the glorious Cimarron Ridge to the east. The little town of Ridgway is in the valley of the Uncompahgre River, eight miles down the escarpment. An ideal place to retire and build that cabin!

That winter Penny had decided to not pursue a career in politics and I had decided to not go back to dentistry full time. We were enjoying life as park rangers and had no desire to be wealthy. We had saved enough money we felt we could get by if we supplemented it with a little income from the Park Service. We made the decision to retire from dentistry the following spring, sell our beautiful home and build our cabin on that Colorado mesa. That left us with the chance to get law enforcement commissions and take the positions that we coveted as back-country law enforcement rangers. We found there was a law enforcement course being offered at Hocking Technical College in Nelsonville, Ohio that winter and enrolled.

Nelsonville, Ohio, is a small town in the lovely unglaciated hills of the southeastern part of the state. Our good friends, Gene and Tommy Good, had offered us the use of their rustic little cabin, that we had visited numerous times, in a secluded hollow about 15 miles from town, so it wouldn't be much of a commute to class each day, and we could occasionally make it up to Columbus to see friends and Kristy on weekends.

Classes didn't start for two days, so we took advantage of the time to reacquaint ourselves with the cabin and the immediate area. The property had been named Hyla Hollow after a tree frog from the genus Hyla. The beautiful hollow was inhabited by hundreds of the little gray and green Hyla frogs. Each spring the singing of the romantic croaking frog songs fills the hollow with music. In summer the vocal music of the frogs quiet down and the brook that runs just below the cabin takes over the music-making with its own instrumental symphony. Of course the music of the frogs and brook compete with the voices of warblers, wrens, thrush, sparrows, chickadees, and the multitudes of other birds who live in the hollow through spring, summer, and fall.

Now it was winter and cold, the frogs were hibernating, the brook frozen, most of the birds had migrated to warmer climes where food was available. Chickadees, a variety of nuthatches, purple finches (who look like thick beaked sparrows dipped in raspberry juice), jays, and cardinals filled the niches provided by the feeders we kept filled with thistle and sunflower seed. At night flying-squirrels would, occasionally sail into a lighted, cracked-corn feeder. We hated to leave the hollow to go to class, but that would be our routine for the next eight weeks.

The law enforcement class started with introductions of some of the teachers and each of us. It was a class of fifteen, Penny was the only female, most of the men had graduated from high school a year or two before. The oldest was a 23-year-old Native American, 30 years younger than we were.

We would have lectures from a judge, a prosecuting attorney, a defense attorney, a NPS-LE (law enforcement) instructor, numerous police, sheriffs, and state troopers. There would be classes on CFR 36 (Code of Federal Regulations), basic police work including finger printing, accident investigation, crime scene investigation and analysis, securing a scene, photographing the scene, felony car stop, defensive driving, drugs, stolen property, chemical agents, case incident report writing, radio use and etiquette. Learn how to ask and get answers to the basic questions which are relevant at every incident; what, where, when, why, how and who? I suggested the term "howzcome" to ask of all of those questions.

Just in case that wouldn't be enough to keep us busy, we would have defensive driving classes in a parking lot, hand-to-hand defensive tactics from a martial arts instructor every week, firearms classes, and outdoor pistol and shotgun live-fire every Saturday, with mandatory qualification before graduation. We would have demonstrations of tear-gas and rubber bullets. Then there were scenarios where we would handle a live mock-crime scene.

Classes would start at 0800 and run until 1700 with an hour for lunch five days a week. Then firearms every Saturday from 0800 to 1300 unless it ran later, which it usually did. That would let us have evenings to study our notes and CFR 36, dry-fire the revolver we had brought with us, eat, and maybe even have a beer before we collapsed. Sundays gave us time for peace, the opportunity to watch birds, listen to classical music by a beautiful fire, and enjoy a glass of wine with one of the great meals Penny fixed when she had time to cook.

At our first defensive tactics class the instructor introduced himself and asked for a volunteer. Penny had never been in the military and didn't know that you never volunteer, so a five-foot-five, 115-pound, 50-year-old woman stepped onto the mat facing the six-foot-one, 225-pound, 25-year-old instructor, and two seconds later found herself flat on her back, with her glasses knocked ten feet away. Teacher said, "Never trust anyone, always be alert and ready to defend yourself from any aggressive move."

He helped Penny up and apologized for demonstrating in such an unexpected way. He then showed Penny and the rest of us, how she could have stopped his attack and put him down with a quick grab of his wrist, a turn of her body, and using her hip as a fulcrum and his twisted arm as lever throw the much larger, stronger person over her head onto his back. She could then quickly roll him onto his stomach with his elbow locked, and control him there. We all practiced the move and managed to get the essence of it, if the opponent (one of our classmates) didn't resist too much. He assured us that with practice we would become proficient, and promised to be kinder to Penny the next week.

It was January in southeastern Ohio, and sure enough, the nice weather headed south. After a couple of days of class, we found we would be heading back to the cabin in three inches of fresh snow. We had several miles of gravel and dirt roads to navigate and a steep hill on the gravel/dirt driveway down into Hyla Hollow. Our Chevy van had good tires and positraction, it should do fine. We got as far as the steep driveway, and decided that if we went down we might never get back up. We had better park at the side of the road and not drive the hill. Of course, as soon as we pulled off the road the right wheels were in the ditch, and that was as far as we were going to go. We knew there was an old Subaru Brat pickup with all-wheel drive in the shed at the bottom of the hill, and were confident the Goods would not mind if we used it. We called them for permission. They said, of course we could use the Brat, but warned us it hadn't been used much for years and probably wasn't in very good shape. Boy, did that prove to be the case! It got us to school every day, but had to go to a shop several different times before it would go home. We spent a few nights in a motel when parts had to be ordered for the Brat—her heater never did work. We were thankful to have Brat, but in hind-sight, we would have been better-off to have rented a four-wheel-drive vehicle for the two months.

We were glad the first Saturday firearms class would be inside, since the temperature was not going to get up to freezing. The class was interesting. I was comfortable with shotguns and Penny had used them several times. I had used a revolver, but had never had any instruction in handguns. Most of the kids in the class thought they knew all about weapons of all kinds. The instructors were glad Penny didn't know much about firearms. She could learn the right way, while everyone else would need to forget what they thought they knew in order to learn the proper handling and use of firearms.

First, everyone learns to respect weapons and how dangerous they can be. Then you learn their care, take them apart, clean and reassemble a revolver and a 12-gauge shotgun. Then dry-fire both weapons a bunch of times, until you are comfortable with it. "Damn it, don't jerk that trigger! Squeeze it! Slowly increase the pressure on the trigger until it goes off," was an admonition we heard frequently.

Future firearms classes just got more challenging as the weather got worse, colder with snow and wind! Every Saturday we moved outside for live-firing, and thought we would freeze. The worst Saturday had a high temperature of 16°F and a wind chill of -22°F, with blowing snow. Shotgun education continued with different kinds of ammunition; cracker shells (M80 fire-crackers that are projected about 30 yards out where they explode), rubber bullets, #9 bird-shot, #4 buck, 00 buck and slugs. Then loading, and jacking rounds in and out. Firing was done under the strict supervision of the range master and included standing and firing from the shoulder and from the hip, as well as prone in the snow. We used slugs and #9 bird-shot at paper targets 30 and 15 yards away. In later sessions we would run, loading while we ran and firing from the hip, diving behind some cover and firing from the shoulder. Get up, loading and firing as we ran to a different cover, fire from there, then repeat the process. Just fun in the snow, but boy, did it give us a concept of what a real confrontation could be like.

A man who we decided was a masochist taught us the use of gas masks. He demonstrated how to properly put on a mask. Then he put us in the end of a gymnasium-like room with masks, and fired a gas grenade at us to see if we could get the mask on properly and quickly. All but one of us did, he had to be carried out by two guys who had gotten their masks on properly. The same masochist sprayed us with mace and pepper spray, and shot us in the legs with rubber pellets from a 37-mm riot gun. We didn't like it or him, but, in retrospect, it was some of the most valuable training we had.

This all took place before 9-mm, semiautomatic handguns became the weapon of choice, so we trained using six-shot Smith & Wesson .38-special revolvers, with four or six-inch barrels. We lined up on the firing range, each facing a paper target 30 feet away. The target had the outline of a person on it. Any shot within the outline counted 5 points, anything beyond the body outline didn't count. Having different circles count 5-4-3-2-1 would create a real pain to count the score, and the theory was that any body or head hit with a 158-grain slug would put your opponent out of commission, at least temporarily. Each person would fire 60 rounds in a set with a perfect score being 300. To qualify you must shoot a score of 250 or above. That didn't even sound easy!

The Range Master is in unquestioned control of everything on the shooting range. The quickest way to flunk out of LE school is to not do exactly as the Range Master tells you—no messing around with a loaded weapon. Like a boot-camp drill sergeant, he orders the group, "On my command draw and fire two rounds in three seconds, re-holster, and stand at the ready." Next you hear "Fire!" you draw, fire, and hear a whistle indicating three seconds—time is up before you have lined your weapon up for the second shot. Not many of us had gotten the second shot off before the whistle, so there were a lot of shots following the whistle. That wasn't a problem the first day but he would be stricter about time as we progressed up to the day of final qualifying when there was no give on the three-second rule.

That 60-round set is fired, two or three shots at a time from all sorts of positions, right handed, left handed, from 30 feet, 20 feet, ten feet, even five feet, from behind barricades, or not, mostly standing in the open facing your target, feet spread to shoulder width, your revolver in your dominant hand with the other hand giving support. You end up firing as many as 300 or 400 rounds in a practice day, your hand is bruised from the revolver kick of all those shots, your trigger finger is sore, your arms are weary, you are tired and cold because you have been out in freezing temperatures for five or six hours. You also feel good; you're scores have improved with each set of 60 rounds, you're confidence is higher, you're beginning to think "I am going to make it through this!"

We had scenarios where we were at a simulated crime scene, a car stop, a domestic disturbance, a "nut case" endangering himself and possibly others. How do you and your partner handle them? For a car stop; you and your partner both get out of the cruiser only if there is a second person in the stopped vehicle. Normally the driver of the patrol vehicle approaches the stopped vehicle holding a metal clipboard in front of themself to deflect a shot, in case the stopped driver should shoot. You make no explanation of why you made the stop, you simply say "Let me see your license and registration please," return to the cruiser and check, by radio, with NCIC to find out if the person has "wants or warrants" out on them. If they are not wanted, you return the license and registration to the driver, have a conversation, and either site them or let them go with a warning. If the person is wanted for a felony or other crime, you call for backup and stay in your vehicle.

Domestic disturbances have the potential to be disastrous to everyone involved. So go slow, be careful, don't trust anyone—they all lie! Penny and I were to respond to a mock "Shots fired" domestic disturbance. (The actual scene was outside one of the buildings on campus.) We approached a distraught man standing across the street from a house. He was pointing at the house telling us, "She's in there and has a shotgun! She wants to kill me! She's nuts! She thinks I'm cheating on her." We talk to him, getting him calmed down, and trying to get the full, straight story. He talks, seems to be calming, and tells us a story about marital bliss, raising kids, taking family vacations, and how that started going sour a few months ago. We begin to believe him. Suddenly he points to the house behind us screaming, "Oh God, here she comes with that shotgun!" We turn toward the house where he is pointing. Nothing there, we turn back to look into the barrel of his handgun. Smiling he says, "Game's over you lose!"

OK, we did the first scenario correctly, and got snookered on the second one. Now we have to bring a nut case down from the loft of a barn where he is going to kill any person who climbs up to the loft and then he is going to shoot himself. He claims to be Jesus Christ, and isn't going to be taken to the cross. Penny had an instant plan. She is the mother of three girls, and felt she knew how to handle this nut. She and I walked into the barn, and Penny in a strong authoritarian voice shouts, "Jesus, I'm your mother Mary and this is your father Joseph. Now you quit this foolishness, and you get down here right now!"

The guy in the loft broke up and came down. The judging teachers broke up, and we all had a good laugh. We passed the scenarios test with honors!

We had done well in the two midterms, and survived the defensive tactics course. Perhaps that was due to the martial arts instructor realizing he wasn't up to the job. Things had gone along moderately well with him having us disarm each-other when faced at close range, by a person holding a handgun. He made a final mistake. He had asked for a volunteer a second time, when no one was willing to face him on the mats he picked on Penny again, promising to treat her kindly. He said he wouldn't even touch her. He was going to demonstrate the art of kick-boxing, where he would whirl around kicking his opponent in the head, but he would stay well away from Penny. He misjudged! His heal caught Penny right on the end of her nose, we all could hear the bone crack. Maybe it was just the impact of flesh on flesh we heard, but everyone was aghast. Penny was down, the class was ready to lynch him, but Penny calmed the situation by getting up with blood running from her nose and held out her hand to shake with him. He was not popular with the class anyway, but that kick eliminated him from ever being a successful teacher.

One final day of shooting: We would all be on the firing line until everyone qualified, so we expected it to be a very long, very cold day for all of us. The high temperature for that Saturday was predicted to be 15°F and class was scheduled from 0800 to 2000, in case it took that long to get everyone qualified. Twelve hours in that temperature sounded like we would be lucky to survive, much less shoot well. The wind blew, it didn't snow much, and we all qualified by 1800.

After a dinner break, we went to the classroom for our final exam. Assuming we all passed the final, Federal Law Enforcement School would be complete. Penny and I both felt we aced the final, most of our classmates felt they had passed and wanted us to join them for a celebration. Graduation would be Tuesday, so we had two days to relax and recover before then. We all went to a local pub for beer and fun. Every one toasted Penny for the way she had handled the defensive tactics instructor after he had kicked her in the nose. Penny and I each had only two beers, and felt we had better head back to the cabin sober rather than drive the snowy back roads drunk. We had gotten used to Park Service parties with kids 20 or 30 years younger than we were, and knew how they could end up—time for the old folks to turn in.

Graduation was rather anticlimactic, we received our diplomas, shook hands with our friends and some of the instructors who attended, got some addresses and were glad to have that brief, but tough, phase of our lives completed. Now we were qualified to accept the positions that had been offered to us as law enforcement officers in the NPS! That did make us feel kind of proud of ourselves! Now we could go out and "fight crime," as most rangers like to kid about law enforcement work.

DILLINGHAM

We had visited our daughter, Lori, in Portland, Oregon, for a few days before flying on to Alaska. The spring flowers around her home were in full bloom, the sky had been delightfully clear, and the temperature was in the 70s. Flying into King Salmon that day in early April of 1985, we looked out the windows of the Alaska Airlines plane and realized it wasn't spring, it was still winter; we had traveled back a season. All of the little pothole lakes were still ice covered, snow whitened the north-facing slopes of every hill. When we checked in at the park office, Sally Orot, the administrative officer (AO) said, "This is going to be a strange year." Indeed it was! Weather and equipment problems dominated the season.

Only two months earlier we had completed the federal law enforcement course. Now we had been sworn in as federal officers, and were ready to take our positions as the law enforcement (LE) rangers at the Nonvianuk Ranger Station in the preserve portion of Katmai National Park and Preserve. The preserve is the northern extension of the park proper. It includes Kukaklek Lake which is drained by the Alagnak (or Branch) River, and Nonvianuk River and Lake, plus several hundred thousand acres of surrounding land. The confluence of the Branch and Nonvianuk Rivers forms the Alagnak Wild and Scenic River, which would also be a part of our responsibility.

National Preserves are open to hunting and fishing during state designated seasons. Fishing has always been legal in national parks but hunting is not permitted unless the superintendent specifically authorizes it. Both fishing and hunting in the state of Alaska require state licenses and have strict seasons set by the state.

Before 19 February 2010, law enforcement rangers were the only people permitted to possess a loaded fire-arm of any sort in national parks, the country's most revered natural areas. However, since then, Congress, in its infinite wisdom, deemed it appropriate for anyone to have a loaded weapon with them in a national park. The public and wildlife had been relatively safe from people who felt they had to be armed to protect themselves from wildlife and predatory humans. Law enforcement officers are much more concerned that uneducated people with weapons will unnecessarily shoot an animal or another person than they are a person will be attacked by wildlife or criminals. Now anyone with a fear of being in bear country has the option of carrying a loaded firearm, whether they know anything about guns and wildlife or not. Shooting bears, "In defense of life and property," can be expected to become more common when everyone in the park is armed and dangerous.

Our plan was to get to Nonvianuk by mid May, in time to have everything functional before the opening of rainbow trout season on 8 June. Nonvianuk Lake was iced over until late May that year. Then ice, driven by an east wind, clogged the west end of the lake and the head of the Nonvianuk River until 13 June.

Not to fear, if we couldn't get there no one else could either. We could use the time; there were many things that needed to be done to get ready for the season. We had a lot of gear to gather: our back-pack tent needed all of the seams sealed, we had to check the bottom of the Zodiac (those wonderful inflatable boats made famous by Jacques Cousteau in his TV series on Oceanography) for holes in the hypalon floor and for leaks in the flotation tubes, fowl weather coats had to be collected before somebody living at Brooks Camp grabbed them, boat pillows and life vests were items we needed for the boat. Those were some of the musts for us, and headquarters would probably dream up things for us to do for them until the weather would let us get to Nonvianuk.

Sally, the AO, had arranged for us to be lodged at the Air Force Base while we were in town. Staying on base gave us access to the base NCO Club with all of its amenities. Good food we didn't have to cook ourselves, a party atmosphere every evening if we were interested. So quarters, meals, and entertainment were covered while we were stuck waiting for the weather to cooperate. Waiting for weather was something we were getting accustomed to in Alaska. Not being willing to wait for acceptable flying weather has cost a lot of people their lives!

Our having free time gave the park administration an opportunity to get us to do things they would normally do themselves. The park's Natural History Association's assortment of books and other items for sale to the public hadn't been inventoried for several years, and Superintendent Dave Morris had been getting questioned about it from the NPS district office in Anchorage—they could have the Starrs do that. Dave and Chief Ranger Loren were supposed to represent the park at the spring celebration in the Aleut town of Naknek, 12 miles down the only road out of King Salmon—the Starrs could do that.

The high school science teacher in the town of Dillingham, across Bristol Bay, called the park and wanted the Superintendent to visit the school to explain to the students what the Alaska National Interest Lands Conservation Act (ANILCA) was, and what the National Parks in Alaska were all about. He was strongly in favor of the parks, but some people in Dillingham were adamantly opposed. They feared some of their freedoms might be compromised. It was only a few years since the passage of ANILCA and many Alaskans were still quite dubious of it. Dave knew Penny was a great communicator and had been very involved in promoting ANILCA as it worked its way through Congress, so he asked her if she would be willing to do the Dillingham presentation for him. She would fly across Bristol Bay on a commercial flight, speak to the high school students, stay over night with the teacher and his wife, then fly back to King Salmon the next day. Dave said he would really appreciate it if Penny would do that for him. On that basis, she couldn't turn him down. While Penny was gone, I would be flying to Brooks Camp to help with ranger training. So much for work we needed to do to get ready for Nonvianuk.

When we first arrived in King Salmon several years ago, we became aware of the animosity that many locals had for the Park Service. We would hear whispers of "Park Service, Park Service" whenever we walked into the little store or one of the pubs. Many in the Native population and all of the red-neck population hated the Park Service. They refused to speak to rangers, they just acted like we didn't exist. A few years earlier there had been instances of water being put in Park Service aircraft gas tanks. Now, before flying, park pilots always bled an ounce or two from the wing tanks, so they could visually check to be sure there was no water. King Salmon residents had finally accepted that we were there and were a positive economic factor in the town. Would Dillingham be the same or would we still be resented? Penny was going to be a NPS ambassador. She needed to present and promote the Park Service as one of the really good guys, not as the ogre who was going to take away their hunting and fishing rights.

A few days later she flew to Dillingham on Pen Air's (Peninsula Airways) regular morning flight from King Salmon. The science teacher met her at the airport and explained about the problems he was having with some of his students telling others how bad the Park Service was and how their lands would be taken and their hunting and fishing rights messed up. He was hoping that Penny would be able to explain the reality of the NPS in Alaska and correct the misperceptions.

She had worked up a program of park slides and a talk to go with it. That afternoon as she spoke to the high school science class she noticed the principal was in the audience. After the talk the science teacher and the principal came up to her, complimented her on an excellent presentation, and asked if she would stay longer. They wanted all of the staff to meet her. They would arrange a big potluck dinner party for that evening in the school gym. Penny was sure that Superintendent Dave would give the park's blessing to the idea, but she had to check to be sure. Dave was thrilled. He said, "Stay as long as you want and don't worry about getting back to the park."

Penny told me about the evening. "Of course I was a basket case; I wanted to do a superb job. The potluck was so much fun, I think half of the town was there. I showed slides and talked for over an hour, then answered questions for another hour. I was in my Park Service uniform all evening. The magical thing that happened was, I sat with the town people, and they really came out with questions and conversation, and we developed a warm, open relationship. It was a wonderful evening. The people there couldn't have been more receptive to what I had to say about the Park Service.

"The school principal asked if I would talk to the rest of the students the next day. Of course I would. I already had permission from Dave to spend whatever time I felt would be productive. So I spoke with every class, separately, even little kindergarten and first graders. They loved my stories."

She told me about the one negative incident of the entire trip. "I was out exploring the streets of Dillingham, doing some sightseeing and shopping. A terribly drunk Aleut came up to me and spit in my face. I just wiped away his saliva and walked on. No words would help his problem."

Penny continued, "The trip was a real gift for me, and I feel it began a more open dialogue with Alaskan citizens. The greatest thank you I got was all the fun, sincere notes the little students sent to the park. When they grew up they all wanted to be Park Rangers!"

Park Superintendent Dave Morris was more than pleased.

When he and Chief Ranger Loren heard the story of Penny and the drunk Native, they couldn't imagine how Penny stayed so cool. Dave's report to the regional office in Anchorage got him and the park a letter of congratulations. Penny had an interesting, fun, memorable experience, really felt good about her time in Dillingham, and came home with a couple of pieces of Native art that we still treasure.

Nonvianuk Tent Frame

NONVIANUK (NVK)

The ice on Nonvianuk Lake and the head of the Nonvianuk River finally cleared enough that Pen Air could fly us in to the lake on 15 June. The chance of being resupplied with anything but fuel during the season was next to zero. So we went in with all of our five months supplies. Penny always went to a grocery near our home, filled four or five grocery carts with what she calculated we would need for our time in the bush: canned goods, including some meat, vegetables, and soups, but mostly dry-beans, rice, and pastas. She brought them home along with several empty apple boxes. I filled the boxes, sealed them with strapping tape, and took them to the post office. The postal service would deliver it all to us in King Salmon. That sure beat trying to find a grocery in Anchorage and packing things up there. A catalog food supplier delivers what most of the permanent residents use, but they are really pricey. The little grocery in King Salmon, besides being expensive, is very limited in what they can carry.

With our food, gear, and personal library, we also had a 12-foot Zodiac, a notoriously uncooperative Mercury outboard motor, 40 gallons of fuel, and our infamous beer supply. A lot of supplies, all of which meant we would need to go in a Grumman Goose. The Goose is a WWll vintage twin engine amphibious aircraft with the room and power to cary all of our gear. We had to have something that landed on water, and being amphibious, it would let us get our gear on land without wading, hip deep, with each load.

We had spent the morning getting our pile of gear to the King Salmon airport before our friend Georgie flew the Goose in to pick us up. When Georgie, a Native Aleut, looked at our pile he laughed and said, "White man has much baggage." We had heard him say that before and would hear it many times in the future. He loved to kid us and we kidded him whenever we had a chance. Somehow he had more opportunity to kid us than we did him. The pile was pretty big, but it was what two white people would need for five months, with a little extra just in case Georgie couldn't get us out on schedule.

To get the gear on shore, the Goose had to land near a beach that it could taxi up on. Georgie knew the only such beach was on the north-west corner of Nonvianuk Lake. That put us a good mile from the head of the Nonvianuk River, and the ranger station is a couple hundred yards down, and across the river. With Georgie's help we unloaded that pile of stuff from the Goose, and Georgie was gone.

We assembled the Zodiac, got the outboard mounted, and piled gear onboard, leaving enough room for the two of us to sit and operate the outboard motor. We realized it would take several loads in the little Zodiac so we didn't over load. I connected the fuel line to the outboard, pumped gas into the engine, pulled the starter cord on the Mercury outboard, pulled it again, choked it, pulled, and cursed; pulled, choked, cursed, pulled and cursed again and again—the sun-of-a-bitch wasn't going to start. That outboard had been the bane of previous rangers existence for years, but we had been assured that it had been reconditioned and was "like new." It was my fault! I should have tried it out in town before we left. Never trust anyone else with what could be your life-support!

We walked the edge of the lake in hip-waders, pulling the Zodiac, all the way around to the river and down a few yards to the "Cry of the Loon" fishing camp, hoping they would be able to help us with the motor. The "Loon" or "COL" is on private land owned by Katmai Land (the same people who are the concessionaires of the Brooks Lodge) and leased to Bill Wright of Alaska Fishing and Wilderness Adventures. Bill hires a couple to manage the place: that is, to cook, clean, entertain, be fishing guides, and all else that "managing" entails in bush Alaska. Bill is smart enough to leave the hiring of two young men, usually college students who act as fishing guides and general flunkies, to the camp manager. The camp is "rustic." There is an out house and a shower-house, with an oil stove to heat both the shower house and water. Also a burn-barrel for disposing of burnable trash—all other trash had to be flown out. Cry of the Loon has a capacity of eight guests. It consists of two cabins, each with two double decker bunk beds, and staff quarters in a dining/cooking/gathering building with a nice wood burning fireplace.

Their camp is on the river just at the outlet of Nonvianuk Lake. Meeting the staff there had been one of our first, but not THE first, priority of the season. We walked around the corner pulling our loaded Zodiac and met our four neighbors, who were looking at us like they knew we were lost souls in need of help. We were! We explained about the motor refusing to start, after supposedly being reconditioned by the boat shop in town.

The managers were Tony and Nancy Cooper. Their two young guides for the season were Dave and Kenny. Tony, the boys, and I started working on the motor while Penny and Nancy stood by watching and getting acquainted. Nancy was a little shorter than Penny, about 5-foot-4, and a little heavier, probably 130 pounds. Tony was bigger than me at 5-foot-10 and likely 185. Both had sandy brown hair and great smiles. Tony sported a moderate, neatly trimmed mustache. The boys were bigger and definitely stronger than the rest of us, and seemed more than willing to be helpful. We worked on the damned motor for most of an hour. Did a lot more pulling, choking, and cussing. We changed spark plugs, and even tried a new fuel mixture before giving up. When Nancy heard the story of the infamous outboard she grinned and said, "Well, fuck you very much boat shop." Yep, we were going to get along famously. We all had a good laugh and felt better about being stuck with no transportation.

Tony and Nancy were trying a new experience by managing a fishing camp. They were about our age and were looking into a life-style change like we had made a few years before. We had a lot in common. Tony had been a fishing guide on the Bighorn and Yellowstone Rivers for years, and Nancy was a registered nurse at a hospital in Grand Junction, Colorado, only 100 miles from where we had bought land a year before—we were neighbors. Dave and Kenny were college students who loved to fish, and who Tony knew from the Bighorn River in Montana. Tony had the boys use their boat to take us, our Zodiac, and all of our gear, across to a small gravel beach on the river's far bank below the ranger station. Dave and Kenny even helped us carry some of the gear up the hill to the tent-frame that would be our home for the season.

Without transportation we weren't going to be very functional rangers. We had a ten-watt VHF radio to use for communicating with Brooks Camp and headquarters in King Salmon. We also had five-watt VHF radios that we each carried in a belt holster and used for communicating with each other. Those five-watt radios would reach the park plane if we could see it, but were of no value for talking to anyone who was out of sight. Unfortunately we couldn't use our radios to communicate with the lodges in the area. They all used marine-band radios, which we didn't have. Hal had told us we wouldn't have much luck reaching headquarters with the ten-watt until the repeater on Dumpling Mountain, near Brooks Camp, could be gotten functional, and he didn't know when that might happen. Our luck was due to improve! We reached headquarters on our first try, and let them know the outboard wouldn't start. They agreed to pick it up ASAP, but couldn't tell us when that might be. OK, we were stuck until we had a motor, but there was plenty to do getting the station up and functional until we did have a motor for our little boat that Penny had christened "Das Boot."

As it turned out, the next day Loren, our chief ranger and pilot, flew in to our gravel beach to take the outboard back to town and the boat shop. He would let us know when it was fixed. He was pissed at the boat shop too, and would tell them his feelings in no uncertain terms. They do a good bit of work for the Park Service and should respond quickly—he hoped.

The Nonvianuk Ranger Station is truly deserving of its nick-name "Nonexistant." The rangers are told "Go out there, do your job, and come back alive." We had each spent ten days at the Nonvianuk Ranger Station during our first season in Katmai, so we had a pretty good idea of what we were getting into. That year a single ranger was assigned to the post. Being alone in the Alaskan bush has too many potential hazards and is not approved by the NPS. To cover the park's ass, a rotating assignment of Brooks Camp rangers was sent to NVK. One every two weeks on what is called a ten/four assignment, meaning you work ten days and have four days off. As it turned out Penny and I were now considered to be working that

10/4 schedule, but really we worked 24/7—24 hours a day, 7 days a week. Like firefighters we were on duty 24 hours a day, unlike firefighters we weren't on for 48 hours and off for 72 hours; we were on duty 24 hours every day for nearly five months.

For back country housing, we would be living in the high rent district. (We were charged the same rent for the tent-frame as we had been for the cedar log-cabin with all utilities at Brooks Camp.) The 14 by 16-foot tent-frame sits on a knoll on the south side of the river about a quarter mile down stream from Nonvianuk Lake. Walk through the door onto a plywood floor: to the left are a propane refrigerator and cook stove, and a cast iron sink that drains into a five gallon bucket. The bucket gets dumped out in the brush, well away from the tent. Attached to the rear wall, straight in front of the door, is a small table, with a card-table chair on each side. We remembered the sleeping loft above the table, it had been Greg's domain when each of us had spent time here. To get to the loft we climbed a birch log four or five inches in diameter, with pegs on each side for steps—not very comfortable on bear feet. The loft itself had a double mattress on the plywood deck where we could spread our sleeping bags. There was even a little window in the rear wall, so we could check the world before we went to sleep and before we got up the next morning. We had storage on each side adjacent to the table where we kept all sorts of gear—for us and the boat. Adjacent to the right wall was a narrow single bed, where a guest could sleep. Boots were always left just inside the door. In Alaska everyone removes their boots at the door so as to not spread mud all over.

A hundred-pound propane tank would be flown in—soon. The water for the sink was in the river a couple hundred yards down the hill. We had a Coleman gas lantern for evening light—it wouldn't get dark until late August, but some extra light in the evenings gave us the opportunity to get book work done, personal letters written, or a book read.

Outside there was an elevated food cache that bears couldn't reach, where we stored all of our food. We reached it by setting up a very heavy ladder made of two-by-fours, which we put up and took down each time we wanted something to eat. We had an A-frame outhouse, and a burn barrel for paper and plastic trash. Down at the river there was an erosional notch in the bank just big enough for us to tie-up the 12-foot Zodiac out of the current. The top of the old canvas tent was badly mildewed, so we had brought a treated nylon tarp to make a new roof for our home.

We spent the next couple of days getting the roof tarp installed and the station up and running. Then had time to explore the area by foot. Boreal forest, or taiga (from a Russian Turkic dialect), is the belt of mixed conifers and hardwoods which grows in the subalpine zone all around the world. In Alaska it extends from the southern edge of the Brooks Range to its southern limit in Katmai. So we had boreal forest in some areas, wet tundra below the taiga, and dry tundra above it. If we stayed high we had quite comfortable hiking across dry tundra. We found walking the dry tundra to be a great way to get to know the area. If we talked or made enough noise, we wouldn't surprise a bear and could walk for hours along caribou trails and see all sorts of plants blooming early in their, short 100-day growing season. Dwarf dogwood, with a blossom like the dogwood tree but on a plant that hugs the ground, was just coming into bloom. Alpine bearberry, the plant with the leaves that turn into a brilliant red carpet in the fall, were finishing their blooms, and we could see berries starting to form—they don't make particularly good eating, so we wouldn't be looking for those berries come fall. Mountain avens, or dryas, has long been one of our favorites. It's a mat-forming, ground-hugging shrub that was starting to open flower heads consisting of eight white petals and a clump of brilliant yellow stamen making a striking contrast to the dark background. Golden-crowned sparrows, sitting on the top of low alders would sing, Penny's Jewel Cave saying of "Oh save me" in their sweet descending three-note mating song.

One evening over pizza and beer, at law enforcement school in Ohio with our Indian friend Jim, we had gotten to talking about his heritage and how people had crossed the Bering Land Bridge 13,000 years ago. Jim had a doe-skin medicine bag of "sacred things" that meant a lot to him and to his heritage, that he felt traced back to Beringia. He had asked if we would burry it in a special spot in Alaska where we could assure him it would be "always wild" and a part of his heritage. We took his request seriously and buried the little pouch on the tundra where there was a beautiful view of the Alagnak Wild River and the Aleutian Mountains. It is in a special spot that will always be wild and undisturbed until erosion, possibly the next glacier, takes it down to the sea.

A surprising number of fishermen flew into the river where we could walk down to meet them. Business takes precedence over the pleasure of tundra hikes, so we needed to meet people when they flew in. We got a feel for our duties even without the boat. We always met people in a friendly conversational way, made sure they were familiar with their responsibilities in bear country, explained about trash and how they needed to keep their own picked up, and not expect their guide, or us, to clean up after them. "You bring that bag or can of food in full and consume what's in it; now you, please, take it out empty!" We found out which lodge they were staying with, how they liked it, and checked their fishing license. We always talked with the pilot/guides, got their names and the name of their lodge. After they seemed comfortable with us, which usually required several visits, we tried to get a feel of how they felt they were being treated by the owner and today's guests. Some of the guides would even give us a high-sign if today's clients needed special attention.

Getting tail numbers and descriptions of aircraft associated with each lodge was going to be an important reference for us for the whole season. If we could identify the aircraft, we knew which lodge we were dealing with before we met the people. Employees of different lodges seem to take on the attitude of the owner or manager—follow the laws or ignore them when they think they can get away with it. It didn't take long for us to recognize that different lodges attracted different types of clientele. If we knew which lodge was flying in we could pretty well tell what kind of person we were going to deal with.

After nearly two weeks, we finally got a call from headquarters letting us know that Loren would be bringing our motor to us in less than and hour. Fortunately we were on the beach talking with fishermen and not out fighting crime (exploring) several hours away. We mounted the motor on the transom of "Das Boot" and got it to start with only about 15 pulls of the cord. Loren told us we would have to make-do until he could get a better outboard for us, and flew back to King Salmon. We would make-do. We had the whole lake to patrol, two more lodges to visit, and the Kulik River and Kulik Lake to explore. That is, if we could get the short-shank prop-drive outboard through the shallows of the Kulik River.

It was late June, and we could finally start the season!

Enchanted Lake Lodge

Penny and I had been looking forward to exploring Nonvianuk Lake. It is 20 miles long and must have 100 miles of shoreline. We wanted to know the lake, not just run from point A to point B and back in our little Zodiac. It was glacially carved during the ice age, the Pleistocene Epoch, from 1.6 million to 10,000 years ago,—1.6 mBP (1.6 million years before present) to 10,000 BP—so it was deep and had few islands. In an old book we had run across in the Brooks Camp library, there are pictures of a couple of historic cabins along Nonvianuk's south shore. One had been the year-round home of a family in the early 1940s. They were escaping the draft and earning their living by raising silver fox, a subspecies of red fox (*Vulpes fulva*). We wanted to see if we could find those old places and learn more about their history. We could have a full summer of exploring. Somehow that wasn't our assigned duty, but we would manage to explore while we worked.

Take it easy, get to know our Zodiac, how it handles, and develop some confidence in the outboard, which had a terrible reputation. Then get a feel of the lake and the weather on it—don't do something stupid like running to Kulik Lodge at the far end of Nonvianuk the first day out. Our maps looked like the north shore wouldn't offer much of interest. A fairly steep bank up the side of the U-shaped valley with no significant streams flowing in, so there wouldn't be fishermen there for us to check on. Part way up lake were the remnants of a recessional moraine where the glacier, acting like an enormous bulldozer, had left a large amount of ground-up rock as it paused on its retreat up the valley. That moraine had once reached completely across the lake, dividing it into two separate lakes. Now it had eroded to the place where there were remnant spits protruding from each shore. The north spit was comprised of gravels that contained a large concentration of agates. We found collecting a few of these beautiful varicolored quartz pebbles to be a pleasant diversion from a day of, talking to fishermen, exploring, and "fightin' crime."

The south shore proved to be more interesting. It was not as steep and even had a few flat places, probably morainal material. Those flat areas looked like possibilities for home sites. They were. We tied up the boat and went ashore at every likely looking location. The first one we found with signs of habitation was only a few miles from our station, in a grove of poplar trees fronted by a narrow gravel beach. A few yards in was the remains of a low cabin that appeared to have been occupied not too many years ago. It had three and a half walls and most of a moss covered roof. Inside we found a couple of wooden chairs and a table with mold and lichen growing on them, a set of rusty bed springs, and some kitchen utensils. We harvested, and still have, an old white pottery cup with "Tepco China, USA" stamped on the bottom. It looked like ones we had seen in old restaurants. A rusted out barrel stove still had a blue and black enameled coffee pot siting on it. The one room cabin looked like a place where someone would have sat at night thinking over the days-harvest from his trap line. A hard, lonely life, but one that many men had chosen, and some still do. We wondered about people who chose that sort of life, and suspect there are people who wonder what was in our minds to have chosen such an unusual retirement.

A few miles farther up lake was the south shore's morainal spit, perhaps a hundred yards wide, several hundred yards deep, essentially flat, and covered in grass and brush. In the center were the remains of a log home. It had been built in the fashion of Native barabaras, that is: A hole was dug to serve as the living quarters then a roof was built to cover the hole. This place was mostly collapsed, but I think we figured it out pretty well. The hole, just like that of a barabara, was four or five feet deep with a low pitched, sod covered roof creating an interior with adequate head room except near the walls were beds and furniture would have been placed around a central wood stove. Being below grade it was protected from cold winds and would be warm in the winter and cool in the summer—well, sort of anyway.

There was enough of the original structure that we could imagine what life for a family running a fox farm might have been like. They had shelter, they could cut wood for fuel to keep warm, good water was in the lake a few yards away, but what did they eat? According to the stories we had heard they were raising fox for the fur trade; the fox had to eat too. Both the man and the woman would have spent a lot of time in the summer fishing—like Penny and I did, for food, not for sport. According to the story this couple had two kids. Depending on the kids ages, they would have either been tremendous helpers or a lot of work. The Aleuts fed their sled dogs dried salmon and caribou, probably these people fed the same diet to the fox. Many different berries ripen at different times over summer and fall, so they undoubtedly did a lot of berry picking, while watching for bears picking in the same berry patch. They would have counted on killing a moose or two each fall. We searched around the old cabin and found an area where the vegetation was a little different from the grasses of the surrounding tundra and imagined a garden where the couple grew lettuce, onions, carrots, cabbage, and maybe even some peas. The family led a tough life. We can only imagine what it would have been like to live year-round under these conditions.

Cruising the lake one afternoon, looking for crime to fight, we saw a good looking launch with a brown hull and orange trim. Painted the same colors as Enchanted Lake Lodge's Beaver float planes, we guessed it was probably Enchanted Lake's boat. As we pulled up to them a woman leaned over the gunwale and yelled, "Penny Starr." That was a surprise. We didn't expect a guest at one of the lodges to know us. She turned out to be Judy Ruthven, wife of John Ruthven the famous wildlife artist. Judy had been a dental hygiene student of Penny's at Ohio State. She had heard we were there and insisted we join her and John for dinner that evening at the lodge. We explained we weren't allowed to accept gifts from the lodges. She insisted, and said she would make us her guests. We accepted, explaining that we could have dinner if we presented an evening program, which was not quite so, but we felt it might cover our asses if we were ever questioned.

Enchanted Lake Lodge is on private property, and is owned and operated by Dick Matthews. It is one of the truly high-end, cream-of-the-crop lodges. We had heard tales of the guest list; it included Jack and Barbara Nicklaus, who we had known in Columbus, and actor Jack Lemon, who supposedly came every year. Apparently Dick and his lodge were well known by people who could afford such a vacation.

We pulled up to the Enchanted Lake dock later that afternoon, tied up, and were met by Tom, the skipper of the boat that we had met earlier. He was the lodge's mechanic and maintenance man as well. Apparently, Tom does everything other than flying guests to fishing spots. He offered to give us a grand tour of the lodge and grounds. Great! He had us get on a four-wheeler with him for a quarter mile ride up a steep gravel drive through a forest of pine and birch to the lodge and four cabins, all sitting on the crest of the glacier-carved valley wall. Each of the beautiful cedar log cabins had a living room, bedroom, and full bath with instant hot water. There were a couple of staff cabins a little ways down toward the private lake that Tom said were as nice as the guest cabins. Tom was deservedly proud of the place. He was the one who made it all work so well. Each cabin is located so their view doesn't include another building. They have capacity for 16 guests, four in each cabin, as the bedrooms all have two double beds. Dick prefers to keep it to eight or ten in order to make each visit a more personal experience.

The name, "Enchanted Lake," fits! There is a spectacular five-acre glacial lake adjacent to the lodge, also on Dick's property, from which the lodge operates its two distinctive brown and orange Beaver aircraft. There are a couple of kayaks and a small outboard skiff moored at a dock, for guests to use for fishing, or just paddling around. A year earlier Dick was a bit overloaded one day when he took off in one of the Beavers; he didn't quite clear the trees at the far end of the lake. A float hit the top of a tree, and Dick crashed into the woods. There were no passengers onboard, he was hauling trash out. He wasn't hurt; the Beaver was picked up by one of those sky-crane helicopters and taken to Anchorage where it was repaired in time for Dick to fly it back for the final few weeks of his season.

The lodge building is a gathering room and dinning hall for guests with a fine kitchen behind the dining area. One end of the great room had a large wood-burning fireplace, with comfortable leather chairs around a huge coffee table. The perfect place for conversation and cocktails. Judy Ruthven introduced us to her husband John, the other guests, and particularly to their Cincinnati friends, John Smale and his wife (whose first name I can't recall). A pleasant young woman served cocktails, which Penny declined since we were in uniform. After I accepted a single malt Scotch, she accepted a beer. As expected, the conversation went to a discussion of Katmai, bears, and our work in the preserve. They had a lot of good questions, mostly about bears. They also wanted to tell us about the bear that had been seen on the beach that morning, and get our assurance that the bear wouldn't be looking for them. We were talking with highly educated, intelligent people who wanted to learn about life in the Alaskan bush. When we meet people who show real interest in learning about this piece of the world, it seems to kick us into another gear and we are thrilled to share our knowledge and experiences with them.

We were called to dinner in the other end of the lodge great-room while the conversation was still going strong, but quickly yielded to delicious food. We sat at picnic tables that sat four to a side. The room was mostly glass on two walls looking over the woods and lake below, which gave everyone a spectacular view. Dick Matthews, who was serving dinner wine, described the view when there had been a strong storm a few weeks earlier: white caps on the lake, and the wind whipping trees below the lodge with horizontal rain beating on the windows. We remembered that storm very well. We had stayed in our tent frame, hoping the wind wouldn't blow it away. Tonight's dinner of fried chicken, mashed potatoes, and fresh asparagus was served family style. Without a doubt the best meal we would have that summer.

Penny had been seated next to John Smale at dinner and had been answering a lot of questions from him. As Penny tends to do, she got to asking about the Smale's home in Cincinnati and telling of friends of ours who live there. She asked John where he worked, he replied he worked for Proctor and Gamble. Penny said, "We own shares of P&G, what do you do there?" John smiled and simply replied, "I'm the CEO." We were having dinner with the type of people who we didn't expect to meet on a fishing vacation in remote Alaska.

These were people who we would have enjoyed having a conservation with in any setting, and they were enjoying a fun evening of conversation with a couple of rangers in a beautiful lodge. Dick invited us to come back any time; we enjoyed him and he seemed to enjoy us.

We walked down the drive to our Zodiac, feeling like we had had a delightful evening with friends. As we neared the beach Penny grabbed my arm and whispered, "Do you see that eagle?" I did. It was a mature bald eagle sitting on the beach with a large fish in its left talon. We had been moving slowly and quietly and were only ten or twelve feet away before we had noticed it. It was obviously uncomfortable with us being so close, but seemed to not want to fly off with the fish, likely a lake trout. We stepped back a pace and stood still just watching. The eagle didn't feed, it didn't leave, it just watched us, probably thinking, "Why did these two come along and spoil my evening meal?" We stood still, not speaking, not moving. The eagle stood there watching us watch it; finally it gave up, holding the fish in its yellow talon, it crouched, spread those seven foot wings and was air-born with its prize. We had never been that close to an American bald eagle in the wild before, and probably never would be again. This day had ended up being one of our most memorable days in Alaska, new friends, a delightful meal, good stories, and a close encounter with our national emblem.

Katmai Christmas

Christmas seems to be a universal holiday, at least in the portion of the world we are familiar with, so why not celebrate the holiday and the friendship shared by a bunch of rangers by exchanging gifts while we're all together? Every year we were at Brooks Camp the staff celebrated on August 25th by exchanging fun gifts, either hand made or costing less than $2.00. In those years we had looked forward to the annual celebration. We each drew a name from a hat and decided what we could give that person for fun, as a joke, or something that would perhaps have future meaning. Some of us did skits to poke fun at each other and almost everyone had a little too much to drink. Yes, park rangers do seem to have a lot of parties. Exchanging gifts and getting to know the entire staff, seasonal and permanent better, all in one relaxed setting made for a very positive evening for everyone. Now we were out at "Non-existant"—the nickname the Nonvianuk Ranger Station had been given a couple of years ago, since the place seemed to be forgotten by management—and wondered if we would get a chance to attend the celebration.

Dave had promised he would pick us up for the party even if we were clear up north. He had even drawn names for us so we knew who to make gifts for. I had Kathy Jope, the Resource Management specialist, and Penny had Jim Gavin, one of the maintenance crew. Jim was a serious catch and release rainbow trout fly fisherman and a person who enjoyed a good joke. Kathy was new to her position and was struggling to be taken seriously by the permanent staff.

Now we had to come up with something we could make for Jim and Kathy.

Penny talked a visiting fisherman across at Cry of the Loon into giving her a snagging hook: four large fish hooks, each at least an inch across, soldered together so that it looked like a miniature grappling hook—completely illegal for sport fishing. She tied it to a leader and attached a heavy sinker to a length of 10-pound test line. Sockeye salmon don't feed after they enter fresh water so the Natives, and plenty of others, use rigs like this to harvest salmon illegally with little chance of being noticed by the law. They regularly use this method while gill netting season (a very visible technique) is closed. Throw a weighted snagging hook into a school of salmon and you are bound to hook onto a fish before you get the hook reeled in. Penny was going to pretend she was Jim by putting a sign on her back saying "RED SALMON GAVIN" and acting like she was after any fish in the river. We thought that after a few beers this should be a pretty good joke for a seriously conscientious fisherman.

I had started a scat board, a three foot by three-foot piece of plywood to which I was gluing the turds of as many of the mammals of Katmai as I could find. I had planned to put it in the VC so visitors could see what the different animal droppings looked like, but thought it would make a great gift for Kathy. I figured she would probably put it in the VC as well. I had a wolf turd which looks like the dropping of a huge dog, but full of hair instead of kibble crumbs, a lynx turd as big around and as long as your finger, pointed on each end, and almost all rabbit hair; a hand full of porcupine scat that looked kind of like a hand full of large cashews—well sort of; moose poop, the size of ping-pong balls (they look like particle board when you break them open), and a beautiful brown bear turd three inches in diameter and nearly a foot long. It was mostly salmon bones and grass, kind of loose, so I had coated it with fast set marine epoxy to hold it together. The three species of shrew scat all had a lot of bone fragments and hair. The meadow mouse, three different voles, the northern bog lemming, and ground squirrel scat all look too similar to display each separately (truthfully I can't be sure of which is which) so they were represented by the arctic ground squirrel whose turds are the largest of that group, about a centimeter long and a full millimeter in diameter, and the red-backed vole who's turds are less than a centimeter in length and less than a millimeter in diameter. I knew Kathy would like it and the gang should get a hoot out of it.

The afternoon of the party was cloudy as usual, but the ceiling was falling and we were afraid Dave wouldn't be able to pick us up. About 1600 we heard a plane, and sure enough Dave was putting down on the river. We quickly loaded our presents, sleeping bags, and tooth brushes behind the seats and climbed in. Dave taxied a couple hundred yards back up river to put the nose into the wind, which gave us the room and lift to get airborne before we hit the choppy lake.

We turned and headed south for Brooks Camp, but the clouds had dropped and we couldn't get through the pass. Back over Nonvianuk Lake we looked for a pass to the east that would let us circle back to Brooks, but the clouds were still dropping. Dave decided we had better set down at Kulik Lodge at the east end of Nonvianuk and see if the clouds would rise enough for us to get over the pass. We secured the plane at the lodge's float-plane dock, watched the ceiling continue to drop, and decided we weren't going any farther that day. We walked up to the lodge hoping to meet Sonny Peterson, the owner, whom we all knew well. Sonny was in Anchorage, but his assistant welcomed us, told us we could throw our sleeping bags in an empty cabin for the night, and come up to the lodge for a cocktail and dinner.

We were glad for the warm welcome and did as suggested. We were all in our "civvies" rather than uniform and thought we could go unnoticed, but a couple of German men that Penny had had a long conversation with the day before recognized her immediately and invited us to join them for a drink and dinner. We couldn't very well turn them down, so we introduced our friend Dave and joined them. It only took a few minutes for the Germans to discover that Dave was the Superintendent of Katmai, and a moment more to pull out a fifth of good single malt Scotch Whisky. I can't remember what dinner was, but I remember the single malt was delightfully smooth. The Germans were having a ball getting stories from each of us. Dave and I were getting a bit tipsy, and Penny was enjoying her third Saint Pauli Girl beer when the single malt ran out and we decided we should call it a night. We had missed the Katmai Christmas due to weather, but had had a good evening of telling stories and making friends from another country, and hopefully having made international friends for the NPS.

The next day dawned, not clear, but with a ceiling adequate for flying. Dave didn't want to fly early—give the Scotch at least 18 hours to clear the system before being a pilot. So after lunch (which was offered gratis by the lodge, but we insisted on paying for our meals. The manager wouldn't let us pay for the cabin since it was empty and we slept in our sleeping bags) Dave took us back to our station and took our Christmas gifts to Brooks Camp.

The next time Loren flew in with mail he brought our Christmas gifts with him. Hal had made a sign for me to put up—"NONVIA-NUK DENTAL CLINIC"—with a little sign to hang below reading "DOC IS IN" on one side and "DOC IS OUT" on the other. Dave had drawn Penny as his Christmas gift recipient and had found an old Katmai National Monument poster that pictured Brooks Falls, bears, salmon, and a bald eagle all in beautiful color. He had framed it in old weathered lumber, a real treasure! We had missed the Christmas party, but had given and received and shared with others the meaning and feel of a Katmai Christmas.

A Strange Year

The unusually nasty weather of a late spring had prompted Sally Orot, the park secretary, or "Administrative Officer" in bureaucratic parlance, to comment that she thought this was going to be a strange year in Katmai National Park. It proved to be a different year, but every year in the Park Service has different learning experience for us.

We had been delayed in getting to Nonvianuk by ice and wind. Penny had been sent to Dillingham to talk with the schools about the NPS in Alaska. The Mercury outboard refused to start and had to be taken in for repairs. We met a great couple running Cry of The Loon camp across the river. What next?

We had our tent-frame home up and functioning, but could tell by the weight of the propane tank that it was almost empty. Loren had promised us a new tank soon, but didn't know when that would be. The 100-pound tank that was hooked up when we got to camp had run out and we were on a small spare tank that wouldn't last long. If Loren didn't get us a new tank soon we would be cooking on our white-gas back-pack stove. He radioed one day and told us he was in the air with a 100-pound tank of propane and to meet him at our beach on the river. We were out in the middle of Nonvianuk Lake talking with some men fishing for lake trout. We told him we would be there as soon as we could get back. (Air to ground was line-of-site so we had good clear radio contact.)

I don't like surprises that make you rush from what you are doing. Oh well that's the Park Service—just adjust, and do what you're told! We got back to our mooring slip just before Loren put down on the river. He helped us off-load the 100-pound tank, we secured the empty one in the back of the Cessna, and he took off across the lake.

OK, how do we get a propane tank, that must weigh at least 100 pounds empty, up a steep hill with another 100 pounds of propane in it? Two big, young men had worked here last year and probably just carried the heavy tank up the hill. Neither of us is big or strong, but we do have the ability to think problems through. We had had no problem getting the empty tank down the hill—just lay it down, give it a push, let it roll, and count on it stopping when it hit the brush at the bottom of the path. We tried rolling it up; that worked for a few yards, until we started up the hill, it was too steep, we couldn't do it. We got a length of rope and made a harness for Penny to slip over her shoulder and attached the free end to the neck of the tank. With Penny pulling, me pushing, and the mosquitoes biting, we managed to get it up the hill and onto the platform where it would supply us with gas to run the two-burner stove and cook our morning oatmeal and evening dinners. Those evening meals often didn't happen until late evening, like 2300 (11:00 PM), when we had fishermen or river floaters who had flown in late to talk with. The propane tank also supplied energy to a refrigerator that keep beer and cheese cold. We did have other things in the fridge from time to time, like berries in season, cold salmon leftover from a successful catch, or gifts of fruit, or fish, from river floaters or fishermen.

Insects in Alaska, any place in the north country for that matter, are hard to describe and can be hard to survive mentally and physically. Gnats and Mayflies hatch early and appear in swarms so thick they look like a cloud. If you walk into a cloud of them, or the swarm flies into you, they get in your eyes, nose, and ears. If you open your mouth to curse you get an extra meal, but neither of them bite. They are the food that fish and birds depend on. Then there are the really nasty little no-see-ums that you can't hear and don't tend to see until they have had a piece of you. Mosquito bites tend to itch for a few hours, but no-see-um bites itch like hell for days. Fall brings out the white-sox, a small "black-fly" with white rings on their legs. They have an anesthetic in their saliva, and you may not know you've been bitten until you notice blood running down your neck. A mosquito bite is like having blood drawn, but a white-sox bite takes a chunk of your hide. The next week or longer you will be very conscious of the white-sox bite because it itches like mad and frequently gets infected.

Insects are one of, if not "THE" keystones of the Alaskan eco-system. The millions of birds that migrate to the northland each spring are dependent on the insects for their food supply. Insects are the primary pollinator of fruit blossoms and flowers. The insects in turn are dependent on water where they lay their eggs and where they spend the majority of their lives as larva, feeding on a variety of even tinier life forms and by being food for fish. Some species depend on standing water found in the depressions and pothole lakes left by the retreating glaciers. Others require fresh flowing streams for the larva to live, feed, and finally mature into adults whose only real function is to breed and lay eggs. The propagation of the species.

Fortunately mosquitoes aren't quite as thick as the gnats and Mayflies—damn near though—and they're around until a hard freeze does-them-in. Gnats and Mayflies are short timers, living only a few days or less. We see them only during their spring bloom; the time when they breed, lay eggs, and die. Mosquitoes seemed to be everywhere, but especially near the river and willow brush. We depended on wind to keep them away, but you can't count on the wind blowing when you want it. The best place was in the boat on the lake. Our tent-frame was in a location where there was usually enough breeze to keep the mosquitoes at bay. Mosquitoes have literally driven caribou insane and have run some to death, or over cliffs to their death. There were times that we felt the same way. The day I decided "Das Boot" had to have her bottom cleaned of the algae that had accumulated was one of the worst days I ever had. I had plenty of DEET bug repellent on, but it didn't seem to phase the mosquitoes that day. They had me on the verge of screaming and running; I had to give up on the boat bottom and get away from them.

Mosquitoes hatch from eggs that are laid in standing water, like marshes or ponds, or in a moose foot print in mud that fills with water. It's the female who bites, she must have a meal of blood in order to produce eggs. That blood meal has to come from a warm-blooded animal, usually a caribou, a bear, a bird, or Penny, or me. The male mosquito feeds on nectar, hangs out in swarms, and lives about a week. The female flies into the swarm of males and breeds. After she has had a blood meal, it takes a day for the eggs to develop. She then goes to standing water where she deposits her brood. The eggs hatch in as little as 24 hours into larva which morph into pupa, then into adults. The whole process from breeding to adult takes from five days to two weeks, depending on the temperature. The female lives as much as a month, can breed every few days if she gets a meal of blood, and can produce a lot of the nasty "little fuckers," as Nancy called them. Considering the number of females who have fed on me, does that make me the surrogate sire of a bunch of the nasty little monsters?

Thinking of bugs brings up an encounter we had with even smaller critters. Our only source of water was the river. We had drunk directly from creeks for many years while we were camping with our girls with no problem due to water-borne diseases. So we didn't even think about filling a bucket with water from the wild Nonvianuk River. We both got giardia! Penny had a mild case that put her in bed for a few days with stomach cramps and diarrhea, followed by a week of feeling terrible. I was down for more than a week, with another ten days of going to the out-house every little bit, and feeling like I could die and be happy to have it over with. *Giardia lamblia* is a protozoan that lives as an intestinal parasite of mammals. They contaminate water supplies and attack the small intestine of any mammal that is unfortunate enough as to have ingested it. The illness can last up to six weeks with vomiting and severe diarrhea. We were lucky to get off as easily as we had. It is spread in the wild by humans who carry the parasite and defecate where the feces gets into a water supply. Wildlife drink the water, get infected, defecate, and spread it back to humans, who again, crap in the woods, probably miles away, continuing the vicious cycle.

The river was our only water supply. If it couldn't be used we were going to get pretty thirsty in the next few months. The park administration had been told they should drill a well for the Non-vianuk Station and had put that chore on the to-do list. Not a bit of help for today. We had to have water! While the outboard was in the shop all we could do was dip it from the edge of the river and boil it before we used it. Our access to the river was just below a marshy area. We decided that marsh was the outhouse for some unfortunate sick wildlife who had no option but to poop wherever they were at the time. As soon as the boat was functional we got our water from the center of the river and had no further problems. Well, we did have to carry two five-gallon buckets, three-fifths full of water up the steep hill a couple hundred yards, to camp. We cut an alder pole six feet long, used a life-jacket to pad the center of it, tied parachute cords on the ends and hung the buckets on the cord. Then acted like Chinese coolies getting the water buckets from the boat to camp.

The Merc outboard ran just great after we finally got it started, but it routinely took 50 or 60 pulls on the starter cord to get it going. Penny didn't like that, but was determined to be able to use the boat by herself. Getting it started was her only problem. After it was running she handled it like a pro. We routinely crossed the river to meet fishermen at Cry of the Loon, have evening conversation with our friends Tony and Nancy, listen to fishermen's lies, and tell bear stories which everyone seemed to want to hear. Those evening excursions gave Penny the chance to get used to running "Das Boot" in a fairly sheltered section of the river. The open lake was a different situation where we both felt better with me at the helm.

We got an early morning radio call one day letting me know that my Dad had died, and that Dave would give me emergency leave if I wanted to fly back to Ohio for the funeral. That would leave Penny as the only ranger in the entire Preserve; could she, would she, be willing to do that by herself? We don't like being apart, and she would really be alone for most of a week. She insisted she could handle it, she could run the boat just fine, she had friends a half mile away across the river, and "she was a tough NPS ranger." No problem! I should go home for the funeral, tell all of our Ohio friends "Hello," and hurry back safely.

My dad, Pop, had been born in a two-story log cabin in the hills of Southeast Ohio in 1886. The youngest of 12 children, the only one in the family who ever went to college and made a success of himself. He died three months before his 99th birthday, almost exactly the same age his mother had been when she died. When Pop was 87 he drove his Oldsmobile Tornado from Columbus, Ohio, to Phoenix, Arizona, for a reunion with four of his older brothers. They had a sister still alive, but she didn't join them. I don't know whether she declined an invitation to join her brothers or whether she wasn't invited. Pop had told Penny one time that he had had a very successful professional life, but regretted that his personal life had left a lot to be desired. We knew it was hard for him to see us leave for six or seven months, but he was proud of us for having the courage to do what we really enjoyed. I knew he envied us our wilderness experiences, he had always enjoyed hunting and fishing.

As I was heading back to Alaska after the funeral, I stopped at a roadside farmers' market on my way to the airport, and bought an apple box full of fresh Ohio produce, corn on the cob, cucumbers, lettuce, tomatoes, apples, and grapes. The kid who sold it to me was so excited to have a box of their produce going to Alaska that he called his dad, the owner, to meet me. Of course he had to hear all about where I was taking the box of good things.

This was long before the days of cell phone communication so neither of us knew how the other was getting along. I had worried about Penny being alone, there are so many things that could go wrong when a person is alone in the wilderness. Penny had been concerned about my safety, worried about her own, proud of herself for making it alone, glad to see me when Loren dropped me off, and ecstatic to have the fresh produce. We celebrated by having two beers in recognition of Pop's long life.

Young Bear Joining Us

WE HAD SEEN BEARS A FEW TIMES ON THE LIMITED PORTION OF the river that we could reach with the outboard, but had never had one near our camp. One evening we were pulling into our mooring spot when we noticed a medium sized, light brown, bear grazing only a few hundred yards down stream from camp. We went on to our normal tie-up spot, tied up, and, to our surprise, saw the bear watching us. Not acting aggressive, just standing there, watching, 20 yards away. Normally a bear will leave the area quickly when it encounters a human. Sometimes they take off at a gallop at the first sign of us, and keep running until they are in the next county. Not this guy! We headed up the path to the tent-frame, kind of watching to see what the bear would do. To our amazement he followed us up the path. Well damn! We had never had a bear act like this, he just seemed interested or curious. We went on to our door and watched, he kept coming. When he was about 50 feet away we waved, yelled, and told him to go away. He stopped, looked at us in a curious way with his head cocked to one side like our dogs have done when they didn't seem to understand, then came on. Penny had a rock in her hand which she threw and hit him on the shoulder. He stopped 20 feet away and sat down, apparently to think about it. He seemed to have decided he would come in and have a conversation, he kept coming. By this time I had the shotgun in my hand and fired a cracker shell into his chest. A cracker shell is a large fire cracker, an m80, with a ten-second fuse, so it went bang, very loudly, right between his front feet. I had jacked a round of #9 bird-shot into the chamber, which would be followed by a 12-gauge slug (a chunk of lead almost exactly the size of my thumb) if he didn't take the hint.

We thought we knew brown bears pretty well by now, but this was a totally new and unexpected behavior. Could he be rabid? He (or she) sure didn't act like a rabid animal, he reminded us of a big dog who just wanted to climb in your lap and have his ears scratched. By now he was too close even for #9 bird-shot to not do serious damage. We didn't want an injured bear that we would have to kill, and this guy just seemed to want to be friends. We opened the door, went in and closed the door quickly behind us.

If he came through the door he was going to get shot with the bird shot and a slug, as quickly as I could jack the second round into the chamber. He came up and sat on the little porch, just like we would have expected a family dog to do. More curious than afraid, we kept watch through the little window in the door. He sat there for, probably, 15 minutes and then moved off.

We relaxed and went ahead with our normal evening. Had a beer while we fixed dinner, and talked over the days events, mostly our new friend who Penny had named "Fuzz Bear." We decided he was a subadult, a three or four year old, who had been kicked out by mom when she was ready to mate. He didn't know what to do or where to go. Also, we thought that he had never seen a human before, wanted a friend, and was very curious to see what these strange two legged creatures were. When we went to bed we looked out our little loft window, and there was Fuzz Bear curled up thirty yards away. We saw him almost every day for a couple of weeks, but he never came close again. He slept in the same spot out back every night for a month and then was gone. We missed our friend and wished we could adopt him. He would have made a wonderful pet at our new home in Colorado.

Kulik Lodge is situated on another terminal moraine. This one separates Nonvianuk Lake from Kulik Lake, which is just a few hundred yards up the Kulik River. Kulik Lodge, like Brooks Lodge, is operated by Katmai Land. A company owned by Ray and Sonny Peterson, with Sonny, Ray's oldest son, managing Kulik Lodge and overseeing Brooks Lodge. Ray had been president of Northern Consolidated Airlines, the largest airlines in Alaska after WWII. He merged his company with Wien Airlines, another Alaskan airline, in 1968 and ran Wien Air Alaska until the late 1970s when he sold the airline and retired to handle his fishing lodges.

Brooks Lodge, at Brooks Camp, is on park property and is leased to the Katmai Land Corporation. Kulik Lodge is on a private enclave that, like Enchanted Lake and Cry of the Loon, was acquired before Katmai National Monument was expanded and achieved National Park status. That expansion was a part of the passage of ANILCA in 1980, which preserved over 50 million acres of Alaskan wilderness. Kulik Lodge is on a relatively large enclave that includes an air strip from which a twin engine Navaho makes daily round trips to Anchorage picking up supplies and guests, and delivering departing guests and trash to the Anchorage airport and trash disposal facility. Kulik has capacity for 22 guests and is a very good facility with cedar log cabins that have oil stoves for heat and hot and cold running water in full bathrooms. Not the standard accouterments found in most of the camps and lodges in the area. Kulik has a nice lodge building with a gathering, conversation, and drinking area around a wood burning fireplace, a complete bar, and a dinning room that serves better than average meals.

Katmai Air, also owned and operated by the Petersons, operates from the air strip adjacent to the lodge, as well as from a float-plane dock, and flies a diversity of Cessna aircraft delivering visitors and supplies to several lodges and camps in the area, as well as flying those 22 guests at Kulik to any of numerous locations for day-long fishing trips.

The Kulik River is only a few hundred yards long flowing across the glacial moraine from Kulik Lake. We wanted the adventure of seeing Kulik Lake. Year-end reports of other Nonvianuk rangers indicated that none of them had ever been there. The river is so shallow that the only time it can be navigated is early in the season when the water is high. The Mercury outboard had a short shank but still drew 12 inches of water unless you were going fast enough to be on-step, getting most of the hull out of the water. There was no way I was going to do that on a river I didn't know. The bottom is glacial till with rocks of all sizes. If I hit a rock going full tilt it would break the lower unit and we would be SOL (shit out of luck). Not something we were willing to chance, so we took it slow with Penny hanging over the bow to tell me which way to go to miss the rocks.

We made it, but dinged the prop a couple of times. Damn that is a shallow river. I had to pull the prop and hammer out the blades when we got back to camp. It was worth it though, Kulik is a beautiful glacial lake with no development and numerous feeder streams coming in from the snow fields in surrounding mountains. Those streams are big enough for salmon to spawn in, and they looked like good rainbow streams to us, but guides had told us the rainbows aren't there, so they didn't take fishermen in.

We didn't have legitimate reason to include Kulik Lake on our patrols so we were only there to satisfy our own curiosity and sense of adventure. It is a gorgeous pristine lake with no development and no people—our kind of spot! We spent the day exploring and never found any indication of people ever having been there. The ridge between the two headwaters feeder streams looked like an excellent spot for us to have a retirement cabin. Dream on!

SINCE I HAD BEEN A DENTIST AND PENNY A DENTAL HYGIENIST before I retired and we were both emergency medical technicians (EMTs), we fell into the position of taking care of any medical problem that came along while we were stationed at Brooks Camp. From a fly stuck in a VIPs cheek to broken fillings, loose crowns and abdominal cramps they all ended up being sent to "Doc and Pen." We always had access to the trauma bag in the ranger station and we had our own little dental kit along. We dealt with lots of injuries (mostly minor) and a few illnesses. Most of them were psychological due to being afraid of "things that go bump in the wilds of Alaska". Replacing a broken filling with temporary cement or recementing a loose crown was easy, but all of those little treatments along with Penny's TLC, sure made a big difference to the patients. Instead of having an uncomfortable vacation or work season they could be comfortable until they could see their physician or dentist at home.

Our most fun medical emergency was an Under Secretary of

the Interior who was not a very experienced fly fisherman and had a hook imbedded in his right cheek. The poor man was frantic when he was brought to our cabin one evening, his face was white and he was shaking. Penny talked him down a good bit and gave him a shot of Scotch. I assured him we could remove the hook with almost no discomfort. He relaxed, I took ahold of the eye end of the hook with a pair of needle-nose pliers, pushed the barb end on through his cheek, nipped off the barb, and pulled the hook out backwards. It was over in about 30 seconds and he hardly knew what had happened. Penny wiped his face with an alcohol swab and told him he needed to have a tetanus shot when he got back to Washington. He was thrilled, praised us up one side and down the other, said he was going to write a letter to the Director of the Park Service commending us. I don't think he ever did because we never heard about it, but he invited us to the lodge to have a drink with him. That made for an interesting evening, drinks and conversation with one of our really big bosses.

Our reputation as "Doc and Pen" followed us to Nonvianuk. Jack Holman, the owner of No-See-Um Lodge on the Kvichak River, flew in to see us soon after we arrived. He had a loose jacket crown on a front tooth and didn't want to spend the summer with a wired looking incisor. That was easy to replace with ZOE (zinc-oxide and eugonal) temporary cement. We explained to Jack that it needed to be recemented with permanent cement as soon as possible, but every time we saw him over the next few years he would laugh and tell us the crown was still there just as we had recemented it.

Four men flagged us down one day near Cry of the Loon. They explained they were firemen from Philadelphia, Pennsylvania on a dream vacation they had planned and saved for for years. Now one of them had such a terrible ear ache that they were afraid they would have to abandon their river float-and-fish trip, could we help them? A friend of ours in Colorado was an ENT physician and had given us a dropper-bottle of ear drops, just in case we had such a problem ourselves. Penny administered a couple of drops to the man's ear, put a small cotton plug in and recommended they camp on our beach that night to see how he reacted to the treatment. The next morning he was feeling much better. We told them to take the drops with them, use two drops in the ear, as Penny had done, twice a day, and return the bottle of drops to Park Service headquarters in King Salmon when they finished their river trip. They thanked us and were off on their dream vacation. A week later we got a radio call from headquarters letting us know the drops had been returned with profound thanks from four thrilled firefighters.

Our year at Nonvianuk had been unique and strange in some ways, as I guess all years in the Park Service are. We had made new good friends of Tony and Nancy Cooper across the river at Cry of the Loon, we had done a lot of interesting exploring in the Alaskan bush, had met a bunch of interesting fishermen, both male and female, helped many and been cursed by some. The office, especially Hal who would have to find replacements for us if we declined his offer, wanted to know if we would come back for another year at the Nonvianuk Ranger Station. We told him we would—if he would promise us a river boat. Hal said that Loren had ordered a flat bottomed Jon boat with a 35-horse jet outboard that would be in King Salmon when we returned next April. We said we would be there if the boat would be.

LAW ENFORCEMENT
REFRESHERS

We had brand new commissions our first season at Nonvianuk and weren't required to attend the regional law enforcement refresher, but every year after that we attended the Alaska regional refresher. Those classes were held at a different location each year; which made it interesting and gave us an opportunity to become familiar with different local cultures in the state. Elmendorf Air Force Base, outside of Anchorage, was the most common site, but we also had training in Glacier Bay and Denali, which gave us the chance to become familiar with the most well known parks in Alaska. Probably the most unique location was when we had the training at the regional office in Anchorage, with lodging at a Catholic convent downtown. Every evening of those week long refresher courses invariably ended up with a party. The year at the convent everyone tried to behave while living in a nunnery, and succeeded for the most part. We tried to include our hosts, but try as we might the nuns declined to join us. Even though we knew priests drink, we weren't sure about nuns and were curious. We never found out whether nuns drink alcohol or not. They politely declined our invitations to join us for a beer. Penny, being a "reformed Catholic," had several conversations with the nuns and tried to get them to join a few of us for an evening of just talking, but couldn't convince them.

The convent was in a rough part of town, and Penny ran for an hour every morning before class. She had done that no matter where we were living—except in the bush where game trails weren't conducive to running—that is, until one of our classmates insisted she quit running in that neighborhood. He was afraid she might get mugged or worse, which Penny was not willing to go through again.

We met and got to know rangers whom we had heard of but might never have met otherwise. Most were great people whom we enjoyed. Some became good friends. A few we thought were real jerks—those types you put up with but try to ignore. Hmm, that sounds kind of like the real world. Everyone knew of Penny Starr, the woman with a personality that was always effervesces, the oldest active female law enforcement ranger in the NPS, and probably the oldest active female ranger of any sort. Classes usually consisted of about 15 rangers, all in their 20s or early 30s, mostly tall and fit. Rarely were there more than three women. Then there was us, both on the smaller side and always the oldest by some 20 plus years.

CFR 36 (Code of Federal Regulations pertaining to National Parks) was always covered in depth. After all, that was our bible and the source we went to whenever we had a question about federal law. We had spent the 1985 season at Nonvianuk and would be spending the '86 season there also. Later we would find ourselves taking LE refresher classes before our assignments at Aniakchak National Monument, Great Basin National Park, Glacier Bay National Park & Preserve, the Shelikof coast of Katmai National Park & Preserve, and finally at the Noatak National Preserve, more than 100 miles north of the arctic circle. But, this coming season our jurisdiction would be Katmai National Preserve, the 700,000-acre section added to the park in 1980. Being designated a National Preserve protects it from development but allows hunting and certain other activities within the boundaries. Our authority was CFR 36, which is more than 200 pages of legalese defining nearly everything that is illegal in parks and preserves. It was our responsibility to deal with every incident by interpreting our CFR 36 bible and our own minds as to what action was best suited to the existing situation and would be upheld by a federal magistrate.

We had lectures from state and federal judges, and talks by attorneys. Meetings and discussions with ADF&G (Alaska Department of Fish & Game) and USF&W (U.S. Fish & Wildlife) personnel. One year an ADF&G officer started the session with this announcement:

BEAR ALERT!

ADF&G is advising hikers, fishermen, and hunters to take extra precautions and be on the alert for bears.

We advise people to wear noise-producing devices such as little bells on their clothing to alert, but not startle, the bears unexpectedly.

We also advise you to carry pepper spray in case of an encounter with a bear.

It is also a good idea to watch for signs of bear activity.

People should be able to tell the difference between black and grizzly bear droppings.

Black bear droppings are smaller and often contain berries and possibly squirrel fur.

Grizzly bear droppings have bells in them and smell like pepper.

There were always meetings and discussions with Alaska State Troopers, both Blue-shirts and Brown-shirts. The Blue-shirts are the state troopers who deal with traffic, robberies, murders, and standard criminal problems. The Brown-shirts are the game enforcement division who handle all law enforcement related to hunting and fishing in the state. Rangers are the law enforcement in the parks and handle all crimes that occur in the National Parks (except for fish and game in Alaska, where the state has sole authority). Just exactly where a crime took place can be questionable. Who has jurisdiction over this or that incident is always contentious. We frequently heard discussions about who has what authority and who has this or that jurisdiction. It was, and still is, a bit confusing. There are places where jurisdiction is shared and referred to as joint jurisdiction between state and federal—sometimes we even cooperated effectively.

There were sessions on search and rescue (S&R), defensive tactics in hand- to-hand combat (Penny didn't volunteer to be a victim as she had at LE school), and physical fitness—do so many push-ups, so many sit-ups in 30 seconds, run a mile under 12 minutes. Some of those were getting tough when we were in our 60s.

In a crime-scene investigation there are always a series of questions which must be answered: what? where? when? how? why? who? I suggested we combine all of those questions into one question: "howzcome?" My suggestion got some laughs, some moans, and a couple of, "I like that!" (I still like and use the term.) There was always the old story of the six Ps: "Prior Planning Prevents Piss Poor Performance." In other words, have a plan before you screw up a crime scene by disturbing or allowing anyone else to disturb anything that might prove to be evidence.

The most pertinent and memorable meetings were the telling of actual incidents that rangers or officers had experienced. Jon Peterson, another seasonal ranger, told of his and his partner's horrible experience of arresting a drugged-out man on Lake Mead in Grand Canyon National Park. The man had been selling cocaine to people at a boat-in campground. The word reached the district office, and Jon and his partner were dispatched to handle the situation. When they arrived by boat at the campground they found the drugged-out man unconscious under a tree. Jon couldn't wake him up so they simply carried him to the boat, a 22-foot outboard, and headed back to the ranger station—Big mistake! Part way back, the man regained consciousness. Jon was at the helm in the stern, his partner was on the forward seat, the druggie was laid out on the center seat. The man woke up, pulled a knife, and attacked the ranger in the bow. He had the ranger down over the bow and was about to stab him. Jon had no choice. He drew his .357 and fired two rounds into the man's back, "the center mass." Yes, he died, and Jon will always carry the burden of having taken another's life. We discussed if it was "ranger assisted suicide," but couldn't reach a consensus.

Over the years we got to know Jon well. He is a fine man who has put up an amazing fight against cancer over the past many years. He earned a permanent position with the Park Service, and when we worked the Noatak River National Preserve Jon was one of the best supervisors we ever had. He had been a seasonal ranger until just a few years before and knew the crap we had to put up with most of the time. Jon never got completely over the incident. Many people say, "I could never kill another person." When Penny thinks back to the assault she survived during her first year as a ranger she knows, without question, that she would not hesitate to shoot and kill an attacker.

Nearly every year someone told of a bear being shot "In defense of life or property," as it is referred to legally when someone shoots a bear that they feel is endangering them or their property. That covers a lot of shootings by people who shoot out of fear. Too often that fear is the result of being unknowledgeable about bears, or just, "I am going to do what I want, and screw you and everybody who tries to tell me what I can do!"

Such an incident was related by the ADF&G officer stationed out of Dillingham. One of the more honest fishing guides reported a bear shot by fishermen who were camped along a tributary of the Nushagak River. The fishermen had brought along plenty of booze and used it liberally. They also discovered that if they threw an occasional fish near camp they could be sure of seeing a brown bear up close. A bear that had been chummed-in that way decided to check for more food in the camp. One of the men took exception to the bear coming on into camp and killed it with his 30.06 rifle.

This incident was deemed legal defense of life and property, even though it was done through stupidity.

Fishing with a state license has always been legal in national parks but hunting is not permitted unless the superintendent specifically authorizes it. National preserves are open to hunting and fishing during state-designated seasons. Both fishing and hunting in the state of Alaska require state licenses and have strict seasons set by the state.

Penny had an incident similar to the ADF&G officer's before she had her law enforcement commission, which made a good topic for discussion. It was one she expected to end in the killing of a bear in defense of life and property. She and another ranger, Geof, were camped near the mouth of Big River where it empties into Swikshak Bay on the Shelikof Straights. Swikshak Bay has a large population of brown bears who, at that time, were relatively unfamiliar with people. Penny and Geof were there on an August poaching patrol. Not being law enforcement rangers they couldn't arrest anyone, but they could talk the law, and just the presence of a pair of rangers was expected to deter any poacher who might be in Swikshak Bay hoping to kill a bear.

A group of apparently wealthy Texans was flown in, ostensibly to fish for silver salmon. Each one of them was decked out in fancy new fishing gear, and they brought an immense supply of liquor with them. Actually, a separate float plane brought in a load of single-malt Scotch and Courvoisier cognac. Apparently their goal was to spend their time drinking and having fun; fishing was just an excuse to party. Penny and Geof met them, checked their licenses, explained proper behavior when in bear country, told them about the bears in the area, and made sure they didn't intend to hunt. They admitted they had a rifle with them for personal protection. They were told the weapon must be unloaded and have a trigger lock in place since they were in a National Park—they didn't even know they were in a park. They agreed to the stipulations and had an afternoon drink or six before they went fishing. That night, after dark, the two rangers heard shooting from the camp. On investigating they found the drunk fishermen shooting at liquor bottles, some full, with their hi-powered rifle. Fortunately a bear hadn't come onto the scene and gotten shot.

The rangers could talk and explain, but didn't have the legal authority to arrest. It was long before modern communications and their handheld radios were strictly limited to line-of-sight. They had no way to call for backup. All they could do was talk and that doesn't work well on drunks. They had names and addresses, from the men's fishing licenses, and warned them they would receive citations in the mail—that didn't have any effect on the drunk fishermen. Penny and Geof needed commissions, Penny got hers; Geof never did. He spent a long Park Service career doing resource management, the work he loved.

It was generally agreed, by LE classes and wildlife officers that having a firearm didn't begin to make up for a lack of knowledge and understanding of bears and how to behave in bear country. All of us had incidents with brown bears that demonstrated how important it was to make enough noise so any bear in the area was aware people were present. The bear would take heed and avoid a confrontation. Pepper spray is proven effective under certain circumstances, but in a true attack there would rarely be time to use pepper or a weapon. A true attack, from initiation to contact would rarely take more than one or two seconds. And after contact it is up to the bear. People who have played dead have fared much better than ones who fought. Many of those didn't live to tell the tale.

The story we told of Barrie Gilbert's bear encounter made an ideal example for discussion. We had become friends with Barry at Brooks Camp and related his story. It is classic of how you can get into trouble no matter your knowledge and experience. The season following my encounter with the sow with three cubs-of-the-year (COY) we were in Brooks Camp helping with the training of rangers new to Katmai before we could get to our assignment at Nonvianuk. Dr. Barrie Gilbert was a highly respected bear researcher from Utah State University and brought a pair of his graduate students to Brooks Camp to study social interactions between brown bears and humans. He had read my report of the encounter with the sow and came looking for us. He wanted to hear and discuss every detail of the incident. Barrie had experienced a very similar meeting with a sow and three cubs-of-the-year, but with an unfortunately different outcome. After Penny and I had retold that morning's experiences to him, he explained his meeting with a sow with three cubs to us this way:

In June of 1977 Barrie and his assistant, Bruce Hastings, were researching grizzly bears in Yellowstone National Park. One morning they had their binoculars trained on a single bear, probably a young boar, grazing in a meadow several hundred yards away. A sow with three cubs-of-the-year entered the meadow, chased the boar away, and commenced grazing. (Sows with cubs don't like males around since males tend to think of cubs as a meal. Had the boar been mature she would probably not have entered the meadow at all and Barrie's incident would never have happened.) The researchers watched a while and decided to move along behind a ridge to a better vantage point for observing the family.

A strong breeze was blowing so the men felt it would be superfluous to make noise indicating their presence. Bruce stopped to pee and Barrie went on alone. He crested the ridge and was about to look for the sow, who should have been at least a quarter mile away feeding in the meadow with her cubs. Instead of being a quarter mile away, they were right there and she was charging. Barrie decided he could make it to a tree, not far away, and climb out of reach. He couldn't! She caught him, knocked him to the ground, and started biting him on the back of his head, which Barrie said, felt like an axe against his skull. Thinking of defending himself, Barrie rolled over to kick and push her off. No man has the strength to push a bear. She bit his face, taking out his zygomatic arch (the bone separating the eye and cheek), an eye and much of the flesh of the left side of his face.

Bruce heard sounds but couldn't identify them due to the high wind. He could see the bear had something on the ground that it was mauling. He couldn't see Barrie but assumed it was Barrie that the bear had down. Bruce made a low, loud "Ha" sound, the bear looked up, and ran off leaving the injured researcher, and returned to her cubs,

Barrie was very fortunate to have had his incident in Yellowstone rather than some wilderness area far from help. Bruce radioed for help, and began administering first aid. There had been a lot of blood loss from the terrible wounds to the face and scalp. The little first aid kit they carried didn't have enough of what was needed, but fortunately a life-flight helicopter with paramedics was there quickly and got Barrie to a hospital. He spent nearly ten weeks in the hospital and more than a year having reconstructive surgery to rebuild his face. He still has no eye and not much face on that side of his nose, but he was alive, very functional, and extremely interested in brown bears and how I had managed to survive my attack with no injuries.

Barrie, Penny, and I talked long into the night about how the two incidents that started out the same ended so differently; how he had made three vital mistakes by not making noise announcing his presence, running when the bear charged, and then fighting, all of which are the most natural responses that anyone could be expected to make; how I had been so unbelievably fortunate to have done everything right, except talking to a magpie rather than letting the bear know I was coming, and not gotten even a scratch. I credited my good fortune to park service training and to luck. We both credited not being armed with saving our lives, and the bears' lives as well. Neither of us had the time to effectively use a weapon, and are sure in our own minds had we shot and wounded the bear we would have been killed, the sow would probably have died soon, and her three cubs would have starved to death. Andy Russell, in his book *Grizzly Country* says:

> The mere fact of having a gun within reach causes a man to act with unconscious arrogance and thus maybe to smell different or to transmit some kind of signal objectionable to bears. One must follow the role of an uninvited visitor—an intruder—rather than an aggressive hunter, and one should go unarmed to ensure this attitude.

Each year the fire arms refresher was a mental challenge for most of us, just like it had been at LE school a few years before. Apparently the handgun and shotgun courses are standard because each refresher was similar to the course we had at school. We worked with Smith and Wesson .357 or .38-caliber revolvers (the .38 and .357 both fire .38 ammunition; the .38 will not hold .357 ammunition) with 4- or 6-inch barrels, (the 4-inch barrel was standard equipment, but sometimes we had a shortage of 4-inch revolvers and had to use ones with 6-inch barrels during training.) and with Remington model 870, 12-gauge pump shotguns with 20-inch barrels. The scenario for the shotguns usually were in relation to bear confrontation where the ammunition used depended on the situation. We had access to cracker shells, bird shot, 00-buck, slugs, and sometimes rubber slugs, which were similar to lead slugs but were made of rubber—they would hurt like hell, but were designed to not penetrate. The important things under discussion were when to use which ammunition, how to pre-load the weapon, and how to hand-load under a stressful situation, either with bears or people.

Hand-loading under stress was used in law enforcement scenarios where you are confronted by a bad guy who is firing at you, and you must move and return fire. You start with an empty chamber, five rounds in the magazine, two rounds held between your teeth, and five more in a retainer on the gun stock.

Each year we were presented with a different scenario, so we had to think our way through what we were being presented and how to deal with it. I can still picture one in particular: There is a target, a bad guy, about 75 feet away; he is shooting at me, I am returning fire by firing four rounds of slugs. Then I run toward the target firing a load of bird shot from the hip, the last round in the magazine. I keep running and firing by hand-loading those two mouth-held rounds of bird shot as I run. The bird shot is mostly to deter him from firing while I am exposed, but great if some of the shot hits him. I dive behind a bush 30 feet from the bad guy, load a slug from the retainer on the stock into the chamber and two more slugs into the magazine, fire those three rounds and hope I have killed the bad guy because the exercise is over and if I haven't killed him he has killed me. We find there are five holes the size of quarters in the kill zone of the man sized silhouette, a bunch of little BB sized holes, and two more quarter size holes, but they aren't center mass so aren't killing shots. The bad guy is dead and I passed the scenario, with no holes in me—that time.

Handguns was Penny's favorite part of weapons refresher. She had her own S&W .357 and was good with it, thanks to having taken a class on handguns from a professional handgun instructor and from many hours of dry-firing her weapon. I have always felt a lot of the men, who were big macho type cops, were a bit intimidated by this petite, well, 5-foot-5, 120 pound, woman who still had a great figure in her late 50s and early 60s, and could shoot with the best of them.

The shooting course is known as the PPC (Police Pistol Combat, or Practical Pistol Course, or any of a number of derogatory names). Each of us was issued 60 rounds of .38 police special ammunition to fire at a human size and shaped target at ranges of 50, 25, and 7 feet. From standing and kneeling, behind a barricade, right handed, left handed, full light and reduced light. The target has a center zone about the size of an 8-1/2 by 11-inch sheet of paper, known as center mass and a 4- by 6-inch zone representing the head. Those are called the kill-zone and are scored 5 points, other zones don't score. You're not interested in wounding the SOB. There is a possible score of 300 and a passing grade of 250, you count the holes in the kill zone, multiply by five, and have your score.

The range master is like a marine drill sergeant, nobody questions his authority or what he says. He has the responsibility of ensuring safety on the range, and there are a lot of us firing very dangerous weapons. First we will be shooting from the 50-foot line, we are all standing facing our target. He shouts, "Quiet on the range!" it becomes quiet immediately. He says, "Ready on the range! On my command you will draw your weapon, fire two shots in three seconds, reholster your weapon. Any shots after the three second whistle will be penalized ten points." The next command is, "Ready on the line. Fire!" We do as ordered, there are a couple of shots after the whistle, no one says a word. The next command is "You will fire three rounds in four seconds, reload with five, reholster and stand ready. Ready on the line. Fire!"

We move plywood barricades to the line, shoot "strong hand and weak hand" from behind the barricades. If you are right handed your right is your strong hand, and you are shooting from the right side of the barricade. The barricade is protecting your body and giving your left hand a solid backing as it supports the right. You hold the weapon in one hand and support it with the other. Then we switch and shoot with the weak hand from the opposite side of the barricade. We move up to 25 feet and follow a similar scenario but without the barricade. At 7 feet you don't aim, you just point and shoot. Finally you have fired all 60 rounds. We get the command, "Quiet on the range! Move forward and count your score." Those of us who have 50, or more, holes in our target have the 250 points required and can relax. Those with fewer holes get to go through the whole scenario again. A few with passing grades want to repeat the course just for the practice. Penny always scored over 250 on the first series, but was the first to ask to shoot a second round.

We were offered the opportunity to fire .44 magnum revolvers, 9mm. semiautomatic handguns, and semiautomatic/automatic .223 assault weapons. I don't think anyone declined to try the different weapons at least once. Neither Penny nor I wanted to fire 60 rounds from a .44 magnum. They are heavy, kick like hell, and aren't considered a practical sidearm for routine law enforcement, in spite of Dirty Harry's "Make my day!" affection for the weapon.

The refresher was a time we always looked forward to but were glad to have accomplished so we could get on with the season ahead. It, hopefully, was a good skills refresher and had gotten our head into what we are going to be doing and the problems we had better be prepared to face and deal with in the coming months.

STARR SHIP

Yep, another year at Nonexistent! And Yep, we still didn't have the flat bottomed Jon boat and jet-unit! "It's on the barge coming from Seattle and will be here in a couple of weeks," Hal and Loren told us, "so get the Nonvianuk Station all set up for the season and we'll pick you up as soon as the barge gets here." Having an opportunity to get the station up and running before rainbow trout and visitor season started on 8 June was something we had hoped for last season. So we were glad to have time to get all the pre-season work accomplished before we had to start interacting with fishermen. As could be expected, the weather postponed our flight from King Salmon to Nonvianuk for several days. The wind from the east, kept the lake in whitecaps to the extent that Pen Air wouldn't try to land the Goose on it. So we and our gear sat in King Salmon waiting. Often people get in serious trouble, like dead, when they push to get somewhere when the weather isn't cooperating.

When we made it into the Nonvianuk Ranger Station we found the tent-frame had survived the winter with only a few minor problems, which we corrected quickly. Not only that, but the little 12-foot Zodiac, that we took in with us, had a complete redo on its hypalon bottom and a new short-shank Evinrude 35-horsepower outboard motor that would get us on step (the nose flat and the stern up and planing) in about 10 feet. No more plowing through the water when we had a load. It would run so fast that we almost got in trouble when I started a turn while accelerating; I caught it and straightened out just before we flipped over—Penny had a white face and my hand was shaking on the tiller. We had to learn how to deal with so much power. Best of all, unlike the damned Mercury we had last year, the Evinrude never took more than a couple of pulls on the starter cord to get it running. We would later learn that a 35-horse unit is ideal for a much larger 16-foot Zodiac.

Tony and Nancy Cooper, our buddies from last year at Cry of the Loon, had had a hard time with Bill Wright, their boss. They had threatened to quit before the season ended last year, so we weren't surprised to find a new couple managing Cry of the Loon. The new managers were a fun, friendly young couple, Dick and Helen Lewis from California. They had brought their precocious 12-year-old daughter Janine with them. Janine took to us like we were her long lost grandparents, and we took to her in a similar way. Dick and Helen were both tall, good looking people and Janine was going to develop into a beauty.

Helen had moved from South Africa to the U.S. when she was a young adult. She had been, and still was at heart, an Afrikaner of German decent. She was anxious to enlighten us about the problems between white settlers and the Native population. The Afrikaners had moved in and civilized the country, and were trying to civilize the aboriginals, but the aboriginals wanted their old way of life. I had read Robert Ruark's book *Uhuru* and felt I was somewhat familiar with the Afrikaner side of the discussion. Penny and I both felt empathy for the Native People who had had their land taken and their lives turned from carefree hunter-gatherers to, essentially, slaves who had been given a small plot of land and told to be farmers. However, Helen had stories to tell that would curl your hair—ranch houses burned, women raped, men had their penis and testicles cut off before they were killed, plenty of atrocities on both sides. I had Native American, German, and English grandparents and have feelings both ways. The stealing of a people's homeland was so similar to that of the Europeans taking the land of North American Indians, and for that matter, of the Israelis taking land belonging to the Palestinians, that I could have little empathy for the Afrikaners. We and the Lewis family became good friends, in spite of political differences, and spent a lot of evenings that season talking over the problems and wonders of the world

Surprise! We got a radio message that our boat had arrived and we would be going to King Salmon for a week to get the boat ready, and us up to speed on handling a Jon boat with a the jet drive outboard. A Jon boat is a simple, no frills flat bottom, square bowed, aluminum boat. A jet unit can replace the lower prop unit on most outboards. An impeller pulls water in through an intake grill, forces it through a decreasing diameter chamber by an Archimedes screw, and out through a nozzle at high pressure, which pushes the boat forward. Archimedes (287 to 212 BCE) was one of the great minds of ancient Greece. He was a mathematician, astronomer, and inventor. He once had a need to move water up hill. To do so he invented a screw that fit inside a tube. When the screw was turned it moved water from one end of the tube to the other, regardless of the position of the tube and the attached piping. The Archimedes screw is still used by farmers along the Nile to move water for irrigation. It looks kind of like the old meat grinder that mother had me use to grind up left over meat so she could mix it with some pickles and mayonnaise and make a sandwich spread. The jet aircraft engine is based on the same Archimedes principle by using expanding gasses. The whole idea of the Jon boat and jet unit was to let us go where the water was much too shallow for a prop-drive boat. Last season had proved to us that the prop-unit was worthless in the shallow Alagnak River.

Finally, we would have a boat with which we could see what was happening on the river that had been our responsibility for over a year. A few days later Loren picked us up in the park plane and took us to town. When we taxied up to the park service dock on the Naknek River we could see our boat tied to the dock. We stepped out of the plane and got another surprise. The transom had

its name painted on it: STARR SHIP. Kathy Jope had the maintenance crew paint the name on her stern—the boat's, not Kathy's!
That made us feel pretty good! There were things to learn about
the new boat and motor. It didn't handle much differently than a
keel boat, but we wanted to put some hours on it and see how it
behaved in different situations.

We took STARR SHIP out that afternoon. It didn't like waves
larger than a few inches, but was happy to take us into water as
shallow as four inches where we couldn't have considered taking a
prop-boat. We were well down river on an ebbing tide seeing how
she handled the shallows. So far I had been treating her gently. I
decided to kick it up and see how she took stress. Accelerating hard
I turned left and shit happened. The spark advance linkage came
apart and we went dead in the water immediately. OK, now what?
We had adequate water, but the tide was going out, the current
was running, and we would be sitting on mud flats in a few minutes. All we could do was try to reassemble the mechanism. The
spark advance on a boat is akin to the accelerator linkage on a car.
Advancing the accelerator or the linkage gives the motor more gas
and causes the spark plugs to fire more rapidly. A pretty important
part to have functional—without it you just sit idle. We found that
we could, sort of, fit the ball and socket connection back together,
if Penny held things together while I tightened set screws, and
limp slowly back up river. Any sudden change in acceleration and
it would come apart again. It had taken probably ten minutes to
get it back together—I promised myself we would get faster with
practice. We still had water and were in no trouble, but there are
times and places where this sort of malfunction could be disastrous.

The boat shop in town had a couple of replacement parts they
could sell us, but warned us it was a bad design. The part was plastic
and should be stainless steel. They would order the stainless piece
and it should be here in a week or so. I took the plastic replacement
parts and found I could replace one in five minutes and it would

work fine if we didn't push it. Meanwhile we would continue working with the boat, but we had other things to get accomplished too.

We had requested a 4-foot ice chest that we would use to protect
the gear that we would need to carry onboard; gear such as our
extensive trauma kit, sleeping bags, a tent, spark plugs, motor parts,
tools, spare boat cushions, 100-feet of 3/8-inch braided line, fishing
tackle, and most important, three types of fire starter: a butane
lighter, cotton balls coated in Vaseline and stored in an old 35-mm
film canister, and a steel and flint sparker. To this we added two
35-mm. canisters of strike anywhere matches coated in candle wax,
one for each of us. We had each carried these fire starters for years.
If you can build a fire you can get dry and get warm. Hypothermia
is one of the biggest causes of death in the Alaskan bush so staying
warm is vital, and being wet precludes being warm.

The fire-starters, tools, spark plugs, and spark advance spares
we kept in an old steel army ammo box. The request for an ice chest
was turned down, "No more money in the Nonvianuk budget." I
went to maintenance and appropriated a sheet of marine plywood
and made a box with matching lid that we could secure forward
with bungee cords. It worked just fine, kept things dry and stored
where they would be secure and out of the way.

Superintendent Dave was concerned about us running our
little boat across Bristol Bay, up the Kvichak River, and on up the
Alagnak River to Nonvianuk. He insisted that we fly the route with
him so we could see the terrain and, possibly, some of the hazards
we might face.

From King Salmon we flew west along the Naknek River about
30 miles to the Native town of Naknek. We had run the boat over
that route a few times and thought we were comfortable with it,
but from the air we saw a few hazards that we didn't know were
even there: a couple of sunken logs, a skiff, and what looked like a
sunken barge that Dave thought was from the construction of King
Salmon Air Force Base in 1950. We, and many others, had cruised

right over these without knowing they were there. Obviously they are in deep enough water to not be a hazard. The freighter that sits just to the left of the channel has been there for some time, was obvious, and no problem. It had run up river on a high tide and gone aground when the tide turned and the water went out. Now it sits there rusting. Like many things in Alaska, recycling is too expensive to be an option so broken items are abandon wherever they quit working.

We flew out over Bristol Bay, the part of the Bering Sea and Pacific Ocean which separates the Aleutians from western Alaska. It is deep water, and all we were going to have to be aware of were fishing boats and weather. As we flew north we could see Bristol Bay narrowing to the point that it became Kvichak Bay and eventually the Kvichak River. Approaching the northern end of Kvichak Bay we looked down on about 20 large, white creatures swimming in a school. Dave circled and we watched a pod of beluga whales (*Delphinapterus leucas*) feeding on Arctic cod. Belugas are known as sea canaries since they have the loudest song of any toothed whale. Somehow we couldn't hear them from the noisy Cessna, but hoped to see and hear them a few days later when we were here in STARR SHIP.

The Kvichak River is big and tidal for several miles. We could see a few islands we would need to stay well away from unless the tide was flowing. The river drains Lake Iliamna, by far the largest lake in Alaska, and supports the finest salmon fisheries in the world. At this writing, an international consortium is trying to get the right to build the Pebble Mine, the worlds' largest open pit mine, to produce gold, silver, copper and other heavy metals in the headwaters of Lake Iliamna. Should they be successful, the effluent from the mining operations would find its way into the lake and be the demise of the salmon runs that have supported the diverse life on the Alaska Peninsula for thousands of years.

We flew up the Kvichak a few miles and turned right and up the

Alagnak Wild and Scenic River, which the Natives and locals call the Branch. Dave explained that the Branch River has a unique set of land owners. The Park Service, the BLM, the state, whites, and Natives all own property and no one is quite sure where property lines are, which does make for interesting relationships. The saving grace is that no one is close to anyone else, so there is a lot of open property between neighbors. The BLM had plans to do surveying along some of the river corridor that summer and we could expect to see some of their work over the season.

We flew over several lodges and fishing camps in the lower river, mentally marking where each one was. The lower third of the 80 mile river is a fairly straightforward channel, but looking down on the upper two thirds we could understand why all of the lodges are in the lower river. In Yupik the word Alagnak means to err—to be mistaken. The river is so braided that picking the right channel, one that wasn't going to peter out, was going to be a guessing game for us. The lodge operators had more sense than to put fishermen from the "lesser 48" out into that labyrinth.

We had seen the route and knew a few of the problems we would meet. The stainless steel spark advance piece had come in sooner than expected. We had installed it, and were comfortable with it not disintegrating. Now we had to check tide charts to be sure we would be starting on a rising tide. We wanted to be up the Alagnak far enough to miss the mud flats that would appear in a falling tide. Weather too had to be checked, we didn't want to be out on Bristol Bay in heavy wind. All we had left to do was get STARR SHIP up the river.

THE RIVER

The weather was good! Low clouds hung over King Salmon and the Naknek River with a ceiling of 500 feet, not flyable but with no wind it was very boatable. The temperature was in the 50s, and visibility was unlimited. I was excited; Penny was concerned and probably scared. Our bosses, Dave and Loren, were nervous and worried. They would be in trouble with the regional office if anything happened to us. They had planned to fly over us a few times to be sure we were safe, but the low ceiling precluded that. The Park Service had never had a river boat at the Nonvianuk Station, they were concerned that a flat bottom boat would never make it up Bristol Bay and the Kvichak River—with wind and waves it probably wouldn't. We had a low, but rising tide. Tides in Bristol Bay are some of the highest in the world, fluctuating as much as 30 feet. If we left King Salmon early in the morning we were pretty sure we would be able to get into the Alagnak River before the tide turned that afternoon.

OK let's do it! We were off, cruising down the Naknek before 0800. It took not much over an hour to run the 30-some miles from King Salmon to the little Native town of Naknek where the river meets the sea. As we ran out the Naknek River's mouth into Bristol Bay a little before 0900 we saw the crews of four 35 to 40-foot Bristol Bay trawlers watching us. They were waiting for the beginning of a 12-hour sockeye opening that would begin at 0900, and not a second before. They had their nets laid on deck and their skiffs ready to pull, and set, the nets across the expected path of migrating salmon. These are purse seiners. The nets they use are often 200 or 300 yards long and 50 or so feet deep; the top has floats every few feet to keep it on the surface, the bottom of the net is weighted with lead to hold it down. The skiff, a powerful little open boat, pulls the net out across the channel, time is allowed for the migrating salmon to collect in front of the net. Then the skiff loops the lead end back to the trawler, the bottom of the net is pulled shut forming a purse, and the whole net with, hopefully, tons of salmon in it is lifted aboard the trawler and dumped into the hold.

There are huge fines for having nets in the water before an opening. The crews probably thought we were the law there to see if anyone was cheating. We probably looked official in our bright orange float coats as we entered the bay only minutes before opening time. We smiled to each other, knowing how concerned they were about getting caught fishing too early. We just waved and went on up bay. We were the law and we were official, but they were out of our jurisdiction—a fact we were aware of but doubted if they were.

An hour later we were in Kvichak Bay going slowly and as quietly as we could, hoping to see and hear the beluga whales we had watched from the air a few days ago. Alas, today they were somewhere else in their hunt for a meal. On up the Kvichak we found the mouth of the Alagnak River right where it was supposed to be. We had been looking for Jack Holman's No-see-um Lodge, which we knew was on the Kvichak River, but couldn't find it and decided it was above the mouth of the Alagnak. Jack is one of the good guys among the lodge operators, friendly and as honest as is reasonable among the cut-throat fishing lodge industry.

The Alagnak Lodge was the first lodge we came to after entering the Alagnak River. It is down stream of the end of the Wild and Scenic River, which is the limit of our jurisdiction. We have no authority below the Scenic River boundary and were thinking about how far we could get today, so we didn't even stop to introduce ourselves. We felt a bit guilty and told ourselves we would stop there when we had time on another trip down river. Today we wanted to visit the two lodges that were in our jurisdiction, mostly to see how they would take having another law enforcement agency to deal with. Until now the Park Service had been a nonentity as far as they had been concerned, unless they flew guests into the head of the Nonvianuk River where they could expect to meet us, or to Brooks Camp to view brown bears.

Katmai Lodge, on the lower river, is owned by Tony Sarp, one of two or three of the most infamous operators on the Alaska Peninsula. Ben John was Tony's manager, he had been a fishing guide for another lodge the past few years, so we had met him several times, liked him, and felt he was honest most of the time. We thought he was a decent person working for a jerk. Ben met us with a scowl when we pulled up to the dock. We figured he was having a bad day and was pissed off at Tony who had chewed him out that morning before he took a group fishing. We asked if Tony was back yet and Ben said, "Tony's still out fishing with some BFDs (big fucking deals) from Salt Lake City, who the son-of-a-bitch's playing up to because they seem like big spenders." He went on, "I won't be back to this dump next year. I'm fed up with the shit that Tony hands out. He'll do anything for a buck. He screws all of our employees to reduce his overhead, waters the booze, lies to fishermen, then blames me when people aren't happy."

The lodge didn't fit our idea of an Alaskan lodge. It was more a collection of shacks for sleeping with a beat up lodge building for eating, drinking, and telling stories. The whole place seemed to be typical Alaskan architecture—when you need more room you just add a room to the existing structure without much thought as to how it fits with what is already there. You can see the same architecture in back country Appalachia. Katmai Lodge can handle 32 fishermen (an inclusive term meaning people, that many women find sexist) and would gladly go over that limit if he had a place to sleep them.

What was amazing to us was the fact that when we had met people from the place, last year, most of them were having a good time and wanted to come back. We chalked that attitude up to guests who had never seen a decent lodge and were impressed with the Alaskan bush experience. That and the fact that both Tony and Ben were great story tellers and bull-shitters. Ben invited us in for a cup of coffee and a sandwich. We were chilled and glad to have the coffee, a chance to see the interior, and to pick Ben's brain a little more, but declined the sandwich. We met a few guests all of whom were drinking in mid afternoon—"It's five o'clock somewhere." They let us know the fishing was great and they were having fun.

We wanted to see Branch River Lodge that day too, so we thanked Ben and were on our way, pondering how we were getting such positive comments from people in a place we thought should be condemned. Fun, like beauty, must be in the eye of the beholder, or in the stories that went along with the cheap booze they were pouring down.

We passed a number of Native allotments along the river corridor, some with shacks that the local Yupik Natives use as fishing camps when salmon are running and as hunting camps, especially, for the fall moose season. The moose hunt was going to be interesting for us this year. We had not been able to get down river the previous season, but had met a number of hunters as they flew in to the head of the river before rafting down to a campsite. This year having a john boat would allow us to check on hunting down river.

Branch River Lodge is on a Native allotment, the land is leased by Dr. Robert Di Vito, a physician in Seattle, Washington. We had met Bob Di Vito, Jr. last year and knew he managed the place. We found it interesting that Bob was the only lodge operator or guide we ever met who didn't bad mouth his competitors. The Di Vitos run a clean, not fancy, reasonably priced lodge, one we would not hesitate to recommend. They can handle up to 16 guests in comfort if not class. No one was home except the cook Alice, and Sally, the gal who waited table at meal time and cleaned rooms and the lodge between meals. They greeted us and suggested we stay for dinner since it was getting late. They knew Bob and the other guides would be back with their fishermen shortly and would like to meet us. We told them we would be back one day soon and thanked them for the invitation.

Just as we were about to leave, Van Hartely, owner of Branch River Air, landed his red-over-white Beaver on the river and taxied up to the dock. He was bringing two new guests to the lodge and expected Bob to be back by now. We met the guests, a couple from Arkansas, who had never been to Alaska before, and were excited to meet a couple of park rangers. She asked, "Is there a National Park around here?" We were itching to get going but felt we had to take time to "meet and greet" this couple and give them our friendly, informational beach speech—and yes, we have an unfriendly speech that has to be used for some people. This one was mostly about bears, which is what they wanted to hear. Educating the public was the most important part of our job, and a part we enjoyed. We usually leave the fishing license, safety, and toilet explanation to the guides. Sally was there to greet the new arrivals, Van had to keep going, and we wanted to be on our way too, so we wished them well and pulled out thinking about a spot for the night.

Van and Hugh Hartely are co-owners of Branch River Air and do most of the flying for the three lodges on the lower Alagnak River. Their Beaver and their tan and orange Cessna 206 were planes we saw regularly. One of the Hartleys had "dumped" (a term that means wrecked, but not as seriously as crashed) the 206 early last September, but had it operational by hunting season. These operators have a season of about 100 days to earn their year's income, so they can't afford much down time.

It was getting late and we were whipped, so campsite here we come. It had been raining lightly since we left Katmai Lodge and we weren't going to be too picky. There are a number of islands in the river, the upstream end gets flooded and scoured in spring breakup every year, so that should provide a site with a breeze to keep the mosquitos away and not much vegetation to fight. We skipped a couple of spots that didn't suit us and found one that looked good, ran the boat up on the gravel, tied her to a sturdy root, and were there for the night. The rain stopped before we had the tent up; it looked like a high pressure system was moving in because a low sun was peeking under the clouds illuminating the bright red fireweed blooming all across the island tip. Fireweed has deep horizontal roots that allow it to survive fires and floods. It is often the first vegetation to return after a fire, thus the name. A brilliant rainbow formed an arch across the river to the east, and we were home-alone on a wild Alaskan river! Our rainbow held and formed a double rainbow. I mixed our evening apple cider with cold river water and added a shot of brandy. We toasted each other and enjoyed the view and the brandy while sitting shoulder to shoulder on the beach watching the rainbow slowly fade as the sun dropped into the forest behind us. Tomorrow we had the braids to do, we would worry about that tomorrow. Tonight was for us to enjoy.

THE SUN WAS UP LONG BEFORE WE WERE. THIS FAR NORTH THE SUN is only down for a few hours at a time from late May to early August when Alaska starts "screaming toward total darkness." Today it was shining brightly, which is rare and something that we really appreciated. We lay in our bags listening to a yellow warbler singing to us from a dwarf willow a few yards away. Our bodies and emotions pulled us toward love, our minds reminded us we had the braids ahead of us.

We had most of the river miles of this trip behind us. Today we had the 25 or 30 miles of braided river channels and then several miles of open but shallow river to run before we made it back to our ranger station. We had canoed and rafted a lot of rivers with our girls over the years, but those were all heading down-stream which made the braids, usually, easy to read. Running upstream against the current was going to be a totally new way of reading water and current. Where a stream runs across alluvial plains of glacial out-wash it is going to change its course every time there is a significant rain. Maps are of no value when looking for the right channel. The biggest braid showing on the map was there then, but gone, perhaps, the next day.

After our normal breakfast of instant coffee, tang, and oatmeal with raisins we packed up and headed into the spaghetti bowl of braided channels. This was no time to be slow and cautious since a slow boat draws more water than a fast moving one, so I put the hammer down and picked the channel that looked like it had the most water. The channel split and split again, then merged and split. It was going to do this for the next 25 miles. Nothing to do but keep going and hope we didn't screw up. All went fine until we found ourselves in a channel that quit. We slowed and moved up to the end for a better look. Penny, in the bow, said, "There's a couple of inches of water, maybe four feet wide, that hits an open channel in a few yards." We had heard about riding your own wake, where if you can keep the jet unit in the boat's wake you have enough water to run. You can only get in your own wake by turning pretty hard. "What the hell!" The worst that was likely to happen was we go aground, are stuck, and have to get out and push the boat to deeper water—we hoped. "Let's try it." We drifted back a few yards, moved left, I twisted the throttle handle hard, angled for the opening full out, turned sharply left as we entered the too-shallow area, kept the jet in the wake and sailed through like we knew what we were doing. "Yee-haw! That was more fun than a roller coaster! Let's take a break and catch our breath," the boss said. That suited me. We were both grinning like little kids, but I could feel my heart pounding in my throat, and my hand was sweating on the throttle.

It was time for Penny to learn to read the braids. She took the helm, twisted the throttle, and headed us into a stretch of open water. She is more comfortable moving a bit slower than full speed, unfortunately that draws a little more water. I suggested she hit it before she went into the next braid, she did and we sailed through beautifully.

Those 25 or 30 miles of braids proved to be more like 40, but we were through the worst of them before we got to what is technically Katmai National Preserve. Somehow there is no big sign proclaiming, "You are Entering Katmai National Preserve." Penny jokingly said, "Damn, we should take care of that and put a sign up! A big one."

We weren't at all sure where the boundary was. We could make a good guess but that was all. According to our map it was 7.5 miles, by raven, below the confluence with the Nonvianuk River. Of course the raven can fly straight, we had to wander all of the meanders of the river. We knew exactly where we were when the Alagnak turned left and the Nonvianuk came in from the right. Like Yogi Berra said, "When you come to a fork in the road, take it." The same attitude applied to the river. We took the fork with less water and felt like we were almost home, we were going to make it. Dave, Loren, and Penny hadn't needed to worry.

We had noted several locations that would require further investigations in the season ahead: several Native cabins, the ruins of two cabins, a Russian Orthodox graveyard sitting above a cut bank where it probably wouldn't last much longer, a place that looked like it had been used as an illegal spike camp, and a log cabin that appeared sound. It was getting late, but that cabin was something we wanted to see today. It was on the left bank, the bank on your left when going down stream, so today it was on our right. It was only ten or so miles down from Nonvianuk Lake and our station, so we stopped to check it out.

It was sitting on the inside of a river bend, well up from a cut bank, an ideal location if you wanted a clear view down stream. It had a big moose skull hung from the ridge poll above the door, and several more along the first rafter. Who ever had lived here had depended on harvesting a moose every fall to feed themselves through the long and very cold winter. The cabin had a galvanized metal roof, badly rusted, but that metal roof is what had allowed the cabin to last 50 or more years. Inside it wasn't much, about 10- by 15-feet, a bunk made by tying two-inch alders together with raw hide for the head, foot and sides, with smaller sticks tied crosswise making a platform for sleeping off the floor, a barrel stove, and a table made of more sticks. Carved into a wall, Penny found, "Dec. 1943 kulled a wolf, so kold." Why were people in a place like this in the middle of winter? Were they hiding from the law or the draft? They wouldn't have had a trap line since they were several hundred miles from Anchorage, the only realistic market for furs. Many questions, no answers. We could ponder and speculate but would never know.

The trip had taken a full two days, had been fun, with scary spots, interesting people, a delightful evening camp, and a lot of education for us. We had taken 35 gallons of gas with us and used over 30, that is way too close to running out for any river trip. By our best estimates, from what others told us about river running, and from our experience with the outboard last season we had figured 20 to 25 gallons should be just right,—wrong! Apparently the jet unit uses a bunch more fuel than a prop unit. All season long we ran with 35 gallons on-board when we left home; 15 gallons in a bladder tank behind the rear seat, two 6-gallon Evinrude gas tanks, also behind the seat, and two 5-gallon Gerry cans strapped to the forward side of the storage box. We averaged between 20 and 25 gallons running a round trip of the Alagnak Wild and Scenic River.

Reading the river correctly can only come with experience. We had been amazingly lucky. River runners we knew in Colorado had told us, "If you're experienced you will have no problems; if you aren't you soon will be. Just miss the rocks that show and keep the hammer down!" At the end of the season we would write a

Season-end Report with advice for those who would follow us. It says, "Unless the water is low there are no real problems. Above the confluence the Nonvianuk has many faces, normal river, a series of "S" curves, quiet water, white water, and boulders. Below the confluence with the Alagnak there are braids—take your choice—there are snags and a few sweepers that could sweep you under, but mostly nice river."

OVER THE SEASON WE MADE NUMEROUS TRIPS DOWN THE RIVER interacting with everyone we met, answering questions, educating, and giving advice, mostly about bears and the river. We visited the lodges every trip, learning what we could about each operation from staff and guests. Our first impressions were strongly upheld and reinforced. The Di Vitos at Branch River Lodge ran a respectable sport fishing business, while Tony Sarp at Katmai Lodge was doing anything he or his guests wanted, legal or illegal made no difference—"Please the client and make a buck."

We spent several hours one afternoon in the Russian cemetery looking at the grave markers with their triple horizontal bared crosses, the bottom bar tipped to the right. The Russian Orthodox Church, second largest denomination of Christianity next to Roman Catholic, was founded in Alaska by missionaries in the 18th century. These markers were very old, weathered, falling over, and disintegrating. We couldn't read anything, but that was all right, it was a fascinating place. It was being eroded away rapidly by the river, and would be gone before many more years. Those people are gone and all evidence of their existence would soon follow them. There was a cemetery so there must have been a church; if there was a church there must have been a village with people doing what? Why were they here? Where did they go? What happened? Howzcome? More questions but no answers.

The Alagnak branch has at least twice the flow of the Nonvianuk. We ran up it one day just to see it. We had flown over it and knew there was a falls or rapids that would be classified at least a class four. We ran up the lower end of a huge tongue pouring from between a couple of SUV-sized boulders. I noticed Penny was looking scared, she puts up with a lot of things just because she knows I enjoy the challenge, but this was one time I had sense enough to quit before she told me to. I read her face and the river and thought, "That's far enough dummy!"

The spike camp was a problem! A spike camp is one that is left unoccupied for a 24-hour period. We knew this spot was used occasionally but not on a nightly basis. We reported it and were told to keep an eye on it. "Gee, thanks boss!" We tried, but never found anyone there. One time it had an empty ice chest and a pan of dry dog food. That had to have been from the night before or something would have eaten the dog food by now. We threw the dog food in the river for the fish, put the pan in the ice chest along with a note telling them they were illegal and we would be back to check. That probably gave them a laugh, they knew we couldn't do any more than give them a lecture and a citation, which they would undoubtedly ignore.

The years we were there the river was used by the Native Yupik people on a regular basis. Many of them had allotments where they had built a little cabin, most of which looked like shacks to American visitors. Those "shacks" were just fine for their intended use. They were meant as shelter for the owners when they were harvesting salmon and a moose or two that would provide the major food supply for their family through the long winter season. Recent reports indicate "...the Inupiak tribe of the Yupik Native population has dwindled to nearly nothing." The village of Igigik that we had visited a few times, apparently, no longer exists. In 2000 a researcher named Morseth wrote, "It is easy to get the impression that Native People don't use the river much. Charlie Andrews' [one of only two Natives he located on the river] cabin was burned by visitors and then his allotment was again burned by campers. He and his sister have the allotment, but they haven't had the resources to build a new cabin. ...regardless of the impression that the river is sport-fisher's heaven there is not a Native presence except for a few decaying cabins." Douglas Deur, Ph.D., in a 2008 paper titled, Alagnak Wild and Scenic River Resident Study wrote, "Alagnak Wild River involved a landscape that had been historically occupied by a significant and enduring Native Alaskan population. Indeed, some archeological evidence suggests as much as 9,000 years of occupation near the head waters of the Alagnak, while riverine sites on the Alagnak indicate an almost continuous occupation of the river over the past 2,200 years. This long history of human occupation was only interrupted in recent times."

A WHITE OVER BLUE BEAVER PUT DOWN ON THE HEAD OF THE river one morning. It was Tim LaPort of Iliamna Air Taxi with two young couples from Chicago who were in to float the river. We met them at the beach on our side of the river to give our beach speech. As Tim was helping unload their gear he looked at us and rolled his eyes. These four looked like they needed a serious education on the Alaskan bush. Tim left as we were talking and answering serious questions. They wanted to know everything. We talked about: fishing, catch and release, bears, safety, bears, hypothermia, burying their toilet, bears, staying out of Native houses, history, bears, and more for over an hour. They had questions and more questions, mostly about bears. The two women were concerned,— scared would probably better describe them—the men were wound tight. We hoped we had helped these four pilgrims understand what they were doing and would be better for having talked with us. We had our doubts, the women were not happy about being around bears, and in wet weather, the men were excited and not very knowledgeable. They had rented a raft and all of their gear in Anchorage and desperately needed to be with a guide to babysit them. As we bade them good-by and good-luck, it was starting to rain. We wished them well.

We thought we should go down river the next day to check on them, but got busy and didn't get it off the ground. The following day we headed down river knowing we wouldn't find them unless they were in trouble, so we hoped to not find them. We didn't, but we found the trouble they had created: A Native cabin was burned to the ground, it still had warm spots and couldn't have burned other than night before last. It had rained hard the afternoon and evening those four started, they had probably gotten wet and cold, saw shelter and took it. There had been an oil burning barrel stove, which was now badly warped. It looked like they had lighted the stove, let it get too hot and destroyed the place. We went on down river looking for them but never found them. We pulled into Igigik just in time to sit in on a Native meeting discussing the fire.

Fortunately we weren't armed, but my God were they! I have never seen such a display of weaponry. It looked like they were going to war. Eight or ten men sat around the room. Most of them had a side arm and a belt knife. There were a dozen assorted long guns leaning against the wall. A time to be diplomatic, to try and calm the situation. We were upset too; four stupid Americans, who we had tried to educate had really screwed up, and we had to try to placate the victims. Fortunately we had developed a friendly relation with these people earlier. We talked, they talked. Penny is a wonderful communicator and was able to calmly talk the situation down to the point of everyone being greatly disturbed over what had happened, but it was history and there was nothing that could be done to correct it. We emphasized that our future beach speeches would be strong on protecting Native property. We hadn't gotten the last names of the people and knew of no way to trace them. We did know we could have gotten that information from Tim and Iliamna Air, but that would never correct the wrong that had been done.

Civilization was coming, the old way was going. The old way had been stable for thousands of years. It had provided the year-round living resources for a population that didn't fluctuate much. Now change was here and and the old way was finished. How long can the new way last? New and improved, bigger lodges are proposed. How long can the resources last as change continues? What is the future? The proposed Pebble Mine above Lake Iliamna will be the largest and most environmentally destructive open-pit gold mine ever. If that is approved it will end the commercial fisheries of Bristol Bay and the way of life of whiteman's lodges so new to the area.

VISITORS

We met a lot of interesting people as they were flown in to float the Alagnak River. Among the more memorable were two men from Sweden, Erik and Inge, who were dropped off one afternoon by Greg Bell from High Adventure Air, out of Homer, Alaska. They were going to spend the next few hours fishing, camp on our beach, and get an early start down the river the next morning. Their stories told us they were very experienced campers and world travelers. We made them welcome and swapped stories with them, letting them know about life and living on the Alagnak. They started setting up camp as we headed up to the tent-frame to have our dinner.

A knock on our door only a few minutes later surprised us, it was Erik and Inge. Penny read their faces, realized they had a problem, and invited them in. Inge who seemed to be the spokesman said, "Ve haf a problem! Ve haf a big problem! Ve haf no sleeping bags."

Penny said, "No problem, Greg will still be in the air and we can reach him on the radio. Your bags are undoubtedly still on the plane, and he just missed them while unloading. He can bring them back."

"No, no." Inge explained, "Ve remember ver dey are. In Erik's living room, behind his big chair."

OK, that was a problem, but we could solve it. We had two spare sleeping bags in case our boat bags got wet. We explained, "You take these two bags, use them on your trip, and return them to park service headquarters in King Salmon at the end of your trip."

Well they weren't sure, "Greg vil pick us up at Katmai Lodge in six days. Vil he take us to King Salmon?" Erik wanted to know.

"Lets see if we can reach Greg by radio." I said, "He may still be in the air."

Luckily, we reached Greg before he got back to Homer. He assured us that he would take them to King Salmon, but he would have to charge for the extra flight time.

"That is OK!" both of our Swedish friends said in unison, so it was settled. Erik and Inge could use our bags, drop them off at headquarters and Dave or Loren would bring them back to us the next time they were out here.

We never saw two people look so happy. They thanked us profusely, took our spare bags, and headed down the hill to their camp.

It wasn't five minutes later that there was another knock at our door. Inge and Erik were standing there again. This time with huge grins on their faces. Erik had a king salmon filet in his hand and Inge had a bottle of Ballantine's Scotch in his hand.

"Could ve fix dinner for us and haf a drink to celebrate?" Inge wanted to know.

Never would Penny and I turn down such an offer. Penny said, "Wonderful! Come in! What can we do to help with dinner?"

"Ve saw you haf an oven, could ve use dat to cook in?" Erik wondered.

"Of course, what else can we do?" I asked.

"Noting!" Inge said, "Ve cook, you sit."

It had been one of the more delightful evenings of our park service careers. Good Scotch, a marvelous salmon dinner that Penny didn't have to cook, and stories told by each of us until we were all too tired for more.

Early the next morning we waved to them as they headed down river on their dreamed of Alaskan adventure. Two weeks later Loren brought us our mail, our two sleeping bags, and an official note of commendation from Dave that would go into our permanent NPS record. And, a little box containing a beautiful hand-made Swedish knife with a bone and maple burl handle, and a sheath of the same beautiful burl. A gift we will treasure forever.

ONE EVENING WE WERE CLEANING UP AFTER DINNER AND HEARD two rifle shots, it wasn't hunting season and they sounded close. We went out to see what we could see. On the far bank was a familiar looking man in hip-boots waving a rifle. We hurried down, got in the boat and went across to see what was up. We remembered him, he was John, a man who just this afternoon had come in with three "friends" to float and fish the river. We were pretty sure he was guiding the group and needed a license, but they all claimed they were old friends together for their annual week of fishing.

John excitedly told us, Sam the oldest of their group, was having a heart attack, and he had walked back up river several miles to get us. He seemed frantic and exhausted; Penny calmed him down and gave him a drink of water. We all got in the boat and headed down to their camp. It was in a little clearing several yards up from the bank, well above a bear path along the water. Two more men were looking pretty scared, and Sam, with a white face, was laying on a sleeping bag. I grabbed the trauma kit out of the boat-box as Penny walked up to Sam and started talking calmly with him. She held his hand and felt his head as I got the blood-pressure cuff out. Penny told me his temperature was normal, but his pulse was racing. I found his BP was high and asked what his normal blood pressure was. He told us his physician had warned him his blood pressure was getting too high, it had been 200 over 90. I said, "Today it's 180 over 85. Do you have any pain in your chest or jaw, you don't seem out of breath. Tell us how you feel."

Penny had him calmed down and relaxed a bit, and said his heart was slowing. He said, "I'm scared! My doctor told me I was taking a chance coming on this trip."

The two of us talked to him, explained he didn't have real heart attack symptoms. "You don't have chest pain, you aren't sweaty, your not out of breath, and your pulse is coming back down to a good pace. Sure your tired and worried, but we feel you're not having a heart attack." We could see in his face that he was feeling much better.

Sam told us, "I have to admit, I lied this afternoon, and that has bothered me a lot. John is guiding us. We paid him, and when he asked us to say we were all friends just fishing together, everyone agreed and I went along, but I don't lie and that has upset me."

We talked pretty firmly to the group about the problems of being in bush Alaska without a guide. We gave John a citation for guiding without a license and a permit, shook hands with everyone, told them to enjoy the rest of their time, and boated back up river.

Our radio squawked early one morning. A VIP was coming to Katmai with the expressed intent of meeting with Frank and Penny Starr. He would fly into King Salmon on 20 August, be shown around headquarters, flown to Brooks Camp for a tour of the Brooks River and falls, see lots of bears, and be escorted to the Valley of 10,000 smokes. The following day Dave would fly him out to Nonvianuk to see us.

"OK, who is this VIP?"

"He's Al Hendricks, the new Superintendent of Great Basin National Park in Nevada," Sally told us. Al was the man who had given us our first Park Service jobs at Jewel Cave. We had enjoyed working for him at JECA and thought of him as a friend. Was he coming to see friends or did he have something else in mind? We hadn't had contact with him for several years. He hadn't written saying that he wanted to visit us. What was up?

We had talked about where we would work next year, but hadn't reached any conclusion. Our goal was to work the 150 mile coast of Katmai out of Amalik Bay on the Shelikof Straight. Our Katmai friends, Lynn Fuller and George Stroud had spent parts of two seasons there, but that position wasn't going to be funded in 1987, so that was out. We knew we could come back to Nonvianuk, but we had spent two seasons here and were thinking about a different position. We had worked every position that Katmai had except the coast and supervisory, so we probably would be looking somewhere else; back to Yosemite sounded pretty good. If Al was going to ask us to go to Great Basin we would have to give that serious consideration.

Our little tent-frame was kind of tight for visitors. We'd had two pairs of friends visit us for a few days the year before, each had gotten along just fine, but this was a VIP. He would have to sleep in the single bed where we usually piled "stuff." Gene and Eleanor Probasco, old neighborhood friends, and Pat Barron and Bev May, a lesbian couple who were friends from Columbus Audubon, had all been ideal guests and slept on the single bed in their sleeping bags. They had spent two nights each on the little bed with no complaints, so Al should be fine there—we could stash our "stuff" somewhere else.

A few days later Loren flew in with Al for a two day, one night, visit. Al had brought some fresh fruit with him, which made him extra welcome, and Loren had brought mail. We spent the rest of that day and most of the following day showing Al Nonvianuk Lake and the Alagnak River. We followed our normal work routine of patrolling and meeting people. We lunched our normal lunches both days: Sailor Boy pilot biscuits with cheese or peanut butter and a refreshing beverage dipped from the lake or river. The only deviation from normal was having Al along. He spent his time telling us the wonders of, and his plans and dreams for Great Basin National Park in Nevada. It was just over the state line from Utah, the newest addition to the National Park System, and he had just been appointed its first superintendent.

Senator Paul Laxalt of Nevada, was a staunch Republican and Ronald Reagan's closest friend and ally. He intended to make a run for the presidency in 1988 but had never done anything to earn the recognition of the environmental community. He had never sponsored or supported any environmental legislation much less a new National Park. Someone suggested he could make a name with the progressive thinkers by proposing a National Park in Nevada, one to recognize the vast basin and range which covers most of Nevada, half of Utah, and parts of several other states. Not only that, but think of all the publicity he would get as a new park was dedicated in his honor.

Al Hendricks had been the "management assistant" at Jewel Cave for several years. Great Basin National Park was really an expansion of Lehman Caves National Monument, so it made sense to have him as the superintendent. Now he needed a staff he could count on, and he apparently had been impressed by the two of us. The park's dedication in 1987 would be a very big deal. It would be attended by Senator Laxalt and the new Secretary of the Interior, Donald P. Hodel. State and local dignitaries from all over Nevada and Utah would be there, and hopefully President Reagan would make an appearance. Would we please come to Great Basin next year? We promised we would submit applications, but would keep our options open.

The weather was cooperative and Dave picked Al up that after-noon as scheduled. Now we had this season to wrap up. Moose hunting season would be starting in a few days and we could expect an influx of hunters. Our friends Dick, Helen, and Janine, across the river at Cry of the Loon, had given up on a difficult boss and quit in mid-August. They had used the excuse that Janine had to be ready for school early, but they had shared with us that they just couldn't stand what they were putting up with from their absentee boss Bill Wright. We had gotten a similar report from Tony and Nancy last year so we understood, but would miss our neighbors. Cry of the Loon was now being run by one of this seasons young guides and a girl/woman who had been hired as the cook the day before Dick and Helen left. A cook and a guide, both 19 or 20 who had never met, sounded like a potential problem to us; we would see.

Fall in Alaska comes in August. By early September most of the leaves have fallen. It freezes most nights, there is a good coat of snow or "Termination Dust" in the mountains. The salmon have spawned. The bears are fat and laid back, and we are starting to think about heading back to the cabin in Colorado that we had built ourselves last winter. The cabin still had a few electrical connections for me to make, and the final inspection before we could move in. Penny had to get our furniture out of storage in Columbus and on a truck to our mesa before our off-season home would be complete. But those were chores that would have to wait for another time.

We had hunters flying in for the moose season. They had to be met and debriefed. The rights of Native private property was high on our priority list of discussion subjects this year. We knew there would be a camp down the Alagnak a few miles. There is a little lake about a mile up from the river that is ideal moose habitat. It is too small to land a plane on, so last year a camp was established by the river where hunters could take a short, but difficult walk and have a good chance for their moose. Last season we had hiked—bush-wacked is more like it—through willow and alder in hip waders, probably a five mile round trip to that camp—"Hell of a trip." Of course we found no one there, but we inspected the camp and left a letter so there was no question that they knew we were aware of their presence. ADF&G had let us know a bull and a cow both had been harvested there last year. Hunters have to clear any kill through a wildlife officer and have their license and moose tag marked. We were sure there would be a new bull there this year, so it was a likely place for a camp, and this year we would be able to reach it by boat.

"Wanton waste" is, to us, the most disgraceful offense of any hunter. It is when a trophy hunter, rather than a meat hunter, kills an animal and harvests the rack or hide and leaves the meat to rot or be eaten by scavengers. It provides him bragging rights but leaves the habitat deprived of prime breeding stock, and a meat hunter with no winter game in the freezer. In Alaska it is illegal to harvest the rack or hide until the meat has been carried out. That way, if it takes two days to get a complete animal to camp, the part that may be scavenged over night will not be the meat. We couldn't check things like that last year, but this year we could.

Nonvianuk Lake is rather steep-sided and provides no shallows and little place along the shore for willow. Thus there is little decent moose habitat. Which meant we didn't need to spend our time checking the lake and could devote ourselves to what was going on along the river.

Sure enough, the same foursome from Montana flew in to float down to where they could access the little lake. We hadn't met them last year, but they had a good clean camp when we checked it. They were anticipating getting two more moose this season. All of them had licenses, moose tags, and everything in order. They were anxious to get going, but were glad to hear our talk on proper behavior in bear country and Native rights.

Five or six other groups flew in with plans to float and find a likely site, set up and hunt, then float on down to one of the lodges where they would be picked up by the same pilot who had brought them in. We ran the river several times during the season, but never located a camp except for the one by the little lake. There are just too many braids and places where they could have set-up. The lodges told us only one group had harvested a moose, but none of them were too disappointed; they had all had good experiences. The Montana group, whom we had no trouble finding, did get a nice bull and went home happy. Our assumption, and hope, was that the Natives had harvested most of the game for their own consumption. We had noted numerous moose over the season and were sure there had been a normal year of calf production, which would provide good hunting in following years.

Moose season ended the last of September. The young pair handling Cry of the Loon had gotten along OK and had closed up a week ago. Now we needed to take the Jon boat up lake to Kulik Lodge. They had agreed to help us get it secured for the winter and take the motor into their boat-shed where it would be safe and out of the weather. That meant running both boats up the length of the lake to give us a way back to camp. The Jon boat is great on the river but nasty in waves, so we had to do the lake on a calm day—not something you can count on in October. That chore was one that we had been concerned about, but the weather gods cooperated and gave us a calm day. We boated up to Kulik with no problem and got the Jon boat secured. Two days later Georgie picked us and our "whiteman's luggage" up in the Goose.

Back in King Salmon we had to write our season-end report, say goodbye to friends and head home to Colorado. We had talked a good bit about Al's offer of law enforcement and supervisory positions at Great Basin. We had become accustomed to being on our own with no, or minimal, supervision. How would we get along having people around constantly and someone questioning every decision we made? Food for thought over the next couple of months.

GREAT BASIN

It was early April 1987, and we were heading off for another season with the NPS. Leaving our loved little cabin, which looked only a few miles south into the heart of the 14,000-foot San Juan Mountains, had a different feeling this year. We weren't heading back to visit our daughter Lori, in Portland, Oregon, or our daughter Carin in Seattle on our way to Alaska. We were heading west on U.S. Route 50. We had accepted Al Hendrick's request and would be working this season at the nation's newest National Park, Great Basin (GRBA) in Nevada. The park that Senator Laxalt thought would help him become President of the United States.

From our cabin on Log Hill Mesa it was about 30 miles to Montrose, Colorado, our shopping, medical, dental, and commercial center, where we would pick up U.S.-50. We drove down the steep, gravel escarpment road 1,000 vertical feet to the valley floor and eight miles to the tiny town of Ridgway. Here we turned onto U.S.-550 to Montrose and the fabled U.S.-50. The so-called "Loneliest Road in America" runs from Ocean City, Maryland, to San Francisco, California. Through Kansas and Colorado it may be 50 or 60 miles between towns, but while driving the 400 miles of U.S.-50 across Utah we would go through only three towns that the AAA map shows in red, meaning there is an approved motel or restaurant. Nevada has only two towns in AAA red east of Reno near the California line.

The entrance to Great Basin National Park is just a few miles over the Utah line in Nevada. You drive five miles south off U.S.-50, down

NV-21 to the tiny town of Baker—which does have a restaurant, "The Outlaw," where we often went during the season to get something to eat and a beer—then another five miles west on NV-488. For overnight accommodations, there are a couple of motels 100 miles east in Delta, Utah, but none in Baker. The next chance for a motel or meal is 70 tough mountain miles west in Ely, Nevada. If you want to stay in or near GRBA you had better have your camping gear with you. U.S.-50 is, indeed, a lonely road in a lonely part of the country. Lonely only in man's perception. As we would discover; life is abundant and changes as you move to different elevations.

We had spent lots of summers with our girls camping and hiking in Zion, Bryce, Capitol Reef, Canyonlands, and Arches National Parks. So we were familiar with the Red Rock country of southeast Utah. We had camped in the Uinta Mountains and driven through Salt Lake City several times. Every time we drove past the Great Salt Lake we looked up and marveled at the shoreline terraces and wave-cut cliffs in the slopes of the Wasatch Mountains, 1,000 feet above our heads. They are the most visible remnants of Pleistocene Lake Bonneville. The lake had once covered western Utah, eastern Nevada, and southern Idaho, about 20,000-square-miles, essentially the size of current Lake Michigan, but twice as deep. Lake Bonneville (not to be confused with the ice dams that created the Missoula floods) formed about 32,000 years ago, and lasted until 14,500 BP (before present). During the latter years of the ice age, ice was melting and running into the Great Basin, which had, and still has no outlet to the sea. That is, until it filled to a natural dam formed by alluvial fans at Red Rock Pass in southern Idaho. The water topped the pass and rushed westward across the Snake River Plain and along the present path of the Snake River, reducing Lake Bonneville to the size of Lake Erie, where it formed another set of shoreline terraces and wave cut cliffs.

Water continued to flow into the basin, and still does, with its load of dissolved minerals, but eventually more water was evaporating than flowing in. The lake became more saline and alkaline (bitter) as the water evaporated. All of those mineral salts were deposited on the lake bed. The lake gradually shrank by evaporation, leaving the salt flats of Utah and the Great Salt Lake. Southwestern Utah was a geographic and geologic province that we were unfamiliar with so we were looking forward to learning about it.

Five miles west of Delta, Utah, U.S.-50 goes through the little crossroad town of Hinckley, then runs 200 miles to Ely, Nevada, without passing through another town. The Sevier River comes out of the Dixie National Forest a couple hundred miles south, runs north, loops around the Dixie highlands, and runs southwest across the salt flats before it disappears into the dry Sevier Lake. Since it was the spring of the year, there was perhaps a foot of water covering the slight depression of Sevier Lake. We pulled off and watched thousands of water fowl resting on their migration to Canada and Alaska. We passed a few other intermittent (meaning spring only) streams and lakes with migrating water fowl as we drove across the understandably unpopulated salt flats. Finally we left the salt-flats behind and drove into sagebrush country. As we crested a slight rise we saw a ten-mile wide basin of nothing but sagebrush with a ribbon of asphalt running as straight as an arrow to the next rise, which repeated the pattern of a basin of sagebrush crossed by a ribbon of asphalt—the loneliest road in America.

At the Utah/Nevada border we pulled into a parking lot, the first sign of human life we had seen for two or three hours. Someone is always seeing an opportunity to make a buck; this slot machine/gas station/restaurant/bar/whorehouse didn't have anything that interested us, but we wanted to see it, and might as well fill the tank with gas while we were there. They say first impressions are important; our first impression of Nevada wasn't very positive. As we pulled back onto the highway Penny said, "Save me!"

Five more miles and we came to a brand-new sign pointing south on NV-21 that said "Great Basin National Park 10 miles." We turned south to the little town of Baker where there was another sign, not as elegant, pointing west on NV-488 which read "Lehman Caves, Great Basin National Park, 5 miles." The road started climbing immediately, following the flowing Lehman Creek. The vegetation was changing, sagebrush began to thin, grasses were showing up along with brilliant scarlet Indian paintbrush, and mule's ears (named for the size and shape of its leaves) with their big, yellow daisy-like blossoms. We rolled down the windows to breathe the fresh air, moved into a stand of pinyon and juniper, and could see aspen trees ahead indicating water. Farther up, Wheeler Peak was shrouded in a spruce forest. The vegetation was making us feel like the place might be habitable after all.

We parked at the VC and walked in to look for Al. We had just gotten through the door when we heard a familiar voice shout "Penny Starr!" It was Kathy Riley who had been Al's secretary at Jewel Cave and was now the secretary at Great Basin. Her husband Steve had been maintenance leader at Jewel and had accepted Al's offer to be Chief of Maintenance here. So we were with three old friends in a totally new environment.

Al was busy and asked us to come back in a couple of hours. Kathy gathered some paperwork we needed to fill out and took us to see our season's housing, a single-wide trailer. It was a typical Park Service residence: old, beat-up, and still dirty from last year's residents. But it had everything necessary, things we had done without in back-country locations for a few years, like running water, heat, and electricity. It even had an eclectic collection of dishes, silverware, pots and pans, and a patio shaded by a nice Utah juniper tree. Kathy told us the Schwann's Man comes around once a week with most any frozen food item you might want, and the mobile library comes every two weeks. Food and something to read. We could deal with this for a few months and head back to Alaska next year.

We met with Al and found out what our assignments would be. Penny would be the supervisor for the 20 or so seasonal rangers doing interpretive tours through Lehman Caves and above-ground nature walks. She would set the schedules for opening and closing the VC, select who would lead the daily nature walks, who would lead which of the 25 daily trips through the cave, as well as assign them their days off. She would have to learn the cave and the local ecosystem well, because she would be teaching the new rangers how to interpret the diverse basin and range ecosystem and the underground maze with its many different calcite speleothem formations developing from the ceilings and floor as dripping water deposited its minerals, as well as leading tours and hikes herself. As supervisor she had the responsibility of monitoring each of her ranger's work and grading them on their performance. During the days of the parks dedication she would be working as a law enforcement officer, but would have to make sure extra cave tours were available, and she would be the one to take the VIPs on a special tour of the cave. Her immediate supervisor would be Norman, the Chief of Interpretation.

My position would be as Law Enforcement Supervisor. I would supervise one other ranger, who happened to be a retired state trooper and had more law enforcement experience than I could ever have. Why Al put me in charge rather than Hugh is something that we will never understand, but he did. In addition, since Penny and I both had a fair amount of firefighting experience, I would be the fire crew supervisor and have two kids to teach about firefighting techniques. There was a resource management person hired, but she wouldn't get here for a month or so, so I could cover that until she got here. She never did show up. The chief ranger had gotten a job somewhere else and left only a few days after we arrived, so I would be acting chief ranger until a new chief should get here. "Well Shit Sherlock!" (as the saying goes). What had we gotten ourselves into?

BASIN AND RANGE

Penny's first job was to train a crew of new rangers on the dark world of speleology. Having spent two seasons at Jewel Cave she knew this subject well, but she also had to teach the ecology of the Basin and Range. We both were interested in this unique ecosystem, its geology, the plants and animals that inhabit this lonely part of the world. Lonely only as far as humans are concerned; the plants and wildlife had adapted to the unique niches of this desert/mountain environment. Penny had some learning to do if she was going to teach it, and I wanted to know just to know.

I had a lot to learn too. Beyond the ecosystem, I needed to familiarize myself with local law enforcement and fire departments. I had two GS-3 firefighters showing up in a few weeks who knew nothing about fighting fires. The park had inherited an old Ford one-ton, four-wheel-drive pickup truck from the Forest Service when it adopted the land that now was a National Park. The truck had been adapted for firefighting. It had a 250-gallon water tank with a Briggs & Stratton engine to pump the water to a hose-reel and 200 feet of one-inch, red-rubber hose that could be dragged through brush and embers without hurting it, or to a two-inch outlet and several hundred feet of rubber-lined cotton hose for use in a structural fire. The pump had enough power to put a good stream of water through either hose nozzle. An extension had been added to the front bumper to hold a draft pump and hose. We would be able to refill that little tank if we could find a creek or pond. It was a long way from being a great fire truck, but it was as good as the even older brush trucks we had at home on the Log Hill Mesa Volunteer Fire Department.

While Penny was learning the cave, I took the truck down to a little pool in Lehman Creek to see if the draft-pump worked. I had checked the engine in the maintenance yard. It seemed to work fine. Now, if the drafting system worked, I could fill the tank and test the two-hose systems. I was impressed; it all worked, and put out a good stream from either hose. The truck had been equipped with good hand tools, there were several Nomex shirts (those fire-resistant, heat-resistant, light-weight, aramid fiber, yellow shirts you see on firefighters when a wildfire fighter is being interviewed on TV). OK, we had been told that the Forest Service had not been happy when all of those thousands of acres of FS land had been transferred from them to the Park Service. Apparently the fire division that had been stationed here wanted the land protected, whether they did it or we did. They had left us a functional, well equipped truck; I was grateful.

The Park Service assigned days off to everyone. Sometimes you even got to take them. In back country Alaska we never took days off; they were assigned to us but we worked every day. We would see how often we actually got days off here. Penny had been assigned Wednesday and Thursday so I assigned myself Wednesday and Thursday and gave Hugh Monday and Tuesday off—still today, only the permanent staff seem to get weekends off.

On our first day off Al offered to show us around. He took us out into the sage-covered valley to show us how the Indians had trapped pronghorns. We parked our van and followed Al out into the sagebrush valley, where we saw the remains of a low stone fence. Penny said, "That looks like the old limestone fences farmers made in Ohio to separate fields, except this looks like it's made of river-wash stone and isn't high enough to keep anything corralled."

Al explained, "The pronghorns refuse to jump anything, so it didn't take much of a fence to corral them. A pair of simple low stone fences shaped like a huge funnel would let Indians chase a herd into an enclosure where they were easy to kill." The stones looked like glacial out-wash to us, but Al didn't seem to know what they were. Penny asked about the spring flowers. Al named a paintbrush and a lupine, then admitted he didn't know flowers very well. I asked about the types of sage and if the ranchers were trying to control it. We had "big sage" and some "silver sage" in Colorado where ranchers were clearing land of sage by chaining. That is, by dragging a heavy chain between two bulldozers. It looked terrible; it pulled out the sage and juniper trees and let the rancher convert the land to pasture. Al didn't seem to have any idea about what the ranchers were doing and thought sage was sage. We would have to learn the ecology and local ranch life on our own!

There was another place Al wanted to show us. He said, "Lets drive down the road about two miles and I'll show you the Forest Service's 'Trail of the Ancients.'" I parked in a roadside pull-off near a Forest Service sign, "The Mysterious Rock Art," we followed a gravel path that looked quite new. Al explained, "The Forest Service went into a canyon somewhere, cut out a bunch of petroglyphs, brought them here, and made this disgusting damn display. Can you imagine our government allowing something like this?" No, we couldn't! A petroglyph is an art form used by prehistoric Americans. They carved, chiseled, or whatever, a picture into the face of a rock wall, usually a stick figure of a game animal or person. A pictograph is similar except it is painted on the rock rather than carved in. These were exquisite examples of petroglyphs laid out along a nice gravel path through a pinyon stand. I got down and looked at them closely wondering if they were real or modern. Al was vehement about the Forest Service having desecrated a sacred site to bring it here, so I didn't question the authenticity of the petroglyphs. Penny and I talked it over later and decided to forget it, no need to make waves over something like this. We sure hope they are forgeries, and thought they looked too fresh and perfect to have been made hundreds of years ago. Al had told us that there are numerous petroglyph and pictograph sites in the park. We hoped to find them, maybe next weekend.

We dropped Al at his office and decided to take the road up Wheeler Peak. We could see the peak from our trailer home and knew the road wouldn't be plowed out for another month or more, so it was mostly to see what we could see and how far we could get. The park encompasses the southern part of the Snake Range with Wheeler Peak dominating the range. During the ice age there had been mountain glaciers across the high country but not the continental ice sheets so typical farther north. The only glacier that still exists in the entire Great Basin is on Wheeler Peak not far from the Wheeler Peak Campground. Going up the road we checked out the Lower Lehman Creek Campground at 7,300 feet and the upper Lehman Creek Campground at 7,750 feet. Both were typical Forest Service campgrounds; loop roads through a nicely treed area along a stream with pullouts to each site; each site had a fire pit and picnic table. Driving on up the road, we weren't much above 8,000 feet and thinking we wouldn't get much farther before we hit snow when Penny said, "Pull over. Those rocks back there look like a glacial moraine." Sure enough, there was a pile, almost a ridge, of mixed gravel, sand, and larger rock. This had to be as low as the glacier had gotten. That meant the stone wall Al had shown us in the valley wasn't made of glacial rocks, those rocks had to be erosional talus from the mountains.

Just a few days after our arrival the Nevada Mobile Library came around and we asked the driver for books on the area. He happened to have a copy of John McPhee's new book *Basin and Range* and some bird, flower, and tree books. We felt pretty comfortable with birds, trees, and flowers. We always had our own bird and flower books with us, but McPhee's book should teach us a lot about the geology of this area.

McPhee relates traveling across the Great Basin on I-80 with

Kenneth Deffeyes, a senior professor of geology at Princeton University. McPhee was learning geology from an expert and sharing it with us. The Great Basin is splitting apart from the Uinta mountains of Utah to California's High Sierras, not unlike the Red Sea and the African rift valleys—there could be an ocean here some day. These are north-south running ranges, one after another—some 50 miles long, some 100 miles long, with faults separating each range. McPhee described what Deffeyes had shown and explained to him:

> Basin. Fault. Range. Basin. Fault. Range. A mile of [vertical] relief between basin and range...each range here is like a war ship standing on its own, and the Great Basin is an ocean of loose sediment with the mountain ranges standing in it as if they were a fleet without precedent.

There are no foothills, it's all too young. The uplift happened in the Miocene, probably eight to ten million years ago, faulting, rifting, and spreading began almost immediately. As earth's crust stretched from east to west, the valleys dropped and the north/south running mountains lifted. Salt Lake City is sixty miles farther from Reno than it was eight million years ago.

Each mountain range can be considered an island. The plants and animals that inhabit one range have no way to reach another range unless they are carried by bird or human. You can't walk from one range to another without crossing a hot, dry desert floor, and very few mountain residents have that ability. Thus there is an ideal opportunity for speciation and evolution. Not unlike Darwin's Galapagos finches, a mutation might give an animal a slight advantage. The mutant animal would eventually dominate the local niche but be unable to spread to other ranges, thus becoming a new but local species. Such a scenario would take many millions of years.

Most of the rocks of the Great Basin were first formed in the Paleozoic Era between 550 and 250 million years ago as Pangaea was forming. At that time the equator ran through Texas, Oklahoma,

Kansas, Nebraska, and the Dakotas. North of there, what to us is now "the west," was ocean with many archipelagos. McPhee says:

> Then, a piece at a time—according to present theory—parts began to assemble. An island arc here, a piece of a continent there—a Japan at a time, a New Zealand, a Madagascar—came crunching in on the continent and have, thus far, adhered.

Sand collected on beaches, was deeply buried and compacted into sandstone, some of which was metamorphosed into quartzite. Shells of marine creatures were deposited in warm, shallow seas and compacted into limestone; some of that, under great heat and pressure, after being deeply buried, was metamorphosed into marble. Granite, the beautiful white-salt-and pepper rock we knew from Yosemite, forms when magma intrudes deep into the earth's crust with millions of years to cool. These rocks had gone through numerous orogenies, or mountain-building times, over the past 500 million years. Those rock types were now spread throughout the park; limestone and marble in Lehman Caves, granite in the glacial cirques on Wheeler Peak, sandstones, shales, glacial moraines wherever you find them. McPhee goes on:

> Remember about mountains: what they are made of is not what made them. With the exception of volcanoes, when mountains rise, as a result of tectonic force, they consist of what happened to be there.

Those mountain islands run the full gamut of life zones as one drives up the Wheeler Peak road from the valley floor at 5,000 feet to the Wheeler Peak Campground at 10,000 feet. That drive was equivalent to driving north to Alaska. I drove that road several times each week checking the three campgrounds. Watching the changes of the vegetation was like watching spring come a little higher each week. Each plant and each animal had adapted to a specific niche that the habitat provided.

For most of a century the land had been administered by the Forest Service and the Bureau of Land Management. Now it was "Under New Management." The entire park, with the exception of the few acres of Lehman Caves National Monument, had been open to grazing and timber harvest. The harvesting of timber hadn't amounted to much due to the difficulty of terrain and the fact that ponderosa pine, Engelmann spruce, and Douglas fir were not too plentiful and were in scattered stands. Grazing was another matter. Cattle and sheep allotments would continue, and monitoring them was one of my duties. Each allotment was assigned a number of animal unit months (AUMs). An animal unit being a cow and calf, or a sheep and lamb. Supposedly those allotments were based on realistic numbers and represented the "long-term sustainable carrying capacity of the land." It looked to us like the land had been over-grazed for generations. The carrying capacity had been exceeded and was going to continue to decline. The Park Service planned to administer the land as the BLM and FS had administered it. There was not a damn thing I was going to be permitted to do about it. The initialing legislation for Great Basin National Park allowed grazing as before. The land would continue to degrade.

SHERLOCK'S SEASON

"**W**ell, shit Sherlock!" This was going to be a different season. The two of us had worked as a team for years. Now Penny, my partner, my buddy, my wife, would be doing interpretation and I would be doing law enforcement, resource management, and fire control. We were used to spending 24 hours a day together, now we were going back to having "office hours" and would see each other in the evening and for a few minutes in the morning. A big change. We would see!

Penny had a group of young people, most of whom were new to the Park Service, to train on cave and surface interpretation. She and all of her staff were required to wear "class A" uniforms at all times. That meant green wool dress pants, long sleeved shirt, neck tie, a felt flat-hat (that hat is kiddingly referred to in the Park Service as "road kill"), and a wool Eisenhower jacket when on cave tours. I wore the same "class B" uniform we had worn in Alaska—green jeans, a short sleeved uniform shirt, and a ball cap. Seeing me dressed comfortably when she was dressing formally didn't make her day any easier. One of her rangers, Mike, had been at Lehman Caves the previous season and was a real help to Penny and became her friend and assistant.

She had a strange man, Norman the Chief of Interpretation, questioning every decision she made and often changing the week's schedule of assignments after Penny had posted them. He refused to give an explanation of why he had made changes; he just did. He came across as arrogant and not particularly bright. He made up for his shortcomings with bluster. Penny had the courage—the balls—to stand up to him and argue her points. Poor Norman had never dealt with such a strong person, he didn't know how to handle her. He tried to start the rumor that Penny and Mike were constantly at odds. That didn't work since the staff knew Penny and Mike got along well, so he went to his boss, Al, the superintendent, and ask for help.

Penny was called to Al's office and told that, "You are frightening Norman. You're being hard on him. He's very sensitive. Would you please be kind to Norman?" Al had to agree that in every disagreement between Penny and Norman it was Norman who had made the worse decision and Penny had been right. That didn't seem to make any difference, Norman was Penny's supervisor and she was to follow his orders.

That set the stage for Penny's season, and for the young rangers who would have to take Norman's mismanagement and ineptness right along with Penny. Those kids turned to Penny for support. She became councilor, mother confessor, psychologist, and friend; the one they turned to when they were chewed out by Norman.

Since Penny was their immediate supervisor it was her job to critique their cave tours, their hikes, and their evening programs. Penny has the unique ability to critique a presentation in a positive way, of pointing out places in a program where things could be presented more openly and warmly, making suggestions for improvement, and having the person being critiqued appreciative of her help.

The kids would come to Penny, often in the evening, sometimes in tears, for consolation and help, when Norman had chewed them out for some minor mistake. Penny managed to be there for them, but her anger and frustration with Norman increased over the season. She went to Norman, and told him he was destroying potentially good rangers. He told Penny, these people and Penny, had to accept it, he was their boss and they were to do as he said with no question.

Penny began to think of her staff as her people. They had no one else to turn to and they needed help. She had been told on several of those evening meetings with hurting rangers, that they would never work for the Park Service again, that this was the worst job they had ever had. When Norman was told these things about the staff he replied to Penny, "I couldn't care less. There are plenty of people out there who want to work for the Park Service."

Penny's response was, "The Park Service is a small, close-knit organization. Your and Great Basin's reputation as a bad place to work will spread quickly." Again Norman could care less!

Penny took her concerns to Al. His response was essentially the same as Norman's. "There are plenty of people out there wanting to be NPS rangers; they will come. You need to learn to get along with Norman. He's your boss." Neither Al or Norman seemed to consider their reputations with other permanent Park Service personnel. Those reputations would, and did, follow them! We decided Al was in a difficult spot himself; he had a person in a supervisory position who was totally unprepared for the job. Al must have felt he had to support Norman. There are a few misfits in any large organization; occasionally one floats to the top, but usually they disappear quickly.

At the end of a season all Park Service personnel are given grades, from 1 to 5 on their performance over the season. Below 3 is unacceptable, above 4 is what everyone is shooting for and expects. Penny always went on walks with her rangers several times and gave interim grades where she pointed out how to improve their work and their grade. Norman decided that monitoring walks and programs as Penny did was a good idea, although he had probably never done it before, he saw what Penny was doing. He occasionally followed rangers on their walks and met with them afterwards, just as Penny did. But instead of giving help and encouragement he gave ridiculously low grades and a chewing out. Penny would write their season-end evaluations and give them their final grade; then, of course, Norman would change Penny's season-end evaluations to suit himself.

Unlike Penny I was in hog heaven! I had a lot of diverse responsibility but I also had the freedom to do a lot of exploring when time permitted. I would have no supervisor until our new Chief Ranger came onboard, but I had an experienced cop, Hugh, to supervise and would have two young people to introduce to firefighting. Hugh and I had four campgrounds and numerous trailheads to monitor, and only one vehicle to do it with. I wanted to be out as much as I could, I needed to do resource management and fire preparedness as well as fight crime. I needed transportation. Hugh was more than happy to spend time around the VC and housing area, which suited me beautifully. I assigned him to patrol with the vehicle on Wednesdays and Thursdays, my days off, and to be around the VC on Fridays, Saturdays, and Sundays. Thus I had the use of our patrol vehicle, a two-door four-wheel-drive Jeep Cherokee that was one of the most uncomfortable vehicles I ever drove, but it would get me to some interesting places over the season.

The park dedication would be on 15 August. Al wanted to have at least two SET (Special Event Tactical) teams come in to handle the crowds and the potential for "All sorts of crime, and danger to dignitaries and politicians."

I thought, "Give me a break!" but that is what he wanted and I needed to set it all up through the regional office.

The Western Regional Office insisted on sending the two teams out in July to get a feel of what they would be involved with. They would be there for most of a week and I was to make housing arrangements for them. I could only ask myself "Is this a necessary expenditure of scarce Park Service funds or just more bureaucratic bullshit?" The only accommodations closer than 60 miles were our campgrounds, the SET team would have to camp. They needed to bring their own gear and food. We could supply the space and water but that was it. These "elite" NPS protection officers knew, or at least felt, that they were very special and deserved special treatment. "Sorry the only commercial accommodations are in Ely more than an hour away," I told my contact in the regional office.

It occurred to me that I had better get to know the White Pine County, Nevada, sheriff too, so I called Sheriff Robert (Bob) Sampson in Ely, Nevada. He was eager to help and wanted me to come over for a meeting, so we set a date for that. I mentioned to Al that I was having a meeting with Sampson. Al told me that was fine, but I was not permitted to park the patrol car at any commercial establishment in Ely, "It might not look good."

"Save me!" I thought, He is worried about someone seeing a Park Service vehicle at a commercial establishment but not at all concerned with the reputation he is building with his staff and the Service in general. Besides that we see USFS vehicles at stores all the time.

Luckily, Sampson and I got along fine. He deputized me that day and would deputize Penny and Hugh the next time he was in the park. He took me to lunch and showed me where the IGA (International Grocers Association) store was. After Bob and I were finished, I went to the IGA, parked in their parking lot, got supplies, felt smug, and drove those 60 interesting miles of steep winding mountain and open high desert roads back to the park.

We had four free campgrounds in the park, all inherited from the Forest Service, and free because we didn't have the personnel to properly monitor them and collect fees, much less service them. They have water, fire-rings, picnic tables, and cold water rest rooms. I made a point of getting to each a couple of times a week to make sure everything was OK, no fires other than in the fire-ring, no one in trouble, no one lost or hurt. The Baker Creek Campground was a couple of miles south down a dirt road, in sage, pinyon pine, and juniper with a little grass—ideal rattlesnake habitat. Since we were in the middle of "open range," it was a place where cattle could be counted on to drop a lot of cow-pies. It wasn't really funny, but

Penny and I had to laugh when we got negative comments from people who had been afraid when they heard animals in the night or had stepped out of their tent into a fresh cow-pie. "Come on, you're camping in the real west now!" I'd say, and then apologize and explain about the cattle. Every once in a while we had a snake bothering people in the campgrounds that I had to snare and relocate—the snake not the people.

One morning I came across a couple in their 70s whose small camper had a flat tire. I had been told I was not to give help to anyone with car trouble other than calling to the garage in Ely. The garage would send someone over the mountain, as soon as they could, to make whatever repair was required. This old couple was going to have to pay a couple hundred bucks to have a tire changed. I thought, "To hell with the chicken-shit regulations! I can change that tire, have them on their way, and make a couple of people feel good." I changed the tire, was praised all the time I was working, thanked profusely, offered twenty dollars, which I smilingly declined, and had the great pleasure of having helped two really nice people.

I had forgotten the incident when a week or so later I was called to Al's office. He told me that he had received a letter praising me for my help. "That help," they said, "had allowed them to have a marvelous time in Great Basin National Park." They went on and on about the park, the Park Service, and me. They were so pleased with the experience that they were sending copies of their letter to the NPS in Washington DC and to National Parks Magazine. To myself, I had the laugh of the year, Al had to congratulate me, but couldn't miss the chance to give me hell for disobeying orders and not calling the garage in Ely when there was car trouble. The Park Service tries to support local business when reasonable; I didn't feel this had been a reasonable occasion.

MY TWO YOUNG FIREFIGHTERS, CATHERINE AND SEAN, arrived ready and anxious to learn about firefighting. They each might have reached their 20th birthdays, but they didn't look it. Both were fit and strong. I wouldn't be able to keep up with them which suited me just fine. They could do the hard work and I could supervise. Of course on a fire everyone works equally hard.

They came at a good time. We had completed two days of intensive training when we got a call to a fire on the edge of town. The local volunteer department was on it, but wanted us to back them up. On-the-job training can be the best way to learn many things. This brush fire had started with a man burning brush in a field behind his house. Sparks had jumped to a fence-line with the winter's accumulation of tumble-weed piled against it. It quickly ran 50 yards, and was now in a pit close behind his house. That pit was filled with a lot of brush and trash. The Baker Fire Department had the original brush pile out, was on the fence-line, and running a hose to the pit. I made sure the smoke from the burning pit was blowing away from us, and had Sean take the rubber line to the windward side of the burning pit to contain the fire. I told Cathy to take the two-inch cotton line and wet down the side and back of the house. I started the pump and charged both lines. Their first fire, and both did exactly as they were told without questioning orders—they were going to be just fine.

Later back at the barn, as we were reviewing the incident, Cathy wondered why I had wanted her to wet the house rather than directly fighting the fire. I explained cooling the house may-well have saved the house and all of us from a, potentially much worse fire. The fire had been quite hot and radiant heat could easily have ignited the wooden structure only a few yards away. One other point this fire brought out was the danger presented by trash and junk. Junk could be anything from tin cans to old tires to toxic chemicals. "Never let yourself be in smoke from a junk fire or a grocery truck." I told them, "It could contain most anything."

We were fortunate in that we had a couple of other minor brush fires that gave us all practice. Cathy and Sean got experience with the hand tools we had on the truck: beater/swatters, shovels, brush rakes, and my favorite the Pulaski—like a double bladed axe with one blade turned 90 degrees to make an adze.

One afternoon about 1630 I was finishing an afternoon of "fightin' crime" and wishing Penny could be with me. I had driven the dirt road up Snake Creek to the Shoshone Creek trailhead without seeing any sign of anyone. I had taken a delightful two or three hour hike, watched a pair of red-tailed hawks float lazily, communing with the gods—I am not sure if it was the hawks or me communing with the gods—and watched a coyote take down a jackrabbit. Now I was heading home for the evening. The radio squawked. It was Kathy at the VC letting me and my fire crew know there was a fire on Forest Service land 20 miles west and a quarter mile north off U.S.-50 up a little dirt road. The Forest Service needed us to be first responders since it would take an hour or more before they could get there from Ely. "OK, we'll be on our way as soon as I can get back to the barn."

"Cathy, Sean! You copy that?"

Sean replied, "We copy."

"I'll be there in 10. Pick me up at the VC," I said.

"Will do. Sean clear."

Great, the kids were learning proper radio procedure.

We found the fire in sage, with scattered pinyon and juniper trees, not far from a stand of ponderosa. It covered about ten acres and was spreading fast. It was much more than we could handle alone; we needed back up. I radioed the park and told Kathy we needed help and to let the Forest Service know that this had the potential to be a problem.

Thankfully, the wind had gone down for the evening. I drove our brush truck around the south side of the fire to get between the burning sage and pinyon/juniper (PJ) and the stand of ponderosa. If the fire could be kept out of the ponderosa it would keep things much less complicated. Cathy took the rubber hose on the reel and sprayed the edges of the fire as I drove the truck and Sean followed Cathy, clearing brush and sage with a pulaski, and starting to create a fire line. We had a chance of keeping the fire out of the ponderosa, but we were running out of water. Some locals were watching us and let me know the nearest place with water we could draft was almost back to the park.

About that time Al and Steve showed up in Steve's maintenance truck. Al took command and saved me having to decide whether to drive a half hour each way for water or forget the truck and fight with hand tools. He said we would just fight with hand tools until the Forest Service crews showed up to take over, which they did shortly. They had the manpower and equipment that we lacked: like a 10,000 gallon water tanker, 20 professional firefighters, three brush trucks, and a bulldozer on the way. Their chief took over as Incident Commander (IC) relieving Al who had relieved me a few minutes before. My crew took a break while Al got orders from the IC.

Just before 1900 Penny, Kathy, and a few others from the park showed up with food and a 30-gallon water cooler for us. Oh boy, was that appreciated. Our canteens were nearly empty and we were hungry, dirty, and sweaty. We were going to spend the night, and the Forest Service kitchen might not get there until morning. We took a break, ate, drank, and rested for a half hour, then went back to the fire-line until we were called off due to darkness.

In the dark we could see the fire grow. Not like a nice little bonfire. The fire was now primarily in dense stands of PJ forest and was getting into the ponderosas. It had a front several hundred yards long and was advancing into the ponderosas. Trees were crowning explosively and throwing sparks like the 4th of July. Nothing could be done in the dark so we needed to get some rest and be ready for tomorrow. We didn't have sleeping bags and it was going to get cold so Cathy, Sean, and I slept—sort of—in the cab of our truck.

By dawn the FS kitchen crew was there making pancakes and bacon and lots of coffee. We were sure glad to have that support in place. I'd had a terrible night sleeping sitting up in the cab of the fire truck with two other people. I had spent many waking hours trying to figure out how this fire started and having no success. There had been no one burning in the area and no lightning recently. We learned that, not only had the fire grown over night, but that we had another fire a half mile north. Sounded like arson! The FS had requested additional fire crews, and air support, and had investigators searching for an arsonist.

Al kept us as a crew of five and told us not to take orders from anyone but him. That sure simplified things, and let me know that I was just one of his crew and wouldn't be the one to make decisions. We had been first responders and had kept the fire from spreading much until the pros arrived. Al kept us clearing brush on the windward side where we were safe.

The fire grew all day, to some 10,000 acres and was classified an "Expedition Fire." Several "Hot Shot" fire crews were called in. Bulldozers were brought in to cut wide fire lines through the forest. I hated to see those beautiful ponderosa being cut and bulldozed, but it was necessary if the bigger forest was to be saved. Aircraft showed up and made water and fire-retardant drops. Early on the second day, when the fire was about 18 hours old, supplies like I couldn't imagine were brought in, including disposable sleeping bags—no pads, but tonight we would be sleeping horizontal and warm. It's wonderful how much a little thing like a cheap sleeping-bag can be appreciated.

We spent two more days on the fire hacking, digging, swatting, sweating, and cursing. Finally Al told the IC he needed to get his crew back to work at the park; could we be released? We knew we had the fire surrounded and expected it to be called "Controlled." So yes, the IC released us. We had been on the fire-line for over 80 hours. Now to get a shower, go to Baker for dinner and a beer, tell stories, get to sleep in a bed with my buddy, and be back on duty "fightin' crime," by 0800 tomorrow.

IN THE MIDDLE OF JULY THE "MONSOON SEASON" STARTS PRODUC-
ing afternoon storms, thunder, lightning, and rain with the possibility of flash floods. Up on Wheeler Peak that meant hail, sleet,
snow and exploding rocks from lightning strikes. Hikers were
warned to take extra precautions. They had always been told to
expect wind and cold and to be prepared for bad weather on the
mountain. We recommended that people always have rain gear, a
warm jacket, and plan to be off the mountain by 2:00 p.m. during
the monsoon season.

After 1600 one afternoon a couple stopped at the desk to report
that as they were coming off the Wheeler Peak Trail they thought
they heard someone calling "Won't somebody help me!" They had
called back, had spent an hour searching and yelling but heard
nothing more. Al was away on vacation and Norman was Acting
Superintendent, he happened to be walking by at the time, so the
desk ranger asked him what to do. He said "Call Penny!" and disappeared.

Penny was called to meet the couple reporting the incident and
get more detailed information. She got their names and address,
and a better idea as to where they had been at the time they thought
they heard the call, as well as their feel as to the weather they had
experienced on the mountain. A storm had gone through that
afternoon, rain, sleet, wind, and hail, but it hadn't lasted long—
quite normal for this time of year. It was getting late. A search
party needed to be sent out, cave tours had to go off as scheduled,
and I needed to be contacted. Penny told Norman he would have
to handle the VC and cave for the rest of the day. She radioed me
that she and Mike were organizing a group of off-duty rangers as a
search and rescue (S&R) team. Were there other things she needed
to do from that end?

I told her to get the search party going as soon as she could, to
call the sheriff's office in Ely to let them know our situation; we
would fill them in as soon as we knew anything. I was in the south

end of the park and would start checking the campgrounds for a missing lone camper as I made my way up to the Wheeler Peak trailhead. She should interview everyone they met coming off the trail, and check all cars parked at the trailhead. All of which she knew and had most of it started.

I thought if the lost hiker was with someone they would have notified us of a problem by now. So I was looking for a camp set up for one person, probably a small tent, with not much gear. I didn't find a camp that looked like it was occupied by a single camper, without the single being present, until I got to the Wheeler Peak Campground. By then, Penny had radioed me that all of the cars at the trailhead had been accounted for; either the reported person had made it out or had walked to the trailhead. It was getting late, the sun was down, we didn't have much time before we would have to call off the search due to darkness. I was looking at a small tent, a Buick parked beside it with Ohio license plates, and no one around. Campers next door said it belonged to a man in his 50s who had left, on foot, to hike to the top of Wheeler Peak right after lunch. This sounded like a real possibility. I radioed the VC and told them to call the sheriff and ask them to run the license plate. I don't like endangering rescuers while searching for someone in trouble, so I called off the search until morning. We would meet at the VC at 0600 tomorrow.

A woman came up to me and related that she and her friend had been coming down from a hike to the peak when they met a man in jeans and a T-shirt going up. They asked if he had rain gear and a hat, and mentioned that it looked like a storm was brewing. He said he would be fine, that he wouldn't need more than he had on, and that he was an experienced mountain hiker. This had to be our lost hiker. I got as much description as I could; he was older, nearly six feet tall, looked fit, didn't have the gear he needed, and wasn't interested in instructions from a couple of young women.

That evening Penny got a call from Norman: She would not

be participating in the search, even though she and I were the only experienced S&R rangers. She was to manage the VC and the operation there. Others could do the search and rescue but Penny was needed to keep the park running properly. Being a good ranger Penny accepted his orders, but found herself thinking that Norman had just admitted he wasn't capable of running the park with Al out of town.

I spent the evening organizing the next day's S&R. I talked with Sheriff Sampson. He had run the license plates and had the information on the owner, Jerald Keys from Ohio. He told me he had the White Pine County Sheriffs Posse lined up to be with us by 0700 and was working on getting a team of inmates from the county jail. I had Cathy and Sean from my fire crew and several off-duty rangers who were willing and anxious to help, but Norman wouldn't permit any rangers who were on the duty roster to participate. "We can't disrupt the park's normal activities." We would have two S&R teams on the mountain by 0700, and perhaps the prison crew by noon. I couldn't think of anything more to do that night besides getting some rest.

The next morning our crew of rangers was joined by Sheriff Sampson and his posse, with the promise of the prison crew joining us for the afternoon, bringing the number of searchers to nearly 30. We spent the day scouring that mountain without finding any trace of the missing man. Bob Sampson and I conferred and agreed to continue the search tomorrow with whatever crew we could gather.

At 0700 on the third day three teams of eight started out, not as enthusiastically as the day before—to find a body. No one was considering we might find Keys alive. The BLM sent a helicopter to help in the search. About 1030 the pilot radioed us that he was hovering over what looked like a body. The Sheriff's Posse was about a mile from the location, got there quickly, and reported that indeed it was Jerald Keys.

I never saw the body, but Sampson told me the man had sustained numerous minor injuries in a fall, but that none of them should have been life threatening. We agreed that a real will-to-live must have been missing in the man; he just gave up. Sheriff Sampson was my hero—if there can be one in such an incident. He identified the man from the license number I had given him, he supplied two S&R crews, one of which recovered the body, and he even accepted the responsibility of notifying next of kin. The park and I would have been lost without that man.

I put in for overtime pay for the rangers who had spent two and a half days doing difficult S&R. Al declined to even consider my request. "All of them volunteered to work!" Overtime pay for extra duty such as fires and S&R is standard in every governmental service that I am familiar with. Al and everyone who had been on the big fire last month had received overtime pay.

AL LET ME KNOW THAT THE NEW CHIEF RANGER WOULD BE ARRIVing in Salt Lake City, but didn't have any way to get to the park since he was flying in and would be joined by his wife and two kids as soon as their house was ready. Would I drive to Salt Lake and pick him up? I agreed that I would do that if I could use Al's Nissan sports coup rather than the rough riding patrol car. Al made a face and reluctantly agreed. I went in uniform—green jeans, a short sleeved NPS shirt, and ball cap—and had a little sign "FREET," so that Bruce Freet would be able to recognize me, since I had no idea what he looked like.

That proved to be a good day for us both. We became friends right away. I explained the terrain and beauty of the park he was coming to, what housing was like, and the personnel he would be working with. I tried hard to keep my personal experiences and biasses out of the conversation, but Bruce was sharp enough that, I am sure, he read me better than I would have liked.

Bruce and his wife, June, and their two little kids, Seth and

Laura, were assigned a permanent house with a fenced yard not far from our trailer. June had gotten the kids a kitten to occupy their interests while Dad was away getting established at his new assignment and their new home. A few days after June and the kids arrival, the kids were in the yard playing; the kitten was investigating its new surroundings and discovered something alive to investigate. That something alive turned out to be a rattle-snake, which didn't care to be investigated by a small feline, so it bit the cat. The cat screamed, the kids screamed, June came out and screamed. Bruce happened to be home at the time, heard the commotion, ran into the yard, recognized the problem, grabbed a hoe and killed the snake; problem solved.

Well, not quite: Everyone was crying, the kitten needed a vet, and the chief ranger had killed an animal in a national park. June and the kids eventually calmed down; Bruce took the kitten to a vet not far from town; I wrote a case incident report explaining the killing of wildlife in the park as "Defense of life and property." That seemed to cover the bases except that the cat needed to have a shot every day and none of the Freets were up to that. I had given thousands of shots during my years as a dentist and was glad to give the kitten its daily shot. Penny and I visited the Freets every evening for a week or so, to tend the patient until it died of snake venom. Those visits frequently included a beer and conversation, which resulted in a lasting friendship among the four of us.

SHORTLY AFTER THE FREET FAMILY'S ARRIVAL I WAS CALLED TO the superintendent's office. Al said, "The Keys kids are coming to see where their father died. I sure as hell can't take time to see them, and Bruce just got here, so you handle them. Here's the letter they sent. They should be here Monday."

Sure enough, first-thing Monday morning Steve and Bayla Keys showed up at the front desk. The ranger at the desk radioed me that they were here. I met two nice looking young adults, probably in their early 20s, who were sad but wanted to pay their last respects to their father. They wanted to see where he had died and wanted to take his last hike, the one to the top of Wheeler Peak.

I agreed to take them up the Wheeler Peak trail as far as they wanted to go, show them where their dad's body had been found, and get them off the mountain before an afternoon storm caught us. They had shown concern about weather, neither looked like a serious hiker, their dress was barely adequate, and neither had a pack to carry water and protective clothing. I asked if they had better shoes with them, they did, and each had a small day-pack to carry a jacket, but no rain gear and no water bottle. They hadn't thought about lunch. I said, "There is a little sandwich shop here in the visitor center, you can get sandwiches and an apple there. You two get changed into hiking clothes, bring your packs and jackets, and pick up a lunch. I'll get water bottles and meet you here in half an hour."

We loaded into the patrol car and drove the 12 miles and 3,400 feet in elevation gain to the trailhead. They proved to be more interested in the country than I had expected. Bayla wanted to know what she was seeing as we drove, so I named plants and explained why they lived where they were. The drive from the valley at 5,300 feet to the trailhead near the timber line traverses quite a variety of habitats. The sage of the valley soon gives way to a pinyon-juniper forest. For a way the road follows Baker Creek with enough moisture to support aspen trees. Farther up we went through a zone of short mountain mahogany trees and shrubby manzanita bushes and on into a deep forest of blue spruce and Douglas fir. The trailhead and nearby campground are in a subalpine forest of limber pine, aspen, and Engelmann spruce. All of the life zones that change depending on soil, sun, moisture, and temperature were represented; like driving several thousand miles north, passing through differing life zones from the dry valley of Nevada to the tundra of Alaska

From the trailhead, it was several miles and another 3,000 feet in elevation to the top of Wheeler. We put on our packs and started out, they both seemed a bit hesitant but insisted we go. Bayla, in particular, wanted to know about the Indian culture. I suspected she was trying to keep her mind off the reason they were there. So as we hiked up the trail their father had taken, we talked about natural history and the Fremont Culture. The people who had lived there from CE 1100 to 1300 and the Shoshone and Paiute people who had occupied the area from 700 years ago until white men forced them out recently. Those Native Peoples had irrigated the valley to grow corn, squash, and beans. They gathered pinyon nuts, they hunted mule deer, elk, and bighorn sheep in the mountains as well as pronghorn in the valleys.

When we got to the location where their father had fallen they both wanted to rest a while. I decided it was an opportunity for me to shut up and let them think. In a few minutes they wanted to go on up to see the top. Just a half hour later, when we were about half way up, Steve decided he wanted to have lunch. While we sat and ate, they talked about "Dad." He had been a hiker for as long as they could remember and had climbed most of the fourteeners in Colorado. They couldn't imagine how he had gone without his normal mountain gear and how a fall such as he had experienced had killed him. I couldn't offer them much of an explanation on that, I needed Penny to handle the psychology.

Steve was ready to go on, but Bayla said she would wait for us there. I cautioned her to stay where she was and to stay well away from anyplace where she could fall. She promised to stay right where she was. Steve and I went on, but in another half hour I noticed he was looking pale and needed to stop and catch his breath every few yards. The trail was steep, he had come from near sea level to 11,500 feet, and was pushing himself. At his next stop I queried him as to how sure he was about pushing himself to the top. I said, "Remember your father pushed too hard. I don't want you doing the same thing."

He sat for a minute and finally said, "You're right, let's go back. I don't want to end up like Dad."

AL WAS OBSESSED WITH THE AUGUST PARK INAUGURATION. HE WAS concerned with making sure all the expected dignitaries would be pleased with the newest national park and its superintendent. He had the two SET teams coming, he had ordered fancy new Sam Brown leather law-enforcement belts and holsters for Penny, Hugh, and me. We were to hang our side-arms, extra ammunition clips, hand cuffs, and mace spray from those fancy belts. That was not what we would expect to see in a small out-of-the-way park like Great Basin, but that would be the uniform of the day, along with long sleeve shirts, neck ties, and flat hats. We wore the big belts the days of the inauguration and never again. The local population had been organized to put on a barbecue with all the trimmings, with the park picking up the tab, of course.

In retrospect it was quite a party: a day of people, food, iced-tea, lemonade, BYOB, sun, speeches—every politician from the local mayor and state officials on up to U.S. Senator Laxalt made a speech. I let the SET team handle the law enforcement—there wasn't any. Penny, Hugh, and I handled traffic, and answered questions most of the day. Penny had to take all of the VIPs through the cave. I had a discussion with a group of Nevadans who had a rattle snake cornered and wanted to kill it. One of them insisted, "You have a gun, shoot the son of a bitch!" I got the snake snare out of the patrol car and moved the snake way off into the woods where it would be safe. Perhaps I got lost, because it took me a long time, and when I did get back, the speeches were finished and things were breaking up.

OUR DAUGHTER LORI, HER HUSBAND JOHN, THEIR TWO KIDS, Claire four, and Ethan two, stopped for a few days of camping at Great Basin on their way to spend two weeks at our home in the mountains of Colorado. The next day was Penny's and my Sunday—the second day of our weekend—I borrowed Steve and Kathy Riley's four-wheel-drive Bronco, piled us all in with a picnic lunch, and headed around to an old logging road that would take us up the back side of Wheeler Peak to a stand of bristlecone pine that doesn't get much visitation.

The bristlecone is the longest living plant known—some species of fungi may be much older. "Methuselah," a bristlecone pine living in the White Mountains of eastern California is 4,789 years old and currently the oldest known living plant. The grove that we visited three quarters of the way up Wheeler Peak is where a few years earlier a graduate student from the University of North Carolina, who was working as a forest researcher, had been coring a really old-looking tree, known as Prometheus, to see how old it actually was. The coring tool got stuck and the Forest Service gave him permission to cut the tree to recover the coring tool. Tree rings on the stump showed that when it was cut in 1964, Prometheus had been 4,844 years old. Oops!

We had a wonderful day looking for the stump and just enjoying the uniquely and beautifully weathered trees, alpine violets, and buttercups. Claire heard a funny whistling sound and tried to find what had made it. She was sure the sound had come from the scree at the base of a cliff. We all listened and heard it again. We couldn't see it, but Lori explained to her that she had been privileged to have heard a pika, a tiny member of the rabbit family that lives in alpine rock piles, where it gathers grass to dry and make hay for its winter food supply.

The mention of food made us all remember that it was past lunch time. While we were having our sandwiches, we noticed a golden eagle circling over head, undoubtedly looking for its lunch. I suggested the eagle was wondering if Ethan might be small enough for the eagle to carry home. Lori gave me a look and a "Dad!" We all chuckled.

The next day Penny took them all on one of her tours of the cave. That evening Claire decided she was a ranger and mimicked the things she had watched her grandmother say and do that afternoon. She put on quite a performance, dancing around our deck exaggerating Penny's movements and expressions. We all laughed with her as she showed some of the unique points of Penny's cave tour, such as spreading her arms and shouting "Stop!"

There was one of Great Basin's frequent but brief thunder, lightning, and rain storms right after Claire's performance. Lightning streaked through the clouds, thunder like cannon-fire boomed almost instantly. The storm was right over our heads. The kids were scared, but amazingly, from the comfort and security of their parents arms, they watched one of nature's most magnificent performances and heard Lori explain the beauty and importance of this act of mother nature. Within minutes of the lightning show nature performed another miracle, the setting sun broke out from under the clouds and gave us a fantastic rainbow over the ridge to the east. And I recited:

Somewhere over the rainbow, skies are blue
And the dreams that you dare to dream, really do come true.

Somewhere! But not this season in the nation's newest National Park. Penny had a difficult supervisor, who made her position of supervising the interpretive staff of new rangers, a tough job. I had a very interesting position with numerous diverse responsibilities. Al was in a strange spot; he had to manage a new park and deal with Norman, who he knew was incompetent, but would probably be his assistant for several years. I'm glad I didn't have to supervise Norman, but wished Al would be much more firm, and not let him get away with the crap he was pulling to cover his incompetence. Great Basin National Park is one of the more beautiful of the little known and rarely visited national parks. We had some wonderful times there, but Penny's experiences with Norman precluded our considering another season.

Our contracts were complete on Labor Day. We had been asked to stay on through the end of September. We declined. Many of Penny's interpretive rangers had been asked to stay on longer; most of them declined. Al's and Norman's attitude of "There are plenty of people out there wanting to be rangers," was leaving them with a very short staff to finish the season.

We were back on Hwy 50 headed east on the loneliest road in America when Penny made a pronouncement, "I will never work Park Service again!"

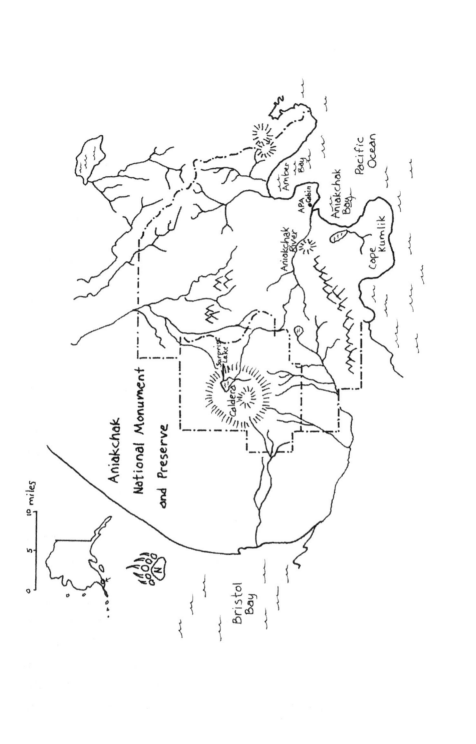

Aniakchak National Monument and Preserve

10 miles 5 0

Bristol Bay

Pacific Ocean

Amber Bay

APA
Cabin

Aniakchak Bay

Cape Kumlik

Aniakchak River

Surprise Lake

Caldera

N

BACK TO ALASKA

Following our frustrating season at Great Basin, Penny had made the pronouncement that she would never work Park Service again. Somehow David Manski hadn't heard about her decision. During the winter of 1987–88 we got a call from David wanting to know if we would be interested in working at Aniakchak National Monument and Preserve (ANIA) next year. The monument is near the lower end of the Alaska Peninsula, more than 100 miles south of Katmai, and known for the miserable weather so close to the Aleutians. Most of the monument is beyond the treeline, the southern limit of wooded country, again due to the wet, cold, windy climate of the Aleutians.

David had gotten to know me in 1985 when I had been assigned to protect him and another researcher from bears while they were doing a three-day research trip on fungi in the marshy northern part of the Katmai Preserve. That had been an interesting three days. The two of them knew their subject well, but hadn't a clue about bears or navigating the wetlands we would be exploring. They were scared of bears, didn't know Alaska, wore hiking boots and carried heavy hip-waders. It seemed they were always changing their foot-wear and still had wet feet. I wore good fitting knee-high Servus Neoprene rubber boots (known as Extratough's or as Alaskan tennis shoes) the whole time and had dry comfortable feet. I carried a shotgun and my minimal backpack. They carried huge packs, with a lot of gear they "might want." They fixed fancy evening meals and were harassed by mosquitoes, I had simple dehydrated meals I could fix quickly and escape to my tent, away from the evening mosquitos. Mosquitos are almost always bad in Alaska, but we were intentionally working wet areas where the swarms here were huge and voracious.

We knew Aniakchak was administered by the Katmai staff and operated out of the office in King Salmon, so it was the home base of Aniakchak rangers. On the phone David let us know there was a new administration at Katmai now. He had replaced Kathy Jope as head of resource management and would be the manager of Aniakchak National Monument. He told us he had heard good things about us from Kathy, Dave Morris, and the rest of the former Katmai staff. He thought we might be interested in being the first rangers to be stationed, for a full season, at the most remote and least visited park in the U.S. National Parks system.

David described the work he hoped we could get accomplished over the season: conduct inventories of raptors, seabirds, and marine mammals along Aniakchak's Pacific coast; record data on nesting site locations, abundance, and breeding success of nesting birds, especially raptors; classify and describe vegetation communities, compare them with existing LANDSAT imagery, record dates of first blooms, collect and organize an Aniakchak herbarium. We would also conduct a small mammal survey and patrol costal waters to contact commercial fishermen and other visitors to learn about their knowledge and past uses of the Aniakchak area. We should inform them about NPS rules and regulations. And no, he didn't expect we would be able to accomplish everything he would like done, but we could get a good inventory, a base-line data, on which future abundances and changes could be based.

Holy-heifer-dust! That sounded like six seasons worth of things to accomplish. OK, we had something serious to consider. Penny had made a meaningful statement when we were leaving Great Basin, would she be interested in this proposal? David told us Katmai's new superintendent was Ray Bane who we had met our first season in the Park Service. He is the one who had stimulated our initial interest in Katmai. The new chief ranger was Steve Hurd, he had been lead on one of the SET teams at Great Basin, and David himself as resource management specialist.

David's job at Aniakchak was to send a team whom he felt would be competent to do the work and be capable of living and working the full season under the conditions existing at Aniakchak. There had been other rangers there for brief stays over the past years. Our friends Lynn Fuller and George Stroud had been there for three weeks in 1983, and David Manski himself had been there for ten days last year. He felt we were the most competent and dependable couple he knew of and wanted us to make Aniakchak our home for three months or longer. Penny asked him to call us in 48 hours. We had a lot of thinking and talking to do.

We thought. We talked about the experience that Lynn and George had related to us. They had a pretty rough time at Aniak-chak, but were glad they had done it. We talked about the negatives we had experienced last season at Great Basin. We remembered all of the wonderful experiences we had enjoyed in Alaska, the time alone, depending on each other and no one else. Those memories of our Alaskan lives will always be important to us.

At home in Colorado one fall, after we had returned from a marvelous season of being by ourselves for months, an acquaintance, who had spent the past season in Honolulu, Hawaii, asked Penny if returning to the tiny town of Ridgway, Colorado, hadn't been a cultural shock to us; it had been to her. She had been in a large city surrounded by many people every day, we had been alone in the Alaskan bush, and yes, it certainly had been a cultural shock for us, but the opposite of the shock she was experiencing. We appreciated quiet and solitude; she appreciated crowds. We read the Aniakchak bulletin:

Located about 400 miles southwest of Anchorage on the Alaska Peninsula, Aniakchak is one of the most remote and least visited units of the National Park Service system. The isolated location, expense of getting there and persistently miserable weather probably account for the limited number of visits. Unlike most parks outside Alaska, Aniakchak has a vast wilderness area without developed facilities. You must, therefore be prepared to meet Aniakchak's challenges on nature's terms; conditions conducive to hypothermia, high densities of brown bears, violent weather, extreme remoteness and few other people are the norm, rather than the exception.

The bulletin went on to tell that summer high temperatures average from the upper 40s to low 50s. "You should expect most days to be overcast and wet. Violent windstorms, low ceilings, and rain should be expected, so plan on delays getting to or from Aniakchak." Penny had a long phone conversation with Lynn Fuller and got her impression of her and George's experience at ANIA. David called exactly when Penny had asked him to. We accepted his offer. I guess we were addicted to the culture that we had found in the seclusion of the Alaskan bush—with the caveat that he enroll us in the law enforcement refresher session that spring. That would be an expense he had not counted on, but felt it would be a distinct advantage to have rangers who were not only biologists but law enforcement officers too.

Now we had questions: when did he want us to get to Katmai? Would we have accommodations in King Salmon? What boat would we have at Aniakchak? When would we go to Aniakchak? David had answers: our EOD (entry on duty) would be 5 June. While we were in King Salmon we could live in the vacant house that had been occupied by our former boss, Hal Grovert. We would take a 16-foot Zodiac inflatable boat with us when we flew to Aniakchak. We would go down as soon as weather permitted.

We had experienced enough of life in bush Alaska to be

demanding. We wanted to do an aerial survey of the 70-mile coast we would be expected to patrol. That would give us an idea of the general lay of land and sea, and give us a chance to locate raptor nests that might not be visible from a boat. We wanted a primary motor and a small kicker as a back-up motor for the Zodiac, just in case the primary failed. We wanted to land and inspect the old APA (Alaska Packers' Association) cabin that would be our home, and hopefully fly up the Aniakchak River to land in the caldera of the Aniakchak Crater. That caldera is six miles in diameter and 2,500 feet deep, a part of the volcanic "Ring of Fire" which surrounds the Pacific Ocean. The huge caldera was the basis of President Jimmy Carter's 1978 decision to proclaim the 601,294 acres of caldera and surrounding land as Aniakchak National Monument and Preserve.

David couldn't promise all of that. He was sure he could get us the flight to see the coast and up to the caldera. Landing at the cabin could probably be a part of that flight but would depend on conditions when we got there. He already had a 30-hp Evinrude outboard for the Zodiac and would see if he could get a small outboard for a backup.

FOLLOWING THE LAW ENFORCEMENT REFRESHER COURSE IN Anchorage, we had ten days before our EOD date at Katmai. That gave us an excellent opportunity to relax, catch our breath, and visit Alaskan friends. Lynn Fuller (who Penny had talked to about ANIA and is one of our friends from our first couple of seasons at Katmai) lived in Palmer, only an hours drive from Anchorage. We rented a car and drove up to visit her for a few days, hoping to pick her brain more about the time she and George had spent at Aniakchak. We wanted to hear more about what would be our home for the season. She expounded at length on the weather they had experienced: cold, wind, rain, and storm most of the time they had been there. The old bunkhouse we would occupy was so big and so drafty they couldn't heat it so they froze. They had slept on a pair of plywood sheets laid on the open ceiling joists so they would be safe should a bear decide to visit. It was either sleep up there or lay their sleeping bags on the floor. "Very encouraging!"

We drove back to Anchorage with mixed emotions about our coming season. It would be our biggest challenge so far, but offered wonderful rewards, a chance to experience and observe a new environment in depth.

That afternoon we caught a commuter flight to Kenai where our old friends Al and Donna Franzmann picked us up. We had been close friends with them since our Air Force days at McConnell AFB in Wichita, Kansas, during the mid 1950s. Al was the base vet and I had been one of the base dentists. Since then, Al, Penny, and I had furthered our educations; Penny and I for the joy of learning about the natural world, and Al upgraded his doctor of veterinary medicine by getting a PhD in wildlife ecology. He became the director of the Alaska Department of Fish and Game's Kenai Moose Research Center on Alaska's Kenai Peninsula and a world-known research biologist.

We managed to spend a few days with the Franzmanns on most of our many trips to Alaska. The four of us always enjoyed time together and Al was anxious to share his work with us. Over the years he took us along on flights to radio-locate moose that had been fitted with radio emitting collars. We joined him on helicopter flights to tranquilize moose, brown bear, caribou, and Dall sheep by shooting them with tranquilizer darts from a moving helicopter. The helicopter would land, we would hike to the location of the downed animal and make sure it was sleeping soundly before we handled it. Then do a physical work-up consisting of a blood sample, several measurements (weight when practical), extract a premolar to age the animal, check for parasites, eyes, ears, rectal temperature, and general apparent health. The ADF&G team always clipped on plastic ear tags and tattooed the inside of the lower lip with an identification number so that a history of the animal would be available if it was trapped again or harvested by a hunter. We frequently placed radio collars on the tranquilized animal or replaced existing collars on previously collared animals. Finally we gave an injection to reverse the tranquilizer, waited for the animal to recover enough that we were sure it would be alright and not be taken by a predator before it was able to defend itself, then got the hell out of there before a very unhappy animal was completely mobile.

Both Al and Donna prided themselves on living off the land. They had a magnificent garden of vegetables and berries. All of their meat was wild and harvested by them: moose and caribou every year, black bear and Dall sheep some years, and plenty of small game, mostly grouse and rabbit. I have eaten, and enjoyed, a lot of small game that I hunted, but nothing as delicious as the big game they harvested each year. The Franzmanns always had a freezer full of game meat, berries, and vegetables which they proudly shared with us. Wild meat, home grown potatoes, vegetables, and berries make a wonderful diet, and some of the most delicious meals we have ever eaten. We envied them living on a diet like our ancestors had, but reminded them that the exploding human population precluded very many people having such a diet. We had long discussions over controlling natural predators like wolves who were taking game animals that humans wanted for themselves. We didn't convince them that humans will always want more, and they never convinced us of a need to reduce the number of natural predators to supply more game for humans.

Normally we had to fly back to Anchorage to catch a flight to King Salmon. A few years before this year's visit to the Franzmanns, Katmai Chief Ranger Loren Casebeer had been one of the instructors at the regional LE course and would be flying the park's plane to King Salmon the same time that we would be flying down. He offered to pick us up from the little lake that the Franzmanns' property backed onto. We suspect Loren merely wanted the opportunity to meet the famous wildlife biologist. His picking us up had been greatly appreciated, it saved us the price of a commercial ticket.

This year we would be flying commercial. Mark Air had direct flights from the Kenai airport to King Salmon. We took that rather than fly back to Anchorage to get the Alaska Airlines flight that we had taken on most previous trips.

Aniakchak Caldera

CALDERA AND APA CABIN

We flew from Kenai down to King Salmon on a gorgeous day. Under clear sky we looked north and saw Mt. McKinley which we always call Denali, the Native name for the tallest peak in North America. Looking to the west, as we flew over Cook Inlet, we flew right beside the famous volcanoes of Redoubt and Iliamna, which define the northeastern and southeastern corners of Lake Clark National Park. A little further south, at the mouth of Cook Inlet, we passed the smoking volcano known as Augustine Island, then over our old stomping grounds of Kukaklek and Nonvianuk

Lakes and on into King Salmon. It's not very often that the sky is so clear and few places offer such breathtaking sights. We decided we were being welcomed back home.

David Manski was in the town of Chignik meeting with the elders of the local Native community, the Koniag Corporation, for a few days and had told us to use his place until he got home. David's hospitality was appreciated, but he would be home in a couple of days and we would need a place to stay for a week or so before we went to Aniakchak. We had been told Grovert's old house was empty and we could use it. It was a completely vacant apartment. We had learned that if you are going to survive in the Park Service—or any where else for that matter—you had better find ways to provide the necessities yourself. We went to the park's warehouse, found a card table, two folding chairs, a floor lamp, and some silverware. We found a double mattress at Casebeer's old house and with a little help from our friends got it to Grovert's. Penny was sure we could mooch some sheets and towels from David and his wife Shira as soon as he got home. Shira and their two little kids hadn't gotten to King Salmon yet, so we would meet them later.

We would be in King Salmon only ten days or so and had a lot of things to get accomplished. We needed to make sure all of the gear we had requested was in our corner of the warehouse, in good shape, and that no one else would appropriate it before we took it to Aniakchak. We had to be careful of things like float-coats because there are never enough to go around and someone would commandeer yours if you didn't protect it, so we took our coats back to Grovert's. Penny needed to make sure the boxes of food which she had bought at home in Colorado and mailed from daughter Lori's in Portland had arrived safely. She needed to seam-seal the tent and do a lot of communicating with Park Service personnel and friends. We checked the stoves and lanterns that we would depend on for heat, light, and cooking.

I put the Zodiac together to make sure all of the parts were there and the boat was in good condition. I took the 30-horse Evinrude outboard and the little kicker that David had gotten for us, down to the river, attached them to a skiff, and ran both of them for a few minutes to make sure they worked properly. The Evinrude had a smoky exhaust, but other than that it ran fine. The old kicker seemed rough, so I hauled it to the boat shop for them to check out. The next morning the boat shop said the kicker was now running smoothly and assured me the smokey exhaust was from gas that had been mixed for a two stroke motor in the tank they had loaned me. I checked the kicker at the river, it seemed to run pretty well on the park gas. The Evinrude still smoked a bit but ran smoothly.

When you may not get resupplied at all, you had better put a lot of time and work into planning and assembling all of the equipment, food, and clothing for a three or four month stay at a bush location. (Thus the famous six P's—prior planning prevents piss poor performance!) That can amount to a sizable pile of stuff. As Pen Air pilot Georgie liked to kid us, "White people take much baggage!"

David had scheduled Joel, the park pilot, to fly us on an eagle survey of the ANIA coast, land at the APA cabin, fly up the Aniakchak River and into the caldera. As can be expected, weather didn't permit the flight the day scheduled, but the next day it was a go. Joel decided to reverse the order of the flight, take us to the caldera first, then the APA cabin, and do the eagle survey last. Weather wasn't good, we flew through clouds, which we don't like doing in mountainous terrain. I sat in the right seat of the Beaver, beside Joel, with Penny in the seat behind me. We were well west of the Aleutian Range so there was no chance of running into a mountain. I shouldn't have been worried, but every time I looked at Joel he seemed to be asleep. The instruments showed that we were maintaining altitude and heading; the right seat has a wheel and pedals just like the pilots; I had flown several times, so "Ha-cunna-matta!" (Swahili for no-problem-man).

Thankfully, I didn't have to fly. Joel opened his eyes before we reached the caldera rim, dropped us over the edge, circled the three-acre Surprise Lake, to get the wind direction from the waves, and landed on the flat ash and cinder floor of the volcano. Surprise Lake is the the remnant of a large lake that once filled the caldera and is the source of the Aniakchak River. As Penny and I got out to explore, Joel closed his eyes.

The caldera is six miles in diameter, a really big one. That must have been one hell of an eruption 3,700 years ago, many times the size of the Mt. Katmai eruption of 1912. Standing on the crater floor we looked up to the rim 2,000 feet above our heads; the floor is 1,100 feet above sea level. In the center of the caldera is Vent Mountain, a volcanic cinder-cone itself, with a 200-foot deep central crater. There are hot springs all over the caldera floor. The water from them had once accumulated and formed a lake 1,000 feet deep. It overflowed the rim, producing a tremendous flood and creating the Aniakchak River and gorge. The river can be, and has been, floated, but it wouldn't be this year. It has class III and IV rapids in its upper 15 miles then widens and meanders 12 miles across the lowlands to empty into the Pacific Ocean 200 yards south of the APA cabin.

We walked along a crystal clear, very warm stream that joins the Aniakchak River inside the caldera. We had no idea what sort of dissolved minerals the stream contained, probably all sorts of nasty heavy metals. This one tasted very acidic and must contain a good bit of dissolved iron because the gravel in it is stained a hematite red rather than the yellowish of the ash floor it was flowing across.

There would be a team of biologists doing research in the caldera this year. Kristine Sowl, a generalist, and Will Cameron, a limnologist, would fly into this desolate place around the same time that we went to the coast, camp for two weeks, and do a biological inventory of the caldera floor. We didn't see a lot for them to inventory and didn't envy them a bit. We got to know and like Kristine while we were in King Salmon and have continued to follow her career as a biologist and manager of several different remote National Wildlife Refuges in Alaska.

Joel was yelling at us, "Let's go!" so we made our way back to the plane for the next leg of today's exploration, the APA cabin, that would be our home for the season.

We flew right through "The Breach," a 1,200-foot deep cut in the caldera wall, that was cut by the over-flow, and straight down the Aniakchak River canyon to the coast. Somehow neither of us had a burning desire to float that river; it looked rough, cold and really wet. The only reason we could think of for going down it would be to say you had done it. Once we had been inclined to take challenges like that just to see if we could do it, but like the saying about Alaskan bush pilots, "There are old bush pilots and bold bush pilots, but there are no old bold bush pilots." We had matured enough that we were "the old rather than the bold bush rangers."

We spotted a cow moose and yearling calf feeding on willow buds on the lower river and a single bear near the mouth. The tide was out, exposing a broad sand beach and a series of reefs near shore. There was a west wind coming off the mountains and down the river. Joel circled out over Aniakchak Bay, came back into the wind, put down on the east/west running beach of the south facing bay, and taxied up to a creek only a few yards east of the cabin. The two of us piled out, excited to examine the ocean-front cabin and surroundings. Joel closed his eyes.

The Alaska Packers Association bunkhouse had been built, in the 1920s, to house workers who maintained salmon traps and harvested the fish, mostly salmon, which were trapped. Several rows of poles had been set off-shore across Aniakchak Bay. When salmon were running, huge gill-nets were strung from them. The mesh of the net is sized so that only the head of the fish goes through, the netting catches in the gills, and the fish is stuck. Men in boats then drag the nets across the boat and pick the stuck fish out of the netting.

Fortunately only a few remnants of those traps were still in existence. A basaltic dike runs several hundred yards from just east of the rivers' mouth to a mass of basalt that is an island at high tide. The dike afforded enough protection from wave action to allow several stumps of those old posts to still be sticking up on this low tide.

Penny and I walked down the beach and up 100 yards through four-foot tall beach grass to the cabin which was about 30 feet, or so, above high tide line. Calling it a cabin was certainly a misnomer, the place was more like a barn. It was an L shaped building about 40 feet wide by 25 feet deep with a 25 by 25-foot room—that we used as a shed—in front, all one open space. The ceiling joists were eight feet above the floor and open to a pitched roof another ten feet up. If my calculations were correct, we would be living, and trying to stay warm, in a very well ventilated room of about 10,000 cubic feet. Keeping warm was going to be a challenge. We could see a hundred or more holes the diameter of a finger in the rusty galvanized metal roof. Lynn had told us they were bullet holes; pilots flying over liked to shoot at the roof just for fun. I looked at the interior walls and floor and realized they had been made of 1 by 2-inch clear #1 redwood. "You can't get wood like that anymore," I said. We had put a redwood deck on our Colorado cabin last winter and the best 2 by 4 redwood I could find had lots of knots in it. At least half of the wall paneling was missing. Lynn had told us hunters and fishermen had torn off the wall paneling to use for kindling to start beach fires.

The 15 by 25-foot deck was in real need of repair. One corner sagged at least six inches and most of the decking, again clear redwood, didn't reach the front edge of the frame, which left unsupported boards to be careful of. I am not sure what happened to that decking, probably a combination of weather and people giving it rough treatment over the years.

Running a few feet from the east side of the "cabin" is a little stream about eight inches wide. We followed it up hill a way and found the creek's source was a spring. I tasted it, it couldn't have been better, so I decided it could be our drinking water. "Not so fast!" Penny said, "Sure, it will be a great water supply, but we should still run it through the Katadyn water filter. We can't take a chance of getting giardia again or something even worse out here."

"Yes sir, mam," I agreed.

Up the hill to the left, toward the river, and about 100 yards away, was an outhouse that looked like it was ready to collapse. We hiked up an overgrown path to check it out. Sure enough, on closer inspection it looked like it was ready to collapse. We would need to build a new one.

Joel was standing beside the Beaver looking antsy. The tide was rising, the sea was getting closer, not close enough to be a concern, but we still needed to do the eagle survey and he wanted to get going. I wanted to eat first but he said we could eat while we were flying. He had eaten while we were looking the place over. Penny suggested we check Amber Bay to the north and east before we finished Aniakchak Bay, then around Cape Kumlik, and southwest to see Kujulik Bay at the southwest corner of the park. Joel said, "We'll do Kujulik and bag the rest of it."

Both of us said, "No! This trip is primarily to do an eagle nest survey. We'll fly the whole damn coast, low and slow, just like David said." Joel was pissed. He wasn't used to rangers not letting him have his way, but he agreed to do what we demanded.

He taxied to the far end of the beach to get the the nose into the wind, turned, and roared up the beach and off. We were headed southwest so we continued in that direction. We spotted three eagle nests and five mature bald eagles near the mouth of the Aniakchak River, then one nest and two eagles by the lake at the base of Cape Kumlik. The cape is too exposed to provide the needed shelter and there is no stream for fish, thus no fish-eating eagles. We noted a small herd of caribou on the beach of Kujulik Bay and a pair of eagles over the bay but couldn't find a nest. We turned and retraced our flight back over the cabin and around the cape between Aniak-chak and Amber Bays, noting a pair of rough-legged hawks south of the Aniakchak River. Two good streams flow into the base of Amber Bay, with good eagle habitat in the area between and around both streams. We found several nests and saw six eagles, a young bull moose, and a sow with two cubs in Amber. We flew on east to the end of the unnamed cape, saw an eagle, and knew that the end of the cape was the boundary of the monument, the end of our territory, our jurisdiction, and our responsibility for this season. We didn't see a place in any of the three bays that would provide shelter for our boat. That worried us; no cove, no safe place to moor. The boat would be exposed to the weather no matter where we anchored it.

Joel turned north taking us past the Twin Peaks, a part of the Aleutian Range at the base of our unnamed cape. We flew on north over Mother Goose Lake and on to King Salmon. That had proved to be a very productive flight, we had seen 20 bald eagles, 10 eagle nests, two rough-legged hawks, 15 caribou, a single bear, a sow bear with two cubs-of-the-year, and three moose—a cow, a yearling, and a bull with sprouting antlers. We had seen our season's home: a building with many shortcomings, a landscape like no other we had experienced, open bays which had no safe place to moor a boat; we understood why there had never been rangers assigned here for longer than a few weeks. By the time we landed in King Salmon Joel seemed to have gotten over being mad at us for insisting we fly the whole coast, so Penny invited him to join us for dinner at the Kingco Bar and Grill.

APA Cabin

To Aniakchak (ANIA)

Today, 17 June 1988, was the day we would fly to Aniakchak for the three-month or so season. We had our pile of gear stacked on the taxi ramp at the King Salmon Airport. Four months of supplies: the Zodiac (in two huge neoprene bags), two outboards, assorted radios, our food and personal items, and all of the research paraphernalia that David felt we needed to accomplish his wish list. Added to this were five 20-gallon cans of boat gas, ten gallons of kerosene for the "Kerosun Heater," two gallons of white gas for our cook stove and lanterns, and finally three sheets of 1/2-inch plywood for a new outhouse that David wanted built.

Early that morning we had gotten a call from the Pen Air office letting us know the Goose was in Anchorage for its 100-hour inspection required by the FAA, so we would be flying in the much smaller Wigeon. Okay, the four-foot sheets of plywood would fit in the Goose but not the Wigeon. I had to cut the plywood sheets into two-foot wide sections. We had planned on the Goose; the Wigeon would require two flights to get all of this "white-man baggage" that we were taking. Georgie would have a field day kidding us when he showed up. We busted our humps dividing the gear into two piles. Not just two piles but one pile that we would need right away and the other that we could get along without for a few days, should the second flight not be made today. Georgie missed his chance; Oren Seybert, the owner of Pen Air, flew in to get us and explained that Georgie was in Anchorage with the Goose.

As almost all Alaskan pilots do, Oren helped us load. He wanted to make sure the weight was properly distributed to balance the aircraft. Oren was satisfied and we piled in. It was Penny's turn to fly in the copilot's seat, so I sat behind Oren next to a window. We each had good views and Oren, unlike Joel, kept his eyes open across the peninsula, over the Aleutian Range, and down the coast to Aniakchak Bay. The sea was almost calm and we would be landing not long before high tide. On our approach we noted eagles by the river's mouth, flushed a sizable flock of pigeon guillemot, and saw two seals near a reef straight out from the cabin. Our wildlife counts had started and we hadn't even landed yet.

Oren knew where the reef was and stayed to the right of it, landed the amphibious Wigeon with a splash, taxied toward the beach, put the wheels down, gunned the engines, and roared up onto the beach. The three of us unloaded more quickly than we had loaded, piled everything on the beach, and Oren was gone before the tide changed. He let us know he wouldn't be back today, the tide was nearly full and would be falling before he could load and get back. He promised, weather permitting, he would be back tomorrow before high tide with the rest of our gear. You don't put an amphibious aircraft on a beach during a falling tide. You might not get it off until you have another rising tide to help float the plane off the sand.

We looked around. We were alone in the wilderness—where we belonged! It was a nice day. It wasn't raining and the clouds were at about 10,000 feet. An otter sat on a rock eating a fish and watching us; our first sighting of a sea otter. We could see a pair of bald eagles fishing by the river's mouth and some ducks near the island. We could watch for hours, but we had better get to work carrying the gear up to the cabin. We could identify the ducks another time.

We got all of our "stuff" into the cabin, found a pair of metal card-table chairs and a card table that would do for the office. We had a roll-up camping table to use for meals and evening cards. We set up a ladder made of two-by-fours, checked out the loft, and carried our Thinsolite pads and sleeping bags up to our elegant bedroom. The floor of the loft/bedroom was two 4- by 8-foot sheets of 1/2-inch plywood laid on the open ceiling joists of that huge room. Over our heads were the rafters and sheet metal roof with many bullet holes. Penny suggested we could watch the stars at night. I suggested we tape the holes to keep the promised rain out.

It had been a full day. Penny had packed sandwiches for dinner. We took the sandwiches, a box of wine, our Sierra Club cups, and binoculars out to the deck for our evening repast and to see where we were. Behind the cabin a steep rise of a couple hundred feet leads to a basaltic bluff that goes to the left (west) as far as the river and to the right all the way to Amber Bay and beyond, including the cape separating Amber and Aniakchak Bays. A few miles south Cape Kumlik juts out into the Pacific Ocean.

Dinner was marvelous, a meatloaf sandwich, half an apple, and a cup of "fine" red box-wine. With our binoculars we checked everything we could see from the deck and found our otter sitting on the same rock. Something wasn't right, sea otters (*Enydra lutris*) don't climb out on rocks to eat, they live almost exclusively in the sea and eat while floating on their back. Their diet in these waters would be sea urchin, clams, and other mollusks and echinoderms. In our excitement we had wanted to see animals we had never seen before so we jumped to the conclusion that we had a resident sea otter. That's okay, a resident river otter (*Lutra canadensis*) is fine too, and sea otters would come later. Otter's home had to be in the river, but his fishing grounds included the bay near the river's mouth.

About that time the ugliest red fox (*Vulpes vulpes*) either of us had ever seen walked along the beach a few yards away. He was shedding his winter coat and had tufts of hair hanging like big, dark cotton balls from his side and belly. He looked at us and yipped, both of us yipped right back. He sat down and gave us a curious look, walked towards us, lifted his leg and peed on a log at the edge of the beach, moved a few yards and peed again. Was he marking his territory? We thought so. I decided I should mark our territory too. Somehow I didn't have the bladder control that the fox had. He could pee just a squirt a lot of times—an ability that Penny suggested I work on. It proved to be interesting though, every time Foxy came by he would sniff every spot that I had marked, lift his leg, mark the same spot, move on and mark every place that I had marked. He never crossed into our marked territory. We, however, crossed into his every day.

A few days later a bear wandering down to the beach from above the cabin was seeming to stop and pee every little bit. Was he marking territory the same way? I had better try to mark our territory all the way around that big old building. Now that was going to take a lot of urine from me; I would need to recycle more beer than we had. Hmm, not a practical solution, so I marked near the porch and down to the beach to see if our marked territory would be respected. I kept it marked as well as I could, which wasn't very well. Foxy never crossed our boundary. Bears crossed into our marked territory several times over the season. Penny was fascinated with the project but wasn't willing to be a participant, beyond observing.

Which brings up the outhouse and its repair or replacement. It occurred to us that we could solve the toilet problem by not using the outhouse. We would use one of the three-gallon buckets the boat gear had been packed in as a toilet. It worked fine! Put a little sea water in the bucket, use it for a toilet, put the lid on, and once a day take it to the beach and bury the contents in a hole in the sand in the intertidal zone. Mother nature would recycle our excrement and provide nutrients to sea-life. We requested a toilet seat, and to our surprise, one was sent down in a few weeks.

The morning of our first full day at ANIA we awoke to wind, a gentle rain, and a pleasant morning to get the cabin organized. "Let's have breakfast first," Penny suggested. Oatmeal with raisins had been our standard breakfast for years and sounded good to me. It only took a minute to realize that none of our silverware had made it on yesterday's flight. "Just adjust" has always been a standard phrase for us; OK, adjust! We both carried Swiss army knives with us as a standard part of our dress, so we walked to the beach, found a couple of pieces of drift wood the right size and carved ourselves spoons that would work fine for breakfast, and lunch too if we decided to have Ramen with our Pilot Biscuit and peanut butter. If we were going to have peanut butter we would need to get it out of the jar, we better carve a knife too. If the rest of our stuff didn't show up today, we would "adjust" some more.

Meanwhile let's clean the place and decide where to put things to make it a comfortable, functional home. We had plenty of space; no problem there. The building was in the shape of an "L." One window faced the beach, the another was around the corner of the L and looked along the the wall with the first window in it. In front of the windows would give the best light and be a good place for the tables. There was a counter to the right of one window that we would use for our kitchen. So the dining room would be next to the kitchen and consist of the camp table we had found in the King Salmon warehouse and the two folding chairs that had been left here. The card table that had been here would sit in front of the other window and be our desk—chairs we would have to move back and forth. We put spare boat cushions on the chairs to keep our butts off the cold, rusty steel seats. The Kerosun heater would be at the center of wherever we were spending our indoor time.

While we were sweeping and cleaning we noticed a distinct odour de feces in one corner. We had company! A pair of porcupines (*Erethizon dorsatum*) had established residency under the floor. Not only did they stink but, in July, every night for a week or ten days we listened to the wild sounds of porcupine courtship and mating—grunting, singing, growling, wrestling. It didn't sound very sexy to me. Our evenings entertainment did get old by the time we were ready to sleep. Mating must have been consummated because the sounds did quit eventually, but the aroma continued; just adjust! We got used to it after a few weeks; interesting how human senses eventually ignore continuing stimuli.

We opened up and cleaned debris out of the little stream that ran beside the cabin. It proved to be the best source of drinking water we ever had in Alaska. It also became our refrigerator. We sat a 20-gallon steel drum, that had a bear-proof lid, in the stream and put everything that needed to be kept cool inside. It worked great. We kept a red cabbage wrapped in several layers of newspaper for six weeks.

We tried to quit working for the government by 1800 hrs., have dinner, and take a relaxing beach walk. We told ourselves we would just enjoy our evenings, we wouldn't even collect data on plants and animals. Of course, evening proved to be an excellent time to observe wildlife, and a beach walk a chance to see animal tracks, what was blooming, and what sorts of flotsam and jetsam had washed up. When we got back to the cabin we couldn't resist recording everything we had seen.

The evening of our first full day we stood on our front deck and heard a golden-crowned sparrow and a savannah sparrow singing, they seemed to be trying to out-sing each other—music for our ears. Fireweed and cow parsnip were in bloom all over our front yard. We noted the two huge eagle nests in the cliffs near the river's mouth and a smaller nest on the island, which was being worked on by a pair of rough-legged hawks—a pretty nice welcome. We walked along the path through tall beach grass to the beach, turned left and walked most of a mile to where the beach peters out and more basaltic cliffs curve out to the cape. Looking up at the cap rock we could see a different texture. It didn't look like basalt, we could see striations in it like it was sedimentary. We would check that out another time.

There were lots of sizable drift wood logs all along the beach, but not a tree growing anywhere. We were beyond the tree-line. The weather here was extreme enough that trees couldn't survive the cold and strong winter winds. All of the logs piled at the high tide line had been carried here from across the Gulf of Alaska by winds and currents. We sat down on a three foot thick log to watch and listen. A hermit thrush sang from the bushes behind us, a king fisher flew by with a fish in its mouth, foxy yipped and made us wonder if he could have a den in the rocks. Penny pointed out a beautiful dark burgundy chocolate lily, she leaned down to smell it and remembered why it is also called "skunk lily." As we walked back toward the cabin we saw a pair of sand-hill cranes circling above the river. A colony of bank swallows were working on nests near the top of the cliff, there were pigeon guillemot and red-breasted mergansers on the water. Hundreds of gulls were feeding on what must have been a school of small fish in the bay. A pair of semi-palmated plover were scurrying along feeding at the water's edge as a wave receded. They were probably feeding on tiny arthropods and insect larvae that were feeding on microscopic critters, perhaps protozoans, in the sea water. Oh, my God, did we have a lot to see, learn, and report. These are the sights, sounds and experiences that make us love this life. The challenge had begun.

THE STORM

David had given us specific instructions to check in by radio every morning at 1000 hours, so setting up the radio had to be done right away. The VHF radio had a long antenna that had to be strung from the end of the building to a tall pole supported by a pair of guy-wires and staked down. We wondered who would run into the system first, so we tied some red flagging to the pole and support wires, hoping to warn the bears and caribou about the new obstructions. We also wondered how good our radio contact with King Salmon would be. It had been poor when we were at Nonvianuk and this was several times as far and across the Aleutian Range of mountains. As it turned out radio contact was terrible and not something we could count on. It was not unusual to go five days without radio contact with the office.

Having a functional base was primary in having a successful season. After creating living quarters was accomplished, getting the Zodiac ready was our next priority. There was no safe spot anywhere in Aniakchak Bay to moor the boat. It was wide open to any storm. The river would have been ideal, but the bank of the river on our side was a 50-foot high basaltic cliff. There was a good anchorage across the river, but of course we couldn't get there without the boat. We had been supplied with the mooring system that other people had used. It consisted of a pair of concrete-filled #10 cans with an eye bolt protruding from the top. The cans were to be buried in the sand ten feet apart and well below high tide line. A ten foot line connected the two cans. A 20-foot line with a mooring buoy was to be attached to the eye of the near-shore can. We were to tie our bow line to the buoy and consider our boat anchored.

I didn't like that way of anchoring our 16-foot Zodiac but couldn't come up with an acceptable solution, so we would use the "tried and true" method of others. I questioned that it would hold in a storm, but David said it had held while he was there. Lynn had told us she and George had used that same system without a problem.

There was a 12-to-15-foot (vertical) tide and at least 200 yards of exposed sand at low tide, so not to worry, sort of in the middle of the tidal zone would give us access and as much protection as anywhere. We each had chest waders that came up nearly to our armpits; we wouldn't be able to reach the boat when it was in more than four feet of water, and it would go dry before low tide. We would have to go out and return when the mooring spot was in more then one foot, but less than four feet of water. That didn't give us much of an operating window unless we stayed out a full tide cycle. We wouldn't be able to do a lot of boating with those restrictions and we felt a major part of our assignment should be done from the boat.

On a low tide we dug holes in the sand and buried those two #10 cans in line with the prevailing wave direction. We attached the lines and mooring buoy and were ready to put the boat together. Assembling a Zodiac is not a problem if you do it right, follow steps 1, 2, 3, 4, & 5. If you do 1, 2, 4, 3, 5 you might as well start over. We had used a much smaller Zodiac at Nonvianuk. This was a 16-footer and twice as heavy as the 12-footer had been. We decided to put it together in the intertidal zone next to the mooring buoy and let the tide float it rather than us trying to drag it into the water. It all went smoothly, almost like we knew what we were doing. We mounted the two outboards, loaded the gas tank, connected the gas line, and waited for the tide to launch her. Penny, of course, christened her "Starr Ship II," but we seemed to refer to her as "the boat."

We had seen some salmon jumping and thought there would be

a commercial opening soon, which meant there would be trawlers for us to check on. Salmon spend several years at sea growing and maturing. When they reach maturity they recognize the urge to mate and head for to the stream where they hatched. They collect by the thousands along the coast, migrating to their natal stream. This is the time when they are subject to commercial harvest. The timing of legal harvest is controlled by the Alaska Department of Fish and Game and known as an "Opening." Openings can be of most any length from a few hours to several days, depending on the strength of the salmon run, and can be called with little notice. We would need to find a way to know when there would be an opening. We hoped the Park Service office would keep us informed, but doubted we would get up-to-date information.

We wanted to be comfortable with the boat and the waters of the bay before that happened. As soon as the water got deep enough to put the Evinrude-30 down, we climbed in, fired her up, and went exploring. Penny said, "Let's check out the cape by Amber Bay first." I turned left and twisted the throttle. The boat jumped up on-step, and we were off, planing across the calm bay. That end of the bay was not far off and we could see a kelp forest with lots of tan balls floating in it. I slowed down and drifted closer. The brown balls turned out to be a raft of female sea otters loafing on the surface. With our binoculars we could make out several pups resting on their mothers' chest. Now we really did have sea otters to add to our mammals list.

The giant kelp, a form of brown macro-algae, creates shelter for the otters and is food for sea urchins. The otters eat the sea urchin and keep the system in balance. When hunters over-harvested the sea otters, from the late 1700s to the early 1900s, the urchin population exploded and nearly destroyed the kelp forests which serve as break-waters for bays all over the northern Pacific, from California around the Gulf of Alaska and down the Aleutian chain.

The sea otters weigh 20 to 40 pounds making them the largest member of the weasel family and the smallest marine mammal. All other marine mammals have a thick layer of fat insulating them from the cold. Sea otters, like the rest of the weasel family, have a thin layer of fat and depend on the densest fur of any mammal to keep warm. They can, and do, walk on land but spend nearly all of their time in the ocean. After all, that's where their food supply is; the sea urchin, an echinoderm (urchin and sand dollars); mollusks (squid and snails); and crustaceans (crabs, shrimp, and barnacles). Sea otters are one of only a few animals that use tools. They lay a rock on their chest and pound the sea urchin against it breaking them open, then pull the animal out of its shell with their front teeth. Babies are born in the water most any time of year and weigh three to five pounds. The newborn's fur is so fluffy that they float like a cork and can't dive, which allows mom to go fishing for a few minutes with the pup safely floating wrapped in a kelp frond.

We could watch these guys for hours and would over the season, but we needed to get a better feel for the boat and check the rest of the bay. Between our mooring and the river's mouth are those basaltic dikes that lead out to the island with at least one other dike between us and the island-dike. When they were exposed there were always waves breaking on them; they would destroy an outboard and tear the bottom out of the Zodiac if we hit one. Something to stay well away from until we were sure just where they were.

That reef system formed by the dikes provided good shelter for lots of glaucous-winged and mew gulls, red-breasted mergansers, and those pigeon guillemot we had seen when we landed the other day. A bald eagle, near the island, was being attacked by the two rough-legged hawks who had a nest on the island, and were probably afraid the eagle would take their chicks. The big hawks are distinctly white and dark with a dark belly and wrists, white wings and tail, except for the striking and definitive dark tip to the tail feathers. They kept diving at the eagle until the eagle rolled onto its back with those huge talons pointed straight up and nearly caught a hawk as one of them flashed by.

A pair of harbor seals were watching us as we rounded the island at the river's mouth. I stopped and we sat watching them watch us—that old game of "watchin' you watchin' me." The current and tides form a long sand spit, almost a barrier island, just across the Aniakchak River. We could see something big on the spit, "Lets check that out!" we said in unison.

As we got close Penny yelled, "Oh, my God, it's a whale!" We were on a high slack tide, neither rising nor falling, so I just nosed the boat up on the sand and threw the anchor onto the beach. As we piled out to examine this creature we noticed lots of bear, eagle, and raven tracks in the sand all around the thing. It had attracted lots of scavengers looking for a meal, but it appeared to be almost intact. We were surprised that it was not torn apart until we got a whiff of it. It smelled worse than rotten garbage. It made the porcupine stink seem almost pleasant. It had certainly been dead for a good while and probably washed up here in a storm long after it had died. The whale was light brown, (probably bleached) 25 or so feet long with a small dorsal fin which made it a minke whale, the smallest of the baleen whales. A pretty exciting find and one that we would love to know more about, but it smelled so bad that we weren't about to examine it closely.

We had explored too long and missed the tide! Our mooring would be in 10 or 15 feet of water—not a good place to step out of a boat. We would have to stay out until the tide dropped to less than four feet, the deepest we could go in our chest waders without filling them with cold, salty water.

"Let's check the river," I said. "It should be deep now and we can get pretty far up."

Penny's turn, "Okay, but we have to pay attention to the tide. We sure don't want to get stuck up river in a low tide."

The lower Aniakchak River runs across several miles of flat

boggy terrain covered with willow, rye grass, and cotton grass. It was ideal moose habitat, and apparently good caribou (*Rangifer tardandus*) habitat too, there was a bull and a yearling feeding on new buds. We slowly motored up stream until my navigator suggested that was far enough. "We don't want to get stuck when the tide gets low," she reminded me.

We turned and headed down stream. With the motor running only fast enough to keep the boat steerable we were quiet and didn't disturb the local residents. A string of mergansers, momma followed by 12 chicks, held against the left bank and watched us drift by. A kingfisher flew right over our heads with a fish in its mouth, probably going to feed the nestlings. A cow moose and calf walked across the river like they were walking across the tundra. Those long legs are wonderfully evolved for moving through forest, thicket, and water much more easily than we could. There were tracks of a sow and two cubs-of-the-year on the left shore heading down river. A golden-crowned sparrow was singing from the top of a willow, a fox sparrow from another. Near the river's mouth there was a pair of red-throated loons—the first time either of us had ever seen red-throated loons. A busy place, this river.

The tide was dropping. We should be able to tie to the buoy and step into a water depth our waders could handle. "Let's call it a day," Penny said. That was fine with me. We saw a few salmon jumping as we rounded the island, reminding us we might expect a commercial opening in a few days.

As we walked up the beach Penny looked so happy, I had to ask, "What are you so happy about?"

Her smile grew and she said, "I just am! This is so wonderful, the two of us all alone in the natural world, counting on each other and no one else." It had been an idyllic day. It was 21 June, the summer solstice, and our un-anniversary. We had been married 32-1/2 years ago on the winter solstice. That evening we sat on the deck with a cup of wine, and celebrated our good fortune in having found each other. I put a Willie Nelson tape in our little radio/tape player and we danced to "Stardust" as we watched the moon come up over the Pacific Ocean.

The next morning the wind was blowing hard from the north. The waves were big and getting bigger, as usual they were from the southeast and were breaking several deep along the beach. The boat was taking a terrible beating, waves pushing it one way and wind pushing it another way. The wind was so strong that it was hard to stand on our deck. We made our way down to the beach and nearly got knocked down by the wind.

As we watched, waves were braking onto the boat filling her with water. There was nothing we could do with her in deep water except watch. As the tide ebbed she hit bottom with each wave trough. That looked like it would quickly destroy her. Losing the boat would be a real disaster.

We had to try to rescue her. We got dressed in chest-waders and as soon as the tide was out far enough we waded out. A wave caught us and nearly dunked us. I held Penny's arm and she held mine. We had to save the boat, but we had to save ourselves too. We clung to each other and reached the windward side of the boat and hung onto it. By pulling on the bow line I moved us seaward until I could reach the buoy and untie the line. Now to pull the boat to shore against the wind one way, the waves another. We were nearly to shore when I slipped and went down on one knee, Penny tried to help me up, but we had to hold onto the boat's painter. In the process we both took sand and water into our waders. About the same time a wave broke over the boat's stern and dumped several inches of sand into her; that was as far as we could move her. I thought, "Damn it! We should have left her alone, she probably would have been alright. Now we have to take it all apart clean out the sand and reassemble before the tide comes back."

We stripped off our waders, dumped them out, and put them right back on. We needed their protection since we would be on our knees getting the sand and water out of the boat. We pulled the gas tank and the outboards, wrapped them in tarps, and stashed them in the grasses well above high tide. The wind was nasty but it wasn't raining. We had several hundred pounds of sand and a lot of water to get rid of and only a few hours to do it. I dug down to the drain plug in the transom and pulled it, that let most of the water and some of the sand escape. We had a shovel but didn't dare use a sharp object inside the boat, so Penny went to the cabin for a couple of pots to scoop and dig with. We dug down to the floor boards, pulled them out, and kept scooping until we had her as clean as we could get her. Now we needed to rinse out the last of the sand, but the sea water was too turbid to use. Enough already! She would be safe if we drug her above the high tide line. We were exhausted, and the tide was coming. Maybe tomorrow would give us calm and clean water to rinse her with, and time to do it right.

We went to inspect the mooring, and sure enough one of the cans had pulled. Had the second pulled before we moved the boat there is no telling where she might have ended up, on one of the reefs probably, and our season would have been ruined.

That evening we decided we would have to move the moorage to the other end of the bay where the kelp forest would provide some protection. I devised a mooring system in the form of a triangle with the apex on the beach and the base as deep as we could get it. It would require: one iron stake, two 25-pound Danforth anchors with 20 feet of chain on each anchor, two mooring buoys, and at least 600 feet of 3/8-inch braided nylon line. The anchors would form the base in deep water, and be set 100 feet apart with mooring buoys attached by 20 feet of line to the end of the anchor chains. The 600 feet of line would complete the triangle with the two anchor buoys as the base and the stake near high tide line as the apex. We would attach a carabiner to the line between the shore and the right-hand buoy, tie boat's bow line to the carabiner; pull on the left line and boat would move out to the right buoy; pull the right line and the boat comes in to us in shallow water.

The next morning we radioed headquarters but couldn't reach them. We tried several times during the day but never did make contact. The following day we had the same results. We wondered what would have happened if we had a real emergency! Finally we had good radio contact with David. We explained what had happened in the storm and our proposed solution. He would need to think about it, run it by Superintendent Ray Bane, and get back to us. David reached us the next day and gave us the OK. It was a couple of hundred dollars of unexpected expense, but he and Ray couldn't think of a viable alternative. The requested equipment would be flown to us in a few days. Meanwhile we had lots of other projects to get started.

Rocks, Plants, Critters, and Fish

We had a couple of days before the new mooring system would be sent down. That gave us the opportunity to work on the herbarium and the small mammal trapping projects. We were both excited to get up on the plateau and see what it was like and what lived there. It would also give us access to the sedimentary deposits forming the upper layers of the cliff of the northeast wall of Aniakchak Bay.

Basalt not only forms the dikes and island out from the cabin, it also forms the wall behind the cabin and a major part of the cape separating Aniakchak and Amber Bays. We could see the basalt dipping to the northeast and an increasing layer of what looked like sandstone forming the upper section of the cliff. The surface of the plateau looked as flat as could be. It all said: ancient lava flow, followed by marine and/or beach deposit, uplift, and erosion. I said, "Let's climb up there and see what we can find."

"OK," Penny agreed, and said, "We can collect some plants at the same time."

Penny packed sandwiches, I filtered a quart of creek water, put the sandwiches, water, camera, binoculars, plant book, and a few plastic bags for collecting plant specimens in our daypacks and we were off.

We climbed up the steeply sloping basalt cliff behind the cabin to the top. A little farther east the basalt turned to vertical cliff and offered no access to the plateau. In a crack in the columnar basalt there was a very small plant with an upright bright blue bell sticking straight up, David's plant book told us it was a mountain hairbell. We climbed on and in a place that had collected a little soil we found a moss-like clump of moss campion, a lovely little flower with small pink blossoms and the wonderful aroma of lilac. Several species of crustose lichen—red, black, orange, and green— were scattered across the face of the basalt.

On top we could look for miles. There was nothing growing taller than our knees anywhere. We sure wouldn't surprise a bear up there! It was a habitat of moist tundra—mosses, lichen, fireweed, lovely low purplish-blooming Kamchatka rhododendron, dwarf willow, horsetail, blueberry, bearberry, nagoonberry (a low pink strawberry-like blossomed plant that, in a couple of months, would produce delicious berries), and a fleshy blue-green plant with a tight cluster of small dark reddish blossoms known as roseroot. The roseroot gets its name from the smell of the root, it does smell like a rose when cut—the way roses smelled before all of the genetic modifications removed the "rose smell." The young roseroot plant is quite edible, and was eaten by the Aleuts either raw or cooked. We tried it raw and decided we could get along without it.

Several hundred yards away a small herd of caribou stood warily watching us. They were mostly cows with young, along with several yearlings, and a few immature bulls. For a moment we were surprised that they seemed so concerned about our presence, then we remembered we were in a preserve where they are hunted and not in the monument where they are protected. We had seen a single caribou on the beach frequently, usually a young bull, perhaps looking for a mate, but this was our first herd. Being hunted would also account for seeing bear tracks on the beach in the mornings but rarely seeing a bear making those tracks. A few days ago we had seen both caribou and bear within a few seconds. A young caribou was trotting down the beach and a little way behind was a young bear loping after it. Every time the bear got close the caribou would sprint away, slow down, and look back. The bear was keeping up but not getting too close. We decided the two of them were playing; figuring out the game of life, herbivore and carnivore.

We had collected numerous plants for our herbarium and Penny wanted to get them in the plant press before they wilted. Since we had made our way to the top of the plateau, I suggested we follow a quite visible game trail along the cliff top to the far end of the bay and check the geology of the cliff. We could see the dip of the dark basalt along the northeast wall with lighter sedimentary, probably sandstone, above. I suggested we put the plant specimens in a plastic bag with water and stash them until we got back. Penny thought that should work but suggested, "Lets have lunch before we hike clear out there."

I never seem to feel hungry, but get grouchy if I don't eat. So I chuckled and said, "Yes Mam, good idea."

The sedimentary deposit was, as we expected, sandstone that appeared to be beach deposits, thick layers, thin layers, some that looked wind blown, and one spot where we saw what looked like wave ripples on a stream bed.

Back at the APA cabin late that afternoon, we were relaxing on the deck identifying the plant specimens we had brought back, when we heard a plane and saw a blue Beaver with white trim landing at the far east end of the bay. It appeared to drop a person off, and was gone in just a few minutes. We were pretty sure it was a state trooper plane, and wondered if they were dropping a trooper for a stakeout. We walked down to find out who was in our bay and what they were up to.

Trooper Bob Mumford was amazed to find out that he wasn't alone and thrilled to be invited up to the cabin for a beer and spaghetti. He thought Penny's dinner sounded much better than the Ramen he had brought and the beer might be better than the creek water he would have. We let him know we limited ourselves to one beer to conserve our supply. There was plenty of creek water that we ran through a Swedish Katadine filter to have with dinner.

Bob had a suggestion! If we were willing, he would convince his boss to use us as the state stakeout. They would bring us a radio tuned to the trooper frequency so we could check in regularly. We should have good radio contact with their base on Kodiak Island and could keep them up to date on commercial fishing in this area. He would see that we were informed of commercial salmon openings at the same time the fishermen were. That sounded good to us. We could help them and they could help us by providing dependable radio contact we could count on in case of an emergency. At dinner Penny decided we could celebrate a bit and opened a box of red wine. We talked through Bob's idea, became real friends, agreed that the state and feds should cooperate more, and had solved most of the world's problems before the wine ran out.

The next morning we surprisingly reached headquarters and let David know about Bob's plan for us to be stakeouts for the state. He told us he would run it by the superintendent, and the superintendent would have to run it by the Alaska Regional office, but it sounded like a good plan to him.

We all decided the chain of command is just bureaucratic bullshit! We agreed with Bob and if it flew with the troopers we would be more than happy to be eyes and ears for them—the Park Service didn't even have to know about it. I don't think it was two days after Bob left when he flew back in with a radio and all the information on commercial fishing we would need. They would listen for us at a specific time, but we should call them any time we had information we felt was pertinent. Bob also brought us some goodies, a jar of peanut butter and a carton of strawberries. We did get the OK from David eventually.

Our small mammal observations had started a week earlier when one morning, very early, we were awakened by the sound of something running across the floor below us. We peered down between the ceiling joists and watched a beautiful brown and white weasel running across the floor, jumping high against the wall, doing a back flip, landing on its feet, and repeating the trick over and over. He was about 15 inches long with small dark eyes, a black nose, and a black tip on his tail, which made him a short tailed weasel or ermine (*Mustela erminea*). In winter he sheds his summer coat and becomes completely white, except for his nose and the black tip on his tail.

He was instantly christened "Ernie the Ermine." He visited us so often we considered him our house pet. He did his back flip game every few days; it must have just been fun. He got almost too friendly on occasion. Once while Penny was cooking she felt something pulling on her pants leg, she looked down and here came Ernie climbing up to see what Penny was fixing for dinner.

David had included ten small mammal traps in our gear. They were metal cones ten inches long with a five-inch diameter opening. We were to dig pits along the mouse trails through the grasses, set a cone in the pit flush with the ground, and check them an hour or so later to see who had fallen in. We were to identify, weigh, and measure each critter, then release it unharmed. We tried to explain to the critters that we would let them go. They didn't seem to under-stand that they needed to hold still as we weighed and measured them. The little bastards squirmed, bit, and didn't cooperate at all with our scientific research project.

We would pull a trap, I would pick up the critter in my leather gloved hand, hold it firmly enough that Penny could, sort of, mea-sure how many millimeters it was from nose to tail, then how long the tail was. We were supposed to measure the hind foot, but that didn't work very well since they weren't willing to hold still. We had a scale like a hand-held postal scale, I would attach a clip to the back of the critter's neck, let it hang and see how many grams the jumping scale indicated. We had forms that Penny filled out for each of them. Then I would cut off the outer right hind toe with fingernail clippers, so we could tell if it was a recapture, and release the poor little bastard.

Most of the little critters were voles; tundra vole (*Zapus hudsonicus*), meadow voles (*Microtus pennsylvanicus*), and the ubiquitous red-backed vole (*Myodes rutilus*). They all had four front toes and five hind toes, one incisor tooth, and three molars in each quadrant of their mouth. The only ones we really got to examine in detail were the few unfortunate enough to die under our care. That did make us feel bad but helped our research—unmoving animals are much easier to weigh and measure than squirming, biting ones.

Give us a break; all of these statistics need to be considered as plus or minus 10%. The tundra voles were 18 cm. long including a 4 cm tail and weighed 50 grams. The fur is dark on the back, sides are yellowish, with a light-tan belly; the ears are set deep in the fur and not very conspicuous, the upper incisors have a distinct groove running down the facial surface. The meadow vole is more chunky at 15 cm. and 60 g. with dark brown fur and a grey belly. The red-backed voles were by far the most common—we had met them all over Alaska. They are smaller and more slender at 14 cm. with a short tail and weighed 30 to 40 g., with a rusty brown back and lighter brown sides. All of the voles eat seeds and berries, store food for winter, and would gladly share our beans and pasta if we didn't protect them. They had to have different niches, which we couldn't perceive, or they couldn't have occupied the same habitat. That was something we would try to figure out.

The Arctic shrew (Sorex arcticus) is a handsome little critter, chocolate brown on the back, with lighter sides, and a cream or nearly white belly. They are 10 cm long, with the 4-cm tail making up nearly half the total length. They only weighed about 10 g (less than half an ounce). The teeth fascinated us—they have 32 just like us—the first thing we noticed was the teeth looked like they had been painted with gentian violet—that purple stain often used in preparing microscopic slides. The central incisors, both upper and lower, are greatly enlarged giving the shrews serious weapons for grasping the insects and small mammals that they consume voraciously. They seemed hyperactive, their metabolic rate is so high they must eat almost constantly. We couldn't leave one in a trap very long or it would starve unless a vole fell in and became the main course of the shrew dinner.

The voles made up the major portion of the diets of our carnivorous friends Foxy and Ernie, and the rough-legged hawks. Owls prey on them too, and are the only known predator of shrews. We have seen bears dig out vole nests, so the arctic carnivore population is deeply dependent on a healthy vole population.

One morning later in the season I had set out the traps and gone back in to join Penny for our morning oatmeal. Penny heard a funny sound outside, we went to the door and looked out to see a bear having his breakfast. He was actually pulling the occupied traps, tipping them up and pouring the trapped critters into his mouth. We couldn't believe it, and didn't think quickly enough to get a picture. The bear had run the trap line in about two minutes and was gone, leaving the traps scattered wherever he dropped them. The next day he was back checking traps, we realized we had better terminate the small mammal trapping or we would have a bear/human disagreement over the trap contents.

David reached us by radio and let us know that he and Superintendent Ray Bane would be flying down that afternoon with the mooring system we had designed. Great! We put the boat together, mounted the two outboards, and let the tide launch her again. The Evinrude worked fine but the kicker wouldn't fire at all. We would let David and Ray take it back to King Salmon that afternoon.

We had become friends with Ray and his wife, Barbara, during the two weeks we had spent in King Salmon before coming down to Aniakchak. So we were happy to see his Cessna circle us and land in the calm sea. Barbara had come along to see what this country and the Alaska Packer's Association building was like. It was a clear, warm day (in the mid 60s) and she saw it in its best light, but she was sharp enough to question us as to how we stayed warm on a stormy day. Penny laughed and told her "We don't. All we can do is huddle around the Kerosun heater in our full uniforms, long underwear, coats, fur trimmed down hats, and shiver."

We unloaded the anchors, chain, and line from the plane right into our boat, and as soon as the bosses were gone, we took it all to the far end of the bay. It went together just as we had designed it. Now we could anchor in much deeper water and pull the boat into shallow water where we could reach her. That would at least double the time we could have access to the boat. The sea otters' kelp beds proved to be a problem though. Every time we had a storm our lines got fouled with loose kelp. That simply meant we had to spend half a day clearing the lines of kelp.

We were back in the boating business before the first commercial salmon opening. It was good timing; there were several trawlers in the bay anticipating the salmon opening that would begin at 1800 that day. The term "trawler" can be a bit misleading in that these boats use purse seine nets for fishing rather than trawling with a long line. More technically: "A trawler is a boat with a displacement hull producing a low speed, high capacity, efficient long range vessel." We visited all of the boats, talked with their crew and skipper, and were invited aboard most of them. That proved to be a wonderful learning experience and a chance to create a whole set of new friends. They knew we represented the law and wanted us to understand the industry from their perspective. I am sure they knew our jurisdiction ended at the high tide line, but they didn't want to get cross-ways with us, just in case.

They showed us their boats, usually about 40 feet long, with the cabin forward, a flat deck aft, where the net is laid out, and a big hold in the center where the catch is dumped. The nets are as much as 1,200 feet long and 40 feet deep with a "cork line" along the top, which keeps it on the surface, and a "lead line" along the bottom that sinks, producing a vertical wall. A powerful skiff tows one end of the net out across the path of migrating salmon. As soon as they think they have a school of salmon trapped, the skiff loops back to the trawler. The lead line, which runs through a series of rings on the bottom, is pulled in closing the purse and preventing the fish from escaping out the bottom. A boom is swung out and, with a heavy duty block and tackle system, winches up many tons of fish, which are dumped into the hold, completing a "set."

Depending on the size and design of the trawler they could hold 50,000 to 100,000 pounds of fish, but couldn't keep them more than about 24 hours—preferably much less that that. It was a long expensive sail back to the cannery in Kodiak so most of these boats belonged to a cooperative with a processing ship in the area. When a trawler filled its hold it would head to the processor. Those ships had huge vacuum pumps with 10- or 12-inch diameter hoses, with which they suck up those thousands of pounds of salmon in a matter of minutes. Depending on the type of processor, the fish are iced for a short time and marketed as fresh, or dumped into a tank of extra salty water called brine, which freezes the fish quickly. The processors take their fish to canneries or transfer them to a factory ship for further processing.

We went aboard an anchored factory ship one day and couldn't find anyone for a few minutes. When a young man finally showed up he explained that the work is extremely hard for a few hours and then there is nothing to do until they get another load. This ship, he told us, could filet and freeze the fish or can them. He carefully let us know most of the crew were sleeping. He didn't seem to be drunk, but he must have been on some drug, he acted like a little kid caught with his hand in the cookie jar. We weren't offered a tour or to meet the captain, but he brought us two frozen rib steaks and a fifth of Scotch whisky that he insisted we take as a token of friendship. He probably was expecting us to arrest him and the whole crew for drug offenses and thought he was buying us off with his gifts. Had he known we were in state jurisdiction waters where we had no authority he might have treated us differently.

That evening we built a nice little beach fire behind some driftwood logs, sipped some Scotch, grilled our steaks over driftwood coals, and toasted naïveté—actually I had a little Scotch and we both had wine with the steaks since Penny doesn't like Scotch whisky or whiskey of any kind. (Scotch whisky is spelled without an "e," other whiskeys include the "e.") Our friend, Ernie the Ermine, showed up to join in our celebration and got to share in the spoils with a couple of scraps of steak.

Looking toward the Aleutian Range southwest of us that evening, we watched clouds performing differently than we had ever seen. A heavy bank of clouds was roiling over a mountain ridge and down a cliff face like an avalanche or waterfall in slow motion; we decided to call them Niagaras. We wondered if they portended an overnight storm and decided to not worry since there was nothing we could do about it. No storm occurred, but we had our first observation of a unique weather phenomenon that we would see a few more times in the future along the Pacific side of the Aleutians.

THE DEAD OUTBOARD

It wasn't more than a week after the state troopers had set us up to report incidents to them when we were on the deck early one morning and noticed a boat we weren't familiar with in the bay. They were pulling up a net full of fish. Nothing unusual about that except it was during a closure. An illegal set was happening and we were watching. With our spotting scope we were able to read the boat numbers prominently displayed on the side of the cabin, as is required of all commercial fishing boats. Using the long lens on our camera, we took several pictures of the incident as proof should it be needed. We had the identification number and photos of the incident, (showing date and time of exposure) all the proof necessary for an arrest. We radioed our trooper contact on Kodiak, notified them of the circumstances, and gave them the registration numbers and description of the boat. They told us they would act on the information and let us know the results.

Several days passed. We were wondering if the troopers had busted the boat on our information or if the boat had gotten away with an illegal set. That morning, before we went on patrol, we heard a plane coming in; it was the state's blue and white Beaver. Bob and his boss got off with huge grins. They told us the skipper of the boat had pleaded "No contest," and been fined $200,000. We thought "Oh, my God, that seems like one hell of a fine." The troopers told us that was pretty standard for fishing during a closure. They thanked us profusely, gave us some fresh vegetables, a six-pack of beer and were gone.

We had built a good relationship with most of the regular fishing crews in the area and were afraid they would be mad and shun us or even damage our boat for reporting the violation. To our amazement, every skipper we talked with thanked us. They said commercial fishing had to be controlled or the fish-stock would be depleted and they would all be out of work. One skipper said, "Those goddamn sons-a-bitches are out of Seattle and have been fishing closed all season. If you didn't catch them we would'a got 'em our selves." That made us feel good, and like we were doing what needed to be done.

Penny asked what they would have done. He said, "You don't want to know, it wouldn't have been legal."

By now the bald eagle chicks were either sitting on the edge of their nests begging for food or had fledged and were following their parents around begging for food. Eagles make the smallest, weakest, most plaintive call of any large bird, and the big fledglings were hilarious with their small begging chirps. All of the eagle nests in Aniakchak Bay, except one, had successfully raised a chick, and two nests had produced two young each. It had been a good year for our national bird here and we were having a ball watching the antics of the eaglets and fledglings as they harassed their parents for food.

We had been so busy with commercial fishing and our local eagles we had neglected what was happening next door in Amber Bay. There were several eagle nests over there that had had eaglets in them the last time we checked. We decided we had better go see how they were doing.

The next morning I was getting our gear ready for a full day in Amber, and Penny was taking the toilet to the beach to bury. While she was digging she caught a glimpse of movement at the mouth of our little creek. She held still watching as a short dark animal came onto the beach. Her first thought was a bear cub and momma would be close-by, but no, it was a wolverine (*Gulo gulo*) and only about 20 feet away. Penny and the wolverine looked at each other, both probably thinking, "I don't like this." The wolverine was between Penny and the shore so she just stood still watching. The wolverine watched a moment then turned, and quickly went back up the creek and out of sight. When Penny came into the cabin I could tell she was excited. Her eyes were wide and she was talking a mile a minute. It was Penny's first sighting of a wolverine—I had yet to see one in the wild—and it was probably the wolverine's first sighting of a human. No harm done this time, but men with traps wanted his hide.

The day had started with a bit of excitement and now we were off to check on our endangered bald eagles. In 1782 the bald eagle was adopted as the U.S. national emblem. It had been put on the federal endangered species list in 1967 and would be removed in 1995, but kept on the threatened list until 2007. Before Europeans began settling North America the bald eagle population was at least a half million, but as human population grew we usurped eagle habitat (along with the habitat of most other wild species) and their populations declined. Eagles and humans competed for the same foods, and humans with weapons at their disposal had the advantage. Westward expansion of the human population removed much of the natural river and lake-side habitat the eagles depended on. By the 1930s people were beginning to recognize the steep decline of bald eagles, and in 1940 the Bald Eagle Act was passed by Congress. That act greatly reduced the harassment and shooting of eagles which allowed them to begin to recover. But about that same time DDT was introduced to control insects. Small mammals and fish consumed the poisoned insects and became poisoned and poisonous themselves. Predators, including eagles, ate the poisoned fish and mammals and were poisoned too. The biggest blow to the eagles and other predatory birds, such as hawks and falcons, by DDT was the thinning of egg shells, which made them susceptible to being crushed by their incubating parents. The chicks that did hatch were weakened by the DDT resulting in a greatly reduced survival rate of the hatchlings.

Almost immediately after getting under way, we had stopped to watch sea otters loafing in their kelp bed and had drifted into the kelp with the motor idling. When we started up again I managed to wrap kelp around the prop and stall the motor. We tipped it up and cleared the kelp but the motor didn't want to restart. It had been smoking a bit since the big storm and had earned the name of "Old Smoke." However, a couple of extra pulls on the starter cord and we were off with no further problem.

As we were rounding the point separating Aniakchak Bay from Amber Bay, we were watching a pair of parasitic jaegers harassing a mixed flock of kittiwakes and glaucous-winged gulls that were feeding on a school of small fish. It seemed like every time a gull or kittiwake caught a fish, a jaeger would dive on it forcing it to drop the fish which the jaeger would then catch and eat. We had wondered about the name parasitic jaeger, but this explained it pretty clearly.

We had seen horned and tufted puffins numerous times, but they seemed especially plentiful today. They were probably collecting dinner for their chicks by diving on the same school of fish that was feeding the kittiwakes and jaegers. In a quiet little bay we watched Kittlitz's and ancient murrelets diving for invertebrates. The sun was shining brightly and we were enjoying near perfect weather with a fair breeze from the north. Our bird observations had been unusually good and now we were paralleling the south shore of Amber Bay looking for more interesting wildlife. A bear was walking the ridge above the beach cliff and seemed to be watching us as we happily motored along watching it.

A few minutes later Penny said, "The motor sounds funny!"

I said, "I know, and it's not pissing." Outboard motors have a water pump that pulls water in, pumps it through the motor maintaining a proper temperature, then expels a constant stream out the rear. Like a stream of urine, and often is referred to as "pissing." Without the cooling of that circulating water the motor will quickly over heat, seize up, and quit. That was happening to us right then. I shut the motor off and pulled the cover. It was too hot to touch.

"Damn! We're in trouble," I said, "This is exactly why we had insisted on a backup kicker." The kicker David had found for us had worked sporadically a few times in King Salmon before we left, but never ran after we had gotten to Aniakchak.

Penny wanted to know if it would start again when it cooled down. I let her know we would try. I was sure, in my own mind, that it would never run again. At the moment we had a more critical problem to deal with. The north wind was blowing us sideways and would soon have us out of the bay and into the open Pacific—next stop Japan! We have a saying between the two of us when dealing with wind in a small boat, "The wind wins!" We knew we had to win this one or we would be in real trouble. Time to paddle as hard as we could toward the shore and the brown bear. We thought he would be the kind of problem we could deal with much better than the open ocean. Somehow paddling a 16-foot Zodiac is not something the manufactures had in mind when they designed it. The 12-foot Zodiac we had on Nonvianuk had oars and could be rowed reasonably well. We both sat astride the bow tubes and paddled hard. We were winning but getting exhausted too.

When we finally reached shore the bear was watching from the top of the high bank. He must have had fun watching those two weird things come in without the roar of an outboard. He apparently got bored because he turned and walked away leaving us with one less problem to deal with.

Now to the boat. We tried to restart the outboard, but it was seized up. I couldn't even move the pull cord; it was completely frozen. We had no radio contact from our hand-held radios. Shit! We were stuck. The damn boat had to be moved above the high tide line, but it was too heavy to drag, so we loosened the outboard from the transom and wrestled that to what looked like a safe spot behind a big log. We removed the two gas tanks we always carried, our emergency kit, and personal gear, and pulled the floorboards Now the Zodiac was light enough that we could drag it up to where, unless there was a big storm, it would be safe—we hoped.

We had a tent and a two-day supply of dry food in our emergency kit, but didn't want to count on someone just happening by to rescue us. We had seen only one private boat all season and there wasn't going to be another commercial salmon opening for several days so there wouldn't be any fishing boats around. We had better start hiking back to the cabin, maybe only five miles, but maybe eight or ten, across the wet tundra. We were in baggy, chest high, canvas waders and would have to carry our heavy, bulky float-coats and the emergency pack. As I mentioned, it was one of those rare beautiful, sunny days with a moderate wind, perfect boating weather. The temperature might get to 70 or even a couple of degrees above—a really hot day on the Alaska Peninsula.

We couldn't walk the beach; cliffs came to the water's edge around most of the cape. We climbed the steep bluff and looked out across the wide open spaces of wet arctic tundra, nothing as high as our waist, and most of it lower than our knees. Penny said, "OK, where do we go from here?" Fortunately we had a topo map and a compass. We could locate our present position on the south shore of Amber Bay on the map, locate the cabin at the mouth of the Aniakchak River, get a bearing from point A to point B, and follow the compass home. All we had to do was follow the bearing of 205 degrees and we would be home, at least that's how I explained it.

We were already sweating in those waterproof waders, but we picked up our gear and started hiking. I had selected a mountain peak on Cape Kumlik on the far side of Aniakchak Bay to use as a straight line target; all we had to do was walk toward that peak and we should intersect the cabin.

It turned out to be a little more of a hike than just walking a straight line.

After only a couple of hundred yards we came across the bear that had watched us struggle with the boat. He was busy digging tubers and hardly paid us any attention. We made a considerable detour around him and got back on track, at least according to my calculations. We crossed a river, three other streams, and had several marshy-swampy muskeg areas to negotiate, either by wading across or making our way around them, which of course moved us off my original sighting line to the cabin—there was nothing distinct behind us that we could use as a back reference-site, just Amber Bay and more tundra. We were hot, sweating, drinking water, and looking for some shade to sit in and have the lunch Penny had so carefully packed for the day. We had those big floppy waders on and didn't need a dry spot to sit, so we just sat down on a soggy hummock and ate.

A few hours later Penny realized we were pushing too hard. We had gone through our two liters of water, weren't sure where we were, and were carrying too much—all of which we would need if we didn't find the cabin. Mosquitoes along the shore had been minimal to nonexistent. Up here in the wet tundra they were thick and voracious, and driving us, especially me, nuts. Penny said, "We had better rest long enough to quit sweating, fill our water bottles from that little creek, and get rid of the tension that I see building in both of us." We had a sack of gorp with oatmeal, raisins, M&Ms, and who knows what else, that we had been munching on so we sat, munched, and talked through our situation. All we could do was continue on our chosen route and hope we came out above the cabin.

We continued our bird observations noting sandhill cranes, a yellow warbler, a lesser yellow-legs and a least sandpiper. Penny noticed a bear a hundred yards away digging furiously. We stood and watched his progress. He was probably digging into a rock-squirrel burrow, throwing rocks and tundra plants all over. He stopped digging, raised his head chewing, and gulped; he had his prize. He looked toward us and went back to digging. OK, we had rested, we slathered on fresh DEET (diethyl-m-tolumide or jungle juice), watched Native residents earn their living, and gotten our minds off our predicament, time to "Head 'em up, move 'em out."

Following our target to the mountain peak for another hour or two we came to the escarpment. The sun had set and light was fading. We looked down and to our amazement there was the old Packer's cabin looking like the Taj Mahal only a stone's throw away at the bottom of the escarpment. Following the line-of-sight to the peak we had selected from the topo map had worked just as it should. I said, "If you can't be good, be lucky!"

Penny said, "That had nothing to do with luck; you figured out where the cabin was and took us there." She was amazed and I was impressed. We had come out exactly where I hoped we would when we selected the route from the map.

Back at the cabin, we put the emergency kit in a corner and kicked off those god-awful sweat-soaked waders and our sweat-soaked clothes. Each of us had a huge drink and a quick sponge bath in cold water. (Penny counted 27 mosquito bites just on my shoulder that had been out of the wind. They had been driving me nuts.) Penny opened a pack of Rye Crisps and a can of salty sardines. We had been close to suffering heat exhaustion from loss of body fluids and salts, the result of working too hard and long, and sweating too much without replacing the fluids and minerals. We sat on the deck for a bit watching darkness settle and thinking how fortunate we were to be experiencing the unique happenings we were facing every day. Then we climbed to our beds on the rafters and slept until nearly noon.

At headquarters, David answered our radio call that afternoon and promised to get a new motor to us ASAP. We fixed a special meal to celebrate being alive—scrambled eggs with extra salt and English muffins. Then spent the day doing nothing.

The next day David showed up with two outboards, the damned Merc 25 that we should have "deep-sixed" at Nonvianuk a couple of years ago and a 10-horse kicker. He had hired a commercial plane and pilot, Randy Arment, to bring him down since the park plane had been flipped a few days before and was in Anchorage for repairs. We quickly donned those damned waders, grabbed our float coats, climbed into Randy's plane, and were on the way. Five minutes later, rather than the eight hours our last trip between Amber Bay and home had taken, we were looking down on our Zodiac. It appeared to be fine. Randy landed; he and David helped us off-load the new outboards and load the dead one in his plane. They even helped us drag the boat to the water and waited while we installed the outboards and made sure they ran before leaving.

We headed home and then decided we might as well finish the patrol we had started several days ago. All of the Amber Bay eagle nests were vacant, but there were several fledglings still acting like they expected to be fed. We went up the larger of the two streams coming into the head of the bay, and made it to an old cabin we had seen from the air. White people must have lived there. It still had some furniture in it: a double bed and a couple of wooden chairs, along with some kitchen items. We couldn't imagine anyone spending a winter in it; you would have frozen. We were glad we had a nice home in Colorado for the winter and didn't have to spend it in a place like this.

The Aleuts built houses called barabaras; they were dug four or five feet into the ground and then roofed. We had located several barabara pits near the APA cabin that had been used during the early twentieth century. They provided year-round shelter from Aleutian weather. This old cabin wouldn't have given the residents adequate shelter any more than the APA cabin gave us. We had spent the summer freezing on stormy or even rainy days, really any day the sun didn't shine—highs were often in the 50s inside and out. The wind came through the walls, and the kerosene heater we had didn't heat beyond three feet. These people couldn't have been much warmer than we were, and they had apparently spent the winter here. "Save me!"

We had run up the river using the 10-horse kicker. Now we were ready to make the run around the cape and fired up the Merc. It ran for a while before it quit and wouldn't restart—here we go again! This time we had a backup, and the 10 kept running. It wasn't strong enough to get us on step but it did get us back to our anchorage in Aniakchak Bay. Dead outboards was getting old!

AN ALEUTIAN FALL

David had gotten another outboard to us within a few days of the Merc dying.

We were sure he had to be tired of our outboard problems, we sure were. Every one he had gotten for us was old but the best David could afford on his Aniakchak budget. This time he found some money somewhere because he sent us a brand new Yamaha 35, and we still had the small kicker which also ran without a problem. With the new outboard we felt like we had wings, we were cruising all over, talking with fishermen on their trawlers, observing birds and sea mammals, and gathering statistics on populations and uses of the Aniakchak Monument.

One day while the "Capt'n Sam" was offloading salmon to the "Melodie Dawn" we were invited aboard by "Capt'n Sam's" skipper, Mike Grunert. He felt like talking. He told us that Pinks were only bringing 47 cents a pound while reds and silvers were bringing nearly two dollars, so they were hand sorting the entire catch of many thousands of pounds of mixed salmon. Normally salmon run in schools of a single species, so this was an odd day for them. While his crew and the crew of the tender were working Mike had a story he wanted to share with us: His mother Viola Erikson had been born in one of the barabaras just above the APA cabin in the late teens or early 20s. Viola's father, Mike's grandfather, had spent winters trapping for furs—red fox, wolverine, river otter, and ermine—all along the coast and on the plateau above. Summers, he fished commercially and fed the family on fish, moose, and caribou. A simple and difficult, but wonderful life. Mike seemed to be thinking of all that his grandparents had missed, and considering all that he was missing with the modern life he was leading. We understood and appreciated his thoughts and memories, and thanked him for sharing.

We had spent time making in-depth observations of the large black-legged kittiwake colony on the steep basaltic cliffs of our little island. Last spring, before we had shown up at the preserve, several hundred of them—probably a thousand or more—had fought over nesting spots on the tiny ledges. There had been more birds than nesting spots, so some had to go somewhere else—or not nest. Our bird-book, *The Birders Handbook* by Erlich, Dobkin and Wheye, told us, the female kittiwake lays two eggs, the first is distinctly larger than the second and hatches sooner, producing a larger chick which is more aggressive, gets fed more, grows faster, and often forces the smaller chick from the nest—an act known as siblicide. Nature can be tough! But, every species produces more offspring than the habitat can support; the most fit fill the available niche-spaces and propagate the species.

The cape leading to Amber Bay consists of a layer of sandstone over the basalt with a layer of dirt and soil on top, which provided puffins a place to dig their burrows. Those burrows are dug horizontally, several feet into the ground on steep enough slopes so our fox friends couldn't reach them. Both Horned and Tufted Puffin are described as, stocky North Pacific species with a thick neck, large head, and massive bright orange and yellow colored bills. Puffin and kittiwake alike eat small fish and marine invertebrates that they collect by diving. Kittiwakes specialize in invertebrates. The puffin harvest mostly small fish. The gulls are omnivores, like us and bears, and will eat most anything they find on the surface.

A young Aleut couple in their small 32-foot Bristol Bay trawler had finished the salmon season in Bristol Bay and decided to come clear around Unimak Island, through the Unimak Pass, 300 miles south of us, and up here to fish for silver salmon. They had heard of Aniakchak National Monument and decided to see what it had to offer. We were glad to see them. They were the first and only actual visitors to Aniakchak National Preserve in 1988. We showed them the APA cabin, and the barabara pits above the cabin, and explained that the actual monument was the caldera in the center of the peninsula and could only be reached by air or a long difficult hike. The coastal area was a preserve and not appreciably different from the southeast coast of the rest of the Alaska Peninsula.

Fall came rather suddenly in mid-August. We awoke one morning to a storm that didn't seem willing to quit. Day after day of clouds, rain, and wind. We were freezing and couldn't seem to get warm other than in our sleeping bags. The Kerosun heater put out a good amount of heat which immediately rose to the roof without having an appreciable effect on the big room we were living in. The temperature inside remained the same as outside—in the low 40s.

Now the seas were too rough to get out much, the delicious nagoonberries and blueberries had been ripe in late July and early August, the brilliant scarlet fireweed had topped out and was now developing little cottony tufts of seeds which the wind was distributing. There wasn't much in bloom, and we were thinking it was high time to shut this operation down for the year.

Not quite yet. Fall hunting season had started and we noticed the skiff off one of the trawlers pull up to shore just across the river, and drop two men who quickly disappeared into the willows. An hour or so later we heard two rifle shots and guessed the men had gotten a moose or caribou. After another couple of hours a shot was fired from where the men had been dropped. Were they signaling to be picked up? We had better find out! We got there in our boat, before their skiff did, pulled into an eddy in the river, tied up, and hiked over. They had the four quarters of a caribou they had shot. No, they didn't have their hunting licenses with them, they had left them on the boat. We let them know we needed to see the licenses before they could take the meat.

They were off a boat we weren't familiar with, and we suspected if they got the meat to the boat they would just take off and we would end up running the trawler down to get its number. The seas were pretty rough and we would be putting ourselves in danger— not a pleasant chase to contemplate. Fortunately they cooperated, went to the trawler and returned with their licenses and caribou tag all in order. Another day of "fightin' crime."

Foxy was still barking to us every time he went past. He now had a beautiful winter coat of reddish fur including a big fluffy tail with a bright white flag on the tip. Something was different! When Foxy peed he squatted instead of lifting his leg—he was she! Ms Foxy was now walking the beach, she must have raised the pups to the age she was comfortable leaving them alone or with their dad. Ernie the ermine had brought his significant-other around too. Ernie and Ms. Ernie had been doing a duet of back flips around the room the other morning, and one of them had come up on our sleeping rafters and pulled on my pajama-shirt collar as if telling me it was time to get up.

I haven't mentioned mosquitoes much because the wind down here, with no trees to break it, was strong enough and constant enough that we rarely had mosquitoes. Every once in a while we had black flies taking a chunk out of our neck, but the most disconcerting insects were the small gray-brown moths and the big blue-tailed flies. Neither of them bit nor seemed to bother our food, but they had been with us all season flying in our face, buzzing around the stove and lantern, leaving their corpses everywhere. They were just plain aggravating. The inside of the cabin apparently provided shelter from predators and some warmth.

Either the moths or the blue-tailed flies, or perhaps both, had been laying eggs all over the windows all season. We never did figure out why they laid eggs on the plexiglas window, but we had to wash them with clorox every week or two to get rid of the thousands of tiny eggs. The moths spent the days hiding. In the early morning and evening light hours they were on the windows where it was light outside. The darker hours they spent flying around the Coleman lantern, driving us to distraction. During the summer the blue-tailed flies weren't around much during the day, but neither were we. Now they were trying to get warm and the warmest place every morning was on the bottom of the boards that our sleeping bags were spread on. We could look over a rafter and see the under side of our bed was covered with hundreds, or thousands, of those damned flies. When we got up the warmth went with us, and the flies would start flying around looking for another warm spot.

The hours of light were diminishing fast, especially in the evening. We were losing several minutes of light a day. It was dark at the time we were accustomed to still being on patrol.

All season we had tried to hear news on the local radio station out of Dillingham. That station rarely gave national or international news, but once we heard the DOW had fallen below 2,000 for the first time in three months. This station was the only communication system available to bush residents, who were mostly Native and people like us. Our communication with the park had been set up for us to call in on a set schedule: Monday, Wednesday, and Friday at 0800. More often than not we couldn't make contact, sometimes for days. I know this story sounds like we could call in and reach David when we needed to, but frequently it took several days. The Dillingham radio broadcast we could pick up most mornings and occasional evenings. When we managed to hear a live voice it gave us a feeling of contact with the world.

Now that it was dark in the evening we huddled around our little battery powered radio beside the Coleman lantern in the hope of hearing most anything. On 19 August we heard an Aleut woman announcer in Dillingham reading the messages that she received and was passing on: "For Ellen in Chignik, from Mary in Naknek,

'Uncle Kitax is home from the hospital.' To Ivan and everyone in Ugashik, from Sue, 'My baby boy was born last night.' To everybody from Willie, 'Last night the Ekuk baseball team beat Clark Point five to one.'" And, as we leaned closer to our fading radio, "To Penny Starr a ranger at Aniakchak National Monument, 'Happy birthday Mom, I love you.' from your daughter Lori." That was the best birthday message either of us had ever received.

When we were lucky we could pick up the evening broadcast of "Radio Reader" with Dick Estel reading a novel. That was like a serial, you had to listen the next night or or you would miss a chapter. When I was a youngster I went to the movies every Saturday afternoon to see a double header movie with a ten minute Lone Ranger or Tom Mix serial between the movies. It cost 10 cents, which was most of my weekly allowance, but I had to go back the next Saturday or I would miss an episode of the exciting exploits of the Lone Ranger saving the beautiful maiden or Tom Mix catching the train robbers. It didn't matter what the movie was, the serial was the reason to go.

The weather had gone from bad to worse. We had completed our baseline surveys of plants and animals, commercial fishing for salmon was about done for the season, visitation had amounted to two people, and we were ready to head home. David had reached us to let us know we would be picked up in three days. We took the boat apart and stored the pieces in their bags. We packed all of the park equipment, including two 20-gallon plastic drums of extra boat fuel—every time a plane came down, for any reason, they brought us more fuel. Everything was ready for our pickup except our sleeping bags, stove, lantern, and food—the items we had to have to live. All we had to do was wait for Pen Air to get there. The Dillingham radio told us the weather in King Salmon was too bad to fly. The weather at Aniakchak was worse. A plane couldn't have landed in the waves we were having, much less taxi up on the beach for us to load our gear and take off. We waited for eleven days after the designated pickup date with nothing to do except try to keep warm and worry about spending the winter here with no food. My mother had a saying, "If you are worried, do something about it. If there is nothing you can do, forget it." A good thought, but somehow, it didn't seem to work here; we couldn't forget about getting out.

Radio contact with David in King Salmon was even worse than normal, we had no clue as to what was being done about getting us out. Finally the Pen Air Widgeon showed up. Georgie radioed us that the seas were too rough, he couldn't possibly land today, but he would be back tomorrow. Tomorrow came. Quoting our log:

30 Aug - Thursday - 0545

…rain, sleet, ceiling 0-0, wind SE 10-15, hi 44 - lo 36." We woke up really hoping, but not expecting to be picked up. Then the ceiling lifted and the Widgeon with Georgie at the controls showed up. He landed in swells that were bigger than he should have attempted, but he made it. We loaded as quickly as we could. It was hard, wet work, in the cold and wind. Penny had a terrible migraine that made the day that much worse for her. Finally, we got everything onboard and Georgie taxied into the surf. (Georgie should probably have refused to take the nearly 150 pounds of leftover fuel on this dangerous flight, but he took everything we had out.) The swells were at least three feet, more than the Widgeon should operate in, but it did and we were airborne with our hearts in our throats. Penny remembers bargaining with God as we took off in those seas. The ceiling was coming back down, we flew just under it, at 300 ft.

Now we had to find an open pass over the Aleutian Mountains. We had lost "the window" through the pass that Georgie had used coming down. Seventy-five miles north, Wide Bay is separated from Ugashik Lake by a low range that Georgie thought would be open enough that we could squeeze through a narrow pass that he knew well. It was, and he/we did. Then it was open country with a ceiling of 800 feet—700 feet less than FAA visual flight regulations allow—with nothing obstructing us all the way into King Salmon.

David met us with a cold six-pack in his hand and a huge grin on his face. An Alaska Airlines passenger plane had just landed, Penny said no to the beer, she felt it wouldn't be proper to drink in uniform with the public watching. I took a beer and David handed an open one to Penny telling her that it was OK today. Georgie, of course couldn't drink, he still had to fly. Our hats were really off to our friend Georgie. He had risked his life, made a dangerous flight, and a scary landing to get us out, knowing it might be another ten days before he would have another chance. David wanted to celebrate, but we had to unload the plane before we could relax with that beer.

David was so excited he could hardly contain himself until we had our work done and could sit and listen to him. Then he announced that Penny and I were to receive "Special Achievement Awards" (a very rare recognition; we never knew of another) at a ceremony in the Park Service Alaska Regional Office in Anchorage. We would each receive an award certificate and a check for $250. And we were being asked to present a slide program on Aniakchak to the Regional Director and the office staff, the hierarchy of the NPS in Alaska. We were dumbfounded, thrilled, excited, and very proud. We were being recognized for doing something that we had done not for glory but because we wanted to know and understand this unique area. For the first time the plant and animal life of Aniakchak National Monument & Preserve had been documented.

David had gotten us a room at the Air Force base in King Salmon where we could work on our reports and the program in peace and quiet. We had a lot to get accomplished before our date with Region. Gear had to be cleaned and put away. Bird, mammal, and plant population statistics had to be completed, tallied, and filed. Season-end reports had to be completed, including justifying all of the outboard motors we had to have replaced. When all of that was done we had a slide-show to put together—without access to the final rolls of slides that wouldn't come back from Kodak in time.

Time was up. Our meeting with the Anchorage office was tomorrow, 12 September, and David was dragging us out the door to the airport. On the flight to Anchorage we had the chance to pick David's brain on what positions would be funded at Katmai in the next few years. No, Aniakchak wouldn't be funded and the Amalik Bay position, the one job we really wanted, wouldn't be funded until at least 1991. We had completed our 10th year with the Park Service but weren't ready to call it quits and really retire. There were still places out there we wanted to see and experiences we wanted to have. We had committed next summer to going to Africa with our friend Gene Good, but were thinking ahead to Park Service positions that we would want another year.

Gene and Christine Good invited us to go to Africa with them for a month next summer, and we jumped at the opportunity. Gene was a professor of environmental biology and had been our mentor and advisor through our second educations in the 1970s—Penny's in anthropology/geology and mine in wildlife management. Gene was not only our mentor, but the four of us had become close personal friends.

Our half hour program at regional headquarters went really well. We answered questions for an additional half hour and were given our awards and a standing ovation for accomplishing a season that many in the regional office, who had spent a few days at Aniak-chak, didn't believe could be done. David took us to a wonderful dinner at the Captain Cook restaurant. He was celebrating too, our success had been a big feather in his cap. The next morning we flew to Portland, Oregon in time to celebrate daughter Lori's 34th birthday with her and her family and to consider our future.

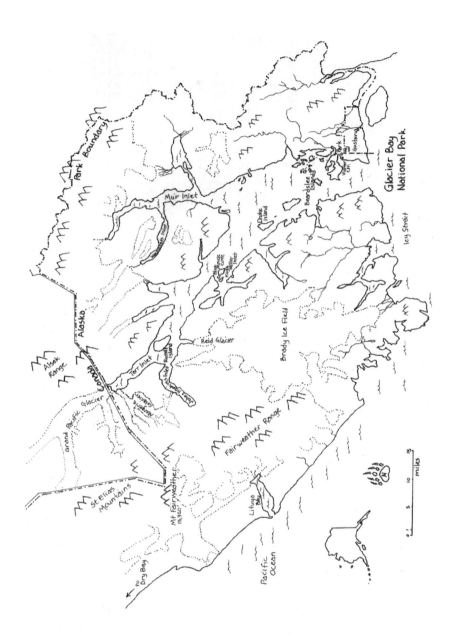

Glacier Bay
National Park

Park Boundary

Alaska

Alsek
Range

Grand Pacific Glacier

Canada

St Elias Mountains

Mt Fairweather
15,320'

to
Dry Bay

Fairweather Range

Lituya
Bay

Pacific
Ocean

Muir Inlet

Tarr Inlet

Reid Glacier

Johns Hopkins
Inlet

Johns Hopkins
Glacier

Rendu Inlet

Brady Ice Field

Drake
Island

Russell
15,638'

Scidmore
Cut
Hugh Miller
Inlet

Beardslee
Islands

Visitors
Ctr.

Gustavus

Icy Strait

N

0   5   10   15
miles

To Glacier Bay

Growing up Penny experienced the ecosystems of the plains and coal-fields of Kansas. I was raised with the deciduous forest and agricultural fields of Ohio. We had shown our kids the diverse ecosystems and habitats of the United States and Canada as we camped and explored with them. While scuba diving in the Caribbean we introduced Lori and Carin, our two older daughters, to a much different ecosystem, the beautiful and intricate coral reefs of those tropical waters. We and our girls had walked the surface of the Columbia Ice-Fields in British Columbia and Alberta, Canada. We had seen surface melt water rushing down a hole in the ice, called a mill-well, and imagined its route through the glacier to the Athabascan River. At night we had listened to the rifle-shot-like sounds of the living glacier as water cooled, froze, and expanded, cracking the ice.

With the Park Service we had experienced amazing diversity, from the speliothems of Jewel Cave to the big trees and glacial carved valleys of Yosemite to Great Basin's sagebrush flats, and up through the biological and climatic changes accompanying elevation changes on Wheeler Peak. In Alaska we had seen and lived in the coniferous forest, glacial pot-hole country, tundra, and the fiords of the rugged Alaska Peninsula.

The summer of 1989 Penny and I went to Africa with our friend, and the mentor of our second educations, Gene Good, and his wife Christine. In an ecosystem totally new to us, we experienced and observed the diversity of life on the high planes and jungles of

Kenya. We and the Goods spent evenings discussing the parameters, diversities, and evolution of life in general and were swapping stories of past experiences.

One evening Gene told us of his experience with a team of researchers from The Ohio State University, as they examined the succession of life after glacial retreat. In the mid-1950s he had been part of a team who had spent several summers studying and documenting vegetation changes following glacial retreat in Muir Inlet of Glacier Bay National Monument in southeast Alaska. They had camped in Wachusett Inlet, a branch of Muir Inlet.

Gene related a hike he had taken his first year there. From the terminus of the Carroll Glacier he walked down Wachusett Inlet for a couple of miles to its mouth in Muir Inlet. Starting on bare gravel and rocks, with no sign of life, except some beginnings of a black algal crust, he moved down inlet to a patch of sand that had been exposed only a few years. It had clumps of moss, horsetail, scattered inch-high fireweed sprouts, and the beginnings of dwarf willow.

As he moved farther on to land that had been exposed still longer he added scouring rush and a small dryas (the low, mat-forming member of the rose family that we had seen so many places in Alaska) to his plant list. Farther from the glacier he hiked through almost knee-high willow, then a stand of dwarf alder, across circular mats of leathery-leaved dryas that had been growing for, perhaps, twenty years. Still farther he came to a small patch of heather. He even found a few finger-sized spruce saplings, and near Muir Inlet a spruce/fir forest was showing signs of establishment. On the opposite side of Muir Inlet he could see a maturing 150-year-old spruce/fir forest. In a couple of miles he had walked through fifty years of plant succession.

When he returned in following seasons, he was impressed by the maturing of the plant life he had noted that first year. He went on to explain the process of succession and made it sound fascinating enough that we thought we would like to see and experience for ourselves what happens on land when a glacier recedes—an ecosystem unfamiliar to us.

TO OUR SURPRISE, WE GOT A CALL FROM GLACIER BAY THAT FALL. The Chief of Resource Management knew of our accomplishments at Aniakchak and wanted us to do similar work the next season at Glacier Bay. We asked about combining law enforcement with resource management. Mark said, no he didn't like law enforcement, that would get in the way of what he wanted done. We told him we needed to think and talk about it.

Penny didn't care for the way he sounded, too arrogant and chauvinistic. We talked it over and decided to see what else we could learn. Penny called the park and talked with Acting Chief Ranger Mike Sharp. Mike was very enthusiastic about the park and explained all the different ranger positions. There would be about 12 interpretive rangers on staff who present evening programs at the lodge and take people on interpretive hikes in the spruce/fir forest and along the rocky beach of the lower bay. One of them boards each cruise ship and interprets the bay to whomever, of the thousands of passengers, is interested. Law enforcement (LE) rangers issue boating and back country permits, monitor the campground, and patrol the bay in cabin cruisers. The lower bay, where many small private boats, fishermen, and tourists, have boating permits would get most of the attention. LE would have a raft, with a little cabin on it, anchored in Blue Mouse Cove, 35 miles up-bay where a ranger would be stationed occasionally. The third group of park personnel, the Resource Management division, has two technicians who do all sorts of odd jobs and some research. This year the division would like to have a second team stationed on a raft 50 miles up-bay looking at plant and wildlife succession and documenting the abundance and location of plants and animals, with particular attention to nesting bird colonies.

Mike and Penny hit it off immediately, he sounded like our kind of guy. He knew of us and encouraged us to apply as LE rangers. Then he had a second thought; if we applied as generalist rangers and were working for resource management, he might be able to pick us up as up-bay LE rangers without Mark getting too disturbed. That way we could be on the payroll as resource management rangers, work primarily by documenting resources from the raft but work as up-bay law enforcement rangers at the same time.

That sounded like a good idea to us. We applied and were accepted to double positions, just as Mike had suggested. We would have our LE refresher in Denali in April, and report to the park for firearms qualification under the supervision of new Chief Ranger Randy King. Then we would be working primarily as resource management technicians under Mark, who we knew nothing about.

Over the winter we looked into the history of Glacier Bay National Park and Preserve (GLBA). When Alexis Tchirikov and Vitus Bering were exploring for the Russian Czar, in July of 1741, their log says, "This must be America judging by the latitude and longitude." No mention was made of fiords or bays. They must have sighted what is now known as Mt. St Elias and the Fairweather Range. In 1778 James Cook commanding His Majesty's sloop Resolution, while hunting for the mystical northwest passage, on a sunny day, hung the misnomer of the Fairweather Range on the range of mountains north and south of 15,320-foot Mt. Fairweather. He too found no bays, but did mention that Icy Straight was choked with ice calving from the enormous glaciers.

Those glaciers were the remnants of the Wisconsin glacial age which had retreated 15,000 to 12,000 years ago ending the Pleistocene Epoch. Between 4,000 and 3,500 years ago an increase in winter snow accumulated, producing ice that was comparable to the Wisconsin Ice Age in the eastern Gulf of Alaska. The ice that covered everything in this part of the world would have been 3,000 to 4,000 or more feet thick , completely filling and obliterating all fiords or bays—Juneau, a few miles south, was under 5,000 feet of ice.

George Vancouver had been a midshipman on Cook's ship in 1778. In 1794, on his own expedition as a British explorer, Vancouver spotted an indentation in the tidewater glacier that would become Glacier Bay.

Trapping for sea otter pelts seems to have been the prominent concern of Russians and Europeans along the northwest coast of North America. Little else is mentioned in print until October of 1879. While seeking to corroborate the 1840 continental glaciation theories of Louis Agassiz, naturalist, explorer, and author, John Muir canoed from Fort Wrangell on Wrangell Island with a pair of Tlingit paddlers and "discovered" Glacier Bay. They found the ice front had retreated 45 miles from the bay's mouth up what would later be named Tarr Inlet. The Muir Inlet, later named for the famous explorer, was not much more than another concavity in the ice front. Muir sent stories of his adventures and findings to newspapers, exciting the public and scientists to see and learn more about this emerging wonder.

On a typical, for him, but memorable day hike Muir climbed (what sounds like) the ridge separating Grand Pacific Glacier from Rendu and Queen Glaciers. He wrote:

> I reached a height of fifteen hundred feet on the ridge that bounds the second of the great glaciers. All the landscape was smothered in clouds and I began to fear that, as far as wide views was concerned, I had climbed in vain. But, at length, the clouds lifted a little, and beneath their gray fringes I saw the berg filled expanse of the bay, and the feet of the mountains that stand about it, and the imposing fronts of five glaciers, the nearest being immediately beneath me. This was my first general view of Glacier Bay, a solitude of ice and snow and new born rocks, dim, dreary, mysterious. I held the ground I had so dearly won for an hour or two, sheltering myself from the icy blast as best I

could, while with benumbed fingers I sketched what I could see of the landscape, and wrote a few lines in my notebook. Then, breasting the snow again, crossing the shifting avalanche slopes and torrents, I reached camp about dark, wet weary, and glad.

Eliza Scidmore read of Muir's recent exploits in the San Francisco Bulletin and was so intrigued that she became one of Glacier Bay's early tourists. In National Geographic magazine she wrote:

Steaming slowly up the inlet, the bold, cliff-like front of the glacier grew in height as we approached it, and there was a sense of awe as the ship drew near enough for us to hear the strange, continual rumbling of the subterranean or subglacial waters, and see the avalanches of ice that, breaking from the front, rushed down into the sea with tremendous crashes and roars.

Ah, to be able to paint pictures with words!

To preserve the glacial environment, Glacier Bay was designated a National Preserve in 1925. With the passage of The Alaska National Interest Lands Conservation Act of 1980, Glacier Bay was categorized as a National Park and Preserve. A new environment, a new challenge! We were excited to experience this place of ice, water, and the succession of life.

INTRODUCTION TO GLBA

In February of 1990 we got a surprise call from Glacier Bay. It was Mike Sharp informing us that the law enforcement refresher would be held at Glacier Bay rather than in Denali as we had been told earlier, so we wouldn't have to report for work until 1 May.

We had decided to drive from our mesa home in southwestern Colorado to Denver, leave our car with friends there, and fly on to Alaska. Our reservations were to fly from Denver to Seattle, on to Juneau, and finally to Gustavus, Alaska, the little town 10 or 15 miles from Glacier Bay, on 30 April. That would get us to GLBA one day ahead of our EOD.

We woke up early on the 29th, looked out the window and said, "Damn!" It was snowing hard and had already accumulated eight inches. We had intended to drive our Chevy van to Denver, but knew it would be safer to use our old International Scout since it had four-wheel drive. It also had a lousy heater/defroster system and antique windshield wipers that sort-of worked. How many times had we told Alaskan visitors to not plan on traveling with a tight time schedule? We had made the same stupid mistake.

I locked the Scout's front hubs because we would be using four-wheel drive all the way. Luck was with us. We followed a snow plow to the top of Monarch Pass, cleaned the windshield, and in first gear headed down the steep, unplowed eastern slope of the Rocky Mountains. The snow built on the windshield, the wipers removed some of it, we had to stop at least every half hour to scrape ice off the windshield. The normal six-hour trip took ten hours, but we reached Denver safely and had a delightful evening with old friends. The next morning our friends dropped us at the airport; we were on schedule when we landed in Gustavus, many hours later.

We expected to be met by our boss, Mark, but he sent Dena and Kitty, the two Resource Management technicians to pick us up. Dena was a tough-looking woman in her 30s with a great figure. Kitty was just a big pleasant kid with a good smile who had never done anything like this before. They drove us to park headquarters where we were to meet Mark as soon as we got there. But Mark wasn't there and no one knew where he was or when he would be back.

Dena took us to our cabin, a tiny A-frame in the woods and told us we might as well see Mark in the morning, since he would have left for the day by now. The cabin wasn't much. It had a sleeping loft with a double mattress on the floor, an oil-burner heat stove, a two-burner propane cook top, a cold-water sink, a little table with two card-table chairs, a beat up old couch, electricity and a few lights; there was an outhouse 30 or 40 yards away. The cabin was always dark and felt damp until we got the oil heater going. Next door was a nice house-trailer where our old friend Kris Fister and her husband Larry Prussin would be living. Their trailer was much larger than our A-frame, and had a phone, an oven, hot water, and even a shower. We envied them the shower. We had to go to the dormitory to get our biweekly shower. Kris was a LE ranger who would be doing boat patrols in the lower bay. Larry was the seasonal head of interpretation for the park that season.

A little before 0800 the next morning we were at Mark's office. The park secretary told us he wasn't in yet. "OK, we'll look around and come back in a while." We stuck our noses into the office across the hall and were welcomed by Superintendent Marvin Jensen. Marv, who was almost as new to Glacier Bay as we were, welcomed us warmly and told us to stop-in any time. He seemed like a very pleasant person and let us know that we didn't have a chief ranger yet, but that Randy King would be joining us in a week or two.

Mark still wasn't in so we wandered down to the dock where we met Mike Sharp, the district LE ranger who Penny had talked with, and the one we would be working closely with, since he was in charge of all boating operations and would check us out on boating skills before we would be permitted to use any park boat. Mike welcomed us, showed us around the dock, and explained boating in Glacier Bay. He seemed like a great guy; tall, lean, with a big mustache and good smile. He looked like a wide receiver on a football team and proved to be very competent with boats. He showed us the dock in Bartlett Cove, which is where all of the smaller park boats and employees' boats are docked, and where our boat would be kept when we were in Glacier Bay between patrols. There is a commercial dock a quarter mile away, near the lodge, where the larger park boats are moored, fuel is sold, and from where small tour-boats operate. All private boats entering Glacier Bay must tie-up here and get a boating permit from the nearby ranger station before entering park waters.

We found Mark in his office when we got back to the headquarters building. He was a nondescript man, nothing significant about him except he seemed preoccupied and didn't want to take time to meet and talk with his new employees. He told us we needed to check-out with Dena on boating this morning and go on an overflight of the park with Mike Sharp that afternoon. When we got back from the flight we should report-in with him to receive further assignments. Hmm, he seemed rather formal and not at all friendly.

Mike had told us we had to check out with him on boats before we got into any park boat. So we decided we had better check with him before we took a boat out with Dena. Mike was still on the dock and said, "Sure, we can check you out right now. Hop in this skiff and each of you run a figure eight course right here."

That was quick! It didn't give Penny any chance to worry about passing a test. We climbed down into the skiff. I stopped to think;

Mike is pretty sharp, he was testing more than just "could we run an outboard?" He wanted to see how we would approach an unfamiliar boat. We had seen Mike in this skiff just a few minutes before so we knew it was running just fine, but I felt we should check it carefully before we took it out. I tipped the motor up, checked the prop, opened the cover, checked spark wires, carburetor, and shift lever. Penny checked the gas tank and fuel line, and found that the fuel line was disconnected at the tank. She laughed and reconnected the line. Mike was probably expecting us to check-out today and wanted to introduce a problem. I checked the drain plug, tipped the motor back down, pulled the starter-cord, listened to it purr, and ran a 1/4 mile figure eight, and traded places with Penny. She pulled the starter-cord and ran the same course. As she pulled up to the dock Mike gave us a thumbs up and gave Penny a hand up onto the dock.

We found Dena at Mark's office and told her we were ready for our check ride. A few minutes later we were back at the dock with Dena and Kitty for our check rides in Dena's messy skiff, not anything like Mike's had been. Dena had been told to take us out into the main bay and be sure we could handle the 22-foot aluminum skiffs we would be working with. She took us out into the bay and told Penny to take the tiller and head up bay. We looked at each other and shrugged; she was having us run before the wind, which was pretty strong. We have always made a practice of starting a patrol by heading into the wind so we would have the wind at our backs returning, just in case conditions deteriorated.

Penny did as told and ran up bay with a building sea for about twenty minutes. Dena seemed to think Penny had demonstrated adequate boat handling, took the tiller, and headed back down bay into a strong wind and three-foot waves. She was taking the waves head on at full throttle. Waves were breaking over the bow and we were all getting a lap full of water from each wave. We had good float-coats on, but not rain pants, so we were getting wet and cold and being beaten badly with each wave blow. I said, "Isn't it my turn to check out." Dena gladly relinquished control of the boat, I cut our speed by half and turned to quarter the waves. The spray and splash stopped immediately, and the pounding was greatly diminished, but we still had an hour of tacking and difficult boating to get back to Bartlett Cove and shelter from the wind and waves.

Nothing was ever said about our boat handling by Dena or Mark, but apparently Kitty had told the story because the next day Mike related the story as he had heard it and laughingly congratulated us on having successfully demonstrated our boating skills.

Mike Sharp was not only the LE and boating ranger; he was a pilot and did some flying for the park. We met him and two other LE rangers after lunch for our overview flight. We drove to the Gustavus airport, and watched while Mike did a meticulous preflight check of the GSA (General Services Administration) Cessna-206. The wind was down and the ceiling unlimited so we should have some great views. We flew west at 3,000 feet over Icy Straight and past Dundas Bay, a large and convoluted fiord that looked like a place we would love to explore. Then we skirted Cape Spencer and flew northwest along the coast. Just below us was fiord after fiord all cut by the glaciers that had flown off the Brady Ice Field. We looked across many miles of an enormous sheet of ice and snow covering several hundred square miles of the southern portion of the Fairweather Range, a truly spectacular mountain range. Our Colorado home is on a mesa at 8,000 feet and looks a few miles to the spectacular San Juan Mountains and three impressive 14,000-foot peaks. Those mountains rise from a base of 6,000 feet and are some of the most impressive mountains in the lower 48. The Fairweather Range rises from below sea level to Mt. Fairweather at 15,320 feet in only fifteen miles.

Up the coast, we flew into Lituya Bay which is a wide fiord about 10 miles long with a glacial morainal island known as Cenotaph in the center. Cenotaph Island was the home, or hermitage, of Jim

Huscroft from 1915 until he died alone there in 1939. The story goes: "Once each year Jim rowed his open boat to Juneau for a year's supplies and his full one year's accumulation of newspapers, which were saved for him at the Elks Club. He read each day's paper one year late and never looked ahead a day. Each Christmas he celebrated by eating his choice of 14 kinds of pie that he made for himself from the local berries he harvested."

In July 1958 there was a magnitude eight earthquake along the Fairweather Fault that dislodged 1.3 billion cubic feet of ice, rock, dirt, and trees from the steep headwall at the terminus of the Lituya Glacier. That sudden collapse created a wave 1,700 feet high that completely denuded the facing promontory. Three boats were moored in the bay at the time, one was smashed where it was anchored, one was carried over the spit at the bay's mouth and dropped into the ocean with enough force that it came apart when it hit the sea. Fortunately, the couple onboard had enough time to escape in their dingy before their boat sank. The third boat was anchored behind Cenotaph Island which spared it from the huge wave. Mike flew us to the upper end of the bay so we could see the devastation caused by the wave that had struck 32 years before. The face of the promontory was as bare as a rock could be. From the plane we couldn't see any recovering vegetation anywhere.

When we got back to the park, about 1600, Mark had left for the day. OK, we'll see him tomorrow! We saw Mike down at the dock and asked him to tell us about Mark. We had gotten the feeling there was no love lost between the two of them. Mike told us Mark had been screwing Dena, who he supervised, for two years—a very big no-no in Park Service protocol, and probably all employee/supervisor relations in any business. Not only was he screwing Dena, he was trying to make-out with the superintendent's daughter at the same time. We were right. Mike had no use for Mark. We were working for two completely different personalities; we needed to get to know Mark and decide for ourselves how to deal with him.

GETTING TO KNOW MARK

We finally met with our boss Mark to get our "assignments," as he put it, for the season. He seemed to want numbers. He wanted us to count every animal in the park: all the bears—black and brown—where they were, when, and what they were doing. He wanted us to count fish in different streams at different times, including how many and of what species. Count the numbers of individuals of the dozens of different species of seabirds, how many were flighted and how many flightless; the same for shore birds. Sit on Drake Island with a spotting scope and count the mountain goats on Marble Mountain. Count the hundreds of nests of black-legged kittiwakes on the cliff face just below the terminus of Margerie Glacier. We were to show up at Mark's office at 0800 every other Monday to get our two-week assignments, load the appropriate gear for the assignment, and head out.

Wow! We had signed up to be bean counters. Not what we had expected, but that was OK because we would be able to observe and learn the Glacier Bay ecosystem in depth as we navigated all of the fiords while doing Mark's counts.

Mark let us know we wouldn't start any counts until the two rafts with little cabins on them had been fixed up, and the ranger raft towed to Blue Mouse Cove, and ours to Russell Island. Blue Mouse Cove would also be home to a fuel barge, where we could refuel when needed. Those little cabins needed a lot of cleaning, painting, and fixing before they were ready to be towed up-bay, so we needed to work on them, but first we needed to get our boat outfitted. Mark told us we would find everything we needed in the park warehouse. We should do that today and tomorrow, because the next day he wanted us to boat to Kidney Island and locate the remains of an old fox farm.

We discovered an amazing collection of stuff in the warehouse that had been accumulating for years and gathered everything we thought we might need: a double fiberglass kayak with skirts and paddles, two tents, two sleeping bags and pads, several bear-proof food containers, two 5-gallon fuel cans, and a mushroom anchor with 100 feet of line. We already had a 5-gallon gas tank and a good Danforth anchor on the boat that Mike had issued us. Quite important in this wet climate was a good sized ice-chest to store gear in—something we had longed for at Aniakchak.

Well Sherlock, if we were going to be navigating all over Glacier Bay we had better get good navigational charts of the entire bay. No, Mark didn't have any. He told us we would have to buy them from the store at the lodge. Mike told us we could print copies of his charts, and couldn't imagine that Mark hadn't provided us with a full set.

Mike had shown us a shortcut from the dock in Bartlett Cove to the Beardslee Islands, where the Kidney Island fox farm was. The shortcut was a tidal channel just a few feet wide in some places, shallow with big rocks in other places, and could be navigated only near high tide, but it would keep us out of the rip tides and the occasional whirlpools in the Sitakaday Narrows.

Early on the assigned day we loaded up and headed for Kidney Island on a rising tide so we could use Mike's shortcut. There were plenty of big rocks to miss, but that route saved us some rough water and probably an hour, well worth taking. The Beardslees looked like very interesting piles of glacial debris, probably a lateral or terminal moraine, with many opportunities to get lost among islands that all look the same. Mike had warned us that magnetic variation was 28 degrees east, so our compass would point to 332 when we were headed what appeared north on the charts. We would have to get to know our charts and this was a good opportunity to start learning. We had good visibility and found Kidney Island right where the chart and compass told us it should be. Without knowing the magnetic variation we would have ended up several miles east of Kidney. Interesting Mark had never mentioned the variation! Was he ignorant of variation or was he messing with us?

Kidney Island is well sheltered behind a group of smaller islands and has an indentation that gives it its name and creates a nice cove where we decided to go ashore. We eased up to the bank of fist sized rocks. Penny stepped from the bow into only a few inches of water, took the bow line and tied us to a substantial alder tree. I had checked the tide chart Mark had given us and figured we had a good hour before high tide. If we were able to locate the fox farm quickly we would be back well before that. We had to be back before the tide started dropping or we would be stuck, but with slack-high-tide time included we should have more than two hours.

What was left of the old fox-farm wasn't hard to find. There wasn't much, just the remains of what had been someone's shelter. I don't think you could call it a house, just a place to get out of the weather. Apparently the owner didn't spend much time there, perhaps just enough to harvest the year's crop of fur. We took a couple of pictures and were back at the beach in less than an hour.

To our surprise the boat was high and dry. We tried to push it down the steep bank, but couldn't budge it. Damn it, what had we done wrong? I examined the tide chart thinking I had misread it; no, I had read it correctly. Penny looked at it more carefully and discovered it was for Juneau tides not Glacier Bay. We both know tide charts pretty well and pay attention to them. I blamed myself, Penny blamed herself; there was no excuse in not confirming exactly what tide chart we had. At the same time we wondered if Mark had purposely set us up. Had he intentionally given us a worthless tide chart as a test, knowing we would be stuck and need survival skills?

We would be there until tomorrow morning's high tide. There would be another high tide later today, but it would be after dark. We weren't about to venture into unknown waters in the dark. So we set up camp and went about exploring the island. It had been ice free for 150 years, so it had time to develop a forest of maturing Sitka spruce, big enough that we couldn't reach around the largest ones. The ground was covered by a mix of sphagnum and club moss and a variety of lichen. There were scattered low, small blueberry bushes, and patches of alder and devils club too dense to walk through, but Mark wasn't interested in plant life so that wouldn't need to be included if we had to write a report.

To hell with Mark! We had a delightful evening. The sky cleared and we could see a portion of a rainbow through the trees.

Somewhere over the rainbow, skies are blue,
And the dreams that you dare to dream, really do come true.

We had neglected to put some brandy in our pack—a minor forgotten item, but a reminder to be careful of what else might have been neglected. A freeze-dried Dinner rehydrated with spring water was fine with us and would be pretty standard evening fare this season. We set our tent well above high tide line and above the near-shore route that bears favor. The layer of moss made an ideal mattress so we slept like babies.

The next morning our boat floated on a rising tide and we took off to explore the Beardslee Islands. They are a group of about 30 islands that, according to Mark, were the remains of a terminal moraine—their location told us some were lateral moraines and some were terminal. The largest, Lester Island, is about five miles long and the smallest is maybe 30 feet in diameter. Everything smaller than that is tidal and kelp-covered with deep channels between the islands. We found a string of small, brightly colored floats along the inner channel. We couldn't resist checking to see what they were. We expected them to be crab pots, so I started pulling up one of the lines tied to a float. I pulled about a hundred feet of line before I met much resistance, then I couldn't budge what was attached. We would ask Mike about them, were they crab pots, were they legal, and what was so heavy?

We expected Mark to be wondering about us when we got back late that afternoon, but he didn't seem to even be conscious of us having done anything the past two days. He just told us that tomorrow we would be working on our raft and its cabin; getting it and the LE raft ready to be hauled up bay in a week or two.

The raft cabins were interesting little structures, almost identical to the tent-frame we had lived in at Nonvianuk—10-by 12-feet, with a sleeping loft, an oil heat stove, and a two burner propane stove. The inside needed painting and the roof was due for replacement. We would be doing most of the work ourselves. While we were replacing the fiberglass roofing, we found a section of roof guttering and a barrel. I rigged the guttering to drain rain-water into the barrel, to provide us with fresh water that would be replenished every time it rained—which was almost daily.

Mike stopped by the next afternoon while we were painting the cabin interior, to inform us that he had the LE training scheduled for this weekend and the following week. Seven of us would be heading for Juneau in two of the Bertram boats on Friday. He suggested we let Mark know the refresher would take a full week. While he was there, Mike told us about the crab pot floats. They were marking the legal commercial crab pots of several fishermen who had state licenses and park approved sites to set their pots. He would appreciate it if we would, when we had time, check the color patterns that identified the fishermen using them and numbers of pots of the different fishermen. That would keep him informed on who was fishing and if they were following regulations. "No," he laughed, we wouldn't be able to pull one up. They were five feet in diameter, made of rebar, and weighed a couple of hundred pounds empty.

Mark hit the ceiling when we told him we would be spending the next week attending LE refresher. He had no intention of letting us take a week off to go to Juneau. We told him to talk with Mike about it, it wasn't up to us. He and Mike ended up in the superintendent's office arguing over our future. Fortunately superintendent Marvin could think straight. He wanted us to be commissioned which would greatly increase the park's LE presence up-bay. Besides that, we couldn't go on a 10-day patrol in this climate without the raft-cabin being in place, and that wouldn't happen until Mike pulled them up-bay after the LE refresher. In reality, we would be in Juneau for kayak training over the weekend then back to Glacier Bay for several days of training and lectures and a couple days of firearms qualifications. Half of the training would be on our lieu days (days off). Mark would only be without us for four or five days of our ten-day work week.

The boat ride to Juneau was a wonderful experience. Penny and I had the opportunity to really get to know Mike and Tom Gage, another of the LE rangers who was with us. I got to know the Bertram, the radar, and how the boat handled seas and fog. We ran out of the bay in light fog, into Icy Strait, and part way up the Lynn Canal before turning into Auke Bay and up to Juneau. Of course, it's all glacial-carved with steep, Sitka spruce-covered slopes dropping precipitously to small wave-cut beaches, then dropping again quickly to water deeper than our fathometer could read.

Juneau is the capital of Alaska sitting on a shelf surrounded by mountains. It is fogged-in frequently which gives state legislators all kinds of excuses for being late or absent. Landing an airliner there is quite an experience for commercial pilots who don't hesitate to abort a landing and just fly on to Anchorage rather than drop over the mountain into poor visibility and a short runway—travel by boat is much safer.

We landed at the commercial dock where Mike had made reservations and walked to a hotel where we also had reservations.

Mike called his wife, Diane Biggie, an attractive, dark haired nurse at the hospital, and suggested she join us for dinner. Diane proved to be a delightful person whom we all enjoyed and became a special friend of Penny—a woman's perspective on Juneau and Glacier Bay National Park was good to have.

Another person joined us for dinner at the Red Dog Saloon; Glacier Bay's new Chief Ranger, Randy King, showed up in time to buy us our second round of beer. Randy came across as a quiet and laid back kind of guy, he told us his wife, Sally, and their year-old daughter, Mackenzie, would be joining us as soon as he got settled in his job and had the house ready. Randy had been a district ranger at Yellowstone, was built like a linebacker, and had a most friendly face. We hit it off immediately.

Bright and early the next morning—well, early anyway, it was dark and cloudy and threatening rain—we all gathered at a meeting room in the hotel for a talk on kayaking. We felt we were familiar with kayaks having used a Folboat, which is a type of kayak, several times at Katmai, but the sea kayaks we would be using that afternoon were a different beast. The first thing the instructor impressed us with was, "You never go out in a kayak in this country without your skirt," a skirt being the water-proof fabric, not unlike a woman's skirt, that fits tight around your waist, covers the kayak's open seat and fits tightly over the cockpit that you sit in. It keeps water out and you and your gear dry. We would be operating in rain and waves and possibly white water. Keeping dry is the essence of surviving boating experiences in Alaska. For that matter, staying dry is extremely important in any back-country experience.

That afternoon we all met at a kayak rental shop on the edge of town for live kayaking. Each of us had our own single sea kayak to work with. (Penny and I have always boated together in one boat, be it kayak, canoe, or whatever the boat was, we had a partner to depended on. This would be a different challenge.) We were shown all sorts of ways to use the double ended paddles to control, guide and keep ourselves upright. Then we paddled around the bay experimenting with kayaks and paddles until the instructor was confident that each of us was comfortable with the boat. Then he showed us how to roll a 360 and come up without drowning. Now each of us was to do a 360 while he was close enough to save us if we couldn't complete the roll. We watched some of our friends struggle to get clear around. One guy had to be hand-rolled when he got stuck head down. At a time like that you learn a lot by observing others' mistakes and thinking about how it had been done by the instructor. I couldn't believe it! Penny and I each completed the roll on our first try.

The next day we had the morning to see Juneau and do some shopping before meeting at the dock at noon for the trip back to Glacier Bay. We had been worried about our hands being wet and cold so much of the time in the open Lund—the LE guys would be operating out of the nice, dry, warm Bertrams. We found good, fuzzy-lined rubber commercial fisherman's gloves. Now we could handle the cold, wet world with warm, dry hands.

Mike had me take the helm on the way back to the park. He wanted me to get the experience of handling a boat in the open sea. It turned out to be a difficult trip in rough seas with current, wind, and me, fighting each other over who would decide where the boat would go. I learned a whole lot about open Alaskan seas and managed to get us safely to Bartlett Cove before dark.

The next three days were packed with talks by U.S. Coast Guard, state law enforcement, fish and game, and our old friend Steve Shakleton who was now Alaska Regional Chief Ranger. Nothing really new, but a lot of valuable things to be reminded of, especially the cold water survival stories from the Coast Guard. Some of them made one wonder—like the fact that the bright orange float-coats we wore all the time just made your body easier to find if you fell overboard.

Firearms refresher was pretty standard. We both were always a little concerned about shooting well, but they say, if you aren't a bit nervous before a performance you will likely screw it up. Neither of us had a problem passing both handgun and shotgun tests. The thing that impressed me was Randy King. He stood next to me on the firing line and was the fastest and most accurate shot I had ever met. You are given two seconds to draw your weapon, fire two rounds, and reholster. Most of us took time to re-aim before firing the second shot and rarely completed the exercise under the two second limit. Randy had his second shot fired and reholstered while the rest of us were squeezing off our second shot. Wow! he was good! I was impressed.

The last afternoon was an "all staff" cold water exercise. The entire seasonal staff met on the dock in survival suits, which are float-coat coveralls—the standard polypropylene jacket with canvas legs. There were 20 or 25 of us standing on the dock. Mike gave a good talk on cold water survival, explained the water would never get much above 40 degrees, and told us all to jump in. Nobody moved, he repeated the order to jump in, and glanced at Penny with raised eyebrows. The 57-year-old grandmother grinned at him and jumped. With arms out and legs spread like she was in scuba gear, her head stayed dry and her vision remained clear. The assembled rangers, all of whom were about 30 years her junior, couldn't back out now and all joined Penny in the bay. We had a great potluck at Randy's house that evening, everyone showed up to toast Penny.

We completed the week by towing the fuel barge and the two cabin-rafts up bay, secured the fuel barge and one cabin at Blue Mouse Cove, and our raft on the inland side of Russell Island, a great location. We were sheltered from wind and close to Tarr Inlet where Margerie and Grand Pacific Glaciers terminate, even closer to Johns Hopkins Inlet with its rapidly calving glacier, and just across from Reid Inlet with the spectacularly beautiful clear blue ice of Reid Glacier, all areas where we expected to be doing much of our work. We would be getting our first work schedule from Mark on Monday, but now we had two days off to recoup after our ten days of rather intense LE refresher.

Heading on Patrol

Patrols

25 March 1990

We were getting ready for our first ten-day patrol. Randy King, Mike Sharp, and Tom Gage were on the dock preparing to head up to the LE raft in Blue Mouse Cove for a couple of days in the Arete, one of the Bertrams, named for the sharp mountain ridge that remains between two glacial cirques. They walked across the dock to see how we were doing. We had a lot of necessary gear loaded in the Lund, including a 16-foot sea kayak. Tom laughed and said, "You two look like traveling Gypsies. Why the kayak?"

I told him, "White-man has much baggage!"

We all had a good laugh, and I explained that to not get stuck by a falling tide, I would pull the Lund up to shore and let Penny off with our camping gear. While she started setting up camp for the night, I motored out beyond low tide, set the anchor, pushed the kayak off the stern, removed a tonneau cover, climbed in, and paddled to shore. In the morning we reversed the whole process.

Penny noticed the kayak skirts were not in the kayak where we had left them last evening when we loaded it. (Without the skirts around us, closing the kayak opening, rain and spray would get everything inside soaked.) Tom said, "I saw Mark on your boat yesterday evening before he and Dena went kayaking. He might have used them,"

Randy walked across the dock to Mark's kayak, picked up a pair of skirts and said, "Are these yours?"

I asked, "Do they have a marks-a-lot star on the inside?"

Randy looked and said, "Yea."

"The son-of-a-bitch used our gear and didn't return it," I said, "And he knew we were going out this morning. I can't believe it!"

Mike just said, "Believe it!"

When Randy asked us what we were doing that day. Penny told him, "We're going up to Drake Island to count mountain goats on Marble Mountain just across the channel. Then if there's time, we'll go up to Hugh Miller Inlet and count ducks, then camp somewhere near there."

"Well," Randy said, "We'll be on the raft in Blue Mouse Cove just around the corner from Hugh Miller. How about joining us for dinner and a beer?"

"Oh boy!" Penny said, "We'll be there."

In a few minutes we were going to run up the Sitakaday Narrows. I was excited and Penny was a bit nervous. There are many stories about the dangers of Sitakaday Narrows, the channel between Young Island, the big island on the east, and Rush Point on the west. There are numerous erratic boulders near each shore, that show on charts but not on maps. (Nautical charts show water depth below high tide, and particularly rocks that may be covered at high tide and exposed at low, while maps show the land above high tide.) Rip-tides and whirlpools are known to plague Sitakaday during flooding and ebbing tides, so we had been warned to plan to use Sitakaday at or near a slack tide. We had managed that up until now, but today we needed to go through on an strong ebbing tide. I wanted to run it anyway, just for the experience and to see what was so scary. Fortunately we have read water in a variety of situations and knew what we were seeing—most of the time. The Sitakaday Narrows aren't particularly narrow, but there are whirl-pools to avoid, a strong current pushing us around, and plenty of threatening rocks near the shores. A lot of water moves through with each tide change, and if it were truly narrow it would really be dangerous water. We had no problem and didn't feel Sitakaday amounted to anything like the hype it had been given, but reminded ourselves to not feel too comfortable in any water situation.

On the way to Drake Island, we pulled into a spot where there were tree stumps that had not been destroyed by the last glacier. We tried to figure out how they had survived. All we could imagine was they were in the lee of Marble Mountain, but we didn't think that was quite an adequate answer. There is another set of interglacial forest stumps in Muir Inlet just above Wachusett Inlet that had been made famous in a series of photographs by Ansel Adams. Gene Good had told us they were drowned when the Wachusett branch of the Carroll Glacier had surged some time in the 1800s and formed an ice dam across Muir Inlet creating a lake that drowned the forest. Perhaps a similar thing had happened here below Marble Mountain.

We found a little cove on the west side of Drake Island where we could see the big limestone rock called Marble Mountain. There was no good mooring spot so we just pulled up on some rocks, put the mushroom anchor behind a rock to hold it, and pushed the boat out into deep water. With this falling tide we would have to push the boat out every little while and keep an eye on it constantly or we would be camping right here tonight. We set up our spotting scope where one of us could watch the mountain and the other could watch the boat, and settled in for goat watching. Three hours later we had seen only two goats and those only briefly. Mark had told us he had seen 12 there, and we were to confirm within 10% of his count. We weren't going to fake results just to confirm his count, so we gave up and left.

On the north side of Marble Mountain is Geike Inlet, a fiord that looked interesting so we turned into it and found tiny Shag Cove cut into the far side of Marble Mountain. We pulled into Shag and found that just sitting in the boat we had a good view of goats with our binoculars. We saw five nannies eating and six kids frolicking and nursing, while two billies were peacefully lying on a ledge above them. The kids were quite young and had probably been born within the past couple of weeks, but were amazingly active—running, jumping, and perfecting their sure-footedness. We watched them for an hour and thought Mark would be pleased that we had found the goats.

By then the sun was over the yardarm. "Let's knock off for the day and head to Blue Mouse Cove and see our friends," Penny said.

I eased up to the LE raft right behind the big Bertram. Penny stepped onto the grill decking of the raft and secured our bow line to a cleat, I killed the motor and secured the stern line to another cleat. By that time Mike was on deck handing each of us a beer and welcoming us to the Blue Mouse Ranger Station. "Come on," he said, "We're about to pull our pots and see what we have for dinner." They had both a crab pot and a shrimp pot set and planned to have a Cajun feast. Mike was brought up in Cajun country along the Gulf of Mexico and loved cooking in the unique style of that area.

We all pitched in cleaning a couple dozen shrimp, cracking almost that many Dungeness crab, drinking beer, getting to know each other, and becoming good friends. Mike proved to be an excellent Cajun chef. We had a great evening with men who have remained close friends for years. Penny said we had better go find a campsite before it got too late, Randy suggested the two of us throw our sleeping bags on the bow bunks of the Arete and have breakfast with them before they headed to Muir Inlet and back to headquarters. That sounded good to us. Before we left the next morning Randy told us to feel free to use the Blue Mouse station anytime.

We were to count waterfowl in Hugh Miller Inlet and its northern extension, shown on our chart as Weird Bay. We decided to leave the Lund tied to the raft and take the kayak across a shallow opening between Blue Mouse and Hugh Miller. That way we would have minimal impact on molting birds and those that would be nesting. There were beautiful little black and white Kittlitz's and marbled murrelets diving for crustaceans in the deeper water of Hugh Miller Inlet; the Kittlitz's almost appeared blue when sun light hit their back.

Weird Bay is a weird bay. It's not much more than a cove, enclosed behind an island and several large glacial erratics. A glacial arm had occupied the bay only 80 years earlier and left a lot of rock when it melted. It couldn't be accessed in a power boat except on a good tide, and that would be tricky. The kayak gave us an easy, safe way in and out, regardless of the tide. We noted an eagle nest in a spruce snag and a yellow crowned warbler singing from the top of the willows along the shore. A pair of blue grouse were going through their courtship. He was all puffed up and strutting, she was pretending to ignore him. In the rear of this secluded bay we found a pair of oldsquaw ducks nesting in the brush and 18 mergansers paddling away from us.

We spent the morning watching a world little disturbed by man. Several cormorants came and went. We saw a shoveler duck and a Barrow's golden-eye, a yellow-rumped warbler and a glimpse of a hummer we couldn't identify for sure. We heard a song sparrow, a hermit thrush, and a woodpecker knocking in the woods.

Lunch might as well be eaten while we were in this peaceful spot, so we got out the pilot biscuits and peanut-butter. Then it was on to Scidmore Bay, just to the west and north of Hugh Miller. Scidmore Bay is named for Eliza Ruhamah Scidmore who was entranced by John Muir's stories and followed him to Glacier Bay in the early 1880s. Many times larger than Weird Bay, Scidmore has a narrow channel that opens into a glacial-debris-clogged upper end. The low meadow surrounding it looked interesting, so we went ashore and found both brown and black bear tracks in the mud. We hadn't expected to see black bear signs any place that is occupied by browns. We'd ask Mark about them.

Tracks of a wolf were exciting, but we were distracted as we followed the wolf tracks into the brushy vegetation. An oystercatcher, a big black bird nearly as large as a crow, with a four-inch-long bright orange beak, was acting like it had a broken wing, and running off into the vegetation. We knew it was trying to coax us away from a nest, so we watched carefully as we pretended to follow the bird. Carefully it didn't get far enough ahead that we might loose sight of it. When we stopped following, it reappeared squawking to get our attention and then limped off again. We never found the nest, but enjoyed the show immensely. A month later we enjoyed the same broken-wing con-game on a different beach. This time there were two oystercatchers playing the game. They are easy to see with those outsized bright bills. One was faking the broken-wing and the other was squawking, and acting like he was leading her away from us into the low vegetation. We stood still, watching as a small black ball of fluff couldn't stand it any longer, came out of hiding, and ran to the frantic parents. All three quickly disappeared into the brush. We stood there laughing, but we had a tide to catch before the cut to Blue Mouse went completely dry and we had to paddle another five miles to get back to our skiff.

Oystercatchers actually do eat oysters as well as many other mollusks and echinoderms. There are two distinct techniques that they use to open oysters: some sneak up to an open oyster or clam, and plunge their long, strong bill between the shell halves and sever the adductor mussel before the animal can close up. Others break a hole in the shell by a series of powerful, rapid blows with that big bill, insert the bill into the hole, and cut the adductor, which allows the shell to be easily opened and the clam eaten. On a later patrol we watched an oystercatcher kill a Dungeness crab by rolling it onto its back, quickly pound a hole in the ventral shell, kill the crab, and then proceed to leisurely eat.

We were to meet Mark the next evening in Reid Inlet. We didn't have a campsite in mind for tonight, so why not stay on the Blue Mouse raft? No one would be there, and Randy had suggested we use it anytime. Good plan! Penny fixed a "fancy dinner" for us since we had a propane stove to cook on rather than our little Svea back-pack stove. She made a big batch of rice and poured a can of Progresso chicken and rice soup over it. That along with a couple of pilot biscuits, those three-inch round, quarter inch thick unsalted crackers that are ubiquitous Alaskan back-country food, made a much better meal than the freeze-dried meals that were standard fare when we were camping.

It doesn't get really dark at this latitude this time of year until it is ready to get light, so we had good visibility of the cove and shore. We had seen a cow moose shortly after we arrived and had been watching for other wildlife all evening. As we were heading to bed we heard a wolf howl. It sounded really close. We eased the door open, stepped onto the deck, and watched a big gray wolf as it nosed along the water's edge. It stopped, looked at us, sat down, and watched us watching it. We watched each other for five minutes or so. The wolf got tired of watching us before we tired of watching him. We couldn't be sure it was a "him," but that seems to be the way we think of mammals unless shown otherwise. He stood up, put his nose to the beach and continued around the point and out of sight.

The next morning we were up and going early. We wanted to see Charpentier Inlet and the seals we had been told inhabited it before we had to meet Mark. Charpentier is the narrow inlet that may have been cut by the same glacier that cut Scidmore—where we were yesterday. We had looked down Charpentier, and wanted to see it, but knew it is was too long to do in a kayak unless we had a full day or planned to spend a night. Right now we had to be at Reid Inlet by 1600, so the Lund was the way to go. Charpentier Inlet is, arguably, the most spectacularly beautiful place in Glacier Bay. A good ten miles long, it winds through a narrow fiord with high, steep spruce-covered mountains rising on both sides. The steep mountains forming the sides continue at the same angle below water and down to depths nearing 100 fathoms. It ends in shallows at a right angle turn where a glacier terminated a few years ago, leaving the mud and rocks it had accumulated over thousands of years.

Several weeks later the two of us kayaked into Charpentier just for the fun of it. As we entered we noticed the activity of some very agitated fish creating riffles and wondered what their problem was. A few seconds later we were surrounded by a pod of orca whales, also known as killer whales. A term that offends many biologists, including us, since they are no more killers than any other carnivorous animal. There were at least ten of them all around us. We sat in the frail little kayak, not afraid but spell-bound, as they swam past and around us for twenty minutes. We found it easy to sex them: the males have much longer, taller, straighter dorsal fins, the females have more curvature to the fin and it may be less than half as tall as the males'. There was one male whose fin was laid to the side, like, as we had heard it described, "a limp dick." He was the old man of this matriarchal family. They may have been here for the same reason we were—to see what they could see. The northeast Pacific orcas normal diet is salmon and we hadn't seen any salmon here. Orcas feed on marine mammals such as seals and sea lion as well, and we had seen plenty of seals in Glacier Bay and expected them to be the target. But we hadn't seen any seals in Charpentier, perhaps the orcas were the reason seals were not showing themselves.

I doubt Charpentier has many visitors. To get into it you must navigate shallow, rocky waters west of Hugh Miller, and most power boaters aren't willing to take the time or risks necessary. We visited Glacier Bay with friends a few years later in a 32-foot Nordic Tug and decided not to try to negotiate those rocky shallow in a rented boat.

Now we did have to get to Reid and find a campsite before Mark showed up. He had given us specific orders to camp on the west shore near the mouth of Reid. He would meet us that afternoon, then motor across to the Russell raft for the evening. In the morning he would pick us up and show us some specific things he wanted done.

The run from Blue Mouse Cove to Reid Inlet didn't take as long as we had expected, so we got there about 1300 with plenty of time to set camp and do some exploring.

We had read of the legendary gold-seeking husband and wife team, Joe and Muz Ibach. In 1940 they had built a cabin near the mouth of Reid Inlet and planted three spruce trees behind the cabin. We wanted to see if we could find their place. That wasn't hard, the spruce trees had grown into the only mature trees in the upper section of Glacier Bay—natural plant succession hadn't brought spruce this close to the glaciers by 1940, and still hadn't in 1990. In fact the glacier had covered this area only a few years before Muz planted the trees and developed a vegetable garden with soil that they loaded in gunny-sacks on Lemesurier Island, where they had a more permanent home, and boated it into Reid. The cabin had been about 10 by 20 feet, but half of it had collapsed by the time we saw it. It still contained a bed frame, a pair of chairs, and trash on the floor that had probably been left by recent tourists seeking shelter from rain. We cleaned up the trash thinking, "You carried it in full; damn it, you could carry the empties out."

Joe had started looking for gold in the area in 1925, found some gold-bearing veins northwest of Reid, established a claim, and started digging. That began a 30-year mining operation that produced only enough gold to pay the smelting costs some years. Not a get-rich operation. Joe and Muz spent their last season at Reid in 1956. Muz died in a Juneau hospital in 1959, and Joe shot himself in 1960. Joe left a note on brown wrapping paper: "There's a time to live and a time to die. This is the time."

Joe and Muz apparently had told Captain Smith, a sometimes mining partner, that if one of them died while they were in the back country together the other would soon die too. Smith remarked, "I think I would feel the same way if I had lived out there all that time with my wife." I personally, understand and agree completely with that sentiment; Penny and I hope to die together.

We had been told to set our camp on the beach close to the Ibach cabin where Mark could find us. A colony of Arctic terns had set up their nesting area in that same location. Those long-range migrators spend their summers in the Arctic and their winters in the Antarctic, some 11,000 miles apart. They have a conspicuous aerial courtship which we were too late to see, but we did get to observe their vigorous defense of their nesting territory. We apparently got too close to their turf and were attacked by screaming banshies; diving on us like they would kill us if they could. We ducked and got the hell out of there. They are monogamous and nest in the same location each year. Why had Mark not known about the tern colony before he told us to camp there? Maybe he didn't know as much about wildlife as he pretended!

The beautiful and graceful Arctic terns have long pointed white wings with a little black on the trailing edge of their primary feathers, a deeply forked white tail, a black crown and nap, and deep red bill, feet, and legs, with a gray body. Truly wonders in flight, they would often hover, looking down into the waters of Reid Inlet, then dive, and invariably come up with a small fish. We watched a parasitic jaeger fly over the tern colony, and expected to see it try to steal a meal from a tern with a fish, but the jaeger moved on. We decided the terns were too aggressive for the jaeger to bother trying to steal from.

By then it was after 1600, the time Mark had told us he would meet us, so we set our little, low beach-chairs—that we had picked up in Juneau—where we could watch the terns and watch for Mark too. Those beach chairs proved to be a wonderful investment; they let us sit in our umbrella-like cooking tent with our butts off the cold, wet ground.

We admired the unusual blue-turquoise clearness of the ice of Reid glacier. It was the only clear ice we would find in any quantity in Glacier Bay. It had no morainal debris except along the edges and consisted of bubble-free ice. Air bubbles, which occur in most glacial ice, had been squeezed out of Reid, allowing ice crystals to grow larger, making for beautiful clear blue ice. Perfect to pour a little Scotch whisky over, if I had any. I mentally put it on the shopping list for someday.

About 1800 we noticed a skiff coming from the direction of Russell Island, its lone occupant standing with the tiller handle in his hand. Standing in an outboard is something that most boaters consider an invitation to a cold, wet death. If you hit most anything you can be thrown overboard with little to no chance of catching your boat. Sure enough it was Mark, and with no flotation device on. "Dumb shit!," Penny muttered and I echoed. We had expected to see him coming from down bay rather than from the direction of the Russell raft, that made us wonder why he might have been to the raft before showing up to meet us two hours late.

His first words weren't an apology for being late, they were, "This isn't where I told you to camp." I explained that there was a tern colony occupying the location he had told us to use, and asked if Arctic terns didn't nest in the same location every year. He looked toward the terns and told us we were still too close and should move our camp. Penny told him the terns had been quite content with us here until he pulled up.

Then she told about the two goats we had seen from Drake Island and all the ones we had seen from Shag Cove. Mark explained that he wasn't interested in our seeing goats from any place other than Drake Island. Our job was to observe wildlife from the same location he had used previously and not to go around dreaming up other locations and screwing up his statistics.

I told him about the assortment of ducks we had observed. Mark wanted to know how many of them were flightless. I said, "We didn't chase them so none of them flew, they just swam away from us."

"Damn it," Mark said, "I told you I wanted to know how many were flightless."

"That's an exact example of what was described as 'wildlife

harassment' by the state troopers at our LE refresher," I said. "We were given specific orders to site anyone we saw deliberately disturbing molting ducks."

Mark was pissed and I didn't want to stress our relationship even further, so I decided to not even mention the bear tracks showing brown and black bears in the same bay. He had once pointed out that black and brown bears never occupy the same habitat. We knew that, but had known of grizzlies and black bears temporarily occupying transitional areas between forest and tundra in interior Alaska as well as Montana and Wyoming. After all he was our boss and we should try to get along since we would be following his orders for the next few months.

Mark must have decided not to push it either and told us he would pick us up at eight tomorrow morning to show us how to count the kittiwake colony he wanted documented and to show us how to measure bear tracks.

He pushed his boat out, stepped in, and was off. Standing in the very stern with the tiller tilted up so he could reach it. He twisted the throttle full on, as he was turning, the boat jumped, veered left, almost burying the port gunwale, the bow shot up, the stern dropped, he almost went over the side before he recovered his balance. Penny gasped. I said, "Dumb shit," and Mark was gone for the day.

The sound of two rifle shots startled us. We looked back at the Reid Glacier and watched a big chunk of ice probably two hundred feet tall and twenty feet wide calving into the bay. What an amazing site. It didn't drop like a rock, it sort of floated forward, leaned over and fell with a huge splash, went under, and slowly resurfaced. Two minutes later a two-foot wave hit the shore where we had stood— good thing we had set camp well up from the water.

Throughout the night we listened to a thunder storm rumble and growl. We expected to see lightning flashing across the sky. But no, it wasn't thunder we were hearing, it was the glacier moving;

it cracked like lightning, it growled like distant thunder. After we realized what it was we relaxed and enjoyed the performance.

Getting up early has never been easy for us, but we needed to be ready for the boss to show up at 0800, so we were up by six to have time for breakfast and to have our camp torn down and packed. We planned to spend the next night at the Russell Island raft where Mark had been the previous night.

Between our camp and the shore there were the tracks of a brown bear and a wolf. The bear had just walked on by, probably nose to the ground smelling for anything that might be edible. The wolf had stopped. We pictured him with his ears perked, looking at our camp. His tracks showed that he had walked a few yards toward us before stopping to pee, then returned to the edge of the high tide line and on toward the glacier.

We measured the tracks in the beach sand. The wolf fore paw, excluding the claws, measured 92 mm (3-3/4 inches) wide and 83 mm (3-1/4 inches) toe to heal, the hind foot was just a bit smaller. The bear must have been a sow or a subadult. The fore paw measured 145 mm (5-3/4 inches) by 140 mm (5-1/2 inches), the hind paw was 144 mm wide and 258 mm (10-1/8 inches) long. We had measured a lot of bear tracks—probably 100—in a variety of locations and surfaces. This morning we were going to have the privilege of being shown how to measure tracks Mark's way.

We had our camp all taken down and secured in the anchored Lund and the kayak pulled up high on the beach. We were looking forward to spending tonight, our first night on "Our Raft" at Russell Island. Mark was more prompt today than he had been last evening—only an hour late. He pulled up and motioned us aboard. Without even mentioning the tracks on this beach we climbed in as he explained that we were going to look for bear tracks in several locations this morning. This afternoon he would teach us how to count the kittiwake colony.

Mark landed us at some interesting beaches of sand and gravel, and one location of mud that led to drying dirt. At the first stop he showed us how we were to measure bear tracks. He pulled out a 12-inch plastic ruler that showed inches on one edge and millimeters on the other edge. Emphatically explaining that "This is scientific work and must always be done using the metric system," he proceeded to lay the ruler across the palm pad of the first bear paw and proclaimed, "145 millimeters, a medium brown bear. You can tell it is a brown/grizzly by the fact the claw marks are as far from the toe as the length of a toe print, while a black bear nail print is much closer to the toe." The claw mark being a toe's length from the toe was an interesting fact that I had never heard expressed that way. The separation of toe and claw in brown bear prints is obvious enough that I had never considered the technicality.

Penny mentioned, "If you lay a straight edge from the bottom of the big toe (the outer toe is the largest in bears) across the leading edge of the palm pad, the small toe will be mostly above the line in a brown and below the line in a black bear print." Mark looked at her like she was speaking Greek. Obviously he had never heard that before.

He wanted all tracks measured across the palm pad, the location, date and time of day, weather condition, substrate, and how old the print was. "You can tell that by how eroded it is," he said. "In this climate they erode pretty quickly. With that information I can tell which bear it is and can figure out how big their territory is." I thought, not without us recording an awfully lot of track sets, and there aren't enough bears here to give that information unless we spend all season looking for bear prints and forget everything else you want done.

I asked about the different measurements we would get from tracks of the same bear in wet and dry mud. "I can tell which bear it is if you give me the information I have asked for," he proclaimed.

"OK," I said. Thinking, bull-shit, nobody is that good.

Mark apparently thought he should offer a token of friendship and gave us a loaf of his home made bread. It looked good and smelled great. Penny said we would have it with the dinner she was planning for tonight on the Russell Raft. "No," Mark said, "I'll be staying on the raft tonight." We looked at each other but didn't say anything, he didn't sound like there was any room for argument.

After some lunch we headed on up Tarr Inlet to Margerie and Grand Pacific Glaciers and specifically the vertical cliff face below Margerie where a colony of black-legged kittiwakes was nesting. He wanted to know how many occupied nests there were each week for the rest of the season. There were thousands of the medium sized, beautiful, white with black wing-tips, pelagic gulls. Hundreds were sitting on nests occupying every crack or ledge that would support a nest. Hundreds more were flying around or diving for small fish, the cacophony was deafening. Mark described how we were each to mentally divide the cliff face into eight sections and count the number of sitting birds in each section. The totals would allow him to know the colony size from week to week and year to year.

We sat there in the unusually warm sun each of us counting each of our imagined sections and writing the number in our note book. The idea was for each of us to count each section, add the section totals, and come out with a grand total which would be compared with the totals of each of us. I came up with 1,372 nesting kittiwakes, Penny had 1,413, Mark had 1,895. "This won't do at all," he declared. "I know my count is right, you can't be that far off. Come back tomorrow and count them again." With that, he fired the motor and took us back to Reid Inlet, with not another word.

We looked at each other, I said, "What an ass-hole!"

A week later, when we got back to Bartlett Cove, we learned that Mark had signed out of the office for several days to teach us how to do research. Several people had noticed that Dena was with him as he headed up bay. No wonder he had been late and didn't want us using the raft, he and Dena had been using our raft as a sex nest.

ATTITUDE ADJUSTMENT

When we lived in Ohio our next door neighbor was a widow, only a few years older than we, with four young daughters. Her husband, a physician, had died of a massive heart attack shortly after their youngest had been born. Mary Ann had to deal with raising those four girls, and the girls had to learn to handle living with a strong single parent. When one of the girls complained about being told to do something or how life was going to be lived in their home, Mary Ann would simply say, "Just adjust! That's the way it is girls! Just adjust!"

Mark left us at our campsite in Reid Inlet and headed back to his sex nest on our raft. We talked our situation over and admitted we were working for an asshole, and had better "Just adjust." Our primary reason for applying for the positions we held was to learn: to learn a new ecosystem, how it worked, and why it worked. We could do that and still survive Mark if we were willing to adjust our attitude. We could accept our assignments, carry them out to the best of our ability, and report our findings. Mark could bitch and curse, tell us how incompetent we were, but we would not give false statistics just to meet the numbers he wanted.

The next morning Penny woke up with a stress induced-migraine headache. She needed to take one of her "Wigraine" tablets and sleep it off. She said, "Go explore Reid while I sleep, but don't go too far and come check on me before long." I told her I would walk to the face of the glacier about a mile away, and be back within two hours.

I headed up the sandy beach and quickly found I was walking on gravel. The beach had been mostly mud by Ibach's cabin at the mouth of the bay, turned to sand then gravel, now the gravel was becoming more course. By the time I got to the face of the glacier there were rocks of all sizes. Time and current had sorted the debris the glacier was pushing and carrying, moving the lighter mud and sand the farthest, gradually leaving heavier detritus behind. Most of the rock was igneous granite, but some rocks were partially striped. Looking closely, with the little 10x hand lens I carry, I could see the feldspar, quartz, and mica crystals were differentiating into separate layers. The granite had been in the midst of metamorphosing into gneiss. It takes a lot of heat, pressure, and time to change one rock into another. So I was looking at really old rock that had formed hundreds of millions of years ago deep under the earth's surface as granite, then been subjected to more heat and pressure which had gradually separate the three crystalline forms into layers of their own.

I picked up more rocks and looked at them with my lens. I was finding an amazing assortment of different colors and textures, all of them igneous. We had a geology book, on the raft that I wanted to consult. That reminded me, I was supposed to check on Penny after two hours and had gotten interested in the rocks and forgotten the time. It was past time to pay attention to my number one concern and responsibility; better get back. I stuffed a few select rocks in my pocket and headed for camp.

Penny was sleeping soundly, so I sat in the sun and thought about the geology of Alaska we had read about and seen in other places. Alaska is not an original part of continental North America. Almost all of it is made up of terranes that have accreted over millions of years. Many island archipelagoes like Indonesia, the Japanese Islands, and Baja California have been carried up here by tectonic plates, creating this most confusing jumble of rocks. The north side of Reid Inlet is granite with intrusions of feldspar and basalt. The south side is metamorphic gneiss, schist, and what is referred to as "undifferentiated metamorphic rocks."

Penny had awakened and was feeling good. She wanted to see what I had seen and look at the vegetation along the way. The tide had been falling all morning and had left several sizable stranded icebergs. They looked big, but as we walked up to them they became huge, some seemed as big as our Colorado cabin. One stood, probably, 15-feet tall and 20-feet long. They all looked relatively small when we met them in the bay. The exposed part of that big one would have been more like 3- by 5-feet. When an iceberg decides to roll over you don't want to be close, they could easily capsize your boat.

Vegetation patterns starting near the glacier and moving toward the mouth of the bay were about the same as starting at the water's edge and moving uphill. Near the glacier there was no vegetation, just rocks and sand. We soon found dark crusts of algae that were holding moisture and forming some soil, mosses were adding bulk and apparently catching wind-born seeds allowing scouring rushes, fireweed, and willow to get a start. We've always appreciated the little dryas, a member of the rose family. It doesn't tolerate moist areas very well, but in wind-blown dry places the delightful little, yellow-flowered, mat-forming shrub, very slowly spreads to create sizable mats where blueberry and crowberry seeds—in bird poop—get dropped. The seeds take hold in the dryas mats and in mosses, other seeds arrive on bird's feet or get shaken from the fur of a wolf or bear, and succession is under way.

Nitrogen shortage is a problem for any establishing plant community, and is especially low in glacial till and outwash. Our little dryas plants and Sitka alder associate with molds and fungi that pull nitrogen from the air and sequester it in the plant's root structures. The alder thickets that we had cursed in the lake country of Katmai don't become real stands until the land has been exposed for many years, but then they can dominate in spots. It's dropped leaves break down, form soil, and prepares the land for the climax forest of spruce and hemlock that we had seen in the lower bay.

Walking back to camp we were attacked by a fierce parasitic jaeger. Penny said, "She must have a nest close, Duck and be careful where you step." We ducked and hurried to get out of her territory. I came within two inches of stepping on a little ball of brown fuzz. It was her just-hatched chick. It was hunkered down, not moving. About that time the male of the monogamous pair showed up to join in the harassment of the two-legged monsters. We moved on quickly, protecting our heads and apologizing for trespassing.

That afternoon we headed into Johns Hopkins Inlet, hoping for a close-up view of this most prolific producer of icebergs. No such luck. There was so much ice floating in that fiord we had a hard time pushing the boat through it. It's about ten miles from the mouth of the inlet to the glacier itself; I don't think we got more than a mile or two. We did get far enough to have a great view of a hanging glacier coming off Mt. Cooper. It was a wall of ice sitting atop a several-hundred-foot-high cliff and calving big chunks of ice into the fiord. Glaciers form where more snow falls in winter than melts in summer. The snow collects, is packed tighter and tighter until it becomes granular ice, then solid ice; the ice sits there until there is enough weight to start it moving down hill. Twelve of the glaciers in the park are tidewater glaciers; that is, one whose nose terminates in tidal water, this was the only hanging glacier in the park, and a spectacular site.

Most of the bergs in Johns Hopkins were white with air bubbles as opposed to the mostly clear ones in Reid. Some had dark sand, gravel, and even rocks in them. That was morainal matter that had been scraped off the side of the fiord. Some bergs had greenish-blackish mater that was stuff, we had been told, that came from the bottom of a glacier. Hmm, we needed to learn more about that. It looked like gravel to us, maybe it was rock scraped from a green mudstone.

Penny pointed to a seal on an iceberg, next to it was a pup that would be only a few weeks old. They watched us pretty carefully, ready to dive if we moved closer. We sat still and watched them watching us, just like we have done so many times with other wildlife. They are happy to leave us alone if we leave them alone. In the days and weeks ahead we would see a lot of seals hauled out on ice, often with young pups. Once we noticed a pup by itself. It had a very cut-up face, a gash on its side, and no mom. Perhaps it had an encounter with an orca or bear and Mom had been killed. It was a pathetic site, the pup had no chance of survival, but that's the way of the natural world.

One day we were slowly cruising along the right bank of Tarr Inlet and saw a big river otter lope out of the water with a fish in its mouth. We stopped and watched as it made its way toward the brush 20 yards away. Suddenly, from, it seemed like nowhere, a big gray and black wolf came charging across the sand to the otter. They fought ferociously for a minute or more. The fight ended with the wolf walking into the brush with its prize held high, perhaps a meal for a litter of wolf pups. If the fish meal had been intended for otter pups they would soon starve or, more likely, be killed by another predator.

Every two weeks we had a few days off to spend back at the A-frame we were paying rent on in Bartlett Cove. Those proved to be pretty full times: we had a report to write, a chewing out to receive for our incompetence, a new assignment for the next two weeks, a boat to clean and get ready for the next patrol, supplies to gather, a day to get clean and warm and usually go to a potluck at someone's quarters. Always a full weekend.

We were impressed by the show of friendship and camaraderie expressed by the other rangers, both interpretive and law enforcement. Apparently they had an understanding of the position we were in with Mark. Every time we returned from a patrol, Chief Ranger Randy King met us on the dock as we were unloading (we were never met by Mark). Randy wanted to know how we were, how our two weeks had been, what we had seen and done. He was interested in us and the park; he wanted, and got, a verbal report of everything going on up-bay.

Randy had rangers up-bay on a semi-regular basis, but they were doing law enforcement and not seeing many of the things we saw. Randy was especially interested in the cruise ships and how they were behaving: keeping the required distance from glacier walls, not blowing horns with the hope of causing a glacier to calve, not discharging trash—the jetsam of "flotsam and jetsam." The biggest problem with cruise ships is the stack-gas they expel. Especially when going slowly, as they must here. Large diesel engines aren't very efficient at low speed and accumulate a lot of unburned carbon in their stacks. Captains like to "Blow their stack" to clear the gunk. This is a big "No-No" in Glacier Bay and carries a heavy fine if caught. Clean air is important, especially in a national park. Frequently there is little wind in the bay so stack-gas and excess carbon can accumulate as nasty air pollution and spoil the place for everyone.

We did get a kick out of the passengers who would gather at the ships railing taking pictures and pointing out "The two people going by in that tiny little boat," or "The two idiots camped over there in this cold and rain. They must be crazy!"

We were working from a small open boat in Glacier Bay, Alaska, where it rains—a lot. Oh my god did it rain! We were supposed to spend the vast majority or our nights camping, which we did, but there were times when it poured rain for 72 hours almost non-stop. Not a good time to spend in a tent. We had two raft-cabins where we could be dry if we could get to one. It didn't take long for us to figure the weather and manage to be near one of those cabins, at least for the night when the weather was foul. More than one morning, we had 10-inches of water in the boat. Most of that had to be hand bailed before we could get the boat running fast enough that we could pull the drain-plug and drain her completely.

Regardless of the weather, nature calls on a rather regular basis, even when you are in a small, open boat. In this weather we dressed to stay warm and dry. That meant underwear, long underwear, turtleneck, uniform shirt and pants, and foul-weather float-coat-suits, with Helly Hansen rain-pants and rain-coats over it all. Now you have to pee! Tough enough for me to get the involved equipment exposed and pee over the side of the boat, but Penny had a bigger problem! She had to take off the raincoat so she could get the suspenders off her shoulders, pull the rain-pants down, unzip the survival suit, take it off her shoulder and arms, pull it down below her knees, unbuckle her uniform pants, pull them down, pull the long-johns down, pull her underpants down, and hang her fanny over the side of the boat. Now she could pee and get redressed.

We were to census the salmon running up a stream flowing into Berg Bay. There are two little lakes a couple of miles up the four foot wide, six inch deep stream where the salmon spawn. We had hiked to the lakes a couple of times. And, at Mark's insistence, we even hauled a four-foot plastic boat through the tangle of almost impenetrable willow and alder, so we could paddle across the lakes and follow a tiny stream on up and get a count of salmon above the lakes—if there were any. There were none above the lakes. The stream above was too small for much of anything, much less a pair of breeding salmon. We had busted our butts dragging the damned boat in to prove what we were sure of before hand. Then we busted our butts again dragging it out. "Just adjust, damn it! Just adjust." We reminded ourselves.

There was a good run of sockeye making its way from the bay up the stream to the lakes. We had our counts and thought Mark might be pleased this one time, even though there were no fish above the lakes. It was 1900 hours; we were tired, the tide was in, and we decided to camp there for the night, even though the willow brush crowding the beach kept us from having our camp as far from the high tide line as we like. Bears walk the shore and our tent was only going to be fifteen feet from high tide line.

We made hot water for tea, ate a cold and dry meal, so as to be sure to not have any food smells around, had a splash of brandy and went to bed. About 2200 we woke up to the sound of a diesel boat pulling in. OK, it was getting dark, a boat was anchoring for the night, no big deal. More sounds out there, what was going on? A good sized trawler was anchored, and people were stringing a long gill net across the mouth of the stream. We had never seen a commercial fishing operation in Glacier Bay other than the crab pots, which we knew were legal, but, we weren't sure about set-netting. We got dressed, walked over, and asked to see their permit. They were Tlingit Natives and informed us it was their right, they didn't need a permit. We thought they were lying but weren't positive so we radioed Mike.

Mike said, "Oh shit! Don't hassle them, I know who they are. We aren't far, Ron and I will be there in half an hour. 701 out." (We all had radio call numbers that were used rather than names in radio communication. I was 712, Penny was 713. That is standard radio procedure used by all parks.)

We weren't going to hassle them and didn't want to chase them away, but did want to talk with them. Penny went to a woman about our age who seemed to be supervising and got into a conversation about Tlingit life and history. I went to the men setting the net and asked about the webbing size they were using. This was a different kind of fishing than we were accustomed to. We were familiar with purse seines used in open water. These were gill nets, set either from shore out into deep water that catch fish migrating along a coast, or, as here, across the mouth of a stream that fish were entering. Fish swim into the net, which has a big enough mesh to let the head through but not the body, the gills get stuck, and the fish can't move in or out. The fish are harvested by dragging the net across the bow of a skiff, pulling the fish out, and dropping them into the boat; going from one end of the net to the other, and letting the net fall back into the water.

About that time Mike and Ron showed up, armed, and ready to make an arrest. We backed off to watch. Mike went directly to the skipper, read him out, gave him a citation, and told him to pull the net and get out of Glacier Bay. Mike knew the family—they were from Gustavus—and felt the park should stay on decent terms with the town and the Natives, so they were allowed to keep the few fish that were already in the net. They would die anyway if released.

We were talking with Mike and Tom as the Tlinglits were packing up. Mike was very pleased that we had made the case for him and was going to credit us in his report to the superintendent.

From the dark we heard, "No damn it! This isn't their job. They work for me doing resources management, not law enforcement!" We looked around and there was Mark, looking and acting like the fool he was proving himself to be. He picked on the wrong person when he decided to tell Mike what to do. Mike let him have it with both barrels, told him we had saved the park from being the victims of a poaching operation that he had heard rumors about; it was now stopped.

Mike and Ron left, Mark stayed. He was furious; he looked like a madman. He had endured being told off by Mike and was prepared to vent on us. He had tried to argue with Mike but hadn't been able to speak. He was probably afraid Mike would flatten him. Now he turned his wrath on us. He ranted and raved about all the travesties we were responsible for, our direct disobedience to orders, our inabilities, and on and on. He ended by exclaiming that we were going to be killed by a bear tonight because our camp was too close to the water. We tried to explain every accusation and couldn't get a word in as he raved on.

Finally he turned, got into his boat, and roared off into the dark. Penny and I looked at each other. We weren't going to get much sleep the rest of the night. We needed to talk this out. I said "Fuck him. We have taken his shit for over three months, I can't take any more."

Penny added, "We don't need this job. Lets get out of here." We'd had it. We had done, seen, and learned what we came here for. We decided that we would write our resignation in the morning and take it to Marvin Jensen.

Marv was shocked, but I can't say he seemed surprised. He asked us to let him think and come back later in the afternoon. We agreed to do that, but let him know our decision was made; we would not work another day for Mark.

We returned to Marv's office that afternoon and found a man who looked drained. He had had Mike and Randy in to talk about the situation he was facing with Mark. Mike told Marvin we were routinely sent out with only rudimentary instructions as to what to do and then criticized for not accomplishing the exact results Mark wanted, and that we were never contacted or checked on by radio other than by LE rangers. Randy let him know he was anxious to have us working full time in the law enforcement division.

Marv apparently thought of us as parent figures. He had always been very friendly and outgoing when we met. Today he talked to Penny like she was his mother. His family were staunch Mormons and considered Mark's life style amoral, but didn't know how to handle it. He told Penny of his concerns for his daughter, who had just experienced a difficult divorce and now was involved with Mark, whom he considered a predatory womanizer.

He and Penny talked on; I sat and never said a word. Finally, Marv seemed to relax, smiled and asked us to accept Randy's offer and to help him and the park through a difficult situation. We accepted his and Randy's offer. We all shook hands. He reached out and gave Penny a hug before we left.

FIGHTIN' CRIME

Our first two seasons with the NPS we had worked at Jewel Cave National Monument in the Black Hills where we had a few joint potlucks with nearby Wind Cave National Park. Jewel Cave had only interpretive rangers, Wind Cave, being a good sized, diverse park, has interpretive rangers and a few law enforcement rangers who patrol the 40,000 acres of open prairie, and several miles of roadway, by patrol car.

There is a sizable buffalo herd on the plains of Wind Cave. The buffalo need to be protected from the people and the people need to be protected from the 2,000-pound wild herbivores. Tourists seem to think of buffalo as big placid cows and don't hesitate to approach for that "great picture." Disturbing wildlife is dangerous, stupid, illegal, and done regularly in most parks by the visiting public. Consequently Wind Cave has law enforcement rangers who try to manage the visitors by educating them—managing wildlife just doesn't seem to work.

At one of the joint potlucks we were having a beer and talking with a LE ranger who was telling of the day he had been on patrol and decided to park in an obvious place just to remind drivers that he was watching them. It being a typical warm day he soon fell asleep. Some time later he was awakened by the shaking of his patrol car. Opening his eyes he saw a huge buffalo scratching his ass on the front bumper. He laughed and told us that was a typical day of "Fightin' Crime at Wind Cave."

We have kidded LE rangers about "Fightin' Crime" ever since.

Frank Starr

Now we were LE rangers ourselves, "Fightin' Crime" at Glacier Bay National Park. Sure, we held federal LE commissions but had always found educating the public by explaining the reason for regulations worked much better than citations. Here too, education was the best approach to boaters who chose to ignore the "No Power Boats" areas where whales frequently feed, and the "No Wake" zones near docks.

There were four LE rangers: our dear old friend Kris Fister from Yosemite and Katmai; Ron Anataya, also a friend from Katmai; Tom Gage with whom we had become good friends here; and Steve Prather, an unusual young man whom we knew nothing about. Now add Penny and me, making a crew of six, and, of course, District Ranger Mike Sharp and Chief Ranger Randy King.

Potlucks are popular everywhere in the Park Service and Glacier Bay was no exception. Randy's wife, Sally, and their year-old daughter, Mackenzie, had waited until Randy was settled in his new position before they joined him. As soon as they showed up Randy hosted a potluck to introduce his family to the rest of the staff. Sally proved to be a winner just like her husband. We four became fast friends right away, a close friendship that still holds. Today, we are retired and Randy is Superintendent of Mt. Rainier National Park and we still manage to get together a couple of times each year. Sally told us, "When we grow up we want to be just like you." Could you ask for a better compliment?

The duties of LE rangers varied and were subject to immediate change to fit any situation. There was an office at the head of the commercial dock, manned by one of us from 0800 to 2000 (pronounced twenty hundred hours), where every boater was required to check-in, get a permit, and receive rules and regulations, advice, warnings, and any information the boater wanted. This position, along with park dispatcher, seemed to fall to Penny since she was by far the most personable and best communicator on the LE staff. I was assigned to boat patrol of the lower bay. We both drew campground duty, dock-patrol, and foot-patrol of the beaches. All of us were assigned to check the campground, the area around the lodge, and especially the lodge employee housing area, where a sow black bear and her three cubs seemed to be finding entirely too much food. Too often bears are provided food by people purposely chumming them closer for a better picture, or by unknowing or non-thinking tourists and lodge employees just being slobs and not properly disposing of trash. One of us, usually Penny, was called out, almost daily to chase the bears who were becoming too familiar with people and people food.

One morning there was a radio call from Kathy, a woman doing whale research in and around Glacier Bay, notifying us that there was a hump-backed whale in trouble. It had a line wrapped around its tail, on the end of which was a large red plastic float that the whale was pulling as it swam and dove. The line would have to be cut, or the whale would become exhausted and, perhaps, starve. She needed a ranger to go with her to cut the line. Mike immediately took charge. He knew I was on boat patrol, Steve was on foot-patrol, and Penny was on office duty. Over the radio, he ordered Steve and Penny to get to the outer dock, told Kathy to pick up Steve and told me to pick up Penny. We would go out into Icy Straight, find the whale, and solve the problem any way we could.

It didn't take long to locate the whale. The poor thing was surfacing for a breath much more frequently than was normal. It was severely stressed by the float it was dragging under every time it dove. Kathy and Steve were in an open Boston Whaler with good maneuverability and easy access to the water. Penny and I were in the Rebound, a cabin cruiser with twin outboards. It was a much more stable and powerful boat, but we didn't have easy access to the water and the line that would have to be caught and cut. Kathy, being a senior whale researcher, took command without discussion which suited all of us except Steve. He would have to snag the line and cut it between the whale and the float, which sounded dangerous and scary to him.

Kathy pulled the Whaler up to the line ahead of the float, Steve reached for the line with a boat-hook but couldn't catch it. We were right behind the Whaler, Kathy moved to the side to give us access, I pulled up closer to the whale, Penny reached for the line with her boat-hook just as the whale dove. She caught the line, but saw the big float rushing at her as the whale dragged it under and let go before the float hit her. On the second try Steve caught the line, took a turn around a cleat on the Whaler's fore-deck and started to cut the line. The whale dove before the line parted. The Whaler and crew were being pulled under just like the float had been. Water rushed over the bow, and splashed into the cockpit; it looked like they were going under. Steve frantically fought the line and got it free of the cleat, barely in time and the Whaler popped right up. They had water in the cockpit that had to be drained but they were safe.

OK, that didn't work. We couldn't think of another way to set the whale free so we decided to try it again the same way, except this time we would hold our boat right next to the Whaler in case they needed rescuing if their boat was pulled under. We saw the whale blow a hundred meters ahead and caught up just as she dove. Now we realized we had to be in position before she surfaced in order to have time to cut her free. We calculated where she would come up and got in position. Somehow she did as we had expected. She surfaced just ahead of the Whaler. Kathy powered up close, Steve caught the line, wrapped it around the bow-cleat, and managed to get it cut before our whale took them under. The whale was free of the float and would not have much trouble with the line which was still wrapped around her tail. Without the tension of the float the line would work loose and fall off—we hoped.

The float that poor whale was dragging was more than three feet in diameter, Penny and I managed to load it into Rebound to dispose of later. We congratulated Kathy and Steve on getting it cut loose without sinking the Whaler, Mike gave us all a well done on the radio, and we headed back to the park.

Penny and I were assigned a four-day patrol of the upper bay in Nevé one of the diesel powered cabin cruisers, just to make a LE presence obvious and to communicate with boaters, kayakers, and campers. We met a kayaker named Christian from New York, New York, who told us he had been out for two weeks and would be paddling around for several more days before returning to Bartlett Cove. He had all his permits but seemed a bit strange. He was wearing this funky, big brown and black fuzzy moose hat with antlers like a little kid might wear. He looked and acted like he was on drugs and sounded a bit incoherent. At the same time he was obviously a competent camper having been paddling and camping for two weeks in foul weather in brown bear country with, apparently, no negative effects. He hadn't done anything actually wrong, so we just let him go with strong bear warnings.

Christian, like many others over the season, had taken his sea-kayak on the lodge's sightseeing boat, Spirit of Glacier Bay, from the commercial dock near headquarters to Tlingit Point, at the confluence of Muir and Tarr Inlets. The Spirit would stop here every day, drop kayakers off at 1000 hours and pick kayakers up at 1500 hours the same day or any day they specified. If kayakers weren't at the pick-up point at the agreed day and time they were reported to the park and it became our responsibility to locate them. Usually they had shown up late, missed their ride, and were picked up 24 hours later. Consequently, we didn't worry until someone was more than a day late. This character had made no pick up date, saying he would paddle the 25 miles of mostly open water back to the campground by the lodge. We made a note to check on him when we returned from this patrol.

Before noon rain started in earnest and poured all day and

the following night, making us awfully glad to be in the enclosed Nevé rather than the open skiff we had used for so long. We got a radio call from dispatch letting us know a couple had missed their second pick up and were now considered overdue and lost. We were to search for them and, at the same time, check on a reported bear-sighting near campers in Hugh Miller Inlet.

We were in Tarr Inlet not far from Hugh Miller. All we had to do was cruise across the inlet and find the campers. We had seen a brown bear there earlier in the summer and had recorded its tracks several times, so we were sure it was a medium to small single bear and should be no problem if the campers were knowledgeable and doing as they should with their food. They weren't hard to find—right where we had expected them to camp in the only decent site in Hugh Miller Inlet. They were a couple from Minnesota. They had a nice, clean camp, well away from the water's edge where the bears tend to walk, and most of all, very knowledgeable about camping in bear country. We had a good discussion of similar experiences canoeing the Boundary Waters Canoe Area, shared between their state and Canada. These people had seen the bear, were aware, careful, and not overly concerned—the kind of people we appreciated having in the park. Apparently a boater had reported seeing a bear in the area of their camp and radioed the sighting into headquarters.

The tide was in and we thought we could make it through the shallows to Charpentier Inlet and Scidmore Bay to check for the kayakers who had missed two pickups at Tlingit Point. Sure enough they were in Scidmore Bay waiting out the rain. They were a young couple from Ohio and didn't like the weather at all. Penny explained the weather was like that this time of year and suggested they would be better off heading back to Tlingit Point where they could camp on high ground and get picked up by the Spirit tomorrow. Waiting for the rain to quit might take several more days. It was late in the day and they promised to head back first thing in the morning. We had seen bears here numerous times and encouraged them to make that trip this evening rather than in the morning. The mention of bears got their attention. They hadn't seen any but had seen some footprints and wondered about what to do if they saw a bear. Penny gave them the whole bear indoctrination—they had skipped it when they got their permit. They decided to head to safer, dryer Tlingit right away.

We felt sorry for them but knew they were damned lucky to not have had a bear encounter before this. We radioed headquarters to let them know the lost kayakers were found and would get the Spirit tomorrow, and that the Hugh Miller campers were just fine. Now we could call it a day. We pulled up to the ranger raft in Blue Mouse Cove and were very happy to not be camping this wet night. Penny would fix a good dinner of her wonderful Mexican beans and rice with some Mexican Velveeta cheese melted on top. Meanwhile I went over to the fuel-raft and topped off Nevé. We would have a cold beer from the stash we had hung in the bay, enjoy dinner, and sleep warm and dry. The life of a LE ranger was a lot more comfortable than the life of the cold, wet, sleep-on-the-ground researchers we had been for several months. The comfort factor was nice, but more importantly, we were now working for two really great bosses.

The next morning the rain had stopped and we motored up to the head of Tarr Inlet to check the stack gas coming from a huge cruise ship that had gone up to show its passengers the face of Grand Pacific Glacier. The ship was running cleanly, and we found ourselves beside the cliff face hosting the black-legged kittiwake colony that we had tried to count so many times. We sat for a few minutes reminiscing about the day we nearly froze in our open skiff under a leaden sky with ice thick around us like we were a lime in a frozen margarita. We had actually been hypothermic that evening as we headed for the Russell Island raft. We were both shivering uncontrollably and felt sort of dizzy. When we got to the raft we managed to get some warmth from the propane cook stove, and drank a bit of hot cider with brandy. I realized my pulse was way up. I checked Penny's pulse and found hers even higher than mine. Had we not had the raft-cabin that night, I fear we would have been in serious trouble.

The radio put an end to our reminiscing. Dispatch was letting us know that a group of ten people from the Wilderness Adventures Camp in Wyoming and their guide, from Alaska Discovery Tours, had been, "Viciously attacked by a huge brown bear." Our dispatcher also told us the group had refused the bear orientation that was required saying their guide Rusty would give it. Yeah sure! We had heard that story before. The "attack" had been early this morning, as they were fixing breakfast; they had all grabbed what gear they could, piled into their kayaks, and fled without trying to chase the bear away or retrieve any of their other items. They had gotten to the Tlingit kayak pick-up point before the Spirit had arrived for the regular morning drop-off, and frantically met the boat as it pulled in, demanding the park do something about the vicious bear.

Spirit's skipper had radioed headquarters with the information that was now being forwarded to us. We were to check it out. Mike Sharp got on the radio and warned us to be especially careful; this bear had a food cache and would be protecting it. We, of course, were well aware of that but were glad to know Mike was concerned for our safety.

The incident had taken place at Ptarmigan Point near Tidal Inlet, about 30 miles from our present location near the Grand Pacific Glacier. We cruised down, found an anchorage, made sure the shotgun was loaded to our liking and working properly, and went ashore. We immediately saw bear tracks on the beach—only 125 mm across—had to be a small sow or subadult; they were easy to follow as the bear moseyed along. We could see where it stopped and went directly up the hill. "Oh Shit." Penny said, "There it is!" It was right above us looking like a big dog having fun, rolling around on a collection of brightly colored nylon stuff sacks. The idiots hadn't even bothered to use the bear-proof food containers that the Park Service recommends and loans free to campers. There was nothing we could do until this young bear finished its play time and left. It had obviously eaten everything and was now enjoying just being a kid. We went back to the Névé and radioed our findings to headquarters.

Now the park had a problem: a bear that had learned it could get food from people. All of Tarr Inlet would probably be closed to camping for we wouldn't care to guess how long. That was up to Superintendent Marvin and Chief Ranger Randy—that's why they get the big bucks. It didn't take long to make that decision. Not a half hour had passed before we were informed that Tarr Inlet would be closed to camping for an indefinite period and that we were not to try to access the spot until tomorrow.

We spent the rest of the day cruising the length of Tarr Inlet, looking into every little cove and fiord, notifying all the boaters and campers of the closure that had been caused by campers not following proper etiquette in bear country. People didn't like the edict, they had planned a great camping trip and were mad at the Park Service and us in particular. We let them know it was the bad campers they should be mad at and explained proper bear country behavior, including our concerns, not only for them but for the young bear that would have to be killed if it raided any more camps.

The next morning we rechecked the entire inlet to make sure we hadn't missed anyone or that someone had ignored our explanation of the closure. No bears, no pilgrims, but a couple of boaters to talk to. One of them told us the Royal Viking Sea, one of the huge cruise ships, had left a large oily slick as they left Grand Pacific Glacier; another item for the extensive case incident report we would have to write.

We still had to get to the site of the bear incident and clean it up. We followed the same procedure as yesterday—hauling the shotgun, wearing .357s, and carrying several plastic trash sacks. We walked up very slowly and carefully, talking loudly so as to not surprise the bear, but expecting to see it protecting whatever was left of its raid. There was no bear to be seen. On a knob was an amazing sight—brightly colored nylon stuff sacks all torn up and scattered around, a torn up fire ring, an aluminum cooking pot with tooth holes, a strip of duct tape, a scrub pad, several spice containers with smelly spice strewn around, a few rice grains, a bit of gorp, a French's noodle soup mix container, a few beans, tortilla shreds, lemonade mix, bits of plastic and foil food-wrapper, and still no bear. God, what a mess. We picked up all the trash and hoped those campers were intelligent enough to realize and learn from what they had done, but doubted it. That sort of people are deniers—they go home and tell wild stories of being good campers who were attacked by a vicious bear.

THE LAST ASSIGNMENT FOR THIS PATROL WAS TO RUN UP MUIR Inlet and check on a group of researchers in Wachusett Inlet who were studying succession following glacial retreat. They were fine and really not finding anything new, but enjoying confirming the way plants and animals gradually re-inhabit a newly exposed area. We told them about our friend Gene Good who had done the exact same work in the same location nearly 40 years ago. Many of them were familiar with the reports of the Good Survey and were comparing their findings with his group's. They told us that succession was progressing just as Dr. Good's group had predicted.

We were well up Muir Inlet and decided to patrol on to Muir Glacier. There isn't much tourist traffic here, Tour boats are prohibited and ranger patrols are rare, but Randy wanted the inlet checked whenever a patrol was in the area. I had always wanted to get a close look at one of the rivers coming out from the bottom of a tidewater glacier. Today there was not much drifting ice near the glacial face, the tide was low, and a cavernous opening with a rushing river was obvious at the bottom of Muir Glacier. We had seen rivers emerging from every glacier we had been close to. I wanted a better look at the opening in the glacier and pulled the Nevé in thinking we might even be able to enter the cave. Penny said, "That's far enough! Lets not do something stupid and get ourselves killed."

That stream had a lot more force than I had expected. I said, "OK you're right. This is close enough," and let the current carry us away from Mr. Muir's glacier.

When looking at a glacier we don't tend to think of it melting, just of it moving forward and calving or retreating. But, glaciers are formed by the simple accumulation of more snow in the winter than melts in the summer. Thinking about a glacier, it makes sense for the ice to melt next to the rock wall it is moving through; the albedo of ice, it seemed to me, should be enough to allow very little surface melting. Not so. The surface doesn't reflect all of the light, some ice melts and forms pools and streams which find a way through the ice. A hair-line crack can be enough to create a hole called a millwell that surface water follows down to the ground and becomes a stream, even a river under a sizable glacier.

"Enough already," said Penny, "Lets call this patrol complete and head home."

As we pulled into the dock at headquarters, what to our wondering eyes should appear but Christian, the kayaking druggie in his silly moose hat, walking away from his kayak and a pile of gear on the edge of the beach. I had to secure the Nevé so Penny hopped off and headed to intercept Christian. "Hey, Christian, you can't leave gear unattended on the beach. This is bear country and it will be torn up before you can get back!" she said, as she caught up with him.

"Fuck you, bitch!" he said, and continued walking toward the campground.

Penny pulled her radio and called for back-up at the campground beach. Mike responded immediately, wanting to know the problem. Penny replied, "Druggie leaving gear unattended."

Penny had caught up with Christian and was trying to explain that, "There are bears in the area and your gear will be destroyed, and a bear will have learned that human gear is fun to tear up. So you have to get your gear off the beach before you go to the campground. I'll help you. We can put it all in the bear-proof cache where it'll be safe."

Christian was getting mad and was yelling at Penny by the time Mike appeared. Without hesitation Mike stepped between Christian and Penny, he seemed to tower over Christian, but Christian kept yelling and swearing at Mike saying that, "There is no way in hell that I am moving that shit until I am damned good and ready." Penny had backed away to let Mike handle the situation, like she knew an experienced LE ranger would.

This time the experienced LE ranger lost his cool and started yelling too. Penny could see this escalating into an impossible mess. All that was needed was for Christian to take a swing at Mike and for Mike to respond in-kind or pull his sidearm. Christian would end up in jail, but Mike's career might be over. Penny stepped between the two bellowing males and said, "Christian, you're under arrest. Put your hands behind your back. Mike hand me your cuffs."

It worked! Christian quit yelling and put his hands behind his back, Mike handed Penny his handcuffs, she snapped them on Christian's wrists. They both had immediately complied when Penny took charge—it was one of those inexplicable incidents, but it worked. I had shown up by then and said, "I'll watch Christian. You two decide how we handle this."

They had a prisoner in handcuffs and no place to keep him in secure custody. The closest jail was in Juneau six hours away by boat. Christian seemed to be coming out of his drug fix, so I sat down with him while Penny and Mike talked the situation over. He told me his name was Christian Z. Smith and he lived in New York City, but refused to tell me more saying, "Name, rank, and serial number only," as if he had been in the military.

By this time the administrators, Chief Ranger Randy and

Superintendent Marvin, had become aware of the situation. Penny and Mike were called by radio and told to report to Marvin's office immediately. They left me with Christian and headed to the administration building.

Mike contacted NCIS for information on Christian Z. Smith of New York City and found that he was a 52-year-old judge in New York, New York. Judge Smith had a 24-year-old son Christian Jr. Sounded like we had an identification of our young prisoner. Marvin and Randy didn't want to make a big deal of this incident, so they told Mike to have Penny cite him for littering and get him out of the park.

Mike and Penny decided they couldn't turn him loose in the drugged condition he was showing. I was told to search his belongings and confiscate any drugs or drug-related material. Apparently he had used it all up before he came back to shore because his gear was all filthy, but clean of any incriminating drug material. He was given his citation and told he was under "house arrest," and would have to stay at his tent in the campground until morning. We weren't concerned with him leaving. There was no place he could go unless he decided to go back out in his kayak, which had been secured in the NPS boat-house where he couldn't get it.

The next morning Penny and I found Christian most humble. He handed Penny a check for the $167.00 fine made out to the NPS, apologized to Penny and Mike, and was given a ride to the Gustavus airport.

That evening Marvin and his wife hosted a potluck for the LE rangers. We all had a good evening; a great feed, plenty of beer, and a lot of fun kidding Mike and Penny about the dangerous "Drug King of Glacier Bay." Randy offered a toast to Mike and Penny for handling the "Serious criminal situation with no-shots-fired, and no-harm-done." Penny in turn offered a toast to "Fightin' Crime in Glacier Bay." Everyone had a good laugh, another drink, and we all went home tipsy and happy.

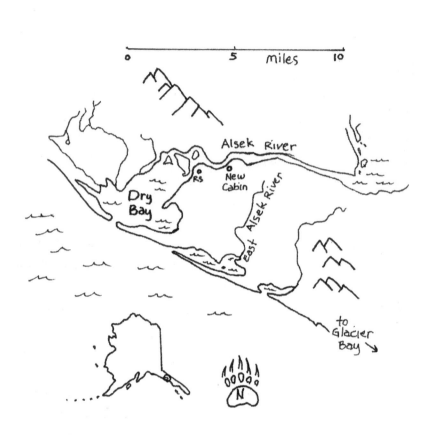

miles

Alsek River

Dry
Bay

RS

New
Cabin

East Alsek River

to
Glacier
Bay

N

DRY BAY

R andy called us to his office; he had a proposition. He knew we
had built our Colorado cabin ourselves. He asked if we would
be willing to go to Dry Bay, in the preserve, for two or three weeks
and build a cabin to be used as a seasonal residence by the Dry Bay
ranger. "No," he said, "It won't have either water or electricity, so
you don't need to consider being plumbers or electricians. I'll send
a carpenter from maintenance and another ranger along to help.
But I really need your expertise. No one else on staff had ever built
anything bigger than a shed."

I said, "We're anything but expert house builders. We've built
one little cabin, but for you," I said laughingly, "and the glory of the
Park Service, we'll give it a shot."

Glacier Bay National Park and Preserve does have a preserve
portion, which visitors and rangers almost never see, and most
don't even know exists. It is quite remote in the very most northwest
portion of the park. I suspect it is actually the delta of the Alsek/
Tatshenshini River but have never found a geologic description
of the area. The Tatshenshini is a serious white-water stream that
was becoming popular with dedicated white-water rafters. Below
the confluence with the Alsek it looses the boulders that create
white-water, but is still a very fast, dangerous stream that forms
the north and west boundaries of the preserve and the border of
Canada.

The preserve's rivers and coast have been used by both Tlingit
and whites for subsistence fishing for centuries. In 1980, ANILCA

added nearly one million acres to Glacier Bay and the preserve portion is a part of that addition. It has a gravel air strip, a wall-tent ranger station, one seasonal ranger, a commercial fish processing establishment, and a bunch of seasonal fishing shacks—we never met a permanent resident.

The East Alsek River, a small stream by Alaska standards, runs north to south through the center of the preserve and provides wonderful salmon fishing when the fish are running and the state declares an opening. As in all of Alaska the state department of fish and game controls the harvest by limiting the openings—the times of legal fishing.

Marvin and Randy had found the plans for a 16 by 24-foot cabin that included a list of all of the material needed for construction. They would get the plans and order all of the lumber and other materials. They had even gotten the Coast Guard to agree to deliver the supplies, by helicopter. We wouldn't have to worry about footers or a stem-wall because this cabin was going to be moveable. It would be mounted on a pair of 6 by 12-inch by 24-foot cedar skids. Thus, in case of a flood it could be pulled to safety by a bulldozer.

It didn't come out until later that Greg, the seasonal ranger stationed at Dry Bay, would be there for a day or two after we arrived, but was going to be gone for a few weeks, so we would need to take over his duties while he was gone. That would be in addition to building the cabin—apparently Randy hadn't been aware of Greg being gone either, one of those last minute developments that do happen.

We flew to the Dry Bay gravel air strip with the food and clothes we figured we needed for a month. Greg met us on a Honda four-wheeler pulling a small trailer. He was about five-foot-ten and well over 200 pounds. He looked soft and the type who would be good with paperwork, but not at all what we considered "Park Ranger material." He would be one of those who would float to the top simply by his paper skills.

We loaded our gear onto the trailer and followed Greg to the tiny shack that would be our bedroom. That shack turned out to be the coldest, dampest damn place we ever slept. Next to the shack was a tent-frame kitchen with a propane stove and refrigerator and an oil-heat stove. the only place with heat where we could warm ourselves or dry our clothes in this place of fog and rain.

As soon as we had our gear stashed he took us to Sitka Sound Seafood to borrow a second four-wheeler and told us to meet him at the tent-frame after lunch. He wanted to show us around the bay, point out what needed to be done in his absence, and introduce us to a few people.

Dry Bay proved to be an interesting place. Seeing it confirmed our idea that the entire preserve is the dirt and sand delta of the Alsek River. It is flat, for this part of the world, and is separated from the Pacific by a sand spit and a lagoon that reminded us of southeast Florida and the Carolina barrier islands—only 50 degrees colder. Two streams run across the preserve, the western one is named the East Alsek River, presumably because it is a few miles east of the Alsek River. We never heard the name of the other. It is, we were told, difficult to access.

The human population seemed to be all seasonal. They were fisher-people, men and women, living in shacks built on the west bank of the East Alsek River. They were fishing for salmon running up the river to spawn. Greg introduced us to a few of them who seemed like good people earning a living by hard seasonal work. Some were teachers, even professors, from the "lesser 48." Some were working hard for the season, but would live in Phoenix and draw unemployment all winter. A typical mix of Alaskans—either PhDs or red-necks.

We met the Dry Bay ADF&G technician, Ben, who was in-charge of directing fishing openings. He had a lot of responsibility: monitoring the salmon runs, counting the numbers of fish going up river, and reporting his counts to his Juneau office. The office calculated when to open the river to fishing and when to close it. Sometimes those openings would be announced only a few hours ahead of time. Ben invited us to help him the next morning when an opening was scheduled for 0730.

Greg didn't have a law enforcement commission but seemed to think he was our boss at Dry Bay. He wanted us to be real sticklers on a whole list of infractions he had observed in the past but couldn't do anything about, such as setting a net too close to another net. They must be separated by 75 or more yards, even a few inches too close and he wanted them cited. We let him know that was not what we were here for. If he wanted them cited, he had better get a commission and be a cop. We would cite if there was a blatant infraction that we had seen and Ben had not, and if it was something Ben wanted stopped.

Meeting several of the fisher-people was interesting but we had been sent here to build a cabin. I said, "Greg, lets go check the cabin site so we know what we are going to need to get done before the Coast Guard helicopter shows up with the lumber."

He seemed reticent to take us there but did. "For God's sake Greg," I said, "you haven't even cleared the trees yet! That was supposed to have been done weeks ago! What the hell have you been doing?"

He couldn't answer. He just sort of mumbled, "I've been busy. I have a tremendous amount of paperwork that has to be kept up. But I did get a chain-saw for you."

Penny kept me from raging on. She said, "OK Greg, you leave in the morning, get us the chain-saw and fuel and we will deal with what you've left us."

The site was about an acre, and covered with young Sitka Spruce two to three inches in diameter right next to the fast, dangerous Alsek River. An entirely different stream than the East Alsek, which was about 100 yards wide and 15 miles long, flowing clear over a bed of sand and gravel, and running two or three knots. The Alsek here, near its mouth, is not very wide, but is a wild, fast-moving stream coming out of the Alsek Range of the Saint Elias Mountains of British Columbia and Alaska. It is fed by numerous glaciers, had a steep cut-bank ten feet high and was running at least ten or twelve knots. Cold, wet, and fast it was something to stay away from.

By now it was late afternoon and Greg had left us puzzling over our next chore. We had to clear the land and build a cabin. Did that make us pioneers? Naw, we would use a chain-saw, assuming Greg had gotten one for us. We realized that the people at Sitka Sound Seafood (SSS) would be our only back-up while we were here. Besides they all seemed like nice kids and had offered us friendship and help, even told us we could use their shower. We had the loan of their four-wheeler, so lets go over and get to know them. We made friends and got to observe the processing of fresh-caught salmon.

The salmon running that time of year were mostly Coho, also known as Silvers. They are beautiful bright, shiny, silver-sided fish with dark bluish-green backs. They weighed six to ten pounds, but could go up to 35 pounds, with nice firm, red flesh. These were all sea-run fish, they hadn't started morphing into the sexually mature animals that change to pink, then red-skinned, with pronounced hooking of the nose and jaws. At the same time the flesh gradually changes to a light, soft texture which doesn't taste nearly as good and doesn't sell at all. They don't start their metamorphoses until they enter fresh water, so these, fresh from the sea, were ideal—and tasted wonderful that evening.

The processing of the salmon was interesting. On a long, stainless steel table three or four people, all wearing rubber boots, heavy Helly Hansen rain pants, and rubber gloves, cut off the heads, collected the eggs, and gutted them. They were run through a machine which removed the scales. Then they were thoroughly washed with fresh water, packed in ice, and refrigerated until the next plane landed to take them to market as "Fresh Caught Alaskan Silver Salmon."

"Enough for today! Lets go fix something to eat and hit the sack," I said, and got no argument from Penny. We had an early morning "opening" to observe and monitor.

The next morning it was raining steadily. We knew we would have a lot of rain to deal with at Dry Bay and decided someone had named it facetiously. Greg had put the chain-saw in the cook-tent, and five gallons of mixed gas outside. So there was no question of how we would spend the afternoon and tomorrow, and probably the next day. This morning we were going to learn about gill-netting on the East Alsek.

We had the park's four-wheeler as well as the one borrowed from SSS so we were independent and each of us could go wherever we needed to be. We headed across the sand road to the river where Ben had asked us to help with today's opening. At the river, all was organized chaos—it looked chaotic but was well organized—people, trucks, and gear everywhere. Nets were laid out on the bank of the East Alsek, skiffs were ready to pull one end of the net out into the river when Ben waved the opening. People were yelling at helpers or cursing other fishers who were in the way. Ben saw us and hurried over to where we were. It was just after 0700 and he wanted us to arbitrate between two groups about to get into a fight over being too close to each other.

Two couples, the Svensons and the Borjkovs, were yelling at each other, saying the other group had to move their nets. Penny and I stepped between them and asked for an explanation. That started the yelling again. Penny took the Svensons, I took the Borjkovs and got their stories. Each claimed they were there first and the other had to move. I got the 100-yard tape from Ben and measured the distance between their beach anchors. Sure enough, they were only 72 yards apart and were required to be at least 75 yards apart. OK they had to move or be cited. Penny and I conferred a moment and told them they both had to move—the Svensons two yards down stream and the Borjkovs two yards up stream. Of course that set them all off, yelling at us. We just said, "Move or we will cite you both and pull your nets for the entire opening." They calmed down and moved their net anchors as we had ordered.

Ben climbed up on the seat of his four-wheeler, ignoring the rain, he took off his rain coat, got soaked, and at exactly 0730, waved that bright orange coat so everyone along the river could see that the opening had started. Each group had a person in a skiff who pulled the end of the net out into the river, dropped an anchor and had the net set. The net itself was called a gill-net; the top line had floats set every few feet, the bottom line had lead weights every few feet, this lets the net hang straight; the mesh of the net is sized to allow the fish's head to go through but not the body, when the fish struggles to get free its gills catch on the mesh and the fish is stuck. The mesh size does a good job of keeping the by-catch low, small fish swim on through, large fish don't get stuck, and bottom feeders aren't bothered except very near shore.

Depending on the run, the net should have a load in an hour or two. The skiff, with two or three people onboard, starts at the river end of the net, they pull it across the bow and drape it across the boat. Working the length of the net, they pulled the fish out, dropped them into the bottom of the boat, feed the net back into the river, and moved along the net to shore. At shore they shovel the fish into a container and haul their catch to SSS, leaving the net in place to refill.

Ben came over and thanked us for our help and suggested we might want to stick around to see the closing of the opening. That's when every net had to be out of the water by a certain time. We thanked him for the opportunity to learn gill-netting, but let him know we had a clear-cutting job that had to be taken care of.

We drove our four-wheelers back to camp, through the steady rain, collected the chain-saw and fuel can, and studied the acre of sapling trees that had to be cleared to make a landing spot for the big Sikorsky helicopter that would bring us the building material that had been ordered for the cabin.

It took a day and a half, but we had all of the trees cut and piled out of the way. It reminded me of a harvested corn field in Ohio, with three inch stumps and shocks of corn drying.

Now we had an opening where the helicopter could land and we could build the cabin with a great view of the Alsek River rushing by. We radioed Randy that we were ready for the material to be brought up, and were told it would be a couple of days, because the Coast Guard was occupied with the rescue of a passenger on the cruise ship Rotterdam. He also let us know that our helpers, Jim and Steve, would fly up the same day the material came. OK, we could just relax and hang out until then.

The weather just got worse. Day after day we had three to four inches of rain—we measured 4.77 inches one day—and were told the helicopter wouldn't fly in that weather. We were accustomed to waiting out Alaskan weather but this was getting to be a bit much. We had a cabin to build and nothing to do until we had lumber to build with. So we visited our friends at SSS. We listened to the bugling and trumpeting of Sandhill cranes gathering for their migration south. The Sandhills have proclaimed their ownership of the tundra marshes and pot-holes for thousands of years, since the retreating ice sheets exposed new land for them to claim. Listening to the Sandhills took us back to *A Sand County Almanac* and the words of Aldo Leopold:

> Out of some far recess of the sky a tinkling of little bells falls soft upon the land. Then again silence. Now comes the baying of some sweet-throated hound, soon the clamor of a responding pack. Then a far clear blast of hunting horns, out of the sky into the fog. High horns, low horns, silence, and finally a pandemonium of trumpets, rattles, croaks, and cries that almost shakes the bog with its nearness, but

without disclosing whence it comes. At last a glint of sun revels the approach of a great echelon of birds. On motionless wings they emerge from the lifting mist, sweep a final arc of sky, and settle in clangorous descending spirals to their feeding grounds.

At night we were serenaded by a family of wolves whose calls communicated all the day's news and views to each other. And to us, if we understood the language.

Finally Randy radioed that the big helicopter would be in that afternoon, and our helpers, Jim and Steve, would fly in that morning. They would be bringing a gas-powered, electric generator and all of the power tools we had requested. Along with an 8- by 10-foot quonset-hut shaped Weather Port so our tools could be stored dry. An hour later Jim and Steve flew in. We had them stow their gear in Greg's tent-frame. We set the Weather Port up and were ready for the Coast Guard.

The big Sikorsky set down right where I, acting like I knew what I was doing and using the motions I had learned on an aircraft carrier, directed. The pilot, a nice looking young woman with the rank of lieutenant, stepped out of the cockpit and walked up to us. Two big guys drove a fork-lift out of the huge stern door. Lieutenant Penelope Erickson told us her crew would put our lumber anywhere we wanted it, then Penelope and Penny found a place to talk while the rest of us got the material off and arranged in the order Jim and I thought would require us to move things the least.

The first job of any construction project is to get the foundation right. Penny and I had cleared and leveled two strips 25 feet long, a foot wide, parallel, and 12 feet apart where the two, 24 foot, 6- by 12-inch, cedar skids had to be positioned exactly parallel and level. We took advantage of the two big Coast Guardsmen and the fork-lift to get the skids moved and properly positioned. That done, we could bid adieu to Penny's new friend, Penelope, and her crew with much thanks.

It had been a long, full day and we were ready to knock off. The rain had almost quit. Penny and Jim walked down to look at the Alsek that was running full and strong against the bank. As Penny stood on the edge, 10 feet above the rushing water, the ground she was standing on must have been undercut, it slumped and she slid down the bank. She struggled to move up the bank, but was slipping farther towards that torrent. That rain swollen, muddy river would quickly take her in her heavy rain gear and rubber boots, to a sure death in a matter of moments, long before any of us could respond. Of course she had screamed as she slipped, and now she felt a strong hand grab the neck of her rain coat, stopping her slide. She looked up and saw the terrified face of Jim lying flat on the bank. He had ahold of Penny and was slowly pulling her to the top. Quite a day; Penny had a new namesake friend and a new hero to thank for her life.

The construction phase of the cabin went quickly and smoothly. Penny and I laid out the floor joists' locations on the header-joists. We carried the 2- by 8-inch by 16-foot joists to Jim, who assembled them with the nail-gun. Then Penny and I made sure the platform was perfectly square by measuring upper left corner to lower right corner then the upper right corner to the lower left corner. If those measurements were identical we had four 90-degree angles to work with and the rest of the construction should go just right. They didn't suit me. I had Jim bang on a corner with a sledgehammer until they were within an 1/8-inch of equal. "Good enough for government work," I proclaimed. The 3/4-inch T&G plywood floor was laid and nailed, and we were ready for the walls.

The walls went just as well. Penny and I laid them out, Steve, the saw-man, cut two-by-fours to length as we ordered; we assembled, and Jim nailed them together with the gun. Steve complained about the odd lengths of two-by-fours that we occasionally ordered, so the idea of king-studs, trimmer-studs, and headers for door and window framing had to be explained. He nodded understanding. He hadn't wanted an explanation, he had just wanted to complain.

The exterior sheathing was a problem. There wasn't any. Randy let us know he hadn't ordered any because the plans hadn't called for it, so we nailed the T-111 exterior siding panels directly over the studs without the sheathing and felt-paper barrier that we knew was needed to keep the building tight.

Ceiling joists of two-by-sixes went up with no problem and we were ready for the rafters. The only real problem with building was the rain; every time we raised an arm, which seemed constant, the rain ran down the inside of our sleeve.

The plans called for a 12/12 pitch roof (a foot of rise for every foot of run). That is steep and tough to build, but it would shed the snow beautifully. The rafters presented a problem for Steve. They had to be notched just so, to fit over the top plate of the walls. Jim cut a template for him and Steve successfully produced the rafters we needed. Penny and Steve handed the heavy two-by-six rafters up to Jim and me to erect from a plywood platform we had laid on the ceiling joists.

The 1/2-inch roof sheathing went well, except Penny and Steve refused to leave the ground and get up on that steep roof. That was all right with Jim and me. We knew neither of them would be able to work in a place where they would be scared. It was tough enough for them to get the sheathing panels up to us.

The metal roofing went the same way. Penny and Steve passed the cut-to-length panels up, and Jim and I screwed them down. Even Jim declined to straddle the roof peak to screw on the cap pieces, so that fell to me. No problem, I thought, but I did manage to sprain my left knee in the process of straddling and unstraddling the peak.

We built the interior wall separating living room from bedroom, installed the windows and door, hung a few cabinets, did the finish trim inside and out, and had a completed cabin in about a week.

One more thing! This spot could be very windy at times. The roof could be blown off, or the cabin itself could be moved if it was just sitting there with no foundation to hold it in place. It needed "deadmen" at each corner. A deadman is a big chunk of concrete which is attached to the overhanging rafters by a length of wire-rope.

Greg had gotten back from wherever he had gone just in time to participate. We told him he needed to dig holes two feet in diameter and three feet deep under the drip line at each corner of the cabin. He didn't like being told to do something, but didn't see an option. We had eye-bolts we set in the concrete that we poured into the holes and heavy eye-screws we mounted in the rafters.

Once that was done, Marvin and Randy flew in to inspect our project. I explained the short-comings of the building: no insulation, no wall sheathing, wind would get in. No problem, they liked it, and we were out of there.

By late September we were back at headquarters in Bartlett Cove. The season was winding down and all of us seasonals would be laid off and head home in a few days. Marvin decided we should have a party, and had an assignment for us. Take one of the boats up bay and get enough fresh glacier ice to make ice-cream for the party.

Parties are always potluck and the ice would be our contribution. That sounded good to us, a last look at the park, collect some ice, which we had done many times for ourselves, and get back early enough for Marvin to make his ice-cream. It was a standard drizzly day with low clouds, but we were in the Arét, dry and comfortable. It was nearly 50 miles to Reid Glacier, where we were sure of getting good clear ice. The Arét cruised at 25 knots, the fastest boat in our fleet, so we calculated it should take two hours up, a half hour to collect ice, and another two hours back. If we were underway by 0800 we should be back by early afternoon.

All went just as planned until we got just south of Hugh Miller

Inlet. There, we suddenly ran into dense fog. We couldn't see much farther than the bow of the boat. We dropped our speed to five knots, then two. The radar showed us exactly where shore was, but which shore? We didn't want to get into Hugh Miller, there were shallows in there. We needed to keep the island at Hugh's mouth on our port, that would get us to Blue Mouse Cove and the ranger raft if we needed a haven for the night. Watching the compass I knew we were turning slightly west, that meant we were probably entering Blue Mouse. Now the radar showed land all around us. OK, if we kept going with land on our left we should emerge from Blue Mouse into the main bay.

As soon as we got out of Blue Mouse the fog dissipated as fast as it had arrived and we were in the clear, and right where we thought we would be. Without the radar we would have had to anchor and wait out the fog. Now it was an easy run on into Reid, scoop up a couple big chunks of ice with the net, put them in an ice chest and head down bay to the party in Bartlett Cove.

Marvin didn't want to call it a season-end party. He wanted to celebrate the birthdays of the two oldest rangers on his staff—Penny and me. We had both had our birthdays at Dry Bay, Penny's 58th and my 60th, without celebrating. Now Marvin wanted to do them right. We were about 20 years older than the next oldest on his staff and, he said, had done more for the park than he had ever dreamed two people could.

It was a typical, fun season-end party, with the extra of Marvin's great ice-cream. The entire staff had been invited. I think only Mark, our initial boss, skipped it. We were amazed and impressed by the friendship and even admiration offered to us. Another season of mixed emotions, but one very rewarding in experiences, new friends, and learning of the workings of the rapidly changing successional land that follows glaciation.

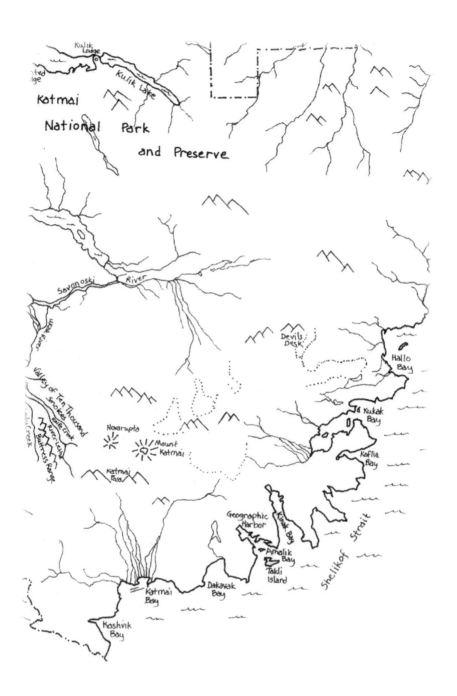

BACK TO KATMAI

We had gotten home from Glacier Bay in October. A couple of months later we had a call from Steve Herd, the new chief ranger at Katmai National Park & Preserve. He had been the captain of one of the SET (Special Event Tactical) teams who had worked with us at Great Basin National Park, so we knew him and he knew us. He wanted us to come back to Katmai and be the rangers at Amalik Bay (AMBA) on the coast of the Shelikof Straight. That was the position we had dreamed of for nearly a decade, ever since we had spent a few days there in 1984 relieving our friends Lynn and George while they had a break.

This would be the 1991 season and there had been no ranger presence at AMBA since 1985. Steve explained that Katmai had gotten a sizable grant from the Archaeological Resources Protection Act (ARPA). ARPA wanted the archaeological sites along the Katmai coast to be examined for evidence of recent disturbance. They also wanted fishermen and the visiting public educated as to the importance of not disturbing those sites.

Steve had read our season-end reports from Nonvianuk and Aniakchak and felt we would be the ideal people to spend a season in the little shack in Amalik Bay and accomplish what ARPA wanted. He told us the shack had gotten a metal roof in 1985, so we wouldn't have rain dripping in like it had when we had been there. He even had a propane refrigerator ordered and would have it installed before we showed up. He wanted us to understand that he expected us to patrol the coast, in a 16-foot Zodiac, every day that weather did not preclude safe navigating. Our responsibility would extend south to the park boundary on Cape Kubugakli and as far north as Cape Douglas. That would be about 100 miles by raven and over 1,000 miles if we patrolled the shores of the 11 named bays in our territory. And no, he didn't want us to try to go clear around Cape Douglas to the northern boundary where the McNeil River Game Preserve begins.

We would need to be in Denali for the LE refresher in late April and in King Salmon by 10 May to help with training. He expected to have two rangers to go to Nonvianuk and two more for Aniakchak. They would need our advice and help.

The National Geographic Society explored the west coast of the Shelikof Strait in the 1920s and proclaimed Amalik Bay and Geographic Harbor the most beautiful harbor in Alaska. They were so impressed that they named Geographic Harbor after themselves. We remembered the cabin could hardly be in a more attractive location. It sits in the very northwest corner of Amalik Bay, at the base of a 2,000-foot cliff of undifferentiated quaternary/tertiary (1.5 to 2 million-year-old) volcanic rock dominated by columnar basalt. At the head of the bay a gradual rise of storm deposited sand begins at the high-tide-line. The cabin sits a couple hundred feet from and probably 20 feet above high-tide. Numerous waterfalls cascade down the cliff face and would provide us with all the water we cared to carry across the rocky beach at the cliff base.

Vegetation is primarily alder with pockets of willow and black birch. Between the tide-line and the cliff is a collection of various size rocks that have fallen from the cliffs. The sand meadows and marshes to the west are covered by lyme-grass, blue joint, cow parsnip and a multitude of flowering plants that change with the season. The neighbors—brown bears, red fox, porpoise, and sea lions—had accepted us before so hopefully they would this year. The bird life, which we would include in our season-end report, would ignore us but give us fascinating hours of watching.

When we arrived in King Salmon we met the other rangers, most of whom would be going to Brooks Camp, and discovered we were the only people on staff, other than the maintenance crew who knew much about the park. The permanent staff all had desks and had never really ventured into the park. None of the seasonals had ever been to Katmai. John and his wife Shakie, who were going to Aniakchak, had been there one season. We didn't need to help with the Brooks Camp crew. They could learn what they needed from the chief of interpretation who had been there only a few months but seemed competent.

The two kids going to Nonvianuk, Cindy, a 20-year-old woman, and Jim, a man a year younger, really needed help. Cindy had never run a boat other than a rowboat at camp, and there was a brand new 22-foot welded-aluminum, flat bottom boat with a cabin and a huge outboard jet motor that they would be taking up the Kvichak and Alagnak Rivers to Nonvianuk Lake. Penny said, "Wow, I wish we had had this boat a few years ago." Cindy wanted me to teach her boating. I did my best. I taught her the bowline and clove hitch—the most useful marine knots that can always be untied even when wet or under strain. Penny and I took her out on Naknek River in the new NVK boat several times. We showed her how to handle it then gave her the helm. She was a good student but needed more experience, preferably in more friendly waters than she and Jim would be in. Somehow Jim just wasn't interested in anything we had to offer them.

John and Shakie had spent one season at Brooks Camp—John as a ranger and Shakie as a volunteer. Neither had ever gotten farther than Naknek Lake where Brooks Camp sits. They wanted to know everything about Aniakchak. We spent two days with them, explaining the place and making recommendations as positively as we could. John was totally inexperienced, and Shakie was a sweet immigrant from India who wanted to please but had no back-country skills. That evening I said to Penny, "I really think they are in over their heads. I'll bet they never go out in the boat, even if they get it assembled."

Then there was a real surprise. The sudden influx of funds from ARPA allowed Steve to hire two young men to go to Swikshak Bay. The men, Jon and Terry, both of whom had several years experience as rangers, had accepted the assignment without knowing what lay ahead. Neither of them had ever been to Alaska before, nor did they have any back-country experience. I had spent part of two days and a night at Swikshak and thought it was a real pit. The tiny "cabin" was in a dense stand of alder and willow. It was about 10- by10-feet with a door, one window, bunk beds, and almost no ventilation. The night I spent there was so stuffy we slept on the roof and got eaten by mosquitos. You couldn't pay me to spend a season there. Add to that, Jon, who was quiet and unassuming but seemed competent and Terry, who was very short, had a big mouth, and was full of bluster and bravado. I couldn't imagine them getting along for a season at Swikshak. Think positive, I told myself, maybe a new cabin has been built in a better spot.

Penny and I have found it frustrating to try to help people who have accepted positions for which they aren't prepared. Some want to learn, some want to look like they are all-knowledge, and some just wish you would go away. This year we had a mixture. They all had a lot to learn about living in the bush with no backup. We had a new section of our favorite park to learn and experience. That fall when we got back to King Salmon, the other back-country teams had all left. We had a lot work to do and never found out how their seasons went. We could imagine Cindy and Jim wrecking the new boat going up the Alagnak River and having to be rescued. Or spending the entire season making-out in the little tent-frame and doing nothing else. We pictured Jon and Shakie never getting out in the Pacific in their Zodiac and worried about them freezing in that old barn of a cabin.

WE HAD REQUESTED A FLIGHT OUT TO AMALIK SO WE COULD SEE the cabin and refresh ourselves on the site. Steve let us know there was a commercial helicopter coming in the next day and he had scheduled it to take us out to AMBA. Fortunately it proved to be a beautiful spring day. The two pilots were nice, friendly young men who were very interested in seeing the famous bay and were glad to have a chance to get a good look at the volcanic mountain range and the bays of the coast, a part of Alaska they had never seen. They seemed to be as excited as we were.

We all had head-sets with microphones. They wanted to be able to talk with us and hear about what they were seeing. As we flew over Naknek Lake, up Savonoski River, and on toward the Aleutian Range they asked questions, and Penny immediately became an interpretive ranger. We had flown this coast several times and had landed in a few of the bays during the four years we had worked at Katmai in the 1980s.

Penny told the pilots, "There is a good pass at the north end of Hook Glacier that is often the last chance to cross the mountains before they close down in a storm. Let's go that way and fly down the coast from there. It will give us a view of most of the coast we will be patrolling." We took it, and Penny continued, "There's Devil's Desk, that 6,400-foot peak with a distinctive cirque someone thought looked like a desk. Let's fly directly over Kukak Volcano. There should still be many feet of snow over everything above 2,000 feet. There, see how the steaming caldera has melted the surface making the snow and ice look like white pillow lava."

On the flats of Hallo Bay there were several bears grazing on young grasses. We turned south and got good views of each bay north of Amalik. Penny called attention to the remains of an old salmon cannery in Kukak Bay and related the letter, she had read in a Park Service bulletin, that had been written by a man on a fishing boat seeking shelter in Kaflia Bay three days after the 1912 Mt. Katmai eruption:

My dear wife Tania:

First of all I will let you know of our unfortunate voyage. I do not know whether we shall be alive or well. We are awaiting death at any moment. Of course do not be alarmed. A mountain has burst near here, so we are covered with ashes, in some places 10 feet and 6 feet deep. All this began on the 6th of June. Night and day we light lamps. We cannot see the daylight. In a word it is terrible, and we are expecting death at any moment, and have no water. All the rivers are covered with ashes. Just ashes mixed with water. Here are darkness and hell, thunder and noise. I do not know weather it is day or night…So kissing and blessing you both, goodbye. Forgive me. Perhaps we shall see each other again. God is merciful. Pray for us.

Your husband,
Ivan Orloff

The earth is trembling; it lightens every minute. It is terrible. we are praying.

One of the pilots said, "Oh my God, that had to be one hell of an experience. I can imagine those poor guys wondering if they were going to live."

We flew over Takli Island and the ten or so little islands that protect Amalik Bay from storm surge and landed in an area of young beach grass, a hundred yards in front of the cabin. We all piled out of the chopper. Penny was talking with the pilots, and I moved toward the cabin. I had gotten about half way up when a brown bear emerged from behind the cabin and stood there looking at us. I waved my arms and said, "Ho bear." The bear huffed and hopped forward. I huffed and took a hop forward. The two of us stood there just looking at each other for several seconds—it felt like eternity to me. Finally the bear turned and disappeared into a stand of alders behind the cabin. I breathed and thought what a stupid thing I had done and said to myself, You dumb shit, you got away with one.

Charlie

One of the pilots said to Penny, "Your husband sure knows bears."

Penny said, "Yes, he sure does," but thought, Frank, you dumb shit, you know that's not the way to meet a bear. She decided, right then, to call that blond bear Charlie—my middle name. She told me the bear and I must be related or it would have killed me.

There were four badly worn steps that we would need to replace, up to a 4- by 4-foot porch and the sagging, weathered door. The cabin proved to need a through cleaning, but was in reasonably good condition. The promised propane refrigerator stood in a corner waiting for us to connect it to a propane tank. In another corner was a low platform with an old double mattress on it. A third corner had a counter where we would put a two burner white-gas cook-stove. The fourth corner had an oil heat-stove. A small window was between the heat-stove and the kitchen counter. A couple of folding card-table chairs leaned against the wall, a 30 by 18-inch plywood table was attached to wall studs under a window beside the door, some shoulder-high plywood shelves above the bed would be our pantry and closet. That pretty well filled our 15 by 16-foot cabin—our home for the next two seasons.

It was still clear and I suggested going back through Katmai Pass. "That will give us an airborne view of the rest of our coastal responsibility. And we can see the route the Aleuts and explorers used between the Shelikof and the old Native village of Savanoski." We flew southwest over Dakavak and Katmai Bays, turned north up Katmai River between Mt. Megeik and the Trident volcano, past Mt. Katmai's crater lake, then down the Valley of 10,000 Smokes, past Mt. Griggs and Brooks Camp, where we had spent two great seasons, and on into King Salmon. We thanked the pilots for a great day. They said, "No, no, we thank you for showing us this amazing country."

Now all we had to do was finish training the other bush-teams, collect our needed gear and supplies, and fly back to Amalik Bay.

Unnamed River

Meeting the Neighbors

Our boss, Steve, had told us he was trying to arrange a radio contact for us in Kodiak, knowing we wouldn't be able to reach him across the Aleutian mountains in King Salmon. Jim Ryan was a retired Park Service superintendent who planned to spend the summer on Kodiak Island. Steve had contacted Jim and talked him into being our contact. Now Jim was in King Salmon, so we got together to see what we could work out about communications. We knew radio contact across the Shelikof and the mountains on the west side of Kodiak Island would make it pretty iffy. We would have a 10-watt VHF base set in the cabin and our personal 5-watt VHF hand-held sets. Jim wanted to set a regular schedule for contact. We agreed to radio him, from wherever we happened to be, at 1700 each day.

We had sat waiting for decent flying conditions many times so the delay getting to Amalik Bay was no surprise. We had all of our gear collected in a hanger for a week. Finally we got the word that today was the day. We and the Swikshak crew would be flying in a twin-engine, amphibious Grumman Goose owned and operated by the USF&W (U.S. Fish & Wildlife Service). The pilot, Jeff Gustofson, had his dog, Donner, riding along and explained, "Dog is my copilot." Jeff decided he had to get all of Swikshak delivered on this load and that there was too much weight to take all of our equipment on the same flight. Our Zodiac and motors would have to be brought out later. We were knowledgeable about weight limits so we didn't complain, but feared it would be a week before the Zodiac showed up.

We used the hour flight to contemplate the season ahead. We had wanted the opportunity to spend a season at Amalik Bay for nearly ten years and it was finally beginning. Jeff made a pass over the bay, scanning the water closely, logging reefs, rocks, and wind before setting down. Jeff banked sharply, put the nose into the wind, and touched down on the water. Spray obliterated our view out the side windows, the Goose settled just like a goose and motored toward shore. We felt the wheels go down, the engines revved, and we roared up on the beach. Jeff spun a 180 so he was headed back to sea and shut the engines down. We were home!

Now came the back-aching part of hauling our gear, apple boxes of food, books, and all of the other things that white-man needs, above high tide. Not all pilots are willing to help off-load supplies, Jeff was. Our four-footed friend stayed onboard while the rest of us carried gear—we didn't want Donner feeding the bears. Good-byes were said. The Goose roared into a rising tide and was gone. We were alone in the solitude and peace that is, to us, the Alaskan back-country. There was a moment when our emotions were a mixture of calm and elation at being just the two of us alone in the wilderness for several months. Then the reality of the getting the pile of gear sitting on the beach up the hill to the cabin kicked in.

As we headed up the path, Charlie appeared from behind the cabin. We three stood looking at each other for, it again, felt like eternity, but was probably fifteen seconds. I said "Hi Charlie," and moved slowly up the path with an apple box in my arms, Penny came right behind me with her load, Charlie watched a moment longer and disappeared into the alders. We breathed a sigh of relief and felt we might have a friendly neighbor for the season.

Frank, Penny, and Amalik Bay Cabin. Photo by Tom Bean.

With the gear in the cabin, we settled down to enjoy the picnic meal Penny had prepared in King Salmon. No need of working until dark, it was June and there were more than 20 hours of daylight. We had the place swept and cleaned up, removed the tarp from the mattress, spread our sleeping bags, and crawled in for the night. We weren't asleep yet when we heard the muffled sounds of an animal turning circles, making a bed behind the cabin. We had walked around the cabin earlier and noticed a bear had a nesting spot right under the edge of the raised cabin. Could it be Charlie's bed room? It not only could be, it was. Charlie wasn't sleeping any farther from me than Penny was. During the night we were awakened by snoring. Penny said, "Is that Charlie snoring?" Yep, it was Charlie.

I hit the wall with my fist and said, "Roll over, Charlie." There was a rustling below me and it was quiet. Charlie had moved and quit snoring. That was an event that would occur every few nights all season.

The next morning it was raining steadily, an excellent day to organize the cabin into a home. As we put things away, every few minutes one of us would look out a window and say, "Look at the harlequin ducks on the bay," or "There's a rough-legged hawk looking for a meal, and a red fox looking for the same meal, probably voles or ground squirrels." Soon one of would say, "Listen there's golden-crowned sparrows singing in the alders."

Charlie appeared out the side window, moved around the cabin to the path at the foot of our steps, and was followed very closely by a big black boar with a scarred face and a missing ear, the marks of previous battles for a lady's affection. He instantly got the name Van Gogh for the missing ear, and we realized Charlie should be called Charlene, since she was obviously a sow in heat (estrous)—she remained Charlie.

All cabin organizing stopped while we watched the enthralling process of courtship. The sow was coy, the boar was patient—for a while. Then he butted her in the crotch with his nose, she scurried down the path and out of sight with van Gogh close behind. We saw similar activity by the pair over the next several days. Never observed copulation, but one evening we were sitting on our little porch watching a magnificent rainbow over the Shelikof when we heard, what sounded like a donkey braying. Penny said, "Hooray! van Gogh scored." We both laughed and toasted the couple. Perhaps Charlie would have a cub or two with her next spring. Assuming we would be back next spring, it would be interesting to see how Charlie dealt with us then.

Van Gogh

The process of creating a baby brown bear, of course, starts with copulation, which we were quite sure had just occurred between Charlie and Van Gogh. Unlike most mammals, brown bears have delayed-implantation; the fertilized egg (blastocyst) does not attach to the uterine wall until the sow goes into her semi-hibernation in late October or November. During a brown bears hibernation blood pressure, respiration, and consciousness remain near normal;

they don't eat, drink, urinate, or deficate. If the sow hasn't gained enough fat and weight to support herself and a fetus, and to produce adequate milk for her cub until they emerge from hibernation, she will abort the blastocyst before it implants. Cubs are born in January or February after a 50 day gestation, blind, covered in fine hair, and weighing about a pound—Mom often sleeps through the delivery. Sow and cub will emerge from their winter den after another three or four months of the cub feeding on extremely rich, high fat, mother's milk and weighing 10 to 15 pounds, full of piss and vinegar and eager to explore the world, but totally dependent on mom for food and shelter.

Charlie and Van Gogh continued their love affair for about a week before he disappeared. Almost immediately another big bore showed up. Hershey was the color of rich milk-chocolate, so the name was obvious. He seemed to be on the beach every time Charlie was, following along at a respectful distance. She acted like he wasn't there, he acted like she wasn't there, both pretending to act normally in a situation where the intent was obvious—known as operant behavior. Finally Charlie had had it. She wasn't interested in more sex. We could see her mouth hang open with saliva running. She was stressed. She growled, and finally charged Hershey, snapping her jaws. He got the message. I pictured her acting that way when I bluffed her a month ago and again thought, you dumb shit, you got away with a stupid mistake.

Another bear showed up, bigger than Charlie but distinctly too small to be a bore, who was an expert clam digger, so she was called "Digger." Everybody dug clams at low tide, most cracked them with their teeth, spit them out, pulled the clam out of its broken shell with a claw, and ate the delicious mollusk. Digger had her own way of cracking a clam shell; after she had dug it up, she would drop it on the beach and bounce up and down on it with her front feet until it cracked, delicately pick the clam out with a claw and enjoy her "clam on the half shell." The dentist in me admired her technique.

Apparently some other bears did too, because it wasn't long before we saw Charlie bouncing on clams.

Young spring grasses are an excellent source of protein (up to 28%) and were regularly grazed on daily by our neighbors. Barnacles were popular with the bears as a meal and source of protein before salmon started running. The bears would simply chew the barnacles off the face of cliffs at low tide. Again the dentist and the dental hygienist thought, how long can their teeth last chewing barnacles?

The day we arrived at Amalik Bay, Maritime Maid, a research vessel out of Homer, Alaska, and leased by ARCO, was anchored just a few hundred yards out from us. We noticed a helicopter sitting on a pad on the aft deck. Pretty fancy, but it was an oil company ship and the cost of research is just a part of doing business. The ship was in and out through the next days rains, but early the following morning the chopper took off, and to our surprise, flew directly to our meadow and landed. We, of course, walked down as soon as the rotors stopped. Lynn, the pilot, stepped out, introduced herself, offered to take us for a ride, and invited us to dinner on their ship. Wow, not what we expected from ARCO but sure we would appreciate getting a ride, and dinner would be a great opportunity to learn what ARCO was up to in the Shelikof.

We had been told that Eberhard Brunner had a camp in Kashvik Bay we would need to check out as soon as we could get down there. Lynn offered to take us anywhere we would like to go. An air-patrol to the south end of our territory would be ideal. She flew us, low and slow, over Takli Island and the little islands dotting the entrance to Amalik. Penny watched for signs of archeological sites. I paid more attention to rocks and shoals that we needed to avoid in the boat. Then around Cape Ilktugitak, across steep sided Dakavak Bay and broad Katmai Bay with the Katmai River braided into many streams running across the ash flows from the 1912 eruption, and on to Kashvik Bay. Sure enough, there was an expansive camp set up on the flats near a river, several 10- by 12-foot wall tents, that would probably house guests, and a large wall tent that we thought would be for dining and general gathering.

We could see a man standing in front of the big tent. We needed to see Brunner's paperwork showing that he had a permit to have this "Tourist Camp" inside the park. Lynn landed not far from the camp, and we walked up to introduce ourselves. Joe, a pleasant young man came to meet us. He told us he was the camp manager, and yes, we had guessed right about the tents. The small ones were for guests sleeping and the big one a gathering hall. No, he didn't know they needed permits to have a commercial camp in the National Park. Brunner had never mentioned it. He would make sure that Brunner got the paperwork all up to date before the first guest showed up in a couple of weeks.

He said, "Brunner plans to be here in a few days, you can see him then. Let me show you our set up." He took us into the big tent which had a large heat stove in the center and a kitchen area at the rear that he was working on. He explained the outhouse, not far from the sleeping tents, had been dug that spring and was for the entire camp. A little creek he showed us came from a spring not far away, and would make a good water supply. It was on the other side of the big tent, well away from the outhouse.

We thanked him for the tour, reminded him to get the permits that were needed, and got back aboard the helicopter. Penny said, "Quite a set up, but I wonder if Brunner intends to get the permits to make it legal? What do we do if he doesn't?" It was in a location we wouldn't be able to get to very often, so it was really up to administration at headquarters.

Flying back to AMBA we were able to make radio contact with park headquarters. No, they had no paperwork from Brunner. And yes, we needed to see him and the paperwork before he opened for business. We also reached Jim Ryan in Kodiak for the first time, and let him know what we were up to.

When we landed in our meadow, Lynn asked if she could pick us up at 1830 for dinner. Penny seemed a bit concerned that accepting a meal would be too close to accepting a gift. I said, "We have business with ARCO. We need to see their papers and explain the rules about disturbing archeological sites, and if we happen to be there as a meal is being served it would be rude to decline."

Penny said, "I guess that's right. We wouldn't want to be impolite."

Lynn laughed and said, "Good. See you at six thirty."

Rather than Lynn flying over, Willie, the cook, and John, the boat's mechanic, came over for us in the ship's launch. They wanted to see our setup; we were glad to show them around. Willie said, "This is neat, but pretty rustic. I'm glad to be on a warm, dry boat."

The evening proved to be very productive. We met O J, the boat owner, and the men in charge of the operation, David J. Doherty, senior geologist, ARCO Alaska; Ron Turner, USDOI Minerals Management Alaska; and the rest of the crew, Scott, Doug, Brian, Drew, and Willie, John and Lynn whom we already knew.

Of course the ship had all their paperwork in perfect order. ARCO and the Department of Interior were working on information necessary for any future oil leases in Cook Inlet and the Shelikof Straight. They explained the entire Alaska Peninsula is either volcanic or accreted terranes that had drifted in over millions of years. This was a trip to confirm the existing geologic maps and add as much new information as possible.

We explained our positions, the need to protect the archeological sites of the area, and keep a close handle on commercial activity in the park. Business was completed and we all relaxed and enjoyed an evening with new friends. Willie served an excellent meal of fresh salad with homemade dressing—the last we would have for months—baked chicken, mashed potatoes, and home-baked, hot bread and butter. None of the crew were more than 40-something and were fascinated by the two of us, 59 and 61, spending a season patrolling these waters in a 16-foot Zodiac. David laughed and said it would be a cold day in Hell when he could get his wife to join him for something like this.

Penny and Zodiak

TOM BEAN

Getting to Amalik Bay and meeting the neighbors was just like moving to a new home anywhere. There were lots of things to accomplish before we had a functional home. Getting the cook stove, heat stove, and refrigerator working came right after cleaning and arranging gear and food so we knew where to find everything. "A place for everything and everything in its place," is one of the secrets of successfully living like this. The cook stove was a simple Coleman two-burner, white gas stove just like the camping stove we had used while family camping for years. The new propane refrigerator was easily connected to a 100-pound propane tank. Remember those threads are left handed, I told myself. Being new, the fridge had a faceplate and several shelves to install. Those chores went quickly with no complications. When it rained we could collect water running off the roof. On other days, we had to carry water from a waterfall a couple hundred yards up the rocky part of the beach.

I remembered the oil heat stove had been a problem several years ago. Now it was a real problem; it smoked badly, spreading soot inside and out. We took it apart, cleaned all the little parts, put it back together and it seemed fine for a day. Then, on a rainy day, it smoked again and fouled our roof-water. We took the entire stove apart and cleaned every part even more carefully, put it back together, and Voila! it smoked horribly. Penny had an epiphany: "How about the oil supply? Could it be fouled?"

"Brilliant, Sherlock!" I said, slapping my forehead.

The oil for the stove was in a 35-gallon drum on a platform behind the cabin, right above Charlie's bed. I climbed up, opened the bung-hole, and got a really rotten smell. (The opening in a steel drum is called a bung-hole, the threaded plug is a bung, there is a bung-wrench for screwing the bung into and out of the bung-hole.) The oil was low, almost congealed, at least six years old, and had been fouled. It had to be replaced with fresh oil if we were to beat the smoking. Fortunately Steve had sent in plenty of fuel for the season. Down in the meadow was a fuel-cache of 55-gallon drums: five of boat-gas, two avgas (aviation gas), two jet/helicopter fuel, and one for the heat stove.

Now all we had to do was disconnect the stove's supply line, roll the drum to drain the old oil—into a bucket, not onto Charlie's bed—roll the drum back, and refill it with clean oil. Well, we did have to get the 55-gallon drum of good oil up the hill and pump from one drum to the other. If you have never rolled a full 55-gallon drum up hill 50 yards, don't! It isn't easy, but we managed it, put the stove-drum back together and pumped it full. Now the heat stove worked fine. We would use the old oil to help our trash burn-up completely. We had made a burn-barrel from an old 55-gallon drum (another interesting chore).

Finally we felt we had a home and could get to work as soon as the park got our Zodiac and motors to us. They had been left in King Salmon because Jeff, the Goose pilot, felt he couldn't carry all of the gear and boats for two camps in one load. Our Zodiac was several hundred pounds that could be delivered later.

We didn't have radio contact with King Salmon or Kodiak. We couldn't reach either from the cabin. We later found we had to be out in the Shelikof to reach Jim in the town of Kodiak, and the Aleutian Mountains blocked all radio contact to King Salmon. So, we could only explore on foot and wait for our Zodiac to be flown in.

On the south side of our little cove was a tide pool at the base of a basalt cliff. It was easy to reach at low tide and proved a fascinating education. Some of the residents changed with every flowing tide. Starfish, or sea-stars, of various color and size changed regularly, and tiny fish came and went. Some creatures proved to be permanent residents. Barnacles, anemone, and mussels were stationary filter feeders that depended on each new tide to bring a supply of plankton. Snails, spiny urchin, and chiton scoured the rocks eating algae and tiny plants. There were hermit crabs running around picking up all sorts of tiny animals to eat. These guys live in the shells of dead snails so every time a hermit crab grows it has to abandon its too tight shell and find a new one that is "just right."—like me buying new pants when my belt tells me I can't wear my favorite pair anymore.

Only a few days passed until a helicopter flew around Takli Island and put down on our beach. To our delight, our old friend Landis Lingrin, who had taken us on numerous memorable rides in his whirli-bird, stepped out. He had brought us our Zodiac, two outboards, and some fresh vegetables. Penny took the vegetables up to the cabin while Landis and I off-loaded the Zodiac and outboards. We had a falling tide, so it would be several hours before we had to have the boat ready for launching. Landis offered to take us for a ride, but said, "I will need to refuel when we get back."

"No problem," I said, "we have our fuel-cache all organized and can give you whatever you need."

Landis took us on another of his wild and crazy rides, skimming the water between the islands at the bay's mouth, around Cape Ilktugitak, up the cliff-face on Dakavak Bay's north face and low over the five-mile-long glacial lake that feeds into Dakavak Bay. Then on down to Kashvik to check on Brunner's camp. We landed expecting to see Joe, and hopefully Herr Brunner himself, but the place was deserted. "Damn!" We still needed to make contact and see their permit. We looked into the tents and found that the main tent seemed ready for guests. The small, floored tents each had two cots, two chairs, a small table, a dresser and a coat rack. Not the Hilton, but it would be an interesting spot to visit for bear viewing and fishing in the river.

Landis dropped us off, took on 20 gallons of fuel and was gone. We only had a couple of hours to get the Zodiac assembled before the tide floated it. It had been several years since we had assembled one of these marvelous boats, but we remembered it well. In fact, I think it was the best job of assembling a Zodiac we had ever done. It does have to be done just right or the floorboards don't fit the rubber floor, so you get pissed and have to start over. That done, we set the anchors for a triangular mooring system like we had developed at Aniakchak. This one, thankfully, was in a good, sheltered location.

Our routine of patrols was quickly established. First thing to do each morning was make sure where the tide was. The boat went dry at low tide so we had to be either at sea or at home during low tides. Unless there was a storm we were going on patrol. We had all of the islands in the bay to check and were anxious to get into the other bays to explore them. Winds weren't a problem inside our bay, but as soon as we got into the Shelikof Strait the wind became critical. We always started our patrols running into the wind, that way we would be coming home with the wind at our back. We could always quit when heading out if it got too rough, but we wanted to make it to our cabin before dark and bucking a strong head wind and waves was no fun—much better to have them at our back.

Amalik Bay has the safest harbor for many miles in any direction. So we weren't surprised one evening when a seiner, the Mikado out of Kodiak, anchored not far out. We were surprised when two crew members, a man and a woman, waved at us as they climbed into their launch and headed for shore. We always look forward to meeting the crew of these boats, but these two seemed to be anxious. The tall good looking woman was standing in the bow waving. I said, "Do we know her?"

Penny yelled, "Margaret!" and said, "That's Margaret Bosworth." Her parents were neighbors and our closest friends in Colorado. We knew that, on a lark, Margaret had come to Alaska and was working on a fishing boat out of Kodiak. She knew where we were working this season and had talked her boss into pulling into Amalik to say hello. The man at the tiller was Pete Hanna, the skipper and part owner of Mikado. Margaret introduced us to Pete. We shook hands with him and gave Margaret a hug.

We invited them up to the cabin. Pete said, "Swell, but we can only stay a minute. I don't want the skiff grounded in the falling tide. But we want you to join us for dinner and see Mikado. Fresh caught sockeye, and Margaret is proving to be a wonderful cook."

Penny said, "Great. What time?"

Pete said, "How about in an hour?"

I said, "We'll be there, but we'll have to stay until the tide is high enough to get back to our moorage."

We met the rest of the crew, Gordon and Keith, had a great meal, and swapped stories about friends and Alaska fishing. Pete told us there would be a 58-hour opening starting tomorrow noon, so we could expect more boats in the bay for a few days. We talked about all sorts of things pertaining to fishing, and Penny mentioned enjoying watching the bears dig for clams at low tide. Pete told us we had cockles, horse, and butter clams on our beach, but no razor clams, which most people prefer. Penny said, "Oh well, we weren't planning on digging clams anyway, leave them for the bears."

Pete laughed and said, "Take a couple of sockeye that we caught this morning. Then you won't even think about clams." We thanked them, wished them good fishing, exchanged hugs, and felt good about our relation with them and the commercial fishing community we were getting to know. The next morning a new bear showed up and was named Mikado in honor of our friends boat.

As we were heading out to orient ourselves on specific archaeological sites the next morning, Katmai Air flew in and landed. We tied the boat back up and went to meet them. A visitor was being dropped off with a pile of gear. We walked up and introduced ourselves. Our visitor introduced himself as Tom Bean. The pilot, Bo, was an old friend. I had done an emergency tooth filling for him in 1986, and told him to get a permanent filling as soon as he could. Bo laughed and said the temporary had lasted three years. Bo told us he was now managing Kulik Lodge and needed to get going. He had to pick up a couple of fishermen in Kodiak, so further conversation was put on hold. We heard Tom tell Bo to pick him up in about a week. "Whoa" Penny said, "You don't leave a pickup date that open." Bo laughed and said he would be back a week from today and took off.

Tom told us he was a photographer on assignment with the National Geographic Society. He and Kim Heacox were collaborating on a story on Katmai National Park for the new book *America's Hidden Treasures: Exploring our Little Known National Parks*. We knew Kim and his wife Melanie. They had been the last rangers here at Amalik Bay in 1985—the first year we worked at Nonvianuk. Tom told us he was married to Susan and lived in Flagstaff, Arizona.

Tom had a Klepper kayak he needed to put together and then find a campsite on one of the little islands. I offered to help with the Klepper and then ferry him out to his site unless he preferred to paddle out. He gladly took me up on both offers, but wondered if he could go on patrol with us today to get an idea of where he was. We were planning on checking on a pair of beached boats we had noted earlier in Geographic Harbor and told him he was welcome to ride along. He gathered an amazing collection of cameras and lenses and secured them in a dry-bag.

The connection between the outer bay and the inner harbor is a narrow channel where we liked to fish for small halibut and watch a family of river otters who were usually out playing this time of day. They were, so we sat and watched the otters, and Tom, at the same time. He must have blown through two rolls of film in a matter of minutes. On into Geographic Harbor we found the two overturned skiffs we had seen earlier, got their registration numbers, and cruised on. (ADF&G later identified them as belonging to Cliff Pulis of Rainbow King Lodge, a typical outlaw lodge operator.)

Tom was having the time of his life. We watched bears fishing at the mouth of the river emptying into the harbor, and showed him an eagle nest on a basalt cliff. It was 1700 and time to try to contact Jim in Kodiak. So, as we went out through the bay, I suggested to Tom that he look for a campsite as we moved through the outer islands. I told him to pick one or two and we would check them on the way back.

As we moved into the Shelikof, Penny noted a school of small fish, which had attracted an arctic loon and several kittiwakes. We routinely saw seals and frequently porpoise. Today was no exception; Tom was excited. We reached Jim in Kodiak and reported that we had a visitor and asked him to have King Salmon check on the boats we had located up bay.

As we headed back in, Tom said he would like to camp where he could see our cabin. I chuckled and said, "Good idea. That way we can keep an eye on each other." We had given him the "Camping with bears lecture," and reminded him that we were beyond the tree-line so he wouldn't be able to hang his food properly. We looked at several sites and found one that Tom thought would be fine. The island was maybe 200 meters in diameter, had a small rocky beach, a flat spot for his tent, and a good view of our cabin. We collected all his gear back at our cabin and got him established at his site.

As we were heading out on patrol the next morning we could see Tom's tent, so we assumed everything was fine. The following morning we awoke to a gorgeous clear sky that was steadily deteriorating. Clouds looking like huge waterfalls, that we called Niagras, were rolling over the ridge to the north, the weather would probably turn wet if not stormy by afternoon. I noticed Tom's tent was not visible, and said, "Hmm, Tom has moved his tent." Penny suggested we check on him as we headed out.

As I was fueling-up and Penny was pumping-up the boat's inflatable tubes that were always a little low in the morning, we saw Tom in his Klepper paddling toward us. As Tom paddled up to us, Penny looked at him and said, "Tom, you look terrible. What's the matter?"

"A God-damned bear got me last night," Tom yelled.

"You don't look like you're hurt," Penny replied in a calm voice. "Slow down and tell us what happened."

"Well," Tom said, "He didn't get me, I was out taking pictures this morning, but he took all my food and destroyed my camp."

That pretty well settled where we were going on patrol today. We collected our shotgun, just in case, and headed out to Tom's campsite. The bear wasn't around, but the camp was a real mess. Gear was torn up and spread everywhere. Tom had done as good a job of securing his food as he could under these circumstances. There being no real trees, he had hung his food sack from an alder that was hanging over a 10-foot cliff. That didn't deter the bear, it had simply torn the little tree down, gotten the food sack and proceeded to demolish everything. Smart bear! If it had killed or injured Tom we would have an entirely different problem to deal with. As it was we had a mess to clean up and three reports to fill out: a case-incident (10-343), a property damage (10-344), and a bear-incident report.

Now we had a camper with no camp, no food, no tent, and no way to reach Katmai Air to let them know that he needed to be picked up. He had his kayak but that was it, and there were still three days before Tom's scheduled pick-up. All we could do was loan him our tent and spare sleeping bag, and feed him until we could reach Kodiak to get someone to pick him up. Tom wanted to sleep in the cabin with us, but we convinced him he would be fine camping in the meadow just below us. That evening we grilled one of our salmon on the beach. Of course Tom was photographing everything. His book has a picture of me grilling the salmon, but refers to it as "...fresh-caught salmon for lunch." After dinner we loaned him a radio to give him a sense of security and said, "Good-night."

Very early the next morning our radio got us up. Tom was on it and in a panic. "There's a bear at my tent!" he was whispering. "It's gonna get me! Do something."

Penny said, "That's the new bear, Mikado."

I grabbed the shotgun, made sure it had a cracker shell in the chamber and another in the magazine, stepped out on the porch, and yelled, "Hey bear!" He looked at me and went on investigating—for about two seconds—then he got a cracker shot in the butt. The cracker exploded and Mikado headed for somewhere else.

Now we needed to feed Tom breakfast. Our standard breakfast was oatmeal with raisins and a little granola sprinkled on top. Tom declined the oatmeal, saying he would just have granola—"Damn," I thought, "our limited granola supply wouldn't last long like this."

As we were fixing the oatmeal, Penny looked out the window. "Damn it, Mikado is back!" she said. I picked up the shotgun, fired another cracker into his ass and yelled, "Hey, bear!" before it exploded—there is a three second delay before the firecracker explodes—and another cracker as he was running down the path. Mikado never came near the cabin again.

Tom asked to go on patrol with us, even though it was raining. We had expected that. That afternoon we had lunch of pilot biscuits and peanut-butter over in Kinak Bay, and watched a bear digging for clams and commented on how they dig like a dog, both front paws throwing sand back between their hind legs until they had their whole head and shoulders in the hole—invariably coming up with a clam. Heading home that evening we noted a blue-hulled boat with gold trim, and the name COHO on the stern, flying the Alaskan flag. As we pulled close we heard a dog barking; sure enough, a Belgian Schipperkey barge dog, had spotted us and was announcing us to the ADF&G crew.

Tom Emerson, Mo Landin, and Pat Holmes welcomed us and introduced us to their four-footed friend, Mickey, who immediately jumped onto our bow and made the rounds, getting his ears scratched by each of us. They were on their way back to Kodiak, had heard we were here, and stopped to say hello. No, they couldn't stay, but they offered us a mess of razor clams. That would solve our problem of feeding Tom tonight.

We had been unable to reach Jim, on Kodiak, since the first day that Tom had been with us, so we asked Mo to try reaching him to get a pick up for Tom. Of course the ADF&G boat had excellent radios, so Mo had no trouble reaching Jim. It took about ten minutes for Jim to call back with the word that Sea Hawk Air out of Kodiak would pick Tom up tomorrow shortly after noon. Not only that, but the pick-up by Katmai Air had been canceled.

Sure enough, not long after noon the next day Kodiak Air was taxiing toward our beach. Mikado was on the beach challenging a cinnamon colored bear that we had not seen before. We had been enjoying the confrontation, but the arrival of the plane made the bears scatter, Mikado to the north and Cinnamon to the south. Two minutes later we were saying goodbye to Tom Bean and wondering if Mikado and Cinnamon would continue to educate us on brown bears establishing their pecking order.

Jim, and his assistant Jackie, had sent us a wonderful care package of two radio batteries, three cans of pineapple, one can of peaches, a sack of lemon cookies, and a can of Chung-King Chow mien, but no granola. Oh well, Tom hadn't eaten it all. Now we could get back to work and investigate our archeological sites.

ARCHEOLOGICAL SITES

In 1983 and 1984, while we were working at Brooks Camp, the prime tourist area of Katmai National Park, we got acquainted with archeologist Don Dumond and his team of students who we called "The Diggers." They were excavating a site on the south side of the Brooks River and were happy to show us how archaeology was done, what they were finding, and how it was interpreted. We, especially Penny, found it fascinating—Penny is only a few hours short of her degree in anthropology/geology. Archeology is the study of artifacts through the excavation of home sites and trash piles, while anthropology is the study of culture and human society. Both relate to people living in prehistoric and historic times.

There were 30 some sites of Aleut settlements in and around Amalik Bay which had been located by archeologists in past years. Dumond, in his book *The Eskimos and Aleuts*, refers to the "Takli stage of the Kodiak Tradition." Takli is the large island at the mouth of Amalik Bay. The Takli stage included many sites on the islands of the outer bay, a few on the mainland and a couple in Kinak Bay. We were to survey those sites for damage by artifact hunters. We had a map, covering 100 square miles, that showed general locations and brief descriptions of the known sites.

We thought we should be able to knock off a site a day with no problem. Yeah, sure! Fortunately we would be here a second season to complete this assignment. We had a topo map showing the locations of the known sites, but translating the map to the sea, the islands, bays, coves, and contours got a bit tricky. We had done the same thing in the Boundary Waters Canoe Area with our kids back in the 1970s and were rarely sure of exactly where we were. Which little bay were we in, was it the one with site 72 or site 75? Finding those locations proved to be an education in itself, and documenting what we found, another education.

Dumond's book told us that the area was inhabited by "at least by 4,000 BC" (Penny and I prefer referencing dates from present time; i.e. 4,000 BC would be 6,000 BP—before present.) Even though the area is considered arctic, it has a mild climate with from 30 to 100 inches of rain annually. We had temperatures in the 40s, 50s, 60s, and an occasional 70. Winter temperatures rarely go below 20 degrees Fahrenheit. We experienced lots of rain, wind, and frequent storms, but no severe temperatures. On calm days the black flies and mosquitoes were terrible, so we appreciated some wind. In the boat we created our own wind. Out where these sites were there seemed to be constant wind, which would have kept all of the flying, biting little buggers away.

Each site was in a sheltered location with a beach where landing a kayak would not have been difficult, and where clams would have been easily available. A couple were on a spit where if one side was windward, the other side was in the lee where kayaks could be launched and landed. Interestingly, none of the sites seemed to have considered access to fresh water a priority; it sure was with us, we had to either collect rain off the roof or carry buckets of water from a waterfall. Spotting a "midden," which looked like a white mound and proved to be a trash heap of mostly clam shells, was an easy way to locate a site. We all create trash; we had a burn barrel to dispose of ours. The Aleuts had trash too. Their trash consisted of many clam shells, the bones of marine mammals, as well as bones of birds and fish. That pretty well defined their diet: animal protein and fat. We found some of the kelp quite palatable, and wondered if the Aleuts might have eaten it to supplement their diets and provide some of the essential vitamins and minerals that would have been missing in their animal diet.

Quoting Dumond:

> In this ice-free maritime region open-sea-hunting tech-
> niques were used by Native Peoples all year round in pursuit
> of resident sea otter, hair seal and sea lion, and seasonally
> in search of migrating fur seals and whales.

Almost none of a sea-mammal was wasted. The meat was eaten, stomachs became containers for water, and made into dry bags for storage onboard kayaks; rainproof gut-skin coats were basic survival items. Skins and furs were used to make clothing. Linda Black, in her article "Aleut: Islanders of the North Pacific" for the book *Crossroads of Continents*, relates, "Aleut men's clothing was made mostly of puffin, murre, and cormorant skins. . . Women's garments were of sea mammal skins—sea otter in the west, sea otter and fur seal in the east." Their kayaks, which they called bidarkas, were made by stretching and sewing sea lion skin over a frame of alder stems. Those bidarkas were the keystone to Aleut life. Their livelihood, their food, their clothing, all depended on access to the creatures of the sea, and their bidarkas gave them access.

We managed to locate the 34 sites that were reported to us as "known or suspected" plus one that we were credited with discovering. Most of the sites had eroding pit houses known as barabaras. They were always on a rise, safe from high water in storms. A barabra is a wonderful arctic design; a pit was dug at least a meter deep and three or four meters in diameter, a roof frame of driftwood or whale ribs was erected and covered with sod and grass. They were ideal for keeping out the winter winds that often raged. We tried to imagine living here through a winter storm and decided that fall storms were bad enough. We were glad we wouldn't be here for a winter one.

At many sites we were able to find quite a variety of tools lying exposed on the surface; percussion-flaked projectile blades with narrow stems that would have been attached to a shaft and thrown using an atlatl, or throwing stick, to propel the shaft; flaked knives and scrapers of various size; a shallow bowl-shaped piece of basalt that had been used as a lamp that burned oil from sea-mammal fat; and pieces, a few centimeters square, of ground basalt with holes drilled in them, which we imagined to be strung and worn around the neck like a necklace.

In 1992 an archeologist was sent to Katmai from the regional office to professionally examine the Takli Stage sites. She visited us for a few days, decided we were doing a fine job, and spent the balance of the season at an office in King Salmon. She was very interested in the site we showed her that hadn't been reported before. She told us it was new and we needed to write it up so she could file it and have it on record as "Starr site 1992."

Starr Site 1992: 31 Aug 1992

Location: On the western most extremity of Kinak Point—the peninsula separating Kinak and Amalik Bays on the western shore of the Shelikof Strait, Alaska.

Significance: Previously unrecorded; within Takli Island Archeological District.

Description: A 30m long, 5m high bluff, the northern half of which is alder covered. The upper 2/3 of the NNW corner is an eroding midden of clam and mussel shells with some mammal, bird and fish bones. Several worked points, both ground and flaked were noted among rocks at the base of the bluff. One point was collected and delivered to Katmai NP&P archeologist Pat McClenahan. It is a 45 mm x 30 mm x 3 mm piece of ground silicized mud-stone with 4 round holes drilled and counter drilled from the opposite side.

To us the most significant find we made was the skull of a terribly deformed human who had reached the age of early adult-hood. The skull cap rose only a fingers width above the eye socket leaving very little room for a brain. The heavy mandible was missing the anterior teeth but had a full compliment of bicuspids and molars with erupting third molars, which indicated an age of approximately 18 to 20 years. The teeth showed almost no wear, showing they weren't used much. Someone had cared for that person for all of those years, probably feeding it predigested food, the same as many wild animals do. We showed the skull to the archeologist, but she felt it was not an item to include in her report to Region. We felt it was of great interest and significance, at least to us it was.

There was a great bonus to all the hunting we were doing for archeological sites; we found all sorts of other interesting sites too. We located a fox farm on Takli Island that had been abandon when the price of furs dropped after WWII. It had a crumbling log cabin where a caretaker had lived and some indication of pens and little dog houses. We rarely saw a fox on the mainland but saw several red fox on the island. We located 13 active eagle nests on the islands and in the bay, most of them active in both 1991 and 1992. All but one of the nests produced eaglets, several had two eaglets. In 1992, we found a rough-legged hawk nest on the mainland, and a peregrine falcon nest out on Kinak Island.

We saw seal and porpoise almost every day. One day we were out checking the south side of Ilktugitak Island looking for a Native site. We didn't find a human site, but we did find a colony of Steller's sea lions. Eight bulls, probably immature since there were no cows, were hauled out on a rocky beach. When we rounded the point I saw them and slowed immediately. They seemed as interested in us as we were in them, all eight of them approached our boat. These are big guys, the bulls are up to ten feet long and weigh around 2,200 pounds, Penny said, "Don't let them get too close, they could flip the boat." I agreed they were not something for us to mess with. I think the sea lions enjoyed watching us as much as we enjoyed watching them.

I commented, "I'll bet they have never seen a boat like this before, or a person up close."

That same beautiful day we were farther out in the Shelikof just enjoying the beauty of a near perfect day when we saw a humpbacked whale spout. We slowly motored over toward where it had been. It had dived so we just let the boat drift. To our amazement the whale surfaced and spouted only a few yards away. We sat still. The whale moved slightly and was against our port side. Penny reached out and stroked the whale's back, stroked it again and again, just like she petted our golden retriever and said, "Oh, my God, I can't believe I touched a whale."

We knew that hump-backs frequently have barnacles on their side and try to rub them off on anything solid. I said, "Maybe she wanted you to scratch the barnacles off her back. Naw, she just wanted to be friendly."

In August of 1991, Jim, our Kodiak connection, let us know a group of archeologists from the State University of New York would be arriving to do archeological research on Takli Island for three weeks. Sure enough, the MV Stormbird, out of Halibut Cove, AK, showed up. They had five archeologists onboard who would be excavating three sites on Takli Island. We met the skipper, Joe and his wife Lynn, who did the cooking and handled mooring lines. Lynn introduced us to Albert Dekin, the "Head Researcher," who in turn introduced us to Mike, Bob, Rusty, and Marion. They informed, us rather formally, they would be excavating sites #22, #71, and #75 all on Takli. We asked to see their NPS papers approving their work, gave them the bear talk, which they weren't interested in, but listened anyway. We asked if they had gone through the shotgun indoctrination that was required for their permit to work in Katmai. They hadn't but Dekin assured us they were all competent with shotguns.

As we pulled away Penny said, "Damn, they're an arrogant bunch. Did you see how Rusty held that shotgun? He didn't have a clue! I'm glad we don't have to deal with them any more."

I reminded her, "Kodiak told us to stay out of their way, but check their sites after they leave." NPS wanted to know the condition they left their excavations.

Our 10-344, case-incident report, that fall told:

Site #22, adequately restored. Site #71 restoration poor; excavation left four to six inches short of refill, dirt and debris left scattered around. Site #75 restoration acceptable, with room for much improvement. Recommend this group be denied future permits.

Kukak Bay

VISITORS

Early in our first season at Amalik Bay we had been exploring up north on a gorgeous day and had gotten all the way up to Kukak Bay. We had crossed the mouths of four bays that we consider fiords, deep valleys carved by glaciers, now flooded by the sea. We had seen tufted and horned puffin, double-crested, pelagic, and red-faced cormorants, a rocky islet with at least 200 sea lions basking in the sun, a pair of sea otters, and had been checked-out by several curious porpoise. Unique wildlife observations always thrilled us and still do.

By then it was late in the day, we were getting tired and needed a place to camp. We knew of an abandoned cannery not far down bay that we wanted to see. It might make an acceptable place to sleep, especially since there were no beaches that would be dry at high tide. The cannery was pretty well shot but part of the floor seemed relatively sound. We looked up, and sure enough it had a roof protecting it from the elements. We had camped in a lot worse places. We spread our foam pads and sleeping bags, fixed freeze-dried dinners, and crashed for the night.

I awoke to water dripping in my ear. With a clear sky, it would be another gorgeous day, so where was the water coming from? There had been a heavy dew overnight, and the roof had a hole directly over my head. The morning sun had condensed the dew, it was running off, and dripping through the hole, wishing me "good morning."

We cruised on up bay with a falling tide and found an enormous tidal-flat that would keep any boat from approaching the Kukak River even at high-tide. Glad we hadn't tried to camp there. We had noticed a 35-foot tall pinnacle of rock standing well out from shore that erosion had worn down to a point. On top we could see the safest eagle nest imaginable with two eaglets standing up watching us. Mom was screaming and diving at us; time for us to leave them in peace.

On the way back to Amalik, we met three kayakers having lunch on a nice sheltered beach on Cape Kuliak. We pulled in to check them out. They told us they were all from Homer, Alaska, and wanted to kayak the coast of Katmai just for the fun of it. They had scheduled Kenai Air to pick them up in Katmai Bay in three days. We made sure they were well aware of bears, had bear-proof food containers, were armed with nothing more lethal than pepper spray, and gave them the Archeological Resources Protection Act story on Native sites. They seemed like good people and told us they would be camping in Russian Anchorage tonight. They had a fourth member of their party who worried them; he liked to paddle hard and should be waiting for them with camp all set-up. They knew a simple problem could be life threatening without a partner near. Would we look for him? We promised to find him and make sure he was safe. We found him just fine. He had camp waiting for his buddies. We gave him the same bear and ARPA warnings, pushing ARPA because we knew there was a Native site here that we hadn't located yet. Then we told him how dangerous it could be to kayak these waters by himself.

Every morning we tried to get the weather forecast on the marine band of our single-sideband radio. This morning they were predicting increasing winds to possible gale force by evening. I suggested we get an early start, we planned to get a good look at Kinak Bay, Russian Anchorage, and Hidden Harbor, and the rest of our neighboring bay.

As I was getting some gear ready, Penny said, "There's a new bear on the beach." We had found that bears come and bears go. A few, like Charlie, were residents but most hung around for a few days and moved on. Today's arrival looked old, her belly hung low and she moved slowly but deliberately. Yes, it was a she, we saw her pee from under her tail (males pee from in-front of their hind legs like most male mammals). We named her "Old Lady. She became a semi-permanent resident and favorite of us both.

We waited until she cleared the beach before we headed to the boat. We always tried to be considerate of the bears, and they seemed to be considerate of us. When they were on the beach we waited; when we were on the beach they seemed to wait. One of those things that worked for everyone.

Kinak Bay is the next bay north, and you can't get there without passing Kinak Point and Kinak Island. Near the Point we watched nine or ten common eider ducks courting. This was a first for us. We had seen the even more rare Steller's eider at Aniakchak, and it was exciting to add the common eider to our bird list. They are big ducks, 24 inches long, with most unusual sloping foreheads. The females were a reddish brown. The males, black and white with a greenish cast to the white neck and back of the head.

We gave the island a careful look and discovered a colony of glaucous-winged gulls nesting on the west facing cliff-face. Both horned and tufted puffin had dug nest holes in the face of the dirt collected above the cliff. A peregrine falcon soared over looking for his meal; we later found its nest in a cove around the puffin point.

The seas were building, but we wanted to explore Hidden Harbor at the upper end of Kinak Bay. You can't see the little harbor until you get right up to it. A narrow channel between thousand foot high headlands leads to a small, beautiful, and very sheltered bay. It wouldn't hold more than a couple of boats, but they would be safe in any storm. A flock of about 70 common merganser ducks were in the harbor—they probably knew a storm was coming and had taken shelter before we had sense enough to.

We had four acheological sites to explore in Kinak, but the wind was building and we decided to check them another day. As we pulled into the Shelikof Penny said, "Oh, God, those waves are big. Can we make it?"

"Sure," I said, "Hang on. These are big swells but they aren't breaking. The wind will be at our back and it isn't far to Amalik." Actually it was a fun ride. We quartered the waves going up from the windward and could sit on the crest like we were surfing. Going down the face was a little touchy. They were too steep to run straight down, so we had to quarter them again and make sure they didn't break into the boat. Penny started with both white-knuckled hands grasping a secure line, but ended the ride with a mile-wide grin.

As we moved into the calm of Amalik Bay Penny said, "Wow, look at those boats." There were four big sloops at anchor, and a dozen or so fishing boats, all taking shelter from the coming storm. We had already talked with most of the fishing boats, so we wouldn't bother them, but the sloops had to be private and should be interesting. The names on their sterns identified them as: HAIDA, KLINGIT, CHUGACH, and ALEUT. We saw a couple of people on the deck of Chugach and pulled up to talk. We introduced ourselves. They invited us aboard and told us they were all with The Nature Conservancy—two couples from Boston and two couples from South Freeport, Maine, along with Philomena Knect, a representative of The Nature Conservancy (TNC) from Kodiak. The 44-foot sloops all belonged to David Rockefeller. He had loaned them to TNC with the idea that his friends would use them to look at land that TNC might protect from future development.

They wondered what we were doing here and were surprised to learn they were in a national park. We had a friendly conversation, and Penny took the opportunity to talk about the archeological sites. She told them of the ancient Aleut home sites in this area, and related the significant value to the history of man's life in this part of the world. She said, "People, like yourselves, go ashore, walk around, and see interesting pieces of worked stone eroding out of a bank or just lying on the surface. Arrowhead collecting in the U.S. has been done for a couple hundred years, but an arrowhead, or any artifact, that has been moved from its original site is of no value to the study of ancient peoples and their culture. A spear point in your hand is an interesting piece of man's ability to work stone, but nothing more. If that point is discovered by an archeologist, its relation to other artifacts, bones, and charcoal from a fire can tell a whole story of human life here. That's why it is so important to not disturb anything above the tide line. If you pick something up to look at, be sure you put it back exactly where it was."

The storm was building, so we declined the dinner invitation they offered, but invited them to visit us at the cabin if they stayed around. They assured us they would move on to Russian Anchorage tomorrow. I let them know they were in a much safer anchorage if the predicted storm stayed around.

They had been an interesting and interested group. Just the kind of wealthy people who would be inclined to collect a few artifacts to remember a trip by and impress friends with. We hoped Penny's talk had convinced them to leave sites as they found them. The next morning the wind was down a bit, and sure enough they pulled anchor and left despite a heavy rain.

THE REGIONAL OFFICE IN ANCHORAGE SENT TWO YOUNG ARCHE-ologists out to document the archeological sites on Takli Island with the hope it would be recognized as an Historic Site. We greeted Ann Worthington, whom we knew from when she worked as a digger for Don Dumond at Brooks Camp, and met Monica Shah a gal we would meet again up on the Noatak River in 1995. They told us they planned to camp on Takli for the five days they were to be here, and would we mind taking them out to Takli in our Zodiac.

We were glad to help them. They loaded their gear in the boat and we all headed out in the rain for the island. We pulled in at the fox farm, thinking that would be a good location for them to make camp. It was early in the season and three bears, in the mating mode, were busy deciding who was King of the Island and would sire the next generation. The gals didn't think they wanted to be dropped off with the love triangle. We agreed, and took them to a site out on the end of the island that didn't have any bears—right then. Penny warned them that a fair number of bears lived on the island and read the concerned expression on both of their faces.

Penny and I looked, questioningly, at each other. Penny said, "OK, tell us about the bear training you had before coming out here."

Ann admitted she hadn't had much bear encounter training since she had been at Brooks Camp eight years before, but felt that having gone through the same training as the ranger staff, she was comfortable. Monica related having gone through extensive training at Denali just a couple of months earlier.

I asked if they had a shotgun. Monica dug through their gear and came up with a standard Winchester-12ga. just like the one we had in the cabin. I asked, "Is it loaded?" They both shook their heads no, so I said "How do you intend to load it, and when?"

Monica said she intended to load the weapon as soon as they decided on a campsite and would load a cracker shell, two rounds of #9 bird-shot, and two slugs.

"Good plan." I said, and asked if they had pepper spray.

Ann said, "Oh yes, and I know how to use it too." Then she showed us a can right in the top of her day pack.

"Good for you!" Penny said. "But are you going to be comfortable camping out here for five days?"

They admitted they wouldn't be comfortable out here with just the two of them and the bears. We suggested they camp in our meadow. We could bring them out to the island every morning and pick them up when we finished our patrol. We decided we might as well spend the rest of the day with them to see what we could learn from working anthropologists.

It proved to be an interesting afternoon of learning for us and teaching and demonstrating for them. We were impressed by the culture and life-style the Aleuts had developed so long ago, but were reminded that their culture changed drastically when Russian fur traders came demanding sea otter pelts and disrupting the Native way of life. Late that afternoon Monica and Ann decided they had enough for their first day, so we took them to our cove where they could set up camp near us. As it turned out they cooked all of their meals with us.

When I mention cooking you probably picture someone fixing a nice meal in a real kitchen. Our kitchen was a two burner Coleman white-gas stove. We fixed oatmeal every morning, with raisins, granola, and powdered milk mixed the day before. Lunch, usually on the boat or a beach, was peanut butter or cheese on Pilot Biscuits. Dinner was pasta or beans and rice with canned soup and a canned vegetable. The girls had freeze dried meals. Any time we caught a fish, or had one donated, we cooked it on the beach, over a drift-wood fire, on a little portable grill—we would never have meat or fish smell in the cabin. We still prefer our fish fresh caught and grilled over a beach fire.

WE HAD GONE UP TO KULIAK BAY ONE DAY LOOKING FOR POSSIBLE Aleut sites. We hadn't found any but had a great day of observing seabirds, sea mammals, and bears. We are always fascinated by bears and could spend all day just watching their antics and interactions. Nothing special today, but we counted six bears chasing fish in a stream at the head of the bay. Perhaps the pink salmon were starting to show up. Harlequin ducks, cute, colorful little guys with round heads and short bills, were diving for arthropods (shrimp and such) in fast surf around rocks. In a little cove several marbled murrelets were after the same arthropods. A flock of a couple hundred scoter were in the bay—mostly black scoter but a few white-winged—and Penny was sure she saw a surf scoter in the group.

It was getting late and we had another great day of seeing and learning in "The Last Frontier." As we pulled into Amalik Bay we saw someone waving to us from the deck of MV Waters. The Waters is a 65-foot ship, operating out of Homer, Alaska, that is rented by a variety of research groups who have projects to examine in the western Gulf of Alaska. This week there were ornithologists from Audubon and U.S. Fish and Wildlife, and David Wolfe, who we knew, from the Alaska Regional NPS office. They wanted information on nesting sites of cormorants, puffin, and glaucous-winged gulls. We told them exactly where to go to see the birds they were looking for, and several others.

As we were leaving one of the women asked what the cruise ship anchored around the point was up to. Penny said, "A cruise ship! Oh my God. We didn't know there was a cruise ship around here." She looked at me, I nodded, and Penny said, "Damn, we're gonna check them out—right now."

The "World Discover" lay at anchor in the south cove of Amalik Bay with a bunch of Zodiacs running around like a swarm of mad locusts. They were going up the channel and on into Geographic Harbor. Their Zodiacs pulled up to a portal the size of a large door, just above waterline. Crew members helped people onto the ship, then helped a new bunch into the waiting Zodiac. We couldn't see any place we could tie up, so I pulled up to the portal, a crewman looked a bit dumbfounded but gave Penny a hand-up. A young woman in a uniform, who had just gotten off the last Zodiac, stepped up and said, "Hi I'm Sally, one of our ship's interpreters. Can I help you?"

Penny said, "Hi, I'm Penny Starr; that's my husband Frank. We're the coastal rangers for the NPS, and I need to speak to your supervisor."

Sally said, "I'll get Susan. She's my boss."

Susan Adie showed up in a minute or two, introduced herself as the expedition leader, and offered to tell Penny whatever she needed.

Penny learned the parent company, Society Expeditions, is German owned with headquarters in Bremen, Germany. Clipper Cruise Lines operates World Discover and several sister ships. Their U.S. office is in St. Louis, Missouri The ship is registered in Liberia and has a crew of 64, with six naturalists. The officers are all German, the hotel crew is American and Canadian, the deck force is Filipino, and they had 130 guests on board. This was the first time they had been in Amalik Bay. They were in Kukak Bay this morning and planned be back to Amalik two more times this season, but not next year. In 1988 their sister ship The Explorer was in AMBA. And, no, they never allow anyone on shore.

Penny said, "I need to see your Commercial Use License (CUL) and I'd like to speak with the captain."

Susan looked confused and said, "Just a minute, I'll check and be right back." Five minutes later she returned with the information that no one knew anything about a commercial use license and the captain couldn't possibly see Penny now, he was too busy.

"OK" Penny said, "You let the captain know, To be legal you must have a CUL. One can be obtained from David Nemeth, superintendent of Katmai National Park in King Salmon, Alaska. The next time you are here I will see the captain! And that woman who just walked by with a Kamchatka Rhododendron blossom in her hand tells me you do take people ashore."

Susan looked dumbfounded, and just said, "Yes mam."

When Penny showed up at the open portal, I pulled our Zodiac up, Penny stepped in, said "Go!" and we were gone. I could see Susan standing watching us pull away, probably thinking, "Damned Park Service is going to be a problem."

They did return two weeks later. We had been expecting them, had been in contact with our office in King Salmon, and learned that, "No, the World Discover did not have a CUL, and had never even applied for one." The office also told us to be polite, but firm, and make sure they were aware they were putting all of Society

Expeditions Inc. in jeopardy of not getting a license to operate in any National Park.

I dropped Penny at their portal, where she found an entirely different situation. She was escorted to the captain's quarters by a smiling Susan Adie and introduced to the handsome, smiling Herr Captain Hienrick, who introduced Naturalist Tim Hosturick PhD. Tim explained that he had talked with the park archeologist who told him the ship must have a CUL. The information had been sent to the St. Louis office and would be acted on as soon as possible.

Captain Hienrick gave Penny a tour of the bridge, offered her some fresh vegetables and a beautiful selection of German wine. "Thank you Herr Captain," Penny said, "I appreciate the vegetables, but will pay your wine steward for the wine." That seemed to disappoint the captain, but he smiled, gave Penny a polite bow and said, "Until we meet again, Frau Starr."

Two weeks later the situation followed a similar scenario. Frau Starr was escorted to the captain's quarters and met by the smiling Herr Captain Hienrick. This time he had reason to smile, he handed her the ship's Commercial Use License with a huge smile and a polite bow.

Penny gave him a big smile, reached out and shook his hand. They both laughed about what seemed like ridiculous government paperwork, but agreed that it was necessary to prevent unsavory people from abusing the resources. Penny casually said, "Now if we could get Herr Brunner, who has a spike-camp down in Kashvik Bay, to be as cooperative our dealings with German tours would be great."

"You know Brunner?" the captain laughed, "He is a scoundrel. He has ads in all the European papers to 'See Katmai's Bears.' All of us in the tourist business know he can not be trusted. Watch him, he gives Germans a bad name."

Penny said, "We will." Then told the captain the story of the three wonderful German "Industrialists" she had taken to The Valley of 10,000 Smokes several years earlier. "They kept having 'A bit of Schnapps' and tried to get me to have some with them. They each had a pair of the most impressive Leitz night-vision binoculars I ever saw. I kidded them about being German U-boat captains. They looked at each other, laughed and said, 'Nein, we are industrialists,' laughed again and said, 'Have some schnapps, Frau Penny.'"

Penny and Herr Captain had a good laugh, shook hands, and parted friends. The kind of ranger/visitor relationship that makes the U.S. NPS respected around the world.

COMPANY

Penny Clemens and Sharon Ruh had been best friends since they had both moved to Upper Arlington, Ohio, the summer before their sophomore year in high school. Now Hal Manhart and Sharon Ruh Manhart lived in Montrose, Colorado, about 30 miles from Ridgway, Colorado, where Penny Clemens Starr and I lived. The two women were still close friends. Hal and I had become friends, many years ago when he and Sharon were dating. Hal was an ENT physician and had a brother Dick, an anesthesiologist, who also lived in Montrose with his wife Marilyn. The six of us often had dinners together, where Penny's and my jobs with the Park Service became a frequent topic of conversation. The four Manharts always wanted to know where we were going to work the next season and claimed they would visit us some day.

Mail showed up at Amalik Bay every time someone had a good reason to fly in, which seemed to be about once a month, or so. In the most recent mail we had a letter from Dick and Marilyn Manhart. They were coming to visit us for a few days. The four of us had discussed such a visit the previous winter, but we hadn't expected them to follow through on the invitation.

Kodiak Air flew Dick and Marilyn in on the day they had scheduled, which can happen, but often the weather causes delays in travel plans. They had brought the rubber boots and rain gear we suggested, plus two grocery sacks of fresh fruit and vegetables and two bottles of wine, all of which they had picked up in Kodiak that morning. We had a of couple spare sleeping bags and Thermorest air mattress they could lay on the floor to sleep, and pile on top of our bed the next morning. That was the best sleeping accommodations we could offer. We had rigged an old sheet around our bucket toilet to provide a little privacy. They knew we lived in the boonies, but I think Marilyn was a bit surprised at how scarce our amenities were. Neither of them had ever carried the toilet to the beach to bury their poop and pee or walked down a rocky beach to a waterfall to get a bucket of water—you become quite conscious of how much water you are using when you get it that way.

That evening Penny and Marilyn were fixing dinner of pasta, ground beef, and cheese with Mexican salsa and fresh salad; I was doing paperwork, and Dick said he would like to go fishing just down in front. He wondered about bears. Penny said, "No problem, they won't come onto the beach if a person is there."

Not fifteen minutes later, Dick ran up the stairs, white as a ghost, and gasped, "There's a bear down there."

We all looked out, and sure enough there was a bear on the beach. Penny said, "Oops! Sorry about that. So much for general rules and bears. That's Old Lady. She's the most laid back bear we ever knew. She's pretty old and may not have even realized you were there. She's looking for the same fish you were looking for."

A few years ago, we had had two sets of friends visit us at Nonvianuk, and realized the best way to treat visitors was to just take them along as we did our normal day's work. This being Alaska, our work was from an open boat so we always dressed for foul weather; we wore rain pants, good rubber boots, and those marvelous orange float-coats with 1/4-inch neoprene rubber lining. We had two survival-suits—float-coats with legs—as spares, that Dick and Marilyn could wear in the boat to keep warm and dry.

So, it being a normal day, we took two empty five gallon gas tanks to our cache of fuel drums to fill. Dick seemed interested, so I had him use the wobble-pump. (A wobble-pump is simply a hand pump with a pipe that doesn't quite reach the bottom of a 55-gallon drum. Gas floats on water and you sure don't want water in your gas, so the pipe dasn't reach bottom.) We carried the fuel to the beach and pulled the boat to shore. As always, the inflatable boat had lost some air during the cold night, so Penny got the pump out of the tool bag, connected it to a low section and asked Marilyn if she would like to pump the boat up. "Sure," Marilyn said, "Show me how."

Penny laid the foot-pump on the aluminum deck and said, "Its kind of like climbing stairs, except you don't go any place. Stand on one foot with your other foot on the bellows-pump; move your weight to the bellows foot, and air blows into the boat; back to your deck foot, and the bellows fills; just like walking up stairs."

Penny released the carabiner holding the boat to the mooring float, I released the latch holding the motor tipped-up, lowered the outboard to the run-position, pulled the starter-cord a couple of times, the motor roared, and we were ready to go on patrol.

There was water in the boat from last night's rain that had to be drained. I accelerated, pulled the drain plug in the transom, the water ran out, I put the plug back and we were on our way. We hadn't been to Geographic Harbor for several days, and needed to see if the Pinks (pink salmon) were running yet. The number of bears at the headwaters stream told us the Pinks were in. Up stream a few yards, there were six single bears fishing, plus a sow with a three-year-old (three-year-olds are usually kicked out in early spring, permitting the sow to come into estrus and mate). Near the mouth of the stream, the poorest fishing spots, were a sow with a yearling and two sows with cubs-of-the-year (COY)—one with twins, the other with a single cub. Marilyn said, "I can't believe this. There are 15 bears right there, and I've never seen a bear outside of a zoo."

We decided it was a good opportunity to record bear behavior by watching for a while. The yearling cub pushed his luck by challenging a subadult, probably four years old and weighing 400 or 500 pounds. The little guy made sure mom was right behind him and charged the bigger bear, ears back and growling as fiercely as he could muster. To our amazement, the big subadult glanced at the sow, who was standing watch, turned and fled. We all laughed, but I said, "What that little one just learned could get him killed if he tried it when mom wasn't so attentive." The poor subadult spent the balance of the time we were there, just sitting on the end of the spit watching other bears fish.

An immature bald eagle landed and took most of the fish scraps that some glaucous-winged gulls were after. It was great wildlife watching, and Penny suggested we have lunch while we were there. Everyone agreed so out came the Pilot biscuits and peanut-butter. This time we had fresh grapes to go with it. Six of those beautiful little harlequin ducks entertained us by fishing for crustaceans in a section of fast water.

Heading back to the bay we watched a mature eagle take a salmon just in front of us and a pair of river otter on the bank eating a fish one of them had just caught. Penny looked at Dick and could tell he was itching to catch a salmon too. She said, "Don't worry Dick, we'll stop on the way in and you can catch dinner for us."

Dick laughed and replied, "No hurry, I can fish later. Just watching all this is even better than fishing."

I decided we might as well check the sea lions on Ilktugitak Island while we were catching up on neglected observations. In the outer bay there were several surf scoters, numerous pairs of Kittlitz's murrelets, a pair of marbled murrelets, and a flock of kittiwake, all feeding on small fish. On the way past Takli Island we stopped to check an eagle chick in the nest we had been watching. It was standing up almost as big as the parent right beside it and should fledge before long.

While we were out in the Shelikof we reached our contacts in Kodiak, Jim and Jackie, by radio to let them know we were still fine, working hard, checking archeological sites, and documenting our observations.

OK, enough already, it was 1830 and Dick still had to catch dinner for us. I headed home to let Dick get his fishing gear and drop Penny and Marilyn off. I took Dick to a point where he could catch a salmon and be able to walk back to the cabin across dry beach. He looked at me as if to say, "Your not dropping me all alone with the bears." I promised him I would be on the beach fixing the fire-ring, collecting drift wood, and keeping the bears at bay. It wasn't a half hour before Dick came across the beach with a huge grin and a nice silver salmon that would feed the four of us that evening.

The archeological site at Russian Anchorage, in Kukak Bay, was our goal the next day. Neither Dick nor Marilyn had any interest in archeology, never-the-less, we showed them a good location for an Aleut camp, but not a permanent home. It sits on a spit open to the sea on one side and beautifully sheltered on the bay side. A seriously eroded midden showed the effect of exposure to the Shelikof seas and winds. There were no barabra pits, which indicated it was not a homesite. A lot of fishermen use the spot for anchorage when they choose to not go around Kinak Point and into the much more sheltered Amalik Bay. We took several photos with the park camera (which recorded date and time of the photo), made a few measurements, and considered the Russian site documented.

For our lunch break we pulled into a beautiful little cove with a sandy beach about half way up the southwest coast of Kukak Bay. It was one of those flawless, sunny days that are so rare and greatly appreciated. Penny and Marilyn had put together a special lunch of the goodies the Manharts had brought from Kodiak: Tillamook sharp cheddar, a fresh fruit salad, and of course, Pilot biscuits.

After lunch we walked a few yards up to the beach grass just to see what we could see. I noticed an area of flattened grasses about five feet in diameter and explained we had found a fresh bear bed that had undoubtedly been used last night. We found nothing else of particular interest, so we headed back out in the boat. I was slowly motoring out when Marilyn said, "Oh dear, look at that." We all looked back to where we had been on the beach a moment ago and saw a big sow with two yearling cubs smelling where we had sat having delicious cheese and fruit.

"OK," I said, "That is a beautiful example of how giving these bears can be. She had undoubtedly been nursing the cubs in that bed we looked at. Had she decided to, she could have had our lunch, or one of us if she really wanted to." We sat quietly, watching the beautiful family examine odors they had never smelled before. I suspect we were all considering the alternatives that mama bear had run through her head before making her decision. In reality she made the decision that kept her cubs from possible harm.

The next day Kodiak Air picked our friends up, and we were alone again. Friends are nice to have for a few days, but the two of us truly appreciated the solitude, peace, and tranquility of this wonderful place.

The survival-suits Dick and Marilyn had worn showed a fair amount of salt from sea water being splashed on them. Rain was forecast for that night, so we hung the survival-suits from nails at the bottom of the steps to get rinsed in the rain.

Early the next morning, while I was still asleep, I felt Penny get up. She rushed to the door, stepped out on the little deck, and yelled, "Old Lady, you're a bad, bad bear! You drop that, right now." Just like she was scolding one of our dogs.

I, of course, was wide awake by then, and thought, "Oh my God, what is she doing. She's gonna get herself killed." I grabbed the shotgun, and ran to the door in time to see Old Lady, about six feet away, drop the survival-suit she had in her mouth, give Penny a look, and mosey down the path to the beach.

EARLY THE FOLLOWING SEASON SHARON AND HAL MANHART FLEW in to Amalik Bay for a visit. We knew both of them were interested in archeology. The four of us had taken several trips together into the archeological ruins of the Anasazi and more recent Native cultures of Arizona and New Mexico. As before, we entertained our guests by taking them on, well, semi-normal patrols. We patrolled to Cape Ilktugitak to check if the eagle nest was active this year—it was. A pair of eagles was busy repairing winter's damage. We would pay attention to this pair all season and watch them raise and fledge two chicks. While we were out there we introduced Sharon and Hal to the sea lion colony on Ilktugitak Island. It was the first time either of them had seen sea lions up close.

They were enjoying the wildlife, but we could tell they wanted to see the archeological sites we had talked about. We headed in to Takli Island and the numerous sites we had examined the year before. The site where the fox farm had been located, had a pair of bears walking the beach, so we headed up to the site in the next fiord. At the head of the deep fiord was a rise—the remnants of an old beach dune. There we located a pair of barabra pits. Neither of our friends had ever seen anything like this before. The Anasazi built their homes high-up in sandstone caves. Here, there were several worked points lying exposed where they had fallen hundreds of years before.

We walked up a little side draw that had an unusual flat floor. Hal moved ahead of the three of us who were examining something. I looked up and thought, Oh shit. I turned to Penny and Sharon and whispered, "Quiet! bear!" I turned toward Hal and, in a firm voice, said, "Hal, don't move! You have a bear a few feet away. It's on that bank to your left rear. It's just standing there watching you. Don't look at it, just very slowly start walking back to us." He did just as I had said. We all held our breath until Hal reached us. The bear continued to stand there just watching us. Finally it turned and disappeared into the alders. We looked at each other, gave a sigh of relief, and then laughed. I am sure it was a subadult who had never seen a human before.

"Lets go have a beer," Sharon said, "It's been a pretty exciting first day. I can't wait to see what you will dream up for tomorrow."

We always note everything we see for Penny to enter in her daily log. On the walk back to the boat we saw some elegant wild flowers: several wild geranium, some purple wild iris, a nice shooting-star, and a gorgeous chocolate lily about a foot tall with several whorls of lancelot leaves on the stem, and two six-petal blossoms the color of rich chocolate. Sharon bent to smell it and said, "Yuk, that smells like shit." Penny laughed and told her it is also called "Out-house Lily."

On the way back to the cabin we saw a lot of the seabirds that we frequently saw, but Sharon and Hal wanted them identified. There were 75 surf and white-winged scoter, several pairs of guillemot, numerous common mergansers, and a porpoise playing off our bow.

The following day the seas were up so we decided to check Amalik Bay and Geographic Harbor. As we were ready to head out, Penny pointed to Charlie and Old Lady on the beach and said, "Lets just wait and watch them." We had already explained we didn't like to go to the beach when there were bears there, not out of concern for our safety, but to show consideration for the natural inhabitants, who seemed considerate of us when we were on the beach.

Old Lady took offense to Charlie being too close and charged the smaller bear. Charlie backed off several steps, then roared and charged back. They didn't make contact but circled each other growling, snarling, drooling, and glaring. They were both permanent residents of the bay and wanted to be alpha-sow. Old Lady, we guessed, had been alpha for a long time, but now, Charlie, the next generation, was ready to claim her supremacy. They settled their differences, for the moment at least, by each walking off to opposite ends of the beach and moving into the alders.

The final day of our friends' visit the winds were calm, and we decided to head out to site 30, where we had discovered the skull of the poor demented young person. Our friends had heard us tell of it and were anxious to see the skull. Site 30 sits on the northwest tip of the easternmost inhabitable island of the Takli group. The approach is steep, across 6-inch and larger surf-rounded rocks, up a 5- to 10-meter ridge vegetated by beach grass, cow parsnip, and other flowering plants that weren't in bloom yet. Several house (barabra) pits were located near the top of a west facing cliff, which gave the best shelter from weather. Not far from the barabra pits there were two large eroding middens made mostly of clam shells, but containing a whole host of marine mammal bones, and the human bones we wanted to examine.

A year's erosion had exposed some additional human bones: the head of a femur (thigh bone), most of a second femur, the maxilla (upper jaw) of an adult, with most of the teeth still in place, and several small bones that had to be tarsal bones from someone's ankle, and the teenager's skull and mandible that had fascinated us, but not the park's archeologist, last season. Sharon and Hal found the skull as fascinating as we had. How could a person with no mental capacity have been kept alive for 18 years in this environment? A true puzzlement!

In the eroded cliff face, about three feet below the surface, we found a layer of charcoal several inches thick and cracked rock from fires that had been used to fix meals hundreds, or even, thousands of years ago. The four of us pictured a family of four or five, one of whom had to be completely cared for, sitting around a fire ring fixing and eating the catch of the day, perhaps clams and a fish. It all might have been cooked in a pot made from the hide of a sea lion and heated by dropping hot rocks into the soon to be seafood stew. Perhaps with some kelp on the side.

We got home to a Wilson's warbler serenading from a bush near our door and a meal of Penny's wonderful mixture of Mexican beans and rice, with a salad of fresh greens, and a bottle of chardonnay that Sharon and Hal had brought from Kodiak. We spent the evening reminiscing about old times together and contemplating the life of the Aleuts who had lived on these islands.

Early the next morning our friends were picked up by Sea Hawk Air, out of Kodiak, and again we were home alone. Our old friends, Gene and Eleanor Probasco, had visited us at almost every assignment we had. They were always a fun pair to have join us for a few days. They had planned to come to AMBA but their son had suddenly developed a serious heart condition; the Probascos would miss our favorite place.

Starr family

WHO IS THAT?

Several weeks after Sharon and Hal left, Stan Steck, the park pilot, landed with mail and several 15-gallon containers of boat fuel to replenish our diminished supply. We and Stan had taken a liking to each other over the past two seasons. We always looked forward to his showing up once in a while with mail, park news, and some needed items. We had burned a lot more fuel than the park had anticipated, and Penny feared we might be in trouble. Stan told us Superintendent David Nemith felt we were doing a great job; the use of fuel showed we were out on patrol a lot. Penny said, "We're fightin' crime every day." We all laughed and Stan was on his way.

The mail contained a letter from our middle daughter, Carin. She was going to show up at Amalik Bay in a week to celebrate her mothers 60th birthday. We had entertained friends and several visitors, but "Hooray!" one of our own kids was going to visit us in The Great Land.

The day Carin was due we skipped going on patrol. In mid-afternoon a blue over white Cessna circled overhead, read the wind direction from the water motion, set down and taxied up to the beach. Penny said "That can't be Carin, there are four people onboard." Ron Edwards, one of Sea Hawk Air's pilots stepped out on the port float, waved to us, stepped into two feet of water in his hip-waders, walked around the plane and reached up to give Carin a hand as she climbed out onto the starboard float. She was waving and smiling, got on Ron's back, and came to shore piggyback.

We were laughing and hugging Carin when Penny looked out to the plane as another woman stepped onto the float and said, "Who is that?" Carin said, "Mom, that's your daughter Lori." Penny said, "Really?"

As Ron was carrying Lori to shore, another woman climbed out. Penny again said, "Who is that?" And Carin replied, "Mom, that's Kristy!"

"Oh my God this is too wonderful. All three of you are here. I can't believe it. Carin, you said you were coming but never mentioned your sisters."

By then Ron had all the bags ashore and was ready to leave. He and I shook hands, Penny was almost in tears and gave him a big hug. Each of the girls hugged him, but before he left Lori said, "You have our pick up on your calendar?" Ron assured her he would be here as scheduled and on-time, assuming the weather permitted flying.

It was a challenging time in each of the girls' lives. Lori (Loran) was managing one of the Grand Central Bakeries in Portland,

Oregon. She had two children, Claire and Ethan, had recently left her husband, and was still recovering from an hysterectomy operation. Carin and her husband Jock Beebe, had recently moved to Toledo, Ohio, where Jock was the CEO of the Jobst corporation, and Carin was on the board of the Black Swamp Land Conservancy. Kristy (Kristin), a UPS driver, and her three quarter horses were living on a small farm in central Ohio. In addition to her UPS job, she owned and operated a traveling tack shop, Silver Starr Tack, and was deeply in the throws of falling in love with Warren Davis, her future husband. Carin had called her sisters and told them they should all visit their parents at Amalik Bay, to celebrate their Mom's 60th birthday.

Kristy claimed, "I couldn't possibly get off work, it would cost too much, and I don't want to leave Warren right now."

Lori said, "I couldn't get off work again, and I can't afford it anyway."

Carin had answers: "This is important. You know how much anniversaries mean to Mom. I just sold some of the stocks that Mom and Dad gave us and will get the tickets." It took a while and more convincing by Carin, but here the three of them were, and we were thrilled.

We each grabbed a load of gear and headed up to the cabin. Lori and Carin had each seen the accommodations we had at Jewel Cave and Yosemite so they weren't shocked by the small, worn, leaky cabin. Kristy lived in an old farmhouse and wasn't bothered at all. She said, "Where do we put our stuff and where are we gonna sleep?"

"Put your gear on that shelf above our bed, then after dinner you can spread your pads and sleeping bags between our bed and the door," Penny told her.

Kristy retorted, "Gee thanks! So, when a bear comes through the door he gets us before he gets you."

"That's the plan," I said. We all laughed, but the girls had heard our bear stories and had to be a bit concerned. Over the next few days they saw a lot of bear activity and grew a bit more comfortable being near big brown bears.

The moon was nearly full, creating tides that were higher and lower than normal. So the next morning, on a negative tide, three bears, Charley, Old Lady, and Digger, were clamming on the beach. Lori pointed out they each had their own technique. Digger clammed in several inches of water. She could see bubbles coming up, didn't hesitate to put her head under water, and would get a clam every time. We had seen her clamming in well over a foot of water, the only bear who clammed that way. Charley didn't get a clam with every dig, but when she did she dropped the clam and bounced on the shell until it cracked; she flicked some shell away, raised it to her mouth and ate. Old Lady dug like a dog, sand flying out between her hind legs. Got a clam nearly every time but wasn't picky about getting it open, sometimes she too bounced on them until the shell broke, and didn't seem to mind getting shell and sand in her mouth along with the clam.

Soon the tide put the clams in water too deep even for Digger, so the bears moved on. Carin and Lori decided to walk the beach, Kristy sat on the roof of the little shed adjoining the deck and wrote a letter to Warren, her new love. She wrote to him every day and was disappointed that she couldn't mail them and sorry she didn't get letters from him.

A few days earlier, Penny had proclaimed, "While Carin is here we don't need to go on patrol. We've worked 60 days straight, we can do anything we want while she's here." I reminded her that "going on patrol" is exactly what we chose to do every day. Seeing and learning about this coastal ecosystem was the reason for our accepting this position, and what Carin would want to do.

After lunch the tide was up so we all went on patrol. A salmon run was starting and we wanted the girls to see bears fishing at Geographic's head-waters stream. There were four small bears working the river, none of them mature. Two of them must have been twins. We had seen them together several times, and now they were sitting beside each other, just watching. We told the girls these guys were still learning how to fish. The pros would show up in a few days when the fishing got better, and these four would need to figure out how the pecking order worked.

This was exciting for the girls, and Penny and I always enjoyed watching bears be bears. We watched these youngsters chasing fish across shallow water, like human children trying to catch soap bubbles floating by. It was comical, a 400-pound bear with wet fur, running through three or four inches of water with splashes flying everywhere and a few fish swimming hard, their backs and dorsal fins above water, dodging left and right. At just the right moment, the bear would dive for its fish, hind legs splayed wide, front paws reaching out, and hit the water with a huge splash as the fish swam on up stream.

Kristy said, "There, that one caught a fish." It had a beautiful silvery salmon in its mouth and headed to shore to eat. It stopped, looked around, and probably realized the other bears were thinking about stealing the fish, so it ran off into the brush before it lost its prize. Carin asked what the gorgeous chestnut colored shore birds pecking in the beach-sand were, Penny told her, "Those are red-necked phalaropes. They come up here to breed but winter in South America."

On the way back to the main bay, we watched an eagle feeding a pair of eaglets in the nest on a cliff, and our river otter family cavorting along the channel. Carin said she wanted to see an archeological site; Lori piped in "So do I," and Kristy gave a "Me, too." So we headed out around Takli Island to site 26, which sits at the head of a cove on the east end of Takli. The entrance is protected by many rocks and reefs that I was paying close attention to as we headed in. Lori excitedly said, "There's a bear swimming. Look, there's a cub following her. I know bears swim, but we are way out here. They must have come from that little island out there."

Penny agreed and told them that we had seen bears swimming plenty of times, but this was the first time we had seen a yearling cub anything like this far from shore. The pair swam right to the place we were headed. We waited for several minutes to give the bears plenty of time to move on before we landed, but I could tell the girls were nervous about following the bears in. I showed the girls the tracks where the pair had moved up a creek, too small for fish to navigate, but they still weren't sure. "OK," Penny said, "Lets walk up on this grassy knoll and look for them."

There was no sign of bears. I was sure they had moved on up the creek to get away from us, but needed to convince the girls they would be safe by the beach. It was an interesting archeological site with several chipped stone artifacts eroding out of a three meter high cliff and a barabra pit dug on top. On three sides were stands of beech grass, cow parsnips, and fire weed, which the girls seemed to be watching carefully to see if the bears were there. Penny suggested we move on and look at the Starr site so the girls could see the site named for our family.

We spent just a while examining a site of no real consequence other than having been discovered by Penny and Frank Starr in 1991. It sits on the southwest corner of Kinak Point where it is nicely protected from almost all weather conditions. We had found it when we noticed clam shells showing through hillside vegetation.

There were several trawlers and a pair of tenders anchored in the bay waiting for the sockeye opening to begin at 0600 tomorrow. A crewman on the deck of the tender Sea Barb was waving to us, so we pulled up next to them. Captain Dick, who we knew, came on deck and told us they had lost their cooling capacity and were going to have to dump the 20 thousand pounds of fish they had in the hold. The whole crew was bothered, the fish were mostly sockeye, which were bringing $1.40 a pound. A few Pinks were mixed in, they didn't matter much, since they were only bringing twelve cents. They were about to dump $30,000 into the bay. Dick said,

"We have a few halibut and will eat some tonight on our way back to Homer. Could you use a small halibut, and how about a sockeye?"

Penny said, "Sure! Thanks, we'll use the halibut tonight and hold the sockeye over for tomorrow. Oh! Would you please dump in the Shelikof and not in the bay? We don't want dead fish washing up in here. They would stink and attract all the bears for a hundred miles." Dick said, "No problem," and gave us the two fish, which we put in a garbage bag, to make sure we didn't get any fish smell on the boat. A bear thinking there was a fish in the boat would be the end of our rubber boat and, probably, the end of our season.

Carin said, "Could we follow them out and watch them dump? It would be interesting to see and would make a great picture."

"You bet," I said, "I think we'd all enjoy watching that." Penny and I had seen it before, but it is such a pathetic sight we felt the girls should experience it. We followed the Sea Barb out and watched as thousands of fish who were alive this morning, came pouring out a shoot on the boat's side. Those fish had been on their way to the stream where they hatched four or five years ago. There, they would have laid the eggs for a new generation. That generation was going to be up to someone else. Sure, they had been caught and weren't going to procreate anyway, but somehow, seeing them just dumped was worse than having them go to market. At least the halibut we would eat in a few hours wasn't just getting dumped.

Dinner that evening was going to be a very special event, a shore dinner prepared by all of us. Lori and Carin fixed a beautiful salad of fresh greens they had brought from Kodiak; Kristy boiled new potatoes; I filleted the two fish and Penny put the salmon in the propane refrigerator for tomorrow and supervised us all while she caught up on family affairs we had missed. I got the little folding grill out of the shed, and we all headed to the beach. Everyone collected small dry drift wood pieces and alder for the beach cooking-fire. Lori, who lived in Portland, Oregon, wondered about a bonfire after dinner like she enjoyed on the Oregon coast, but her parents thought a white-man's fire didn't fit the ambiance here. I said, "After dinner we'll build the fire up a bit and keep it going as long as you want."

I had a good fire going, but needed to get it down to coals for cooking the halibut. My four wonderful women headed up to the cabin to collect the food for dinner, leaving me to tend the fire and think about how I could be so fortunate as to have a wife like Penny and these three beautiful girls who had come all the way to bush Alaska to celebrate their mother's 60th birthday.

The coals reached perfection at the same time the halibut showed up. I had to laugh, because a big hamburger patty came too. Kristy, our meat and potatoes farm girl had brought a pound of ground sirloin from Kodiak. She had a six pack of Budweiser too. Carin and Lori had brought some nice chardonnay, so we each had a choice of beverage to go with our beach-feast.

The weather, since the girls arrived, had been unusually good and this day was ideal. The sun set behind the mountains to the northwest, light would stay with us for several more hours, but the sky was turning a beautiful red-orange creating a magical setting. The girls started singing, "Happy Birthday to you, Happy Birthday dear Mom, Happy Birthday to you," and brought out a sand-in-a-pan cake with 60 candles (we didn't have any way to bake, so a real cake was out of the question). Lori put another stick on the fire; the five of us had sat around many campfires over our years of camping together. We sat on the beach, kept the fire small and friendly, reminisced, and just enjoyed the five of us being together while a Swainson's thrush serenaded us from the brush with its enthralling, ascending spiral of flute-like notes. An evening to remember!

THE GIRLS WERE INTERESTED IN EVERYTHING: BIRDS, FLOWERS, SEA mammals, bears, and archeology. A wolverine crossed the beach while we were getting ready to go out the next morning. We had seen several this season, but it was a first sighting for any of the girls. Lori noticed a golden-crowned sparrow singing "Oh-save-me," from a bush just below the deck and a male yellow warbler with a bright yellow head and reddish streaking on its breast singing in another bush.

On the way to Kinak Bay we passed Kinak Rock and watched a flock of tufted puffin diving for small fish, and flying them to their nest holes for their chicks. A porpoise nosed around us as we idled watching a pair of sea otter lying on their backs with strands of kelp wrapped around their bodies, anchoring them in place. They each had a rock on their chest and were cracking sea urchin, using their fore-paws like hands. In another kelp bed around the point, a sea lion was feeding on—we didn't know what. In Kinak Bay we found a raft of about 300 stocky, short necked, black diving ducks known as scoters, both surf and white-winged, many of whom were molting and couldn't fly. Seals were hauled out, sunning themselves on a rock along the north shore.

In Hidden Harbor there were several bears—a sow with two yearlings and another sow with twin two-year-olds. Carin wanted to know how we knew their age. I explained, "It's just from their size and how they act. The yearlings are the size of a springer spaniel and two-year-olds more like a Newfoundland; Mom will kick them out next spring when she goes into estrous. If you see a sow with a bear about the same size as she, it will be a three-year-old who hasn't been kicked out yet."

Penny said, "Watch the yearlings. In the presence of other bears they will stick pretty close to Mom, and the two year olds will be off exploring."

Kristy said, "Look, that bear has a collar." We could see the collar and yellow tags in each ear. Our friend, state wildlife officer, Dick Sellers, had been out here collaring bears early that Spring and would be glad to know about this one.

In an area of marshy shallows near a creek-mouth we saw four wandering tattlers—gray shore birds about a foot long with 3- or

4-inch legs and a 2-inch bill—wading in sandy gravel and feeding on aquatic insects.

We pulled up on the beach at Russian Anchorage and had a relaxed, leisurely lunch of Pilot Biscuits, cheese, and leftover halibut. Penny suggested we check the archeological site where we had found the human bones. They had all heard about that site in Penny's letters and wanted to see it. So that was the plan for the rest of the day.

Site #30 is on the outermost island of the Takli Island group. It was a beautiful day with little wind so I took us out into the Shelikof far enough to observe seabirds that can't be found near land. We counted 20 ancient murrelets, several marbled murrelets, two Aleutian terns, four flesh-footed shearwater, and six sooty shearwater. The kind of birding you don't get without being at sea. And yes, we had to check the bird book to be sure of their identity. Birder's Handbook told us that shearwaters and murrelets are part of a group of birds that spend their lives at sea and come to shore only to nest and breed. Both of the shearwater species breed on small islets off the coast of New Zealand's North Island and come north to feed during our summer. Marbled murrelets breed in mature coniferous near the Washington and Oregon coast.

We located the human bones and explained our theory of the demented person. Carin, our degreed RN, told us it was what is known as an anecephaly (without brain), an abnormality that occurs during the formation of the brain and spinal column in a fetus. Kristy decided we should call this "Dead Man's Island." It is referred to that way in our year end report.

Lori has eyes like a hawk and sees many things that others miss. We all found various flaked and worn points, but Lori located an area that must have been a workshop with waste flakes and broken or failed points, and a most unusual piece, apparently ground from basalt. It was thin, about 4 inches long, 1-1/2 inches wide, one side had teeth ground into it, like a hair comb, but only a half-inch long.

We puzzled over what it could have been used for; all we could think of was a fish scaler.

Carin and Kristy were identifying wildflowers: the blue and white Nootka lupine were about done for the season, coastal fleabane, a typical Aster daisy with a lovely pinkish cast was plentiful in dry gravel, and a single plant of small frigid shooting star in a protected marshy spot.

Everyone was showing signs of it having been a long day and a full week, so we headed back to the cabin. On the way in, I couldn't resist checking the sea lion group on Ilktugitak Island and the eagle nest on Cape Ilktugitak. As always when we showed up the little colony of sea lions charged out to meet us, or challenge us, which ever it was they had in mind. At any rate the girls had an exciting introduction to sea lions, since I let their charge get a little closer than I should. The two eaglets were getting big and looked like they might fledge soon. The parents weren't around, so they were either out fishing or staying away in hopes the young ones would give flight a try.

Ron, of Sea Hawk Air, was scheduled to pick the girls up at 1400 the last day. That gave us time to get their gear together and still watch bears fishing at the stream in Geographic Harbor. There was not a bear on our beach. With sockeye running the bears had abandoned their activity everywhere except the salmon streams. It was a busy place and we enjoyed the fishing techniques of the adult bears, each of whom occupied its fishing spot depending on the established pecking order. The young ones were busy chasing fish across shallows and challenging each other over fishing spots. It was a typical day of us watching wild Alaskan brown bears, but with the never-to-be-forgotten joy of having our family together enjoying the unique life we parents had chosen for our retirement.

Ron was right on time and our girls were gone. Interestingly, we were sad to have the girls leave that day; we had a wonderful time and would miss them. The old story of fish and friends being welcome for three days but not longer didn't hold for three wonderful daughters.

AND OTHER EVENTS

The 1992 season at Amalik Bay started with an unusual and nearly calamitous event. In 1991 we and our gear flew to Amalik Bay aboard a twin engine amphibious Grumman Goose belonging to the Fish and Wildlife Service. This year, we were on a NPS Goose flown by our old nemesis, sleepy, lazy Joel, who not only seemed to sleep while flying, but also refused to consider the tides. Before we took off from King Salmon, I warned him we would be landing on a sand beach with a rapidly falling tide. He simply ignored me. I shrugged my shoulders and started loading the Goose. Joel moved to the cockpit. I knew he wouldn't offer to help.

Penny and I put a few items through the hatch of the storage area. I climbed in and rearranged them, making space for more gear to be loaded, then climbed out to help Penny load more, a process which had been made much easier last year by the willing hands of pilot Jeff. Actually, all pilots, except Joel, were picky about how the plane was loaded. They wanted to be sure the weight was properly distributed, which affects the balance of the aircraft.

We had a beautiful flight out. The sky was clear so we flew over Naknek Lake and directly up the Valley of 10,000 Smokes, through Katmai Pass to the Shelikof and up to Amalik Bay. We landed and taxied up onto the beach in front of our cabin. With the tide fairly high, we were closer to the cabin than we had been last year. I again mentioned to Joel that the tide was dropping and was again ignored. As expected, Joel sat in the cockpit while we unloaded. Before we had finished unloading, our friend Stan Steck, the park pilot, landed in the park's Cessna 206. Stan set an anchor and hurried over to help unload.

All of our gear was off-loaded and up on dry ground, so I climbed onboard to let Joel know we were done and he was free to leave. He was asleep, so I loudly said, "Joel, we're done. Have a good flight back to King Salmon." He grunted as I left.

The two big Pratt & Whitney engines roared, the tail lifted, but the Goose didn't budge; the engines continued to roar even louder as Joel gave it full throttle. The plane rocked a bit but didn't move. The three of us on the beach looked at each other. Stan yelled in my ear, "Grab the port float and push." I pushed on one float, Stan pushed on the other, the engines roared even louder, but the Goose refused to budge from the sand it had settled into.

I decided Joel and the Goose were there until the tide came back in twelve hours. We three moved up the beach and away from the intense noise. With full throttle, those big radial engines were starting to throw oil. We were picturing the Goose sitting on the beach all season with blown engines. Finally the Goose moved a bit, then more. Joel and the Goose made it to the water; he slacked power for a moment, then resumed full power and was gone.

Stan felt he had to apologize for his fellow pilot. Penny said, "No, you don't need to apologize; that's Joel! We know him. I just hope he didn't destroy that beautiful aircraft."

Stan helped us haul our gear to the cabin, said he had to get to King Salmon to see if Joel made it back, gave Penny a hug, shook my hand, wished us well and was gone.

SPEAKING OF NOT PAYING ATTENTION TO TIDES, ONE DAY WE had headed south to check the salmon run up the river in Dakevak Bay. We had cruised around the cape into Katmai Bay and checked the site of the former Katmai Village, which had been destroyed in the 1912 eruption of Novarupta and the collapse of Mt. Katmai. Penny suggested we go on down to Kashvik Bay and make a surprise visit to Herr Brunner. "Good idea," I said. However, when we got to Kashvik we realized the tide was out, and we couldn't get near Brunner's camp. There were several hundred yards of sand beach between us and Brunner's camp. Well damn! We couldn't put an anchor down and walk in; the tide would be coming back which would leave the boat way out in water that was too cold to swim in.

Penny had a solution, "You stay with the boat. I'll walk in and talk with Brunner." I didn't care for the solution, but couldn't come up with a better idea. I was better with the boat, and Penny was a much better communicator, so we went with her plan.

She had a long walk, probably a half mile, across the wet, almost flat beach, to the creek where Brunner's camp was located, then a hundred yards up the creek, through dense willow brush, with bear tracks everywhere. The creek was too wide and deep for her to wade across, so she yelled until she got the attention of a camp guest. Brunner himself came down to meet the "lone ranger" who had appeared at his camp. He was amazed by her solo appearance, but was willing to listen. Penny informed him, in a loud enough voice that all of his guests, who were watching, could hear, "You and your manager have been told before, you must complete the paperwork and apply to become a legal concessionaire. You are operating an illegal spike camp. You will be cited and never be eligible for a permit in any National Park."

Brunner stormed back, "Damn you, this is harassment. I know Senator Stevens. I'll have you fired."

Penny laughed at him and told him, "Go ahead and call Senator Stevens, I've met him, he's sensible. My life isn't dependent on this job, and Stevens has no option other than to follow the federal regulations in CFR-36 which states 'All concessions in a National Park must be licensed.'" She looked behind Brunner and saw several German guests nodding their heads. They understood Brunner was cheating and putting them in jeopardy.

When Penny got back to the boat she wore a huge grin and told me how Brunner looked dumbfounded, like a little boy caught lying with his hand in the cookie jar. "Now it's up to headquarters to follow up on Brunner, we've done all we can," she said.

On August first 1991 we were awakened by the sound of a train roaring down the fiord from Geographic Harbor. It got louder and louder, the cabin shook, things fell from shelves, rocks and boulders fell from the cliffs above us. After an eternity the sound was gone and everything was holding still (that eternity was probably less than a minute). Finally we realized we had experienced an earthquake in the mountains around us. No boulder had hit the cabin, but there were lots of big rocks lying around that we had not noticed before. Life at Amalik Bay, as far as we could tell, continued as if nothing had happened. All of Katmai's volcanoes are part of the Ring of Fire that circles the Pacific Ocean. We were accustomed to small earthquakes, they are a regular occurrence everywhere along the Aleutian Chain. This one, we learned, was a 5.5 on the Richter scale.

Returning from a patrol of Missak Bay one afternoon, we saw an Alaskan Trooper boat anchored in the bay. We, of course, stopped to talk with the troopers. They told us they were simply making a visible presence so the fishing fleet would know the troopers were paying attention. We motored on down the channel to check Geographic Harbor. As soon as we entered the harbor we saw a trawler, the Odessa Maid out of Seldovia, sitting on the beach—a falling tide had left it high and dry. There were several men on the beach waving to us. We pulled in and could see their problem. There was a hole the size of a soccer ball in the bow well below the water line. The men admitted they had been watching bears instead of paying attention, and had rammed a submerged rock. The boat had immediately started taking on water. Fearing they would sink and knowing the tide was full and falling, they ran the boat onto a shallow beach.

Did we have anything they might use to plug the hole? We didn't, but the troopers might. So we headed back to ask them. Amazingly they handed us a gallon of Wet Zone epoxy and fast-set fixer. They asked if we knew how to use it. I said, "Yes." I had a similar epoxy in my shop at home.

Back at the beached boat, they had a nylon tarp smoothed and wedged against the hole from the inside. They knew how to use the epoxy, but now had another problem; a bear wanted to use the beach. The men were scared and threatening to shoot the bear. "No!" Penny said, "We'll take care of the bear. You fix the boat. You only have a few hours before the tide floats you, and you had better have the hole fixed before then."

We grabbed our shotgun from its water-proof case and moved up the beach toward the bear. We could tell it was getting nervous and wanted to move across the beach, probably to reach the head-waters stream to fish. We have always gone on the theory that "The beach belongs to the bears," but there are exceptions. "Sorry Mr. Bear but you will have to go through the woods to get there." We both talked calmly and softly to the bear, about 20 yards away. In a few minutes he or she, seeming to understand, moved up into the woods and was gone. Penny stayed on this end of the beach with the shotgun, and I moved to the other end of the beach just to make sure another bear didn't come along to disturb the boat repair crew.

Two or three hours later a layer of clear epoxy had been spread over the hole and a second nylon tarp was spread over the bow from the outside to provide some extra protection. The tide rose and floated the Odessa Maid. They headed slowly for Homer about 200 miles away. We wished them well and went home for the night.

Old Lady on a Hot Day

On a sunny Fall afternoon Penny and I had decided to sit on the beach, rest our backs against a big driftwood log and relax. It was warm, hot for Alaska—70 degrees. I was almost asleep, when Penny punched me, "Schuss," she whispered, and pointed to Old Lady walking toward us. Actually Old Lady was simply walking her beach. We sat still, Old Lady walked right past, not 20 feet away, glanced at us and moved down the beach a ways. She walked into the water and laid down. She rolled onto her back and splashed water all over herself. She lay there splashing water for at least ten minutes. Just for the pleasure of it, we guessed, and to cool off on a hot day in her world. We sat still, just watching our friend bathe. Finally she got up and walked on down her beach. We looked at each other, smiled and kissed, held hands, and sat a while longer.

In mid-summer Charlie had stepped on the cabin's bottom step and broken it. We asked Stan for material to build new steps and make significant repairs to the deck. The roof needed help too. We put new flashing on all four edges and caulked several holes. It was September and we would be pulled out in a few weeks. We knew the Amalik Bay Ranger position would not be funded next year. In fact, there were no plans for it ever being funded again. We needed to secure the cabin, not just for the winter, as we had the previous fall, but as securely as we possibly could. We had given Stan the dimensions of all the windows and asked him to have maintenance make plywood shutters for them. By the time we left we wanted this building to be in as good condition as it could be. It meant a lot to us and we wanted it safe.

The bears were fat and still gorging on spawned-out salmon to be ready for their long winter sleep. Bears don't hibernate as other true hibernators do. Their heart rate and body temperature fall, but not drastically. Bears do, however, lower their metabolic rate up to 75%. They don't eat, drink, urinate, or defecate for as long as eight months. They burn the stored fat, recycle the water in urine, and lose as much as 40% of the weight they had at the beginning of their winter sleep. When spring came they would be ready to face a new world.

We too were ready to face a new world. We were in our 60s and had worked every Alaskan Park Service position we were interested in. Perhaps it was time for us to retire and work on our Colorado cabin.

Stan had told us to be ready for him to pick us up on 16 September. The Zodiac was to be left in the cabin—funding to have the Goose pick us up wasn't available so Stan would take us out in two loads in the park's Cessna.

The boat still had to be cleaned up; she had been in the water for four months and had a sizable collection of algal growth and barnacles living below the water line. On a high tide we pulled her up on the beach. The falling tide would give us time to work on her dry, just like the Odessa Maid. We pulled the outboard (it would go back to King Salmon in Stan's first load), took out gas tanks and gear, pulled the floorboards, and rolled her over. Now the fun! That coating of algae and the barnacles had to be scraped off. We had done it several times before. The best way we had come up with was a putty-knife and a lot of elbow-grease, followed by buckets of fresh water from the waterfall—salt water leaves a salty film.

We were ready. Stan flew-in late the afternoon of the 16th, apologized for being late, picked up the outboard and all non-essential gear, and told us he would pick us up early the next morning. We could almost count on Alaskan weather putting the kibosh on that plan. Sure enough, the night of the 16th a real storm blew in from the Shelikof. In the morning, rain and sleet were blowing almost horizontally and the bay was covered in whitecaps—no way were we going anyplace that day—or the next few days either.

We had kept food enough for several days, plenty of water was running off the roof for us to collect and the oil stove kept some heat in the cabin. We were safe and dry with nothing to do but watch the storm and reminisce on what a wonderful retirement we had chosen. Twelve years of seeing, learning, doing, and being a part of the natural world that we have always wanted to better understand.

Finally the weather broke. The sun in the western sky shone under the cloud bank that still hung over the Shelikof and Kodiak Island, creating a spectacular rainbow that stretched across the mouth of Amalik Bay. It lit our favorite place with our love and our hope it would remain the undisturbed wilderness we knew. We stood on our little deck and held each other. We realized that we had indeed flown over the rainbow and experienced dreams that really do come true.

The next morning the radio crackled, Stan announced he was in the air and would be here in less than an hour. It was a brilliantly clear day following the storm. The thermometer told us it was 31 degrees outside and 38 degrees inside. Time to be getting out of this cabin. Shutting down didn't take long. We turned off the propane and oil to the stove, blocked the refrigerator door open, elevated the mattress off its platform, dumped the water container (after Penny had her last drink), and had the shutters almost up when Stan landed.

It only took a few minutes to finish shutting the place down, carry the last of our gear to the plane, and we were flying out of Amalik Bay, probably for the last time. It wasn't easy to leave realizing we were probably leaving the crazy careers that had changed our lives so completely.

Stan recognized we were feeling a little melancholy. He had Penny take the copilot's seat and gave us a most unexpected and appreciated flight back to King Salmon. We flew out over the islands of Amalik Bay, turned and went up the channel and over Geographic Harbor. We turned north and flew up the coast, over the bays and capes we had explored from the Zodiac. He took us all the way up to and over massive Mt. Douglas. We had superb views of Serpent Tongue, Hook, and Hallo Glaciers, and Kaguyak Crater. The Kukak Volcano was smoking and melting the fresh snow that had fallen on it the past few days. On the far side of Mt. Douglas we saw the isolated volcanic island of Augustine. It had erupted on August first and was still smoking and preparing for its next eruption. Stan turned the little Cessna over the McNeil River State Game Sanctuary and flew west. He was showing us all of the places in Katmai National Park & Preserve we had experienced, lived, cursed, and loved. We flew over McNeil River and Paint Creek, between Battle Lake and Kulik Lake, between Kukaklek and Nonvianuk Lakes, down Nonvianuk River, and on down the Alagnak Wild and Scenic River, down the Kvichak River, up Bristol Bay and the Naknek River to King Salmon. We expected to land in King Salmon, but Stan took us on up the Naknek River, over Naknek Lake, Brooks Camp, and the falls on Brooks River before returning to King Salmon and headquarters.

In about two hours we had relived our six years of working, seeing, learning, and knowing Katmai National Park & Preserve like few, if any, others have ever known this magnificent park.

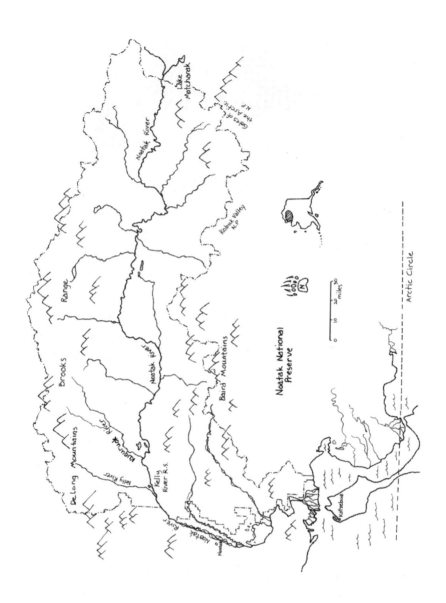

OUT OF RETIREMENT

We had spent two and a half years enjoying our re-retirement. We were adding a master bedroom, laundry, and library to our Colorado cabin. The project was enclosed and the interior could be nearly finished this coming winter. We were planning to complete it when next summer's good weather would let us build a deck and front porch.

In early December of 1994 we got a call from our long time Park Service friend, Jon Peterson. Jon had gotten a full-time position a couple of years before and had just accepted the position as Chief Ranger of the Northwest Alaska Areas, consisting of: Kobuk Valley National Park, Cape Krusenstern National Monument, and the Noatak National Preserve. The three units were operated out of a small office in Kotzebue, Alaska. A park, a monument, and a preserve all with one chief ranger sounds like a pretty daunting job, but each of those "parks" are, considering the immensity of the U.S. National Park system, rather insignificant due to their remoteness and low visitation.

Jon would have one seasonal ranger stationed in the Native town of Onion Portage in Kobuk Valley National Park. The Cape Krusenstern National Monument ranger would be stationed at Anigaaq, a Native fishing site, on the coast of the Chukchi Sea. He wanted Penny and me to be the rangers in the Noatak National Preserve.

The first time we had been in Alaska, when we were visiting our friends Al and Donna Franzmann in 1973, we had heard stories of the Noatak River and had pipe-dreamed of canoeing it. Now we were being asked to be the rangers who would kayak the length of the river and patrol the lower half by outboard boat. We would live more than 100 miles north of the Arctic Circle (66° 33' 45.9" N) and experience an unspoiled ecosystem that supported a caribou herd of 260,000.

Jon let us know the ranger who had worked the Noatak the previous season had been a problem. He had sold and done drugs with the local Natives and given away gasoline to anyone who stopped at the Kelly River Ranger Station (at the confluence of the Noatak and Kelly Rivers) and asked for it. This season's Kelly River rangers would have to deal with a Native population who had learned to think of the Park Service as a supplier of drugs and free gas.

Jon and Kathy had been married just a few months earlier. They were a pair of delightful people. Both in their late 20s, they were good looking, blonde Scandinavians who were physically fit and tall—Jon, 6-foot-3, and Kathy, 6-foot-2. Now Jon was puzzling over who he could trust to handle the Noatak River and the expected Native problems. In 1992 Kathy had been the seasonal supervisor at Katmai. It was her first season there and our second season at Katmai's Amalik Bay. She needed to learn about the wonders of Katmai. We had to get ready for the coast but took time to fill her in on Brooks Camp and the things we felt she needed to know about Katmai. Consequently, she knew us and we knew her. Kathy suggested Jon call us. She said, "I know Penny and Frank are retired, but you know them even better than I do, and I can't think of anyone who could handle this situation as well as they would." Jon liked the idea and called us. Now we had to make the decision. Should we let the house project sit until fall and take on one more season in the Great Land?

We were well into our 60s and knew the physical strain would be tough on our bodies, but the chance to experience and learn another unknown ecosystem was intriguing. The west flowing Noatak River runs through a broad valley, the heart of the Brooks Range, with the De Long Mountains to the north and the Baird Mountains to the south. Its head waters are in the rugged Schwatka Mountains of Gates of the Arctic National Park at over 4,000 feet. It flows 425 miles to Kotzebue Sound and the Chukchi Sea. The Noatak basin is 12.6 million square miles and is the largest undisturbed basin in the United States. There is one small Native village, Noatak, and a few Native inholdings with a fishing/hunting shack. Other than that, the 6.5 million-acre preserve was in its natural state.

Oh my God, could we do this? At the same time could we turn it down?—The house could wait. We would accept Jon's offer and spend one more season as NPS rangers.

Penny went shopping for the food we would need to get us through five months in the bush: dried soups, pastas, an assortment of dried beans, rice, Velveeta cheese, Spam and some other canned meats, as well as canned fruits and vegetables. We would get beer in Anchorage and Jon had promised to get it to us at Kelly River. We got out our uniforms—and yes, they still fit. We pulled out our infamous Svea backpack stove and cook kit with the wolverine tooth-holes through the lid, and all the other gear we would need. We boxed it all up and mailed it to Kotzebue, Alaska.

When our Alaska Airlines flight landed us in Anchorage, Penny looked up at a leaden sky and said, "Hmm, must be Alaska." Law enforcement refresher began on 15 May in Denali National Park with housing in the little town of Healy near the park's entrance. It proved to be an interesting experience. We were glad to see old friends and meet a bunch of new young people just starting their careers. We were now, not 20 years older than the other participants, but 30 to 40 years older. Not only that, I had pulled a muscle in my back and couldn't do the physical fitness tests. Penny could and completed every requirement—except it took her nearly 13 minutes to run the "12-minute mile."

Day one of the refresher started with a massive mock disaster where a small aircraft crashed into a shopping mall. They had every organization they could think of participating: the local sheriff's department, the volunteer fire department, state troopers, forest service, and park service. Everything was chaos for a few minutes until the sheriff took the position of Incident Commander and gave everyone distinct orders as to what they were to do. Having an Incident Commander takes the panic out of a situation. He, or she, is boss. Everyone follows orders and chaos becomes a managed situation.

The lectures were pretty standard fare. A judge told us to not bother siting wildlife infractions. He would dismiss almost all of them; "The wildlife is there for man to harvest," he said. Fish and Game told us to expect a small run of all salmon species this season. Most of the lectures we had heard many times—some entertaining, some boring—but it was good to get us back in the mode of thinking like cops. Firearms refresher was fun. I had the highest score in the shotgun test, and Penny had the second highest score in the handgun qualification, using her personal .357 magnum revolver. The young macho males were astounded that a "little old lady" could out-shoot them.

After the weekend visiting friends in Palmer and Anchorage, we flew to Kotzebue and were met by Jon and Kathy. They took us to their apartment for lunch and told us we would be staying in an apartment in the same building until we could get to Kelly River. Jon told us about his plans for the season. He wanted us to be at the Kelly River ranger station as soon as possible. He had hoped for late May, but the river and Kotzebue Sound were still frozen over. Jon said, "You can't get there until the river is clear enough for a float plane to land you on the bank in front of the station. You'll have to assemble and launch your dock before you launch your skiff. Don't worry, all the parts are up there, and this dock is amazing. You'll love it. You need to get over to the warehouse and collect your gear before other people grab the best stuff. You can do that in the next couple of days.

"Before you go in," he said, "I want you to fly to the little Inupiat village of Noatak for a meeting with the elders. (Inupiat is also spelled Inupiak and Inupiaq. They are a member of the larger Native group, the Inuits.) They need to know there are laws that were neglected last year and will be enforced from now on." He had one more specific request: "The damned porcupines are so thick up there they're chewing up the wooden pilings that support the tent-frames. You need to kill a bunch of them before they destroy the place."

Penny said, "Jon, we can't kill wildlife in a park."

"Wait until you see what the bastards are doing, and besides Noatak is a preserve."

After a pleasant two-hour lunch with Jon and Kathy, Jon took us to the office to meet the staff, get our hand-held radios, a .38 revolver for me, and see the headquarters. The superintendent wasn't around so we would meet him another time. We met Willie, Beth, Pete, and Marion. Even I could feel the seething among that group. We felt sorry for Jon. He would have to spend a lot of time with a group who hated each other and their jobs too. Maybe we didn't want to meet the superintendent. He would be the leader and pacesetter of this unhappy crew.

Apparently, we had plenty of time to see Kotzebue and collect all the needed gear before break-up would let us move to Kelly River. But our first chore was to move into the apartment we would have in Kotz—which seemed to be the way everyone referred to the town of Kotzebue. The apartment was small and dark, but would be fine for a couple of weeks.

We decided to walk to the warehouse. On the way we wandered through town to see what sort of place we were in. Our first impression was that this world was monochromatic. Everything was gray, the sky, the sea, almost all the houses and buildings. We could see the giant white radar dome of the Distant Early Warning (DEW) line sitting at the end of the runway. There were a lot of white, black, and tan plastic bags blowing around. The closest thing to color was the new hospital and the apartment building we were to live in, both of which were a dull, faded red, not far from gray.

Before modern man intruded and introduced metal, plastics, and other nonrenewable items, everything the Inuit needed was biodegradable, either plant or animal, so the unused parts would break down. The little junk they created was left on the ice of the sound; when the ice broke up and went to sea the refuse went with it. Now they had a ten foot tall chain-link enclosure out near the docks where trash was stored until a barge load of supplies from Seattle came in. The trash that hadn't blown away would be loaded onto the barge and shipped back to Seattle. In a couple of weeks there would be a "Pick-up Kotzebue" day when the borough would pay a dollar for each 30-gallon black plastic bag of trash that was turned in. That was evident in the number of partly filled, black plastic bags that were in front of most houses.

We walked Front Street along the channel connecting the Chukchi Sea to the west with Hotham Inlet to the east. The mouth of the Noatak River was a couple of miles north just across the channel—all of which was solid gray ice. There were several brown or black muddy pickups in front of nondescript houses, most up on blocks. The dogs were black and white, kids dressed in dark clothes. A few hundred yards along we came to the one-floor hotel of eight rooms. It had a badly worn carpet in the lobby and a restaurant with the same worn carpet. We were told, "It's the best and only place to eat in town, and no, they don't serve alcohol." We found a store that had a reasonable assortment of canned and boxed food, lots of candy and soft drinks. Their clothes were mostly Helly Hansen rain gear, Carhartt work clothes, high-top tennis shoes, and Extratough rubber boots. They would be getting their winter clothing on the next barge from Seattle. It was beginning to sound like everything came by barge from Seattle. Items that turned over quickly, like pop and candy, were flown in on commercial flights, mostly by

Alaska Airlines from, you guessed it, Seattle, via Anchorage. Like essentially all Native Americans, the Inupiats are very susceptible to alcoholism, so alcohol is illegal in Kotz, which didn't stop a black-market supply of booze from thriving.

Jon had told us we needed to get hepatitis-B vaccines as soon as we got here since we would surely be exposed. He had insisted we get tested for TB before we left home. If we got it here and hadn't been tested to prove we were TB free, the government would say we had it before and deny our claim. We had the tests in Colorado. We walked over to the new hospital and found it interesting. Like all fairly new construction in the Arctic, it was on pilings to keep it up a couple of feet above the ground to protect the permafrost. A heated building in contact with the ground melts the permafrost, sags and creates a mess. The entire new hospital had been built piece by piece in the "lesser 48," similar to double-wide house trailer sections, and shipped up here by barge from Seattle. Just like "Lego" pieces, all the parts had been assembled into the building. The hospital had been designed by an architect from somewhere in the U.S., probably Seattle, but possibly in New York or Louisiana. We went into the hospital and made appointments to get our hep-B shots. While we were there we wandered around and found it was a pretty complete modern hospital. Sure the floors were muddy and already showing signs of wear, but everyone who came in had on muddy boots, including us.

The NPS warehouse was just that—a big, unheated building with gear piled all over with no organization. There were piles of new float-coats, tents, and probably everything we would need. The float-coats were a surprise, they were dark blue, not the international orange that we had become accustomed to. We had always kidded because the U.S. Coast Guard had told us, "The Float-Coat won't keep you alive very long in the ocean, but the orange color will make your body easier to find." It was late enough that we decided we would come back in the morning and set aside what we needed. Penny said, "Just a minute, there is only one coat my size, we better set it aside with my name on it." We created a pile of gear with Penny's small coat and a medium one for me. Clearly marked it, "KELLY RIVER—F&P STARR." We relocked the warehouse and went home for the evening.

Jon had assured us the tent-frames at Kelly River were completely supplied with everything we would need there. "Trust but verify." We couldn't verify, so we better make sure we were self-supporting. We would take a North Face VE-25 tent, sleeping bags, food for the season, and our own back packing Svea white-gas stove and white gas. That would cover our asses, just in case. We would need all of those things on the two-week kayak trip of the Noatak River anyway, so we weren't doubling up on our "white-man's baggage."

First thing the next morning we went back to the warehouse to gather our equipment. There are always new and old items in a Park Service warehouse so the first one selecting their gear is likely to find the best equipment. We intended to be early; we had learned a long time before that being older had advantages and disadvantages, you can't compete physically, but with age comes wisdom, you have to out-think the kids. We wanted to make sure we had good equipment for the river. We unlocked the door, turned on the lights, and headed to the collection of stuff from which we would assemble our gear. Behind me I heard, "God damn it! My coat's gone."

I walked over to our little pile, and sure enough there was one medium float-coat, and no small coat. I pulled my radio, pressed the speak key and said, "700, 710,"

Got an immediate response of "700."

I said, "Location?"

Heard, "Office."

I replied, "Be there in five. 710 clear."

"Copy"

Radio protocol calls for short direct communication with no

more talking than necessary. The caller first identifies who is being called, then identifies himself. Jon's number as Chief Ranger was "700," my call number was "710," and Penny's was "711." That lets everyone with a radio know who is calling who. We didn't want to explain our problem for the whole park to hear, best left for a meeting in Jon's office.

His door was open, we walked in and closed the door. "OK, what's up?" Jon said. We explained. Jon told us there was only one other person on staff who would wear a small. He was a smart-assed little guy on maintenance who had been here last year and had gotten away with all sorts of crap. "Don't worry, I'll get the coat and make sure his boss knows he stole it. Besides he doesn't spend much time in a boat and isn't qualified for a float-coat."

Back at the warehouse, we decided we would have to take our gear back to the apartment to be sure it didn't walk. There were tents of several styles and manufactures, we knew we wanted a VE-25, so we pulled one out with a clean stuff-sack, opened it, looked carefully for any holes or worn spots, and made certain all the parts were there. It was in good condition but Penny always insisted on resealing all the seams to make sure there would be no leaks. We wanted two heavy sleeping bags, it was still freezing every night. We also knew it could get pretty warm after the ice was gone and we had 24 hours of sun, so we should take a pair of lighter bags too. There were plenty of bags, no need to feel guilty about taking four. We would take them back to the apartment building and wash and dry them at the laundromat next door.

There were several Klepper kayaks to choose from, but only one double, and we wanted to be in the same boat. We didn't even consider the singles. The double showed some wear and would need a little refurbishing. That was OK. We knew how from working on the Folbot we used at Katmai.

That afternoon excitement reigned in Kotzebue. The ice was breaking up. Everyone seemed to be on Front Street watching chunks of ice more than a foot thick and as big as a car rushing by. A pretty exciting event, and it meant we would be able to fly in sooner than anticipated.

We let Jon know we were ready to go as soon as we could. Jon said, "Sounds like a plan," a phrase we would hear frequently this season, "but first I want you to fly out to meet the elders in Noatak. I have that all set up for day after tomorrow. I want you to make sure they understand this is not last year when there wasn't any law enforcement up river. They need to know we are required to enforce the state regulations on wildlife harvest. The Natives really have no limit on harvest. They can take fifteen caribou a day and as many fish as they want. They do have to pay attention and not take fish that are under size, but they don't want the little ones anyway. I'll get you copies of the regs. The only thing they are likely to complain about is, they must have Alaskan hunting and fishing licenses. They don't think they should.

"So be at the airport at 0800 day after tomorrow. Jonas, with Baker Aviation, flies a ten-seater out two mornings a week and comes back at 1400. I want you to see the town, especially the clinic. They have an RN, Cheryl, and her aide, Vicky, both nice gals, who will show you some of their problems. Look the village over and meet with the town elders at 1100. Cheryl will show you which house, and maybe introduce you. Meanwhile you still have paperwork to complete."

We nodded our heads, Jon said, "Sounds like a plan."

We chuckled and said, "Sounds like a plan."

NOATAK

We were at the Kotzebue airport well before 0800 and met our pilot, Jonas, as he was loading the Cessna Grand Caravan turbo prop we would ride out to the little village of Noatak. He told us he had flown in Alaska for 30 years and had once been one of those "bold-bush-pilots," who fly anywhere, anytime. He had decided to become an "old-bush-pilot" by flying safe and sane when the weather was flyable. He had flown for Baker Aviation for several years. He flew to Noatak twice a week, to Borrow once a week, and to Nome twice each week. Penny let him know that he was our kind of pilot and we would love to go to Barrow, "The top of the world." "I was there yesterday, and will be going back next week," he said. "Come along and I'll show a different world."

We had done our homework and knew the Inupiats we would meet today were a part of the of the ancient Thule culture that dates back to the end of the ice age 12,000 years ago. The Natives of this part of Alaska had migrated to the mainland from the Bering Sea islands several thousand years ago. They had always been hunter-gatherers. The people we would meet still relied on fish from the river, caribou, moose, and even spring grizzly when they could find one. The grizzlies were up north where the caribou were calving. In the Noatak country they had been hunted to the point of being scarce and were rarely seen.

We flew north up the broad Noatak valley, saw the little village below, checked the wind direction and landed on a gravel strip. One pickup truck and several people on four-wheelers were there to meet the plane. Two young women, each on four-wheelers, were waving at us. We walked over and met Cheryl and Vicky from the clinic. Both round faced, pleasant looking Native women. We climbed on behind them and went directly to the clinic. They were anxious to show us the place and explain the problems they were dealing with.

It was a fine little clinic, well supplied by funds from the borough, through the federal government. They told us alcohol use in the village was down. Alcohol, in any form, had been declared illegal a few years before. Smuggling it in was difficult. It was pretty easy to spot if it was flown in and bringing it 50 miles up river from Kotzebue, by boat, was a pain and not worth it. Drug abuse and STDs (sexually transmitted disease) were out of control. Bringing drugs in by air was pretty easy. Anyone onboard our flight could have had drugs in their pockets or luggage, or it could be in the freight that came with us. They didn't have the authority to search people or freight; could we do that? We hated to tell them the village of Noatak was out of our jurisdiction, and searching without probable cause or a warrant was beyond anyone's authority.

They told us how Native culture had been changed. Their ancestors had been hunter-gatherers, depended on salmon and caribou for their food and shelter. Sure, they still fish and hunt, but most of what they harvest is used to feed dogs. Now much of the food was ordered from one of the bush suppliers and flown in by Jonas. Most of the clothing came from Sears or LL Bean. Even sled-dogs aren't used much anymore. Everyone has a snow-machine and a four-wheeler.

There were only a few jobs in Noatak. The largest source of employment is the Red Dog mine in the De Long Mountains just west of the Noatak Preserve. It is the largest zinc mine in the world and provides a good number of jobs. The mine maintains a port on the northern coast of Cape Krusenstern National Monument that offers more jobs. Of course, all of the high paying positions are filled by whites from the states. The mine and port provided the only local option for Native employment. Some of the men worked there but most of the young people had gone to Anchorage or "outside" (the lower 48) to find work.

We were getting along well with these two young women, so Penny asked, "Would you tell us about the elders we will be meeting in an hour or so?"

Cheryl and Vicky looked at each other, Cheryl said, "Penny, you are a woman and will learn that women have no standing with the elders. Don't let it upset you. It's a fact that we have to deal with every day. Just ignore it. Frank, that grey beard and hair show that you're an elder. They will accept you and listen to what you say. They won't like it, but they will hear you."

"We probably shouldn't tell this," Vicky said, "but the daughter of the Olsons, where you will be meeting, is a classic case of our problem with alcohol and drugs. She went to the borough high school in Kotz. When she finished she couldn't find a job, so she went outside. I'm not sure where, probably Seattle, but she discovered booze and drugs and men. She came home a few years ago with a case of gonorrhea, a baby, an addiction to heroin, and I don't know what else. We try to help her. We've treated the clap, but I'm afraid her drug addiction is beyond what we can do. She needs to go to Anchorage to the rehab center, but she refuses and we can't force her. I'm not sure what her kid has, but he's certainly retarded. She and the kid live with her parents, which has ruined Ohoto and Kunee Olsons' lives. They are still the leaders of the elders, but they seem lost."

The four of us sat and talked. We learned a lot about how life for the Inupiats had changed too fast for many people to handle. There seemed to be no solution. Modern times had come to a part of the world that wasn't ready or able to handle it.

It was time to head to our assigned meeting with the elders. We weren't looking forward to it, but we had better get it done.

Vicky had shown us which house was the Olsons'. The small village had a dozen or so government supplied houses, all identical factory-built, and mounted on pilings a couple of feet off the ground. We walked down the dirt road and up to the door. I knocked, we waited. As I was about to knock again, the door opened. A tiny woman with a round face and no expression looked at us. Penny said, "Hello, Mrs. Olson. We're Penny and Frank Starr. We're here to meet with your husband and the elders." She looked at us, stepped back, and opened the door farther. Her expression never changed. She didn't say a word.

We stepped into the living room and saw a table with four chairs and three older Inupiat men sitting in them. Just beyond the men was a kitchen where the woman who had answered the door had already gone. In a corner near the door was a young woman curled up in a love-seat, sound asleep, or probably out on drugs. She never moved while we were there. As we walked in the three men stood, almost smiled, and introduced themselves. Owliktuk, Kumaniuk, and the host who appeared to be the oldest, probably my age said, "My name is Ohoto. That is my wife Kunee." Kunee looked at us without any change of expression.

I said, "It's a pleasure to meet you all. I am Frank Starr, and this is my wife Penny. We will be the rangers at Kelly River this year, and we wanted to meet you. We want to know what we can do for you and if you have anything you would like to tell us or ask us. We've worked in Alaska for several years, but never this far north, and are excited to see and learn your country."

The three of them sat. I started to step back so Penny could take the only empty chair. I got a poke, a frown, and a look that said, "You sit!" I sat and asked them how the winter had been and if this was late for break-up. We learned the winter had been normal and break-up was when it was. OK, this wasn't going to be an easy or fun meeting. I am not a conversationalist and always count on Penny to lead any conversation. I looked at her and got a slight head shake. I was on my own, Penny and Kunee were women and obviously not going to be included in the talk with these three elders.

From somewhere in the back of the house we heard, "Maw," a minute later, "Maw, food." Kunee picked up a bowl from the counter, poured it full of Cheerios, and walked toward the voice. No explanation was given. We wondered about the hungry voice. Could it be a normal child just waking up? We guessed this was the retarded child of the young woman who was passed out on the couch. We could speculate all we wanted but weren't going to be told anything about the family.

I made small talk, and asked how life had changed since they were young. I could see a little life come into Ohoto's eyes. "Sixty years ago," he said, "I was a boy. We hunted and fished for our food. Lived in a house of poles covered by caribou hide. We made fire to heat our home and cook our food." Ohoto went on, "All our clothes were made of skins and fur that Father trapped. Mother fixed the skins and made clothes. I helped Mother until I was big enough to go with Father. We had dogs to pull the sled. They needed a lot of food, dried fish and caribou. We hunted and fished to feed the dogs and us."

He seemed to be getting in the mood to tell stories; Penny and I were enjoying hearing about his life. Unfortunately, right then Kunee came to the table and handed each of us, including Penny, a small paper plate with a sandwich—two slices of white Wonder Bread with a slice of American cheese—and a warm can of Coke. Story time was over. We all ate in silence.

Penny had stood behind me like the obedient wife that she wasn't, just listening and touching my shoulder. When she finished lunch, I felt her walk away. Knowing her bladder, I guessed she was off to the bathroom. I asked Ohoto to finish his story, but he shook his head no. The elders wanted to know what we would be doing. I started explaining the State wildlife regulations we were required to enforce and felt Penny come back. Her right hand squeezed my shoulder very firmly. Was I saying things that I shouldn't? I didn't think so. Something else was wrong then.

The three elders sat stone faced as I explained, "Native Alaskans are allowed to kill up to fifteen caribou a day during season." (The fall season coincides with the caribou migration south to winter feeding grounds.) I went on, "You are permitted to take fish of legal size any time. The state requires you to have valid, up-to-date fishing and hunting licenses, and we are required to check those licenses."

Ohoto looked at me and said, "You will see our licenses?"

I said, "Yes, that is the law and our duty."

He stood and proclaimed, "You will be very uun-pop-u-lar!"

"I am very sorry you feel that way," I said, "but the law is the law, and we are required to enforce it even if we don't agree with it. We aren't here to win a popularity contest. The state requirements are very lenient. All you have to do is buy a license and carry it with you. I hope we can be friends when we meet you up river. Please stop in to the ranger station any time, and let us know if we can do anything for you. I looked at my watch and said, "We have to get back to the airport to catch the two o'clock flight, so again we thank you for your hospitality." The three stone faces looked at us and said nothing.

I turned to Penny and said, "Time to head home. I'd better pee first."

Penny said, "No, let's go." Her expression said, "Don't argue."

Outside I said, "What?"

"You didn't want to go into that bathroom," she said, "The water doesn't work, the toilet is full of shit. There's even some shit in the sink. That little boy looks hopelessly retarded. That whole family is screwed from white-man's drugs."

Houses had been built for them a few years ago but no maintenance instructions had been included. The water and sewer lines were all broken, frozen, and destroyed. These poor people had their culture killed. White-man had good intentions but didn't know how to do anything except hand out housing and money.

Jonas was standing beside his Cessna when we walked up. He asked, "Are you going to stay up tonight to see the last sunset?"

"What do you mean the last sunset?" we said together.

Jonas grinned, "This is June 3rd. The sun goes down for a couple of minutes around one a.m. and won't set again until the tenth of July. Then we start screaming toward total darkness."

Twenty-four hours of daylight we could handle, but 24 hours of darkness would be a an experience we were glad we would miss. Many of the Natives have trouble with it too. Darkness is credited with being the cause of a lot of alcoholism and suicides among the people of the North Country world wide.

KELLY RIVER RANGER STATION

As soon as we got back to Kotz from the village of Noatak, Penny and I stopped in Jon's office to report on our visit. We expected Jon to be upset by the negative response we had gotten from the elders. Instead he congratulated us on a great job. He had expected us to have a much worse time.

He told us he had planned for us to head to the Kelly River station tomorrow, but had been told the river was too high and fast to land a float plane there. We would have to wait a couple more days. That was fine with us; we still had maps to copy and the tent seams to seal. I also wanted to try putting the Klepper together. The maps were just a matter of finding the ones we wanted in the messy park files and making Xerox copies.

Penny insisted the seam-sealing was a one-person job and suggested I start on the Klepper; she would join me in a few minutes. The Klepper came in three big canvas sacks. One held the rubberized canvas skin which weighed about 35 pounds and folded up to the size of a large sofa cushion. The wooden frame pieces pack into two bags, together weighing over 40 pounds; one containing the struts, which were dowels of mountain ash, just over four feet long. The third sack was smaller and oval and held ribs of laminated Finish birch.

Penny had finished the nasty job of sealing the seams of the tent and rain-fly with a sticky, stinky mixture of volatile chemicals. She mentioned she had gotten some on her fingers and how it burned, but she was ready to see how the Klepper went together. We fitted struts and ribs together with hooks and clips until we had nearly identical bow and stern skeletons. We shoved one into each end of the limp blue canvas skin and connected them in the middle where they locked together like two halves of a hinge. Add three more frames and the coaming pieces (the raised border around the cockpits that keep splashes out) and the Klepper was complete. The first time, it had taken a couple of hours to get right. The second try took less than an hour. We were glad we had worked through the assembly of the boat before being dropped off at the head of the Noatak River—not a good place to learn boat assembly.

Bright and early the next morning we were headed to the warehouse—well, it wasn't very bright there were low clouds, and the sun hadn't set for over 100 hours so it was hard to think of 0800 as early. Anyway, Jon reached us on the radio and asked us to stop in his office. He had a plan! A young ranger named Pete was with Jon. We had met Pete at the law enforcement refresher a couple of weeks ago and had gotten to know him in Kotz.

Jon told us he had us scheduled to fly to the Kelly River Ranger Station tomorrow, and Pete would be going with us for a couple of days. "I want Pete and Frank to fly up early with Buck. You two take the outboard, all the radio equipment and the rest of the government stuff. You need to get the dock assembled and into the water and the boat down the bank so Penny can fly in with John and off-load the rest of your supplies without wading. Pete, you'll only be there a couple of days, but some of those things are too heavy for Penny to handle. Another thing; you'll have ELTs (emergency location transmitters). Be sure they are always with you and turned off unless you actually need to be rescued. I want you each to always carry at least three means of starting a fire: a butane lighter, wax coated strike-any-where matches in a film canister and this flint and steel sparker." He handed us each a metal rod about the size of a finger, connected by a short lanyard to a steel piece that looked like three inches of a hacksaw blade with no teeth. "Scrape the rod with the steel and it makes sparks. Another fire starter I like is loading cotton balls with Vaseline and keeping them in a film canister. If you can build a fire you can be dry and warm and not get hypothermic. Sounds like a plan!" Jon used his term "Sounds like a plan" frequently. Most of the time it came across as a question. This time we knew it was a decision not to be questioned.

We were disappointed to not be going in together but that could be ignored. We still had gear to be assembled, but finally we were heading out of Kotz and back into the Alaskan bush. Penny said, "I'll take care of the tent, clothes and food; you two collect the gear." The gear consisted of a Yamaha 35-horse outboard with a jet-unit and tools, weapons and ammunition, a wobble pump to use in the 55-gallon fuel drums that were already there, the Klepper, and all the radio equipment. We would have better radio equipment and connections with headquarters than we had in many years. Jon had gotten a solar collector that we would mount in an open spot and wire to a 12-volt car battery. That should keep the ten-watt base set well powered and recharge our handhelds all season. Jon insisted everything else was already there.

We don't like going to a camp for four months without seeing it first. I asked Jon if he were sure hand tools, heat and cooking stoves, fuel, kitchen equipment, mattresses, anchors, mooring lines and everything else was there. Jon showed us last year's season-end inventory, listing all the stuff we asked about except rope, so I cut 50 yards of 5/8-inch braided nylon for securing the dock, and 50 yards of 3/8-inch for anchor line. We had all our personal gear and food gathered; we were ready.

The weather looked flyable the next morning so Penny, Pete, and I loaded everything in the park pickup and drove to the floatplane dock. Buck, a jolly, round man with a magnificent reputation as a bush pilot, and a beautiful little Maul aircraft, was waiting for us. He supervised loading the Maul, making sure everything went just right to balance the plane. Jon showed up about the time we fin-

ished with the Maul and told Penny to load the 206. He had to go
to the office. He told Penny that John (the other Jon, an NPS pilot
for Northwest Alaska Areas) planned to get to Kelly River about
1400 so they would take off at about 1330. Pete and I insisted we
help load the 206, but Buck said we needed to go. Penny said, "You
go on, I can load all right."

"Bullshit," I said, "A couple of these boxes are too heavy. Pete
and I can load them in and you can arrange them." So Pete and I
loaded the heaviest boxes into the 206, but Buck was getting antsy
so I gave Penny a kiss and climbed into Buck's plane leaving Penny
to finish loading.

I later heard the story of Penny loading the plane for John. She
figured out just how the load should be distributed. She put the
heavy boxes Pete and I had loaded near the center and the lighter
stuff farther to the rear figuring she and John would be sitting up
front. As she was loading the last of the gear a young woman in
an Alaska Department of Fish and Game uniform walked up and
asked, "Are you Penny Starr?"

Penny stuck out her hand and said, "That's me."

The young woman said, "I'm Betsy Stewart. I'm so glad to meet
you. I've heard so much about you for years, but never expected
to get to meet you in person. All the places you've worked, all the
things you've done that other women only dream of. Like Mardy
Murie, you're a legend in your own time." Penny chuckled and
thanked her for the compliment, but said she didn't think she was
in Mardy's league. The two of them sat and talked about Mardy and
her book *Two in the Far North* and her famous wildlife-researcher
husband Olaus—Olaus and Marty Murie were the primary movers
in getting President Eisenhower to protect the Arctic National
Wildlife Refuge—until Penny realized she needed to go eat before
she picked John up.

Meanwhile, Buck had dropped Pete and me and our load at the
base of the steep 20-foot bank of the Noatak River, just below the

Kelly River Ranger Station. We left the outboard and its gas tank on the bank and hauled the rest of the gear to the top. I wanted to see what the station looked like. We could see it through the trees and followed a path up to a platform raised three or four feet off the ground supporting two tent-frames, one for sleeping and one for kitchen and office. I looked inside the sleeping tent and found two bunk beds and a heat stove. I opened the door to the kitchen and, "Holy porcupine shit," it looked like a thousand porcupines had used the tent frame as an outhouse all winter. The dung was dry so the smell wasn't too bad, but feces was an inch deep on the counter where they had climbed between the wall and the tent, and even deeper over most of the floor.

Damn! Cleaning that mess up wasn't part of the plan, but right now Pete and I needed to get the dock and boat in the water. The 18-foot aluminum skiff, another Lund, was on its side, leaning against a tree. The dock was an amazing invention. It consisted of two-foot, heavy duty, hollow plastic cubes. Each side-edge of the cube had a three-inch fin with a hole in the center. The fins were at slightly different heights so that four of them fit snugly together. A big plastic pin with a bigger head went through the holes locking the four cubes together and left the head flush with the deck. Assembled it made a very good 14 by 26-foot dock that could be taken apart each winter and reassembled the next year, assuming no one lost any of the parts. It had only been used one year and all the parts were there. We rolled most the cubes down the bank and assembled them at the water's edge. I secured the two inboard corners to trees with 5/8-inch line and admired a very functional dock that we could walk on with no problem. We slid the Lund down the bank and moored it to a side of the dock, mounted the outboard and were finished just as John and Penny landed and taxied up to our dock.

It didn't take long to unload and haul all the stuff up to the sleeping tent. John told Pete he would be back to pick him up day-after-tomorrow, and took off.

I was arranging things in the sleeping tent when I heard, "Oh, my God" and a string of expletives. Penny had gone into the kitchen tent! I went over and heard, "This is the filthiest damn place I have ever seen. Not only is there porcupine shit everywhere, there's garbage and trash that I can't believe. We've got to get this place cleaned up. Now!"

I'd been trying to think of how to get the dung scraped up. The tool supply was limited, but I had found a big long-handled axe. I suggested I start scraping shit off the counter, Penny could collect loose junk and dump it into trash bags. Pete was busy installing the solar collector and 12-volt battery for the radios, so Penny and I got to work and had the place clean enough to be functional, except for the floor. We were tired and needed to quit for the day.

Penny had finished the liter bottle of water she had brought and asked if we were drinking straight from the Noatak. I remembered Jon had told me the Kelly River was cleaner than the Noatak so he recommended getting drinking water there and running it through the expedition Katadean water filter. "OK," I said, "Lets see if the boat works and run around to the Kelly and collect some water in the plastic jugs I found." The outboard started on the second pull, and we were off. It was less than a mile down stream to the mouth of the Kelly. We were getting our minds off the filth of the station and seeing a different country. We ran a couple of miles up the Kelly, a beautiful stream of clear, clean, cold water, dipped our cups, had a big drink, and filled the three three-gallon jugs.

Then we just sat and looked. We knew we were way above tree-line, but there were spruce trees along the north bank of the Noatak and up the hill several yards. We could see there were no trees on the south bank, and other than at its mouth, the Kelly was open tundra, not a tree in sight; home for the season.

At the station we had been too busy to appreciate where we had landed. But in the quiet of the Kelly we heard the wonderful ascending flute-like notes of the grey-cheeked thrush and realized we had heard the same song at camp too. We were trying to locate the thrush when Penny said, "Wow, what is that bird?" A little grey and white bird with a bright white rump and black eye streak was bouncing around on the gravel bank grabbing insects. My first thought was a shrike, but no, it was too small and had a straight bill. Later we looked it up and found we had made our first sighting of a northern wheatear, another member of the thrush family.

Back at the station, Pete was talking with Mike and Tommi, a pair of bird researchers who had been dropped off. They told us they would be in for two days each month to trap birds in mist-nets and band them. They wanted to sleep in the tent with us, but Pete told them there were four bunks and three of us so they would have to camp. Penny explained that this was our home for the season and they would need to camp down near the Kelly where there was a pseudo campground. They weren't happy about it but agreed to her request and left us alone.

Penny happened to look at her watch and said, "Oh, my God, it's after midnight." The sun was low in the north but it was still quite light. It struck us; how often does anyone look north to see the sun? Now we understood how the Inupiats were up doing things any time of the 24-hour long daylight.

The next morning Pete wanted to cook oatmeal but couldn't get the propane tank connected. I reminded him it had a left hand thread. He laughed and said, "Thanks, I had forgotten that."

Mike and Tommi had been out collecting birds, and by the time we had finished eating they were sitting just inside the door, in good light, out of the drizzle, sexing and banding a couple dozen little forest birds. Pete went back to setting up the radios. Penny was collecting more trash and I was on the floor with the axe scraping shit. Mike looked at me and said, "Would you please quit that? You're scaring our birds."

I was not having a bit of fun. I started to say, "Take your fucking birds and stuff 'em!" but caught myself and said, "Sorry about that, but this has to be done here, and it's going to be done now; you can take your birds somewhere else." They did.

Penny went to the sleep-tent for something and came back to announce "The tent leaks." Sure enough the canvas was dripping in several spots. Jon had sent a waterproof nylon tarp along so Pete and I needed to install it, but Penny reminded us the seams had to be sealed first. Her hands were cracked and bleeding from having sealed our tent, so the tarp sealing was my project. Penny reminded me to not get that terrible chemical goop on my fingers. "Yes Mam! I don't want my hands looking like yours or hurting like yours must."

About the time we got the tarp on the next morning, we heard a plane buzz us. John landed on the river, picked Pete up and all the sacks of trash; and we were alone again—the way we loved it.

PORCUPINES

We checked the foundation posts on our tent frames for porcupine damage, and sure enough, just as Jon had told us, those wooden posts were pretty well chewed up. Too many porcupines can be almost as bad as too many people. The solution was to reduce the number—of porcupines not people. The number of people will take care of itself eventually, we hope. Pete had shot one out of a tree, and I had gotten another. I was poking at stuff I was burning in the burn-barrel with a big stick and saw another porky on the trunk of a tree not far away. I walked up to it and whacked it hard, on the nose with the poker. It dropped dead. That was too easy and didn't feel right, but the population needed to be reduced.

I have never felt right about killing anything I didn't intend to eat. Carnivores, like many insects, robins, hawks, lions, and humans depend on killing to get their protein. All animals have other animals that prey on them. Large animals have smaller animals living on them; the smaller ones also are prayed upon by even smaller animals and each try to kill the ones irritating them. As Jonathan Swift said:

Big fleas have little fleas
Upon their backs to bite 'em
And little fleas have lesser fleas
And so ad infinitum.

But, only man goes looking to kill things that irritate, or might bite him. We all kill mosquitoes that bite us and flies that irritate us. Some of us kill things that could bite us, like spiders or even snakes. And, woe-be-it to any animal or plant that might threaten something we deem our food. We use insecticides and herbicides to kill whatever might threaten our crops. In Alaska they shoot wolves from helicopters because a wolf might kill a caribou that a man might want to kill. Here, Penny and I are killing porcupines that are damaging our tent frame, and neither of us feel right about it.

Penny was coming up from the outhouse and reminded me we needed to dig a new pit for it. We also needed to set up the shelter for the weather station. That sounded more interesting. We were to record high and low temperatures each day, precipitation, wind, and cloud cover, as well as river level. So far the temperature had been in the 30s and low 40s, with clouds and drizzle or rain most of the time. It reminded us of Glacier Bay—cloudy, cold, and wet. Jon wanted to know the river level changes too. Penny found an ideal two-inch diameter stick about eight feet long. I carved notches in it every two inches (bigger every foot) and set it well into the mud bottom where we could watch the river level fluctuate a foot or more every time it rained up stream.

The outhouse pit needed to be dug, so we took a pulaski and a shovel and picked a spot about ten feet from the old outhouse where we would have a nice view of the river from the throne. We dug through the few inches of sphagnum moss that covered the entire forest floor. It scraped off to ice—permafrost—we attacked the ice with the pulaski and realized it was going to require digging an inch or so, then letting the surface thaw a bit before we could dig deeper. An inch a day process. It was going to take a while to dig a proper pit.

"Company coming," Penny said, as a skiff with two Natives pulled up to our dock. We walked down to meet them and learned they had been up-river and needed gas. I told them we were not a gas station, and they needed to plan their fuel needs more carefully. They told us the ranger last year had given them gas every time they asked for it. Penny told them this year they would not be able to get gas here. "Our boss has ordered us not to give out gas except in an emergency." These two insisted it was an emergency. They couldn't get home with the fuel they had. "OK, we'll give you a few gallons, but remember you can't get it here," she said.

A couple of days later another pair came in with the same story, they couldn't get home without us giving them gas. Somehow these two, an older man and woman, seemed honest. We explained the situation and told them we would let them have five gallons but they had to sign for it and promise to bring us five gallons the next time they came up river. They agreed and promised to tell others that gas was not available at Kelly River this year. To our amazement they brought us five gallons of gas a few days later. Another day a surly looking young man pulled up to shore, and without saying a word set an empty gas can on a rock, and looked at me like he expected me to take it and fill it for him. I stood on shore and looked at him without saying anything. Finally he said, "Gas."

I said, "You can't get gas here this year," turned and walked away.

As I was starting up the path, I heard a shot. Penny had blown a porcupine out of a tree with the 12-gauge. I wondered what went through the mind of the guy in the boat. He may have considered the shot a warning to him.

For years we both have carried little NPS notebooks in the breast pocket of our uniform shirt or jacket to note things seen or heard during the day. They are the source of a lot of what appears in these stories.

For Monday 12 June 1995 it says:

Cloudy, 35/46°, rain .27", crick up 2". Killed porky #5 last night. Rain over night, ran under sill, got boxes wet, put 2 X 4s on floor to store gear on. Dug on outhouse hole & hole for cooler barrel—unfinished due to permafrost. Finished cleaning cache. 1700 two Native boats up river, 1807 same two boats down.

Took a good long walk. Noted: yellow warbler, fox sparrow, glaucous gull, red poll, gray-cheeked thrush, wind flower, yellow anemone, sandhill cranes, sheefish (a member of the salmon family), frigid shooting star, arctic lupine, pink pyrola, red fox, red squirrel, bearberry—has bloomed & has berries and red fringed leaves.

As always, radio contact was iffy. Sometimes we had good contact with headquarters; other times it was weak or nonexistent. Today it was fine, Jon reached us and told us Buck would pick us up in three days to fly us to Lake Matcharak—a half mile from the upper Noatak in Gates of the Arctic National Park. From there we would hike, with our gear, to the river and kayak the 375 miles of the Noatak River back to the Kelly Station.

The station was functional and we finally had a couple of days to explore this end of the river. We wanted to get a feel of it. From shore it looked big, wide, and running fast. Statistics told us the average flow was 16,600 cfs (cubic feet per second) but it sure looked bigger than that from shore, at least 400 yards wide—Jack Nicklaus (the greatest golfer of the time, or perhaps ever) couldn't have driven a golfball across it.

We climbed into the skiff and headed up stream. It wasn't a deep river, it meandered from cut bank to cut bank like most streams, shallow on one side and deeper on the opposite. We could see where the river had cut new channels and left oxbow lakes. Apparently, it changed course with every big flood, just like all the Alaskan rivers we had been on. During the Pleistocene Era, glaciers had carved a huge swath through the southern Brooks Range separating the De Long Mountains to the north from the Baird Mountains to the south, creating the Noatak River valley. The glaciers had even over-ridden the Bairds, eroding them to hills like the old Appalachians, south to the Waring Mountains and creating the Kobuk Valley.

We ran up river, 20 miles or so, to the mouth of the Kugururok, the next big river coming in from the north, and promised ourselves we would go up it one day, but not today. The skiff had oar-locks and a good pair of oars. "Let's kill the motor and drift home," I said. Penny liked the idea. Without the motor we had a quiet world, and could let the current take us home. Well, I did have to row a bit to keep us off cut-banks and gravel bars, but we were soon hearing birds and watching them along the shores. Penny pointed out a pair of birds wading in shallow water. They had bodies the size of pigeons, with long thin bills, long bright yellow legs, and spotted breasts. She said, "Look at the pair of lesser yellowlegs." I asked her if she were sure they were lessers. "Yes," she laughed, "Got ya. Remember at Katmai we never were sure if they were greater or lesser yellowlegs. These are lesser because the greaters don't come this far north."

There was a spotted sandpiper, with dark bars on its brown back and many spots on its white breast, catching bugs. Several beautiful stocky, red legged birds with striking black and white heads and russet backs were flipping stones and eating whatever they found underneath. Neither of us knew who they were. We'd have to consult our *Birds of North America* book at camp. They turned out to be ruddy turnstones, another bird we had never seen before.

We floated and rowed a bit, saw a cow moose and calf eating young willow buds, and were getting close to camp. I was watching a northern harrier skimming over the willow brush of the flood-plane to the south, when Penny said, "Whoa! Can you hold us here? I think that's a herd of caribou at the far side of the river." I back rowed and got us out of the current enough that we could watch about 20 bull caribou (*Rangifer tarandus*), with big velvet racks, wade into the river and swim across. They were on their way to the north slope for the summer of grazing and gaining weight to see them through the winter. The cows, who had migrated north earlier, would have delivered their calves by now and be busy gaining weight and trying to escape from the incessant flies and mosquitoes.

The next morning we were still in bed listening to the rain on the tent when Penny said, "I hear a porcupine chewing on a post right under me." "OK, I better go get him," I said. I put on my boots and heavy Helly Hansen raincoat, pulled the hood up, picked up the shotgun and went out. Porky was under the platform, so I had to climb down behind the walk between the tent-frames and peer underneath. Yep, there it was right behind a post. If I shot with the shotgun I'd blow the post away, so I went back and got Penny's .357. He was still there, only 10 feet away, an easy shot. I leaned forward to get a better view, pulled my hood up to keep the rain out of my eyes, and fired. I had killed porky #6, but he had his revenge. I had the most excruciating pain I have ever experienced. I just laid the .357 on the deck beside me and held my ears, I couldn't hear a thing. The hood had acted as a megaphone in the enclosed space under the platform. The shock wave had blown both my eardrums and left me stone deaf. I knew I would never hear Penny's voice or a bird song again. I didn't hear a sound for three days, but finally my hearing started recovering, slowly, but never fully.

Penny, Frank, and Klepper

THE KLEPPER,
THE NOATAK AND US

The day we were to fly to Matcharak Lake had low clouds and rain. Not a flyable day. The next day was the same. The third day it was glorious, sun and warm, 60°F, almost hot, but Buck was in Nome and not available. Since Buck wasn't coming Jon decided to fly up himself and drop a plastic sack of mail weighted down by two ancient hearing aids, bigger than cigarette packs. The mail was appreciated, but the attempt at making a joke of my hearing wasn't.

That warm day had brought hordes of mosquitoes out. Which

Frank Starr

made us wonder what they would be like in the muskeg up river. We had everything for our river trip ready and secured in dry-bags for most of the week and were getting antsy. My ears had gotten a reprieve, and I was starting to hear a bit. Both of us had been concerned about Penny kayaking an unknown river with a deaf mute. Penny's fingers were cracked from using the seam-sealer, but she wasn't complaining, and we both had our minds set on going.

Finally Jon called on the radio telling us Buck would pick us up that afternoon, and would be bringing a few people from head-quarters up to do needed work that wasn't our responsibility. We made sure the station was secure. Food was all in the cache, the little cooler-drum was sealed tightly, weapons were safely and carefully hidden, and our last six-pack of beer was on ice—on permafrost, hidden under the moss several yards away.

A little after 1500 that afternoon a red over white Cessna 185 pulled up to the dock. We were expecting Buck's Maul and were surprised to see Buck in this old plane. He laughed and told us he didn't want to fly the Maul into where he was taking us. Now that was a real confidence builder. He was dropping us into a place he wouldn't take his good aircraft. We loaded, and were off in a half hour.

We watched the vegetation change; the spruce forest along the river went first; tundra covered the ground into the mountains; willows covered shores, and gravel bars appeared, the river braided; the wide valley became a narrow canyon in one area; the mountains ahead became sharp and much less eroded. We spotted a pair of muskoxen (*Ovibos moschatus*) grazing on the moist tundra. Caribou and these shaggy beasts with their large curved horns are the only arctic ungulates to survive the end of the ice age. They had been hunted to extinction in Alaska, but were reintroduced to Nunivak Island in the Bering Sea in 1935–36, and have spread thinly over the northern tundra since.

During the ice age musk oxen, woolly mammoth, woolly rhino,

bison, and giant elk inhabited a harsh, frigid grassland known as the mammoth steppe, which stretched from eastern France north and east across Siberia to northwestern Alaska. The environment was too harsh for humans. Winter temperatures were similar to the arctic, but on the mammoth steppe there was no fuel to burn or shelter from the elements, both of which we hairless apes seem to need. But the big herbivores had heavy fur to protect them from the cold and wind, and the grasses of the steppe provided needed nourishment.

It's the habitat's productivity that limits the population, not the temperature. Three factors made the mammoth steppe more productive than today's tundra. Dead tundra plants don't have the opportunity to rot and add nutrients to soil, they become water-logged, and on the way to becoming peat-moss, and soon freeze into permafrost. Over the millennia the length of the growing season hasn't changed much, but the steppe's surface was composed of decayed plant life. This became soil, which warmed quickly and supported grasses; as opposed to the tough, long-lived tundra plants which must await the thawing of a few inches of acidic duff before they can start the growing season. Perhaps most important are the nutrients that were available to the plants of the steppe. The grasses of the mammoth steppe provided abundant grazing for the herbivorous mega-mammals. They in turn dropped copi-ous flows of urine and feces which released the phosphorus and nitrogen needed by plants. When man killed the slow breeding big mammals he eliminated the nutrients they dropped and changed the ecosystem from the productive steppe to today's much less productive tundra.

You may wonder about the fate of those mega-mammals. As Peter Ward said in *The End of Evolution* and Tim Flannery says in *Here on Earth*, "Those big animals were all swallowed by a black hole—the one between man's nose and his chin."

Looking down from Buck's plane we saw a pair of tundra swans on a pothole lake. They probably had young with them, but we couldn't see them. Buck was turning to land on a bigger lake, which we assumed was Matcharak. I saw a sizable patch of white blooms. "Must be cotton grass, in a bog left from a pot-hole lake filling in," I thought. Penny, from the seat behind Buck, was waving and yelling to get my attention over the engine noise and pointing to a grizzly bear swimming across the Noatak River, it was the first grizzly we had seen since leaving Amalik Bay three years ago, a positive and promising way to start our river journey.

It was after 1700 as we taxied toward a gravel shore and went through a swarm of flying insects, "Oh God, I hope those aren't mosquitoes," went through my head, but they were. We tried to unload quickly to save Buck having to fight them on his way back to Kotz, but there must have been a hundred or more of the (to use the common NPS vernacular) "little fuckers" in the plane and millions of them after us. These weren't the little ones we were accustomed to. These were "big fuckers," a good centimeter long and looking for blood—ours. A flock of bank swallows and several tree swallows were helping us by catching the mosquitoes as fast as they could.

We put on head-nets and fingerless gloves to cover as much skin as we could cover, (they didn't cover Penny's cracked finger tips) and began hauling our gear across nearly a mile of low-growing tundra, with its foot-grabbing branches of bearberry, dwarf arctic willow, and Eskimo (Labrador) tea, through the taller Alaska willows to the gravel of the river bank. Two round trips through that jungle and we were whipped. But we still had to assemble the Klepper. It's a good thing we knew how it went together. That would have been a terrible place to learn Klepper assembly. We paddled down river a mile or so to a gravel-bar in the center of the river where we could camp and have some breeze to keep the mosquitoes down.

As usual we had too much "white-man's baggage," and too little space to pack it. The bow space, where Penny's feet went, and stern space behind my back, were stuffed, we each had a bundle under our knees, and the dry-bag with sleeping bags was lashed to the deck between us. As we paddled, I realized the boat didn't handle as well as the hard kayak we had used in Glacier Bay, and wished the Klepper had a rudder.

As I was waking up the next morning, I was thinking about the Klepper and remembered John McFee's great book *Coming Into the Country*, and his experience with a double Klepper on the Salmon River, a tributary of the Kobuk not far southwest of where we were. (There are six Salmon Rivers in Alaska, and a bunch of Salmon Creeks.) McFee related:

> We have with us a single and a double Klepper. The smaller one is prompt and responsive, feathery on the stream. The double is somewhat less maneuverable than a three-ton log...Pourchot and I have the double Klepper this morning. The ratio of expended energy to developed momentum is seventy-five to one.

We would have been better off with two single Kleppers, but that wasn't an option, and we don't operate singly anyway.

Taking a leak is about the first order of business each morning. We went out to face the mosquitoes in our long johns, boots, and head-nets. I didn't have to expose much skin to them, but Penny had to pull her long-johns and under-pants down and squat. That made an ideal target for a swarm of blood thirsty demons. The only solution we could come up with was for me to fan her fanny; she did the same for me when I had to expose my butt. That was to be our bathroom experience for the next two weeks.

For many years, when Penny and I were camping, the first meal of the day was always instant coffee, Tang, and oatmeal with raisins. Put water from the river, creek, or spring on to boil, mix a spoon-ful of Tang in a cup of water, and sip that while the water heated. With these damned mosquitoes there was no relaxing over Tang or coffee; it was mix it and dive back into the tent to get fewer bites.

When the water boiled we poured it onto the oatmeal and took the pot into the tent to soak. Of course by that time there were plenty of mosquitoes in the tent too. Lots of them ended up dying in the soaking oatmeal. "They just add protein to your breakfast, Pen," I would tell her. Somehow my humor didn't get a laugh. Penny invariably tried to pick the dead bodies out of her breakfast, but ended up eating many dead mosquitoes. The monsters were so irritating we ended up rubbing DEET, that infamous insect repellant, on our jackets. That helped a lot.

The real challenge, and a lot of fun, was reading the river. It was a two person job, but my responsibility, since I was in the stern seat. It had been a while since we had run a serious river. Not that the Noatak was a rough river. It had a good bit of class #2 water and a spot that could be considered class #3, but most of it was simply reading the current and missing gravel bars.

That first morning we were getting accustomed to handling our "log" and watching a very active arctic tern colony and a pair of yellow-billed loons near shore. Penny yelled loud enough that I sort of heard, "White water ahead," I looked past her shoulder and could see little whitecaps which indicated a collection of rocks— probably dropped by a glacier. That shouldn't be a problem, all we had to do was watch for a wake from water being shunted around a near surface rock. The Klepper only draws a couple of inches and should pass over all but the wake-makers. Suddenly I heard, "Oh shit!" and we sailed over a three-foot waterfall that hadn't given us any notice. The water was high and looked smooth until we were right on it. No harm, no foul. We were learning a different river in a different sort of boat and had gotten away with, at least, that mistake.

We made camp that evening on a gravel bar at the confluence with Tunukuchiak Creek. Penny told me there were white-crowned and tree sparrows singing from the willows and grizzly tracks in mud just above the gravel—a friend to be aware of. Penny's fingers were splitting more, but there was nothing to do for them except dob on some Vaseline.

Another day the river moved into a broad area of the valley, spread out and developed braids. Pick the braid with the most water in it and see where it takes you. Sometimes a braid keeps splitting until you run out of water. This one took us to a calm area, well away from the main channel, but it had good water with a decent flow. A five foot wall of snow was to our right where the river had cut through a bank of drifted snow.

No wind and no bugs, how delightful. A moose and her calf walked/swam across a hundred yards ahead. A lot of ducks liked the area too. We saw a family of pintails and a pair of green-winged teal dabbling in shallows by the left bank. There was a big duck with a light green head, a big black-rimmed white eye-patch and a long sloping bill; it had to be an eider. We had seen plenty of eider in coastal waters, but not this particular one. We hadn't expected to see any eider this far inland. This was a spectacled eider we learned when we got back to camp and our *Birds of North America*. It, as well as the king eider, breeds on coastal tundra and near lakes. The pair is monogamous, but he deserts her when she starts incubating her three to nine eggs. I never have found an explanation of when the pair of spectacled eider gets back together, but it must be the following spring when they return to the same breeding grounds. An ADF&G publication on spectacled eider tells me:

> Spring migration from the wintering area includes multiple stopovers at coastal sites with arrival on the breeding grounds in late May or June. Males leave 1–2 weeks after incubation of the eggs begins. Females and young eiders travel to their wintering grounds in late summer. After spectacled eiders leave the nesting grounds, they travel along established migration corridors in the Bering, Chukchi, and Beaufort seas. Males molt and stage in Mechigmenskiy Bay in Russia, eastern Chukotka Peninsula in Russia, or in

Ledyard Bay, Alaska. The females molt and stage in eastern Norton Sound if they nested in the Yukon-Kuskokwim delta or in Ledyard Bay and Mechigmenskiy Bay if they nested on the North Slope. From these molting and staging areas, the birds will head out to the Bering Sea for the winter.

Several more days down river and we were feeling we could handle the slow responding Klepper. Penny, in the forward seat, always sets the paddling pace. We try to coordinate our strokes—it's kind of tacky to hit your partner's paddle because you are out of step. We had learned long ago that Penny sets a sustainable pace. I start too fast and tire. Today we paddled into what looked like a lake—it wasn't!

We were observing a lone wolf watching a couple of caribou in shallows to the right, when suddenly we were in current moving hard left. I yelled, "Paddle right, get the bow out." Penny paddled hard, I tried using my paddle as a rudder to get us farther into the current, but the "log" was committed to going sideways. We slammed into the gravel-bar and broke one of those long struts; not something we could ignore without taking the chance of puncturing the Klepper's skin, so we pulled up on shore to examine the damage and figure out what to do about it, the wolf and its contemplated meal long forgotten.

Well shit, Sherlock, we had a problem! The strut was broken in three places. By the grace of God, or our guardian angel, we had included a tube of five-minute epoxy in the little emergency kit, as well as some nylon cord. We found several strong thin willow sticks, cut them about eight inches long, added two spare aluminum tent stakes, and used those to make the three splints we needed, bound it with cord and glued it all together with epoxy.

Now we could relax and wait for the epoxy to set. We were careful to not get any epoxy on Penny's poor fingers, they looked terrible, cracked deeply and hurt like hell. We even tried Duct tape to hold the splits in her fingers together. There was enough wind to keep the mosquitoes away and it wasn't raining, so we could check our surroundings and see who and what lived here. It was becoming a broad valley with eroded mountains not far to the north and south. We climbed up the bank and found a fat, pink, wooly flower about 10-inches high, with pinnately divided leaves—a wooly lousewort. The name comes from old time Europe when sheepherders thought the plant harbored lice that infected their sheep. The long root is a good source of starch which the Inupiats used regularly until white-man introduced grains in the form of flour, bread, and cake. In a kind of boggy place we found a low reddish blooming rhododendron known as Lapland rosebay and a heather called bog rosemary. Soaring overhead was a golden eagle with a small animal in its talons, probably taking it to his nest for his mate and their chicks. As we were admiring the eagle, a pair of parasitic jaegers started harassing the much larger bird, hoping to get it to drop its meal. Kleptomania is the way most jaegers and skuas get a lot of their food. Stealing works well when the victims are gulls and smaller birds, but it didn't work with the big eagle. He just ignored them and flew on.

We went on down river and camped on a gravel bar, at what we thought was the Anisak River. There are a lot of streams emptying into the Noatak from both north and south. The maps we had were not too accurate, being from very old surveys, so perhaps it was the Anisak. It didn't make much difference, except the Anisak is about half way down river from Matcharak Lake. We would know exactly where we were when we got to the Kelly River Station—it had the only dock above the village of Noatak.

One evening we had stopped on a gravel bar at another stream and were setting up camp. We had the tent assembled, but not staked (the fly is what gets staked and we hadn't put that on yet). I had gone just a few yards to the Klepper to get the sleeping bags, when, through my deaf ears, I heard, "Help!" I looked up and saw

Penny running down the beach after the tent, which a sudden gust of wind had picked up and was taking toward the river. If we lost the tent we really would be in a world of hurt. White-man doesn't do very well without some form of shelter. Penny caught the tent just as I caught up with her, and just before it went into the river. Just a little excitement to get the adrenaline up after a full, tiring day.

We have a saying about boats and wind, "wind wins." This river trip was no exception, and the wind seemed to be in our face most of the time. I had hoped for a breeze from behind to help the current get us down river, but the Noatak runs west, and west wind is the common wind. On another day the sun was bright and the west wind was blowing stronger than usual, making the Klepper even more difficult to control. To have any control we had to keep the boat moving faster than the current, so the wind in our face was making that tough. We rounded a bend and found a strong, steady wind we couldn't make headway against. We paddled hard for perhaps 20 minutes and decided we had better go ashore and let it calm down.

It didn't. There was probably a low pressure system in the Chukchi Sea, because the wind just got worse. We sat in the lee of some dense willows and had our lunch—Sailor Boy pilot biscuits with peanut butter and some dried fruit. We had been out for about ten days, sitting in the bottom of a boat in cold water and working hard. We hadn't counted on burning as many calories as we were, and hadn't brought enough high calorie food. We should have been on a high-fat diet like the Eskimos use. We were burning a lot more calories than we were taking in and loosing weight. Not a good plan!

Clouds came in around 2000 and the wind dropped some. I suggested we get back on the river. Penny said, "For God's sake, it's after eight o'clock. Let's call it a day." Her good thinking, again, prevailed without an argument from me. We set our tent in the lee of the same willows, had our freeze dried dinner with another pilot biscuit (no brandy and cider on this trip), watched the clouds get heavier and rain start, and went to bed.

The next morning we awoke to the sound of clomping all around. Penny thought a herd of caribou were out there, I decided it was a flock of sandhill cranes or the Brants geese that had landed near us last evening. We very quietly unzipped the tent and rain-fly and peeked out; there was a couple of inches of snow and it was sliding off the willows with a plopping sound—no caribou, no geese, no sandhill cranes. We laughed, put on our boots, and went out in our long-johns to shake the snow off the tent.

According to our maps, the last obstacle on the river was the Noatak Canyon. We weren't sure what to expect. This river had been done a number of times, and we had never heard of the canyon being a big deal. The broad stream narrowed as it moved into eroded hills. Around a bend we entered an honest to God canyon with vertical walls cut through rock that had been warped and, perhaps, metamorphosed. It looked like twisted, multi colored taffy, sort of a paisley pattern.

The river took a hard right as it bounced off a vertical wall. We needed to stay away from the wall, since the clumsy Klepper wouldn't turn as sharply as the river. We had to cut the inside of the turn and thought it looked smooth. Penny paddled left, I swung the bow right, and we slid to a stop on a big flat boulder that had about an inch of water flowing smoothly over it. Fortunately, it was a bit rounded. We held our breath and slid off, the bow buried, water rushed over the foredeck, hit the coaming and splashed into Penny's face, but we were on our way. We had gotten away with another mistake, not something to count on. If it had rolled us over, that probably would have been our end. We couldn't have rolled the big heavy Klepper a 360 like we had the little single kayaks at kayak school five years ago. Upside down in a fast, cold river? I question whether we would have made it.

That afternoon was one of those rare, beautiful, sunny days with a good breeze behind us. The river was straight and the current was helping us along. Penny's fingers were bad, hurting like hell, but she wasn't complaining much. If we were reading the maps correctly we only had 20 or 30 miles to go. It was late. We had made at least 30 miles today, including the canyon. The river was wide with a grassy flood-plain on the left. We saw the first real sign of habitation in over 300 miles of river, a roof on four posts sitting on a knoll above the flood-plane. The grassy area looked like an ideal spot for, what we hoped would be our final camp, and we needed to check the structure anyway.

Natives have the right to claim a piece of land, called a Native Allotment, for personal use. This place was a good example. It was a beautiful spot, and the owner had started to build a cabin. We beached the boat and climbed up the bank to the cabin site. Pilings had been set and a floor laid, well off the permafrost. The four corner posts and roof and two rows of logs had been erected recently, but the floor was weathered, it had been exposed for at least one winter, and probably more.

We set camp and relaxed on the first grassy place we had seen in fifteen days. We wished the sun would go down and give us a dark night for sleeping, but that wasn't going to happen for a while. Tomorrow we would be home!

The Noatak had been kind of a mixed bag, but an adventure we will always remember. We had kayaked nearly 400 miles of a seldom seen—by white man—river, fed thousands of voracious mosquitoes, seen much of the impressive diverse plant and animal life of the Brooks Range, sat, freezing our asses for many hours, in the bottom of a canvas boat in 35 degree water, and lost over a pound a day due to not planning on burning so many calories while keeping warm and fighting wind in a log-like kayak. There had been moments of exciting, near panicky, thrills and hours of hard work.

GRAND CENTRAL STATION

As we finished the last miles of the Noatak River trip we noticed a camp on the north shore and stopped to see who they were. Alison, Kerry, and Andria met us and let us know they were a tree-coring team from the University of Alaska-Fairbanks. They were researching the ages of the white spruce and other tree species to work out the vegetational succession since the end of the ice age. They had only been there a couple of days and were getting comfortable with their work, but were concerned about bears. We assured them the grizzlies were scarce; they were on the north slope harvesting new-born caribou, and were heavily hunted along the Noatak, so they probably wouldn't even see a bear in the few weeks they would be here. We gave them the standard bear informational talk anyway.

We knew we had made it back to the Kelly River Station when we saw the white spruce hanging over the water just up stream from our dock. There were two men standing on the dock fishing as we pulled up. One of them took our bow line and secured us to a cleat. They introduced themselves as Bob and Wade, the Arctic char researchers we had been told would be here. They were a couple of nice young men who were getting paid to fish the Noatak, something they would gladly pay to do if they didn't have these jobs. That sounded just like us and the jobs we had held for the past fifteen years—the opportunity to have your avocation be your vocation. They told us they were camped in our pseudo campground, and were expecting five bird-banders to show up any day with a 12-foot

Weather Port to use as shelter for their banding work.

Bob and Wade fished on down river. We gathered our gear from the Klepper and headed up to the tents. "God damn it!" Both tents had been trashed by the work crew from headquarters who had been here while we were gone. There were empty cans and food packages in the kitchen and a dirty shirt in the sleep tent. I'll admit we are more fastidious than most about a clean, neat camp. After many years of camping we are well aware that a place for everything and everything in its place lets you know what you have and where to look for it—no rummaging, and a clean camp doesn't attract bears, insects, or rodents.

We cleaned, Penny put a batch of her Mexican beans on to soak. Penny's Mexican beans have alway been a staple for us, a mixture of kidney, Anasazi, red and white pinto beans and black beans, that she soaks for 24 hours, then cooks on low heat with a whole yellow onion and assorted Mexican spices for about 12 hours. Ideally served on a tortilla with fresh, cut-up lettuce, carrots, and green onions spread on top and slathered with Mexican salsa and plain yogurt. The fresh vegetables and yogurt weren't an option, but rice and beans make a complete protein and we did have Velveeta cheese and a jar of salsa to spice it up. Tomorrow we would eat well. Tonight it would be a can or two of something with taste and calories from the cache. Meanwhile having a beer and sitting on the dock on our beach chairs, with an east wind keeping the mosquitoes away, sounded like a good way to celebrate our completed river trip.

I went to my secret permafrost-cache for a couple of beers, and, "Oh no, the sons of bitches stole our beer!" I yelled. Penny called back, "My float-coat is gone too. I wonder what else has been stolen." We started checking and found both hand-held radios and their spare batteries were gone, as well as the Danforth anchor from the Lund. We were sure the crew from headquarters were the culprits. Stealing wasn't a trait of the Natives, they had plenty of opportunity but had never taken a thing. The SOB who had stolen Penny's coat when we were collecting gear in Kotz was our suspect. It was too late to reach anyone at the office but maybe we could reach Jon. He frequently kept his radio on. Amazingly we had good radio contact. Jon answered right away, welcomed us back, assured us he would handle the situation and bring our gear to us tomorrow, along with a case of beer. Obviously, Jon was well aware of the personnel in the office and didn't question who had taken our gear and beer.

The next morning we boated down to a gravel beach near the Kelly River to meet Jon who flew in with Richard (another park pilot) in a wheeled Cessna on "tundra tires." Those oversized tires allowed the plane to land on gravel bars, sand beaches, and even tundra under the right conditions. They had brought us some fresh vegetables, two cases of Rainier Beer, and a sack of mail. Jon laughed, and said, "Look what I found," as he handed Penny her float-coat, and me a new Danforth anchor and our hand-held radios and bat-teries. "The same kid who took your coat before took all your stuff. I'm trying to get him fired, but he has some sort of weird connection with the superintendent." Jon let us know that four people from the office would be coming up over the fourth of July weekend to fish. They would camp, but had the superintendent's permission to use the Kelly River Station's kitchen—our kitchen.

Back at camp, Penny was going through the mail, and handed me an official letter form the U.S. Government. "Is the IRS looking for us?" she asked.

I opened the envelope and laughed. "Oh my God! I'm old! This is my official notice! It's my Medicare card, proving that I'll be 65 in two months."

Apparently the superintendent had given the five bird-banders the same kitchen privileges as the office people, because when they showed up they acted like our kitchen was community property. We made sure everyone understood they were to keep a clean kitchen, do their dishes, keep all food in the cache, and stay out of the sleep tent. There had been almost no rain since we got home and the river was dropping a couple of inches every day, exposing wide gravel bars along every river mouth. Not only that but the wind was from the east and the mosquito population was down considerably. Hmm! I think we were sent to float the river two or three weeks early.

On 2 July, several planes on tundra tires landed on the far bank of the Kelly River's mouth. We boated down to talk with them and were told a bunch of Inupiats were getting together to celebrate the nation's birth and reaffirm that the Inupiat Nation had been here hundreds of years before the United States had even been thought of. We welcomed them and told them to contact us if there was anything we could do for them. They had an interesting collection of aircraft: two Cessnas, a 120, and a 185 tail-dragger, and a Piper cub. But a beautiful bright yellow biplane was the one I wanted to know about. The owner, a very proud young man, told me it was a World War ll Stearman he had found in Seattle, where he lived. He had flown up for his family's 4th of July celebration. We all had fun discussing old aircraft and laughed over some of the tales they told. I encouraged them to keep a clean camp and have a wonderful, safe, sane, and reasonably sober holiday.

Willie, a man we liked, was the dispatcher at headquarters. He reached us on the radio on 3 July, telling us the four people from the office were flying into the Kelly River bar, and asked that we pick them up and give them a ride to the campground. We could do that. But I told Willie, it seemed kind of a waste of our time. It was less than a half mile from the bar to the camp. This was at the request of the Superintendent, Willie told us.

Sure enough, an hour later Richard called to say he was landing with the four office staff. The two men and two women were people we had met but didn't know. They seemed like four nice enough young people who were looking for a fun few days. We gave them the standard camp rules and bear warning. We explained how important is was to keep a clean, odor-free kitchen, checked their fishing licenses, and told them to contact us if they had problems or questions.

We didn't like being in a camp full of neophyte visitors. We had expected to be in an isolated spot in the Brooks Range where we would be completely alone. Now it was starting to feel like we were managing a resort, so we got in the boat and went on patrol, hoping to find everyone gone when we got back—if we stayed out late enough. "Lets go up the Kugururok River," Penny suggested, "We both wanted to check it out last month." We planned to get a really good look at the Kugururok. It was the next sizable river above the Kelly—there are 16 major rivers running into the Noatak. We had done the Kelly, tried to anyway, several weeks ago, but it braided out after a few miles and was too shallow to get far up.

The sun was shining and a nice breeze from the east kept the mosquitoes down. Penny commented what a delightful day it would be to kayak the Noatak. It was also a delightful day to run up any river in NW Alaska. We took it slow and enjoyed the peace of a quiet river with no one else around. We spotted a family of loons as they ducked into reeds. I killed the motor, Penny dropped the anchor, and we sat to watch. After a couple of minutes the family reappeared, two adults with two chicks perched on momma's back. We speculated they had a nest back in the shallows. Loons typically build their nest on floating vegetation at the edge of calm, shallow water. These loons were different looking. They had slim straight bills and grey, rounded heads. Definitely not common loons who have dark heads and heavy bills, and certainly not yellow-billed loons. We had our *Birds of North America* along, which told us they were probably Pacific loons, but could be Arctic loons. The two may be indistinguishable except the Arctic's dark neck shows green, not black. We thought we had seen a flash of green but couldn't be sure.

Cruising slowly on up river we saw a good stand of fireweed and watched a pair of belted kingfishers hovering over the river. Every minute or so one would dive and come up with a fish. We were surprised when they didn't fly home with the catch to feed a nest full of hungry chicks, until I remembered kingfishers feed young by regurgitating partly digested food. I referred to the one with with the rusty belly band as "he." Penny reminded me the female belted kingfisher is the colorful one.

The river was getting shallow, but we were having a great day and wanted to get farther up. There were braids ahead, I gunned into the one with the most water, swept around a curve and ran out of water. The jet unit sucked up gravel and quit. "OK, smart ass," I said to myself, "are you going to be able to fix this?" I tipped the outboard up, stepped into a couple of inches of water and pulled the stern up on the beach where I had good access to the jet unit. Penny too wanted to know if we were going to be able to fix it or if we were rowing home.

I could see the jet unit was full of small gravel. There is an intake grill to keep gravel out but it doesn't stop gravel under a half inch in diameter, so we were full of small stuff. Water is drawn into the unit through the intake grill by an impeller, which is driven by the engine's drive shaft. The water is then forced through a nozzle at high pressure, pushing the boat forward. There were four bolts holding the grill in place. I figured, all we had to do was take the bolts out, remove the grill and get the gravel out of the screw-like impeller. That worked fine except the gravel had been sucked well up the impeller, which is a tapered Archimedes screw that pressurizes water and moves it to the nozzle. "I have to take the impeller out too," I told Penny. "You might as well take a nap or a walk."

The sun was warm, the breeze was keeping the mosquitoes away, she watched me a while and laid down on one of the seats and was out instantly—a calm, relaxed mind lets you do that. By the time she woke up I had the jet unit cleaned and back together. Penny suggested we take a walk. "Sounds like a plan," I said.

We had a copy of Verna Pratt's *Field Guide to Alaskan Wildflowers* with us and decided to check flowers. We had only taken a few steps when we both pointed to a ten-inch tall daisy-looking flower with lavender rays and a yellow center that we had seen all over Alaska except in Glacier Bay, Penny said "Siberian aster," before I could say it. A few feet away was a patch of nagoonberry. They look like strawberry plants, have pinkish blossoms and delicious red raspberry-looking fruit. The blossoms were about gone and the berries were just forming. We'd look for berries in a month or so. In a meadowy area we saw an evergreen plant with spikes of flower stems sticking up ten inches. The pink flowers, scattered along the stem, had round, hanging heads with long stamen sticking out. I couldn't remember seeing it before, but Penny did. Our book said it was pink pyrola. The meadow also had a lily with clumps of yellowish green flowers on long stems that we remembered—"death camas." Under comments our book told us: "EXTREME CAUTION: Highly toxic poison which causes vomiting, lowered temperatures and breathing difficulties."

A flock of buffy little birds with red caps and black chins landed not far ahead. They were redpolls and we couldn't be sure if they were feeding on seeds or insects. We hoped they were collecting the mosquitoes that were down out of the breeze. OK, were they common or hoary redpolls? They are described as very similar and they do interbreed; the most significant difference is the common has more reddish on the breast and streaking on the sides. We couldn't see any red on these breasts, so we called them hoary redpolls. Besides we had never seen hoary redpolls before.

The sun was getting low. It wouldn't set for a week yet, but the light was fading and we wanted enough light to read the river. We had seen several ptarmigan on the way up river. Were they rock or willow ptarmigan? All ptarmigan, white, rock, and willow have feathered legs and feet, and molt three times a year, matching the habitat, darkly mottled in summer, finely mottled in fall, and white in winter. A gyrfalcon sailed over the Kugururok, undoubtedly looking for a ptarmigan and not caring if it were rock or willow.

We would let today's "which ptarmigan" question remain unsettled.

It was after 2200 when we got back to camp, we would grab a quick beer, a meal and crash for the night. As we walked up the path Penny said, "What's that smell?" I could smell it too, it smelled like grease and civilization. The cook tent was a mess, "Those bastards fried steaks in here," I said. "They'll have every bear in a hundred miles checking us out. I'm going down and hang them!"

"Slow down," Penny said, "Remember we've always found it's best to cool off for a day or two before you respond when you're mad."

She was right again. "OK," I said, "I'll sleep on it and kill them in the morning."

We slept in, I cooled down, and by the time we walked down to the river path I had decided I would simply reexplain the problems caused by food smells in bear country. Before we got to the path I looked at the dock, and saw no boat. Son of a bitch! Could those idiots from the office have decided the whole station was theirs to use as they pleased? Now Penny was pissed too. That boat is our life-line and what we worked from every day. If it was damaged our ability to function here was shot. It was my turn to cool us down. "Lets not jump to conclusions. Come on, we'll walk down and see if they're still at their camp."

They weren't there, but one of the bird-banders was in the Weather Port doing paperwork and told us they had gone fishing, but didn't know where. He also let us know his work was going well and they would be finished by the end of July. We had gotten along well with this team of banders and had learned a lot about arctic birds and the art of bird-banding from them. We walked on down to the Kelly River. The Native gathering had several more planes sitting on the beach. It all looked peaceful, the Inupiats were behaving. We sat on a rock and talked. These kids weren't bad or stupid like we had been saying to ourselves. They were just young and uneducated. We needed to ease off.

A flock of Bohemian waxwings flew into the willow brush behind us—cedar waxwings don't come this far north—probably looking for berries or catching insects, mosquitoes we hoped. We wandered on up the bank of the Kelly. It's interesting how the mind adjusts to not being able to do what you know you should do. Without the boat we couldn't go on patrol, couldn't talk with the Inupiats, or do anything that two back-country rangers are hired to do. We took the day off and had a pleasant afternoon of wandering along the bank of a river in Alaska's Brooks Range. A cow moose and calf waded across the river and into the brush, an Arctic fox found a dead fish at the river's edge, and a golden eagle cruised by. We found bear tracks in mud and had a delightful day all thanks to those four kids taking the boat without permission.

We had gotten back to the station and had our dinner before the kids pulled up to the dock. Penny had suggested we not clean up the previous night's mess in the kitchen tent; we'd have them do it. We had grandkids nearly their age. Perhaps these four could learn something from two seniors. They obviously hadn't learned from their parents.

Finally we heard them coming and met them at the dock. They must have read the expressions on our faces, because the boisterousness we had heard approaching wasn't there as I picked up the bow line and secured it to a cleat. "Have you ever seen what a grizzly can do to a camp that smells like food?" I asked. "Jon has a video that you need to watch as soon as you get to the office. It will show you what this place would look like if the bears weren't on the north slope, and they aren't all up there. We were walking up the Kelly this afternoon and found tracks of a good sized Grizz. We were just lucky that Grizz didn't come by last night. There wouldn't be anything left of this camp, and Penny and I would probably be dead, or a bear would be. We're all going up to the cook tent and you're going to clean it properly!"

They all four looked humbly chagrined and headed off the dock.

"But first," I said, "Is that the way you're leaving the boat that you took without permission? Look at the trash! And were you going to leave us with empty fuel tanks?"

"No sir," seemed to come from four mouths simultaneously, as the young men grabbed the fuel tanks and the women started collecting trash.

Penny took the women (girls) up to the kitchen and I took the men (boys) to the fuel cache. I wish I had heard the lecture Penny gave those girls. It was hard to think of them as men and women. They were a long way from being competent to live in bush Alaska.

The place was clean, their trash had been burned in the burn-barrel—there was no way, except time, for the smell of fried meat to not attract a bear. The kids were gone, we sat on the dock, had a beer, and hoped we didn't have a bear tonight.

Sometime during the night, with the sky like dusk, Penny punched me, "There's someone, or something, digging around out front." We got up and looked out. There was a dark form by the burn-barrel. Of course it was a grizzly bear. It knocked the barrel over and routed in it for the steak it could smell on partially burned paper.

Damn it. Why hadn't I given closer supervision to the kids burning trash? I grabbed the shotgun, made sure it had #9 bird-shot in the chamber, and fired a round into Grizz's butt. I hated to do it. It was only doing what came naturally—going after the food it smelled. We watched it disappear into the woods and hoped it had been reminded to stay away from anything that smelled of humans.

The next morning Willie reached us on the radio to let us know Jim Rude, a commercial pilot, would be landing on the Kelly bar about 1500, to pick up the four office personnel. Would we please deliver them and their gear a bit before that? And Jim would be dropping off four pilgrims who were coming in to look for the Asian tit.

The four office kids didn't mention the shot they must have

heard this morning and I didn't either. I dropped the four kids and met the four pilgrims coming in. A change of guests at "Starr's Kelly River Guest Lodge."

Three of the new guests were very serious birders who had heard a report that the Siberian tit had been seen here last year, and wanted to add it to their life-list. James was a mail carrier from Iowa City, Iowa; Elaine and Mark were members of the San Fransisco Symphony Orchestra; Tom was a man they had met in Kotzebue who was just traveling around Alaska. The three birders felt they needed someone to protect them from bears so they had hired Tom to come with them.

I gave them the whole "Camping in Bear Country" speech and gave them a ride to the camp area. They seemed to be extremely pleasant people, nearly our age, and wanted to talk and ask endless questions. I took a liking to them and invited them up to meet Penny after they got their camp set up. They really liked that idea and said they would be up shortly.

Due to Grizz having visited last night and the fact that I was going to be gone a while, Penny had put on her sidearm. The pilgrims showed up almost before I did, noted Penny's weapon and immediately wanted to know if there were any bears around. She had to admit that the only bear we had seen near here had been last night. The six of us ended up talking and becoming friends. They told us about their lives and Penny told them about ours. Of course bears came into the conversation, and we could talk about bears for hours. It came out that Tom knew nothing about bears. He had borrowed a shotgun from someone he knew in Kotz and really had no idea how to use it, much less how to deal with a bear if they saw one. We explained that a clean camp with no food smell was their best protection, and beside that, a weapon in the hands of an inexperienced person was more dangerous than a bear. Everyone looked at Tom and laughed. He was a nice guy and fun to have along, so I suggested he put the gun away and just be part of the group. Tom chuckled and agreed to stash the shotgun.

They were to be picked up in three days, wanted to find a Siberian tit, had no way of getting farther than the Kelly River, and were scared of bears. We both enjoyed them, felt sorry for them, and decided we could be good samaritans and show them around.

We boated them to several locations they thought looked promising and got an education on the Siberian tit: It is a member of the genus Parus as are chickadees and titmice, they look like chickadees but aren't as colorful. The primary difference in appearance between the Siberian tit and the boreal chickadee is the white cheek patch, which is larger on the tit. They both nest in old woodpecker holes lined with moss and fur, lay four to nine white eggs finely marked in reddish; eggs hatch in 14 days; the young are altricial, eat insects, especially spiders and their eggs, seeds, and berries. Boreal chickadee young are fed for 18 days before fledging, no one is sure how long Siberian tit young are fed before fledging.

The three birders were talking encyclopedias. We tried to pick their brains about many other birds, but they were intent on the tit. We saw lots of chestnut-backed chickadees, which look and act just like the Siberian tit until you get a good view of them. Their darker head and reddish back make it a chickadee and defiantly not a tit. We had fun and learned a lot. They had a good time in the Alaskan bush, but never saw a Siberian tit.

NATIVE SKIFFS WERE GOING UP AND DOWN RIVER SEVERAL TIMES a day. We saw a boat of paddlers going down river every few days, some of them stopped to check-in with us, some of them we met as we were on patrol, and a few went by without us meeting them. Since Jim Rude was the pilot who seemed to have a corner on the market of flying people up river, we had talked with him about where he was dropping them. "Most of them are dropped in Pingo Lake," he told us, "It's between the Aniuk River and Makpik Creek, but don't look for it on your map, it won't show. The Inupiats call it that because there is a pingo near by." (A pingo is a mound of permafrost covered earth. It can be a couple hundred feet high and 2,000 feet in diameter.)

Most of the floaters we met were interesting people who had come up here for the same reason we had: to see and experience this unique country. They used different sorts of boats that all had to be portable by small aircraft. Most were inflatables that were blown up with a foot-pump. Everyone using a blow-up boat complained about the wind pushing them around. There were collapsible canvas canoes and a couple of single Kleppers.

A Lufthansa captain and his adult son stopped in one morning. They were having a wonderful time, but the son kiddingly complained about being starved. They hadn't brought much food, "Dad said we would eat fresh Alaskan fish every day, but in a week we've caught one salmon and lived on gorp."

A group of ten young German men, all in single Kleppers, wearing German olive green uniforms stayed in their boats and told us how wonderful their Kleppers were, "The only way to travel on a river," they told us. I stood on the bank well above them with my arms folded projecting my impression of authority, and never mentioned our problems with the double Klepper.

The most interesting group was four young men from Boston. Jim had dropped them on Pingo Lake, made sure they had all of their gear out of the plane, and promised to pick them up in Noatak in ten days. They had two double inflatables that they had rented in Anchorage. When they assembled the boats they discovered they had everything they needed except paddles. That was a problem! But one of them had an eight-inch folding knife that had a saw as one of its blades. They cut willow stems with a forked end, Duct taped the four boat seats to the forks and had pseudo paddles. They were having a ball, had caught a few Arctic char and couldn't be happier with being on the Noatak River.

The National Weather Service sent Chris and Scott into our

station to do a few days research on Arctic climate. We picked them up at the "Kelly Airport" and took them to the camp. They had been told they could use our kitchen. "Here we go again!" I thought. We gave the "camping in bear country" talk and invited them to use the kitchen with a bunch of restrictions including, "Meat must be cooked on the beach." They said they were well aware of food and bears, and hadn't even brought any meat. We showed them our daily weather readings, which they said would be included in their reports. They proved to be welcome guests who didn't stay long.

A group of "Diggers" was working on archeology up river near the Noatak Canyon. A helicopter pilot had flown supplies into them and radioed us in desperate need of fuel. There was a drum of jet fuel in our fuel cache, so Penny told him to put down on the Kelly bar and we would bring him 30 gallons. It turned out he was a friend of our helicopter pilot buddy, Landis, so we swapped a few stories and added another pilot to our list of friends.

It was August, fall was in the air and the leaves were changing on the alders and willows. The mosquitoes had suffered a good freeze and were all but gone. Maybe the crazy siege of visitors to "Starr's Kelly River Resort" was finally over and we could find time to relax and enjoy our season on the longest unaltered river in the United States.

Caribou Harvest

HARVEST

As we were having breakfast, on a rare morning that we had the kitchen to ourselves, the radio came on with, "Kelly River-Base."

Penny picked up the mike and replied "Kelly River." (My poor hearing had made Penny the permanent keeper of the radio, and years later the phone.)

Jon, in Kotzebue, told us he and Susan Morton, an archeologist from the Alaska regional office, would pick us up at the Kelly bar in a helicopter at 0830. "Be armed, just in case," he said. We would fly north to an archeological site that had been clouted and be back before dark—the sun had finally set, for a few minutes, a couple of weeks ago, and now NW Alaska was "screaming toward total darkness," at about nine minutes a day.

We always kept essentials in our day-packs: fire starter, gorp ("plenty of snacks"), bug dope, bottle of water, and rain gear. We added a lunch of peanut-butter sandwiches and dried fruit, put our .357s on our belts and were ready. It was un-Alaskan, but we walked down to the Kelly rather than boating.

The chopper setting down blew sand and gravel that hit us in the back and felt like being peppered by bird-shot. We climbed aboard, took seats, and buckled up. Helicopters, and most small aircraft, are so noisy that conversation is impossible without headsets. The pilot, Jon, and Susan had them, but another man and we did not, so we sat and watched the tundra roll by. We flew north-northeast for nearly an hour before landing near a little lake.

Jon introduced us to Susan; we remembered each other from the time she and we were examining archeological sites at Amalik Bay. She had records showing this site, and told us site locations were public information, and thus, accessible to anyone. Steve, her assistant, pulled out a USGS topo map that showed the little lake was named Kaiyak. Their theory was someone had flown in last summer, landed on the lake, and proceeded to dig up a couple of barabra pits and the midden where, hundreds of years ago, an Inupiat family had thrown their trash.

This clouting had happened a year ago, so we weren't expecting to meet bad guys today and didn't need to be carrying our heavy weapons. Ours came off and went in our packs, Jon left his on.

GPS was new to us; it had been developed in the 1970s and 80s, but the final satellite hadn't been launched until a year ago (1994), and it would be another year until the DoD (Department of Defense) turned off "Selective Availability." Until then GPS signals were controlled by the U.S. military so as to not give truly accurate readings. Susan had a hand-held unit and was walking the perimeter reading latitudes and longitudes for Steve to record—we were well above 68° north and almost 162° west. We set pins at each spot they recorded, measured elevation differences from the known elevation for Kaiyak Lake, and photographed everything with Susan's camera.

Penny had picked up an owl pellet on the midden that we wanted to examine. At our lunch break we had the chance to dissect it while everyone else was resting. We were pretty sure it came from a snowy owl, "Okpik, the white owl," the Inuits call it. It could have been from a short-eared owl, but we had examined a lot of those pellets at Katmai, and felt this was too big for a short-eared. An owl pellet is a mass of undigested food, mostly skin, fur, and bones, shaped like an elongated egg that is regurgitated. We should be able to tell what the owls up here were eating. Picking it apart with my knife, we found what we expected, fur and an assortment of little bones, probably all from voles, except one part of a mandible that had sharp, purple teeth. The owl had caught a shrew.

The area showed a good bit of disturbance. A lot of digging had been done, but no one could be sure what might have been taken. Susan was sure, in her own mind, that a lot of valuable Inupiat artifacts had been stolen. The chance of identifying the perpetrators was about zero, and proving anything in court would be impossible. We had documented the incident and identified the location. That was all that could be done, so we packed up and climbed back into the helicopter for the ride back to camp.

AUGUST HAD A SPELL OF BEAUTIFUL WEATHER, AND WE REALIZED this weather was expected in August. A lot of people were floating the Noatak and let us know they had been advised to come now because weather could be counted on—cold but often clear. We were on the river every day, and had a lot of boaters stopping in the ranger station to talk.

Our friend Willie, the dispatcher, caught us one morning before we headed out to let us know three interesting men would be flying into the "Kelly Airport" and bringing a present from him. The three men were good friends and interesting people: two physicians from Seattle, Gene Turner a pediatrician, and Pete Toomey an orthopedic surgeon. The third was Pat O'Hara, a National Geographic photographer working on a book about Beringia. They wanted to learn about the area and the river, and asked if they could ride with us for the day. "Sure," we said, "Somehow the campground is empty right now. Climb in, we'll drop your gear and take you on patrol with us."

We went up river, checked a Native boat with two people, two butchered caribou, and no hunting licenses (we had given up on Natives having licenses). Our visitors seemed more interested in us than in what they were seeing. Both physicians were fascinated that I had given up my practice to work for the Park Service. They understood my attitude, but how had Penny been willing to do the same thing? They would love to do this kind of work, but there was no chance of their wives giving up their comfortable social lives to live in a tent and work for a few bucks an hour.

When we got back to camp that evening we invited them to bring their food and come up to the station, and we'd have dinner together. They brought a bottle of single-malt Scotch and a tape from Willie. The tape was by Nana Mouskouri, a woman we had never heard of, but Pat said, "Wait until you hear this. She has the clearest, sweetest voice you ever heard." And indeed she did. Gene poured Scotch into three coffee cups, and poured Penny one of our beers. I put the tape in the radio/tape player that we had carried with us for fifteen years and listened to Nana sing, "Autumn Leaves," "Over the Rainbow," "The Wind Beneath My Wings," "My Own True Love," "Falling in Love Again," and more. I don't know what or if we ate that night, but the music will always be with me. Penny has been the "wind beneath my wings" since we first met, and I can't hear that song without being on the Noatak with Penny.

THE FREEZES WE HAD HAD KNOCKED THE MOSQUITOS DOWN BUT didn't seem to have bothered the no-see-ums or the black flies. They were snapping at us even more fiercely.

Fall became even more pronounced as moose season opened. That meant hunting patrols for us by boat or, when weather permitted, with Richard in a small Piper Cub. The Cub is a great little aircraft, very light, made of aluminum tubing covered in fabric. This one was painted army brown, so it probably had been acquired from the military where it had been used as a trainer and a spotter of all sorts of enemy goings-on during WWII. Several models of the Piper Cub had been manufactured. Richard said this one was an L-4. The standard small narrow tires had been replaced by large fat tundra-tires which allowed it to land on short soft sand beaches or even tundra. It could fly low and slow; Richard told us it had a maximum speed of 80 mph and a stall speed of 40 mph.

Low and slow allowed us to get a close view of any camp we spotted—when we could find one. Seating was tandem (fore and aft) with barely enough room for two small people and our day-packs. Richard insisted we wear our .357s; he carried his in a shoulder holster where it was out of the way. He had a Winchester .30-06 strapped, butt forward, to the right strut where he could reach it quickly if it was needed.

Hunting guides had developed campsites that they used every year, and Richard was aware of most of them. They were in moose habitat which meant near a river or lake with good stands of willow and scrub birch for browse. He would pick one of us up on the Kelly River beach and fly out searching for an occupied hunting camp.

These were not Natives or Alaskans hunting for winter food, but hunters from anywhere in the world looking for a trophy moose. Dall sheep were hunted in the steep mountains of the eastern preserve, but the Cub didn't have the range to get us there and back, so we would have to let the State "Brown Shirt" Troopers monitor them. We would be interacting with moose hunters, most of whom would be legal and willing to spend a lot of money on a hunt. Richard figured the cost per pound of moose meat to take home would be at least $200. They were here for the experience, the fun, and bragging rights of camping in the Brooks Range, and the possibility of shooting a trophy moose.

Richard had explained that these guides liked to hunt early in the day so they had plenty of time to butcher and retrieve any moose they shot. By the time we located them they would be back in camp. It was always interesting to see the look we got from the men in these camps as we stepped out of the little plane. Seeing park rangers in the role of game wardens was not something they expected. Well, seeing anyone doing law enforcement out here was not expected.

Richard and I looked like people who might be wildlife cops. There was nothing notable about either of us. I was 20 years older, but we looked similar, the same size, both had grey hair under the NPS ball caps, Richard had a grey mustache and I had a grey beard—I never shaved in the back country. It was Penny who was the surprise. Hunting up here seemed to be a man's game. She was a good cop, and Richard let her take the lead. She always wore a big smile, introduced herself, shook hands with everyone, asked to see their hunting licenses and game tags. (Alaska sells special permits for each species that may be hunted. When an animal is killed the tag must be attached to the carcass, identifying it and the individual who shot it.) When there was game in camp we always made sure it had the proper tag—a caribou tag on a moose carcass was a common trick. Penny made sure to check everything and give a compliment when things were done well. She always came back to camp with interesting stories about the people she had met and their feelings about hunting in the far north.

Her favorite was a group of four men from Pittsburgh, Pennsylvania, who had saved for several years to be able to afford this expensive experience. They had a big moose dressed out and hung, probably 900 pounds of meat and bones, and a head with a 63-inch rack. That wouldn't be much of a trophy to real trophy hunters, but to these four office workers it was a trophy they could brag about for years. They were as proud and excited as little kids, and spent a half hour explaining the hunt to Penny.

During these hungting patrols, we both enjoyed flying low and slow over tundra in the little Cub. We saw trails threading north and south from the crest of the Brooks Range to the Noatak River, and probably the same on the north slope running to the calving grounds on the Coastal Plain of the Arctic Ocean. These were the migration routes of the 500,000 member Western Arctic caribou herd. They had migrated from their wintering grounds in the southern Brooks Range to the north slope calving grounds in April. Soon they would begin their migration south.

After two weeks, Richard decided we had contacted all of the camps and guides at least once, so it wasn't necessary to continue the flying patrols.

A few days later as Penny and I made our way down the bank to the boat to go on patrol I heard, "Ow, damn!"

I looked behind me and said, "What?"

There was an expression of pain on Penny's face. She said, "I slipped on the bank and hurt my knee. It'll be all right. Let's take a boat ride."

We had only gone a few miles up river when we saw a small herd of bull caribou standing on the far bank. We stopped to watch as they waded into the river and started swimming across. Before the caribou got to mid-stream, three boats with two Natives in each showed up. They moved up stream of the caribou and to our amazement, every one of them pulled a gun and started shooting the caribou in the head at point blank range—less than five feet. We had heard stories of caribou harvest, but now we had witnessed the way it was done.

Almost all of the carcass drifted to shore in a matter of a few hundred yards. We met the men on the beach to check hunting licenses, and of course, no one had one. Somehow they all had forgotten to bring them, but, "No problem," they had them at home. By now we knew full well that Natives having hunting and fishing licenses was a farce. They had no intention of ever complying with white man's harvest laws.

The hunters—no, "the shooters"—pulled the bodies up on the bank. Some of them cut the jugular to bleed the animal out, some didn't. (The meat of a bled-out animal should last much better.) Then severed the trachea and esophagus, cut through the belly skin, from the crotch to the sternum. They were careful to not cut stomach or intestines and foul the meat. They reached into the thorax and pulled out the lungs, guts, and other organs, kept the heart and liver, but left the rest on the beach for scavengers. The body was skinned, but the hide was usually left by the gut-pile. The head was removed and the body quartered. Interestingly to us, the heads were turned over, the base of the skulls removed and the brains carefully harvested. Brain stew was a religious feast of the fall harvest and a thanking of the animal for its gift. The heads were positioned in threes, making a triangle that stood on the antlers. Brainless heads with sightless eyes looking to the sky.

Nearly every day a few Native skiffs would go by with the bodies of as many caribou as they could hold. The Inupiat were legally entitled to harvest up to 15 caribou a day, but their boats couldn't hold more than two or three carcasses, so the harvest was sustainable without endangering the herd.

Jon reached us the next day to let us know he had a plan. The scuttlebutt was the caribou migration was starting early and would be crossing the Noatak 100 miles up stream from the Kelly River. We should go up river, establish a camp, and monitor the Native caribou harvest for a week or ten days.

OK Jon, we could do that. It was mid September, freezing every night and getting up to the low 30s most days; the river temperature was dropping: 35°F this morning. Today was a gorgeous cold Indian summer day. The mountains all had termination dust half way down. This was going to be another winter camping experience. We well remembered our hunting patrol at Katmai, when we had been dropped off by a lake for a ten-day stake-out, but got weathered-in and had to be rescued by helicopter after 18 days.

We would need to take a lot of fuel to run up river 100 miles, patrol for ten days, and come back down. We had gone up beyond the canyon several times and knew that trip burned 20 gallons. We had better take at least 50 gallons. We didn't have that many gas cans, so we'd have to use an empty 55-gallon fuel drum—we had several. I rolled one down the bank and set it in the Lund. Now we had to fill it, five gallons at a time. Carrying two five-gallon fuel cans down that steep bank was a bitch. I asked Penny to let me carry them down; her knee was hurting her, but she insisted she would carry her share. We both carried them one at a time until Penny's knee gave out and she almost fell down the bank. That did it. I said, "We need to cancel this patrol. I think your knee is injured, not just strained. We don't want to do more damage."

"No," she insisted again, "I really want to do this last hunting patrol."

The next day was still beautiful. Sunrise was the most brilliant scarlet sky either of us had ever seen; it turned the river bright red. I remembered the old mariner saying:

Red sky at night,
sailor's delight.
Red sky in the morning,
sailors take warning.

I quoted that to Penny, we chuckled and I finished loading fuel, gear, and extra food and helped Penny down the bank and into the boat. We cast off just as a huge, ominous dark sky moved in from down river. We must have looked like vagabonds. To see around the 55-gallon drum I had to stand. Penny and our gear were jammed forward. We ran up river about three hours, well past the canyon where a huge rock was standing five feet tall on an inside bank, the one that nearly killed us in the Klepper.

"Enough," chief-navigator Penny finally shouted. "That storm has been chasing us all day and is going to let loose any minute. And right there is the best looking campsite I've seen for an hour." It was a protected sand beach on the inside of a bend and had a quiet eddy down river a few yards where we could safely moor the boat. We had seen two Native boats heading down river as we were on the way up, we waved, they waved; neither had any game.

I nosed into the beach, Penny carefully climbed out with the bow line. Hmm, she normally jumps out and pulls the boat up while I tip the outboard up. I asked how the knee was feeling. She replied, "It's OK. Well it hurts, but not too bad. I'm OK."

We set camp back among the willows where we would be well away from wildlife traffic on the beach and protected from wind, should it come up. Penny noticed a single Siberian aster still in bloom, it was out in the open, about ten inches tall with lavender rays and a yellow center. A falcon circled overhead. We decided it was a merlin. It didn't act like a peregrine and sure wasn't a big gyrfalcon. In the sand there were fresh fox tracks, day old tracks of a small bear and cub, and older tracks of two wolves, but no caribou or human prints.

It was turning colder and looking more like rain, so we fixed a quick meal of Ramen noodles and smoked salmon. We did have a cup of rehydrated cider with a shot of brandy. The rain was starting and we were glad to be settled in for the night.

During the night Penny woke up needing the john. It was cold and raining hard, not an ideal time to go out to pee. Fortunately we had brought along "Little John," a joke gift from friends. It was a urinal with a capacity of a liter and had a female adaptor, so it was useable by either of us. On this trip it was going to be regularly used by us both.

When morning light came, I was cold in my down bag but climbed out, unzipped the tent flap and rain fly, stuck my head out, and said, "Oh my God, there's ice covering everything, but it's clear and should melt quick."

Penny said, "Here, empty Little John and get back in your bag for a while." I did, and we talked about the situation. We decided to let the sun do its thing, and go on patrol after it melted out. We wouldn't break camp. We'd use this as our base and patrol up and down river checking on hunters.

The sun did its thing and melted the ice, but it didn't warm up much. We patrolled up river, didn't see any caribou and found only one group of Natives in a camp. They told us, "The 'bou must be down river." They would stay here one more day and head home if they didn't show up. We spent the next few days looking for caribou and hunters, and found both to be rare. Several evenings when we returned to camp, we found bear tracks along the beach, and one morning there were tracks showing that two wolves had checked us out. Their tracks indicated they had walked clear around the tent. What were they thinking?

One evening as I was securing the boat, and getting food for dinner (we kept the food in bear-proof containers stashed in the willows) I heard, "Ow, damn! That hurt."

"What happened?" I asked.

"I just turned wrong, I think my foot hung-up on something, but it hurts like hell. It'll be OK in a minute." She had set our beach chairs up and was sitting in one by the time I got there. "It's feeling better already," she lied. I sat with her. We watched our lone aster swaying in the breeze, its head was bent and the petals were making graceful arcs in the sand each time it turned. A wolf howled in the distance and was answered by another.

Jon had given us surplus army sleeping bag covers of insulated canvas, I slipped our regular bags into them, hoping that would keep us warmer tonight. They worked, and we slept nice and warm.

Some time during the night Penny shook me. I, of course, thought her knee was causing enough pain that she needed something. She said, "What's that weird light?" There was the strangest light fading and brightening, and moving around.

I opened the tent and looked out; draperies of red, blue, and green light were rippling and waving in the northern sky, almost overhead. It was the most magnificent display or aurora borealis, or northern lights, either of us had ever seen. We turned so we could lie in our warm sleeping bags and watch the display with our heads out under the stars. They were like the big velvet draperies that decorate theaters. They moved in waves, nearly dancing at times. Colors changed, especially the reds and burgundies, almost turning violet, they brightened and faded with each wave. "Do you hear that?" Penny said. I concentrated, and yes, there was a buzzing, whooshing sound, like you might hear from the wings of humming birds.

Charged particles—electrons and protons, technically referred to as solar wind—are constantly launched from the sun. Those particles can penetrate the Earth's magnetic field only near the poles. When they collide with oxygen molecules, above 150 miles, they produce red light. Charged particles colliding with oxygen below 150 miles produces green light, and blue light when the particles collide with nitrogen in the low atmosphere.

The traditional lore of Inupiats, and Inuit of eastern Canada, explains the auroras are torches lighting the pathway to heaven for fallen warriors. To us they were the culmination of following our rain-bow through 15 years of wonderful places and amazing adventures we had experienced with the Park Service.

We watched the aurora slowly fade, the music softened, the perfor-mance ended, and the stars became brighter. Penny asked which star was the North Star. There were so many stars, I had to find the great bear (Ursa Major), or big dipper, constellation to be sure which was the North Star. A line through the two stars of the outer edge of the dipper point to the North Star. I found it and helped Penny locate it. It was almost straight over-head, the highest we had ever seen the Polar Star.

The next morning, Penny's knee was swollen and not getting better out here. The hunting patrol had been fruitless. It was time to wrap this patrol up, close out the Kelly River Station, and head south.

Penny and Frank's Last Day as Rangers

FINIS

B ack at the Kelly River Station, we found it had been taken over by Amy, Diane, and Kara, three more researchers from Anchorage. We moved in, they moved to the weather-port, but continued cooking and killing time in our kitchen. De ja vu, all over again. Nice kids, but we were glad to hear they were only going to be around for a few more days before their season ended, and we would finally be alone in the wilderness.

According to Jon's plan we would be picked up on 23 September. That meant we had a week to take inventory, finish the multitude of regular reports and the season-end report, get the boat and dock up the bank, and close the place down. We would need every bit of that time, but we still had crime to fight. Fortunately Penny's knee seemed better. She was still limping but insisted on going along when I went out in the boat.

A lot of caribou were being harvested right around the station—in the river from boats, often with handguns, and in the woods with rifles. We saw caribou every day and heard shots frequently, sometimes we would go to check on the shooters. The Inupiats never had licenses, but we knew that and had given up on demanding to see them. The thing that bothered us the most was the use that would be made of the meat. Except for the back-straps, which we knew were excellent when properly prepared, it went to feed sled dogs.

One day as Penny was coming back from the outhouse, she looked across the river and was amazed to see two grizzly bears on the far bank. They were the first bears either of us had seen near here since I had peppered the one at our burn-barrel. She called me and we enjoyed watching them cleaning up a gut pile. Bears are solitary animals; two being together in fall wasn't about sex; they were probably litter mates, three or four years old, just hanging out together for comfort and support.

Several hours later we heard the report of a heavy rifle. Sure enough, two men in a skiff pulled into the bank by a down bear. "Damn it! Why do they shoot bears?" Penny said. We both knew Native Alaskans always shoot any bear on sight. Nevertheless we needed to check on them. We got in the boat and headed across to talk. No they didn't have licenses, and of course they had shot the bear, "That's what we do with bears." It was a small Grizz, probably one of the pair we had seen earlier. It had a beautiful blond coat that the men were carefully skinning out; they could sell it to a white hunter or tourist for a lot of money. The skinned out body looked so much like a human that, again we were shocked. It took us back to the execution of Sister our first year in Alaska.

The weather had been cold last week, in the 20s every night and not getting above freezing in the days—I measured the river water at 31°F one morning. We had used the oil heat stoves a lot, and refilled the tanks to make sure we didn't run out and there would be a good supply for next year's rangers. To our surprise it warmed up and was in the 50s and even low 60s the next week.

We had two late season visitors that Willie hadn't warned us about; he probably didn't know either one was around. Cape Smithe Air pulled up to our dock one afternoon and dropped off Robin Winks. The pilot promised to be back by 1800, well before dark. Winks introduced himself as a member of the NPS Advisory Board, and explained he was looking at park operations in Alaska, and the Northwest Alaska Areas was on his list. He had heard of Frank and Penny Starr for years, and thought this was an opportunity to meet us and get our take on the area.

Robin had heard of problems in the Kotzebue office and asked for our anonymous input. We admitted we had never met the superintendent, and knew there were problems. We felt Jon was in over his head and was responsible for more than he was prepared to handle—he seemed to be the only one really doing the work of administering the three park areas.

Robin let us know Katmai was having administrative problems too. There had been several changes of superintendent and he feared the park was drifting without adequate guidance. We remembered back just 12 years to when we were first at Katmai. There were six permanent staff members: Superintendent, Chief Ranger, District Ranger, Chief of Maintenance, Resource Management Specialist, and Secretary, operating out of a two-room office and the maintenance building. When we were last there, three years ago, the Park Service occupied the second story of a new office building with 20 some permanent staff, each sitting at a desk looking at a computer. Unfortunately, the number of field rangers dealing with visitors was essentially the same, even though visitation had grown considerably. Bureaucracy in action!

We talked all afternoon about the parks and NPS policies of the places we had worked. We learned a lot about the Advisory Board and the current status of parks in Alaska. Unfortunately, the Advisory Board is just that—"advisory," with no clout. We suspect he got the information he was looking for about NWA (Northwest Alaska), and had our take on other Alaskan parks.

Early one morning a blue and gold Super Cub buzzed us. We recognized it as a trooper plane, so I hurried to the dock in time to catch the bow line on the starboard float as it pulled up. The trooper climbed out with a big smile, stuck out his hand and said, "I'm Curt Bedingfield, you must be Frank Starr. I've heard stories about you and your wife and wanted to meet you, and figured this was a good chance." Penny was standing at the top of the bank, she waved and said, "Come on up. I have coffee brewing."

Curt, too, just wanted to talk. He had first heard of us when he was stationed in Kodiak and we were at Aniakchak. The whole Kodiak office knew we had been instrumental in the troopers getting a conviction on a trawler fishing during a closure. We shared deep concern over the rarity of an Alaskan judge giving a significant fine, much less jail time, for any wildlife infraction. We had a great morning of hearing and telling stories about Alaska—good guys, bad guys, the land, the wildlife, and the changes that were happening in the Great Land. Curt had the same complaints we had and had heard over the years. He related several stories of having strong evidence of illegal hunting only to have a judge throw the case out on a technicality, or impose a ridiculously low fine.

That afternoon, in late September, we were amazed by a brief summer thunder storm followed by a brilliant rainbow. It arched across the river with distinct bands of red, orange, yellow, green, and purple. Its reflection in the calm river smoothed the colors and sent chills up our spines as we held hands and thanked the gods for letting us have—and survive—the experiences we had over the past 16 years.

Willie reached us that evening to let us know Buck would be in the next day to pick up the outboard, the 10-watt radio and solar collector, and other park property that needed to go to Kotzebue. We could throw in some of our personal gear that we wouldn't need. That would be the end of our boating; we had better head up the Kelly to collect enough good water to get us through until we left.

With the outboard gone we wouldn't use the boat again. Our toughest closing chore would be getting the boat and dock up the bank where they would be safe for the winter. OK, Sherlock, how do the two of us haul a several hundred pound boat up a steep 30-foot bank? Strength wasn't an option, we didn't have it. It was a matter of figuring a way. Dock and boat had gone down hill easily; just push the dock pieces off the edge and collect them at the bottom. Pete and I had secured a stout line to the bow of the boat, wrapped the free end around a tree, pushed the boat off the bank, then played out line as the boat slid down the bank.

We had a come-a-long, a poor-man's winch—you crank a handle like a jack-handle, which retrieves a cable several inches per crank. This come-a-long only had 10 feet of cable to retrieve before it had to be restrung. We roped the come-along to a tree, and strung a line from the come-a-long's hook to the bow-eye of the boat. Penny cranked the come-along, and I laid small, round logs in front of the boat to make a smoother path, and gradually the boat came up to the tree. We turned it on its side leaning it against the tree where it should be safe all winter. We simply pulled the dock pieces up, several at a time.

The reports, hand written in triplicate and always a pain, we whipped out quickly. We were sure no one other than, perhaps Jon, would ever see them. We did an inventory of every item in the place: propane tank, and stove, white-gas lanterns that had not been used until August but were getting a lot of use now, pots and pans, and all sorts of things that next year's rangers would need. We always kept the place clean and neat, which, we felt, was important to an efficient operation, so we didn't need to clean house. Tomorrow would be 23 September, but we had heard nothing about our pick up. "We'll see," Penny laughed when I asked her if she expected to leave as promised.

My field notes for Tuesday 26 September say:

Temp—46/63, ceiling–2,000, visibility–10 miles, wind–calm, river–up, rain until 1400, no boats, no planes, sky cleared.

Finally, Willie, at the office, let us know to expect Buck that afternoon. We got the last of our boxes to the beach set them on rocks under a tarp and crossed our fingers that Buck would show. He did, at a quarter to six, under beautiful clear skies.

The 40-minute flight to Kotzebue took two hours. We landed with just enough light to be safe. Buck's Maul had headphones and mics for each of us, so we could talk with each other on the flight. Buck didn't follow the Noatak River back to Kotzebue Sound, as we expected. He told us he wanted us to see some different country, and took us southeast to the snowy Maiyumerak Mountains and down the confluence of mountain and plain. Buck said, "Look ahead and up." There were hundreds of sandhill cranes flying south too, they were much higher than we were, but the long, trailing legs identified them. In our minds we could hear the sound of their prattling voices as they discussed whatever migrating cranes discuss. Buck circled a pot-hole lake and pointed out a flock of tundra swans. He thought, and we agreed, the recent warm spell must have delayed their migration, they should have left a couple of weeks ago. They would winter on coastal estuaries and slow rivers in western U.S. or along the Chesapeake Bay in the east.

The plains spread south and east to the Noatak River. There were literally thousands of caribou spread across the tundra, migrating south for winter food and shelter. It reminded us of the African Serengeti and the wildebeests we had watched migrate to greener grasses years ago. I mentioned the similarities of this tundra and the Serengeti plains. Both support tremendous herds of grazing herbivores that migrate seasonly. The herbivores, in turn, supported many predators: bears and wolves in Alaska; lions, leopard, cheetah, and hyaena in Africa. They each fill specific niches and keep their ecosystem in balance. Too many or to few of each predator or prey species puts the system out of balance. Darwin's second premise is that all living creatures produce more offspring than the environment can support. Too many herbivores will overgraze their pasture, and too many carnivores will harvest too many herbivores. The natural world must, and does, maintain the balance to sustain a healthy ecosystem—unless we humans interfere.

Buck turned into his final approach to the seaplane base in Kotzebue, splashed down, and pulled up to his dock. He stepped out and secured his port float to cleats as I stepped out and helped Penny down. Buck had told us he would take us to the bunkhouse where we were to stay the few days until our EOD (end of duty). Penny said, "Buck, would you join us for dinner at the Bayside?"

"I'd love to," he replied, "but the Bayside had a plumbing problem and is closed for a few days."

"We'll see if it reopens before we leave. We'd like to spend an evening with you. You really made this season for us," Penny told him.

As we expected, the bunkhouse was a mess. No surprise. We'd clean it up tomorrow. Penny went into the bathroom to pee and wash her hands. "Damn it!" I heard, "There's no hot water, and I really want a shower tonight."

"Well, we need to eat something too," I said. "We can have Pilot biscuits with peanut butter and some dried fruit. Sound like a plan?"

Sarcasm came to me from the bathroom, "Wonderful, just like we were camping-out in the wilds of Alaska."

Penny took a cold shower, and I took a cold sponge bath before we crashed for the night. At the Kelly Station, we could at least heat water and have warm sponge baths. So much for being back to civilization.

At the office the next morning we told Jon about the lack of hot water in the bunkhouse. He promised to have maintenance take care of it and told us we had appointments at the hospital to have my ears examined and Penny's knee X-rayed and checked over. The reports the following day were not encouraging. My ears were both seriously damaged. The hearing loss would be permanent and progressive. I should see an audiologist as soon as I got home to find out the depth of loss and what could be done. Penny's knee showed a torn ACL (anterior cruciate ligament). That ligament is crucial in stabilizing the knee when turning and would require surgery to repair; so she should see an orthopedic surgeon as soon as she got home. Our bodies were showing the wear and tear we, and the Park Service, had put them through.

We met with Jon that afternoon, turned in all our reports and got our final evaluations for the season. Penny always worries about being judged and graded. Today she was elated by perfect scores on her—and my—performance evaluations. Jon knew we had some tough times and appreciated how we handled the Inupiats and gotten the NPS into a much better light with the locals. He asked us to join him and Kathy for dinner and the evening.

We had known Jon from several years of law enforcement refreshers, and Kathy from Katmai a few years ago. There were endless stories to relate and laugh over, remembering people and places we all knew. A good evening with old friends. An evening of eating, drinking beer and wishing each other well in the future.

Our last day in the National Park Service, 30 September 1995, was a Saturday, a LEW day, a day off, the first one we had had since mid-June.

We were in the office for the final time. Buck happened to come in for some reason; he looked at Penny and said, "The Bayside is open. How about meeting me for dinner?"

We both used Jon's infamous phrase and said, "Sounds like a plan."

We all laughed and agreed to meet at seven.

Penny and Buck were in the mood to swap stories, and I was glad to listen and put in an occasional word. Buck was in his early 50s, had a summer cabin here, but called Redding, Pennsylvania, home. Bush flying was almost done for the year; he would head home in a week or so. He spent about six months here being a bush-pilot and the other six months at home where his favorite pastime was reading; it didn't make much difference what, he just loved to read. His wife had died a few years ago and he had no kids. We felt sorry for him. He should be a lonely man, but seemed happy, perhaps it was the life he wanted.

Buck wanted to know about us. What had gotten us to the Noatak? Penny told about our first trip to Alaska in 1973 to visit our friends Al and Donna Franzmann—Al managed the Kenai Moose Research Center. The stories they told and the wildlife we saw on that trip convinced us that Alaska was in our future. We promised ourselves to see the bears of Katmai and float the Noatak River. Those promises became dreams that—some way, some day—would come true. In 1973, seeing and experiencing Alaska as NPS rangers was not a consideration. I had a dental practice to run and a living to earn. Penny had a home to manage, and we had three wonderful daughters to rear.

Ten years later we were asked to accept ranger positions at Katmai, and our Alaska experiences were off and running. Over the intervening years we had been places, seen and learned things, and had experiences that people can only dream of or read about. We had seen and learned the workings of the natural world—of geology and life. Now those Park Service days were coming to the end, but we had flown over the rainbow and the dreams we had dared to dream really had come true.

Remember today for it is the beginning of forever.

Made in the USA
San Bernardino, CA
26 March 2018